# English Teaching in the Secondary School

## Linking theory and practice

### Third edition

Mike Fleming
and
David Stevens

LONDON AND NEW YORK

First edition published in 1998
by David Fulton Publishers

Second edition published 2004
by David Fulton Publishers

This edition published 2010
by Routledge
2 Park Square, Milton Park, Abingdon, Oxon OX14 4RN

Simultaneously published in the USA and Canada
by Routledge
270 Madison Avenue, New York, NY 10016

*Routledge is an imprint of the Taylor & Francis Group, an informa business*

© 2010 Mike Fleming and David Stevens

Typeset in by Palatino and Helvetica Neue by Prepress Projects Ltd, Perth, UK
Printed and bound in Great Britain by MPG Books Group

*British Library Cataloguing in Publication Data*
A catalogue record for this book is available from the British Library

*Library of Congress Cataloging in Publication Data*
Fleming, Michael (Michael P.)
English teaching in the secondary school : linking theory and practice /
Mike Fleming and David Stevens. — 3rd ed.
p. cm.
Includes bibliographical references and index.
1. English language—Study and teaching (Secondary)—Handbooks,
manuals, etc. 2. Language arts (Secondary) 3. English language—Study
and teaching (Secondary)—Great Britain—Handbooks, manuals, etc. 4.
Language arts (Secondary)—Great Britain. I. Stevens, David, 1947– II. Title.
LB1631.F625 2010
428.0071'241—dc22
2009019251

ISBN 10: 0–415–56022–5 (hbk)
ISBN 10: 0–415–46502–8 (pbk)
ISBN 10: 0–203–86614–2 (ebk)

ISBN 13: 978–0–415–56022–1 (hbk)
ISBN 13: 978–0–415–46502–1 (pbk)
ISBN 13: 978–0–203–86614–6 (ebk)

# English Teaching in the Secondary School

Now in an updated third edition, *English Teaching in the Secondary School* is a comprehensive guide to the theory and practice of teaching English. Presenting an informed view of current educational policy, the authors provide advice to help students creatively and independently interpret government initiatives and incorporate them in their teaching practice. With practical ideas for use in the classroom, extensive discussion of theory and opportunities for reflection and critical thought, the authors guide students through the whole process of English teaching in the secondary school.

This edition has been fully updated to include:

- a chapter on research and writing for M level students;
- references to the Every Child Matters agenda;
- updates to the KS3 and 14–19 curriculum;
- revised GCSE specifications;
- an emphasis on creativity, flexibility and learner engagement;
- reflections on the impact of globalisation and technology on literacy.

Written in an accessible style, with a wealth of advice and ideas, this book forms essential reading for practising teachers, lecturers, PGCE students and those undertaking initial teacher training, and is suitable for those engaging in M level study.

**Mike Fleming** is Director of Postgraduate Studies in the School of Education, University of Durham.

**David Stevens** is Course Leader PGCE (secondary) in the School of Education, University of Durham.

# Contents

# Acknowledgements

We owe a considerable debt to the teachers and student teachers with whom we have been fortunate to work. Don Salter read an early draft of the book and made encouraging and helpful suggestions. Kath Herring, Maggie Wilson, Helen Simpson, Louise Horwood and Katie Rowland provided ideas for particular chapters. We are grateful to Marianne Fleming, who helped to prepare the manuscript.

Thanks to The Invisible for drawing my attention to the O'Donohue quotation on p. 246.

# Introduction

*Language is a labyrinth of paths.*
*You approach from one side and know your way about;*
*you approach the same place from another side and no longer know*
*your way about.*

Ludwig Wittgenstein, *Philosophical Investigations*

IN ORDER TO ENGAGE ACTIVELY and critically with the ideas in the introduction readers might find it useful to think about each question before reading the section that follows.

## Aims

### What do you think is the central aim of English teaching?

The central aim of English teaching is at one level very straightforward and uncontroversial. At its simplest, the purpose of English as a subject is 'to develop pupils' abilities to use language effectively'. However, below the surface of that apparently incontestable and transparent statement lie all sorts of conflicting opinions, ideologies, methodologies and philosophies. What precisely is meant by the various terms within the statement? For example, it is only relatively recently that English has included speaking and listening as an important aspect of what counts as 'using language'. The inclusion of reading has been less controversial but there has been no similar agreement over what should be read, or indeed what exactly is involved in the process of reading. Presumably the idea of 'responding to language' is implicit in the word 'use'. Does 'using language effectively' mean using language 'accurately' or should the emphasis be on 'appropriateness' to specific purposes and contexts? In order to use language effectively how much knowledge about language is necessary and what form should it take? To what degree does explicit knowledge about language improve its actual use? The word 'develop' as opposed to 'teach' does not make clear what the primary role of the teacher should be in the whole enterprise: as instructor, creator of contexts, facilitator or adviser. Implicit in these concepts are contrasting theories of the way language is acquired and develops.

Even the name of the subject 'English teaching', as will be discussed further in Chapter 1, should not be taken for granted. 'English teaching' is often taken to mean mother tongue teaching but, owing to migration and international travel, many pupils in the contemporary secondary classroom learn English as a second language. This makes increasing demands on the teacher. A new project on language education led by the Council of Europe uses the term 'language as subject' to acknowledge the fact that in many situations the main language(s) of instruction in a school will not be the mother tongue of all pupils. The project also identifies intercultural and plurilingual education as key aims of 'language as subject' teaching.

The impact of changes in the modern world such as globalisation, technological advances and evolving definitions of literacy have an impact on the aims of the subject which need to be considered. This third edition of the book has also addressed a number of national changes that have been introduced since the second edition was published in 2004. These include the Every Child Matters agenda, changes to the Key Stage 3 and 14–19 curriculum and revised GCSE specifications. There have also been changes to the standards for the award of qualified teacher status and the development of many PGCE courses as a Masters level qualification as well as the introduction of a national Masters in Teaching and Learning qualification for all new teachers. These developments have been reflected in this new edition. Perhaps more significant than any one, single policy initiative has been the recent increased emphasis on creativity, flexibility and learner engagement. These developments are welcome and have always been seen as central elements of the aims of good English teaching in successive editions of this book.

It would be churlish not to welcome the emphasis in the most recent 2007 version of the National Curriculum on the enjoyment of learning and the creation of confident, engaged citizens. The acknowledgement of the place of creativity and imagination specifically in the statement about the importance of English is also welcome. However, a note of caution is needed. In the last 20 years since the introduction of the National Curriculum it has been not the programmes of study in English that have had a negative impact in the classroom, but rather the regime of high stakes national testing that has had such a narrowing effect. The decision to abandon SATs at Key Stage 3 is therefore a significant step in the right direction. The view has been expressed in previous editions of this book that external, prescriptive frameworks do not prevent good teaching. It is also the case that rhetoric on its own does not guarantee good teaching. It is important that beginning teachers understand key principles and key tensions in the subject and do not embrace practice in an unthinking way.

As with English teaching, the central purpose of this book – to help readers to become more effective teachers of English – has hidden complexities. The word 'effective' is not neutral but can be interpreted differently according to individual values and beliefs. Most people would agree that a balance between theory and practice is necessary in writing about English teaching but it is much less clear what that balance should look like. A comprehensive, practical, no-nonsense guide has an obvious appeal but may run the risk of fostering the idea that learning to implement 'a practice defined by others' is more important than independent, critical thinking (Goodson 1997). Good theoretical writing often has significant implications for practice but it is not always possible for newcomers to teaching to see those connections or make them relevant.

Another development since the second edition of this book is that there has been an even greater proliferation of English resources on the Internet, including plans for lessons and schemes of work. There is then no need for any new teacher of English to be short of ideas for lessons. However, ideas for lessons and schemes of work are not in themselves enough. They need to be interpreted and understood on the basis of sound principles related to purpose and pupil progression. They have to be adapted for particular contexts in relation to the prior learning experiences and individual needs of the pupils and the experience of the teacher.

In attempting to fulfil the main aim of this book the practical suggestions and examples have been provided within a broad framework of discussion. Our intention is to seek to promote in the reader a critical distance from both theory and practice. 'Critical distance' does not necessarily always mean disagreement and it certainly does not mean blind cynicism to new ideas, but it does suggest a stepping back from the more pragmatic and functional preoccupations one inevitably has as a teacher in order to think about issues of value and purpose. The suggestions for lessons and schemes of work and the lists of approaches to topics are intended to serve not as practical imperatives but as invitations to thought.

The aims of the book, then, can be summarised as follows:

- to provide students, newly qualified and experienced teachers with a comprehensive practical guide to the teaching of English in secondary schools;
- to foster understanding of key principles related to best practice in English;
- to provide specific practical ideas in a way which links theory and practice;
- to stimulate critical discussion and reflection on the teaching of English;
- to provide a guide to the major issues and available literature on the teaching of English.

These aims are closely related. It is possible to provide a comprehensive guide to the teaching of English in a book of this length only by including detailed further reading sections which point the reader towards more specialist authors within each topic. It was not our aim to offer a 'grand theory' of the teaching of English but nor was it our intention to offer simply a bland and 'balanced' guide to the field. The book is written from a particular set of beliefs and convictions about what English as a subject should be and what good teaching entails. Indeed the objective of seeking to stimulate critical thinking would hardly be possible if there was no sense of unifying perspective.

### Reflect on your own experience of English lessons in your secondary school career. What aspects did you find positive or negative and why?

When people are asked to reflect on positive experiences of English, it is likely that a whole variety of types of activity will be identified. Effective English teaching is not about one set of narrow practices but is more about engaging the learner in meaningful and purposeful activity. Along with most teachers we see a place in the contemporary English classroom for a wide variety of approaches to the subject, such as whole-class teaching, group work, knowledge about grammar, shared reading, dramatic presentations, poetry writing or punctuation exercises. Too often, debates about the teaching of English in the past have centred on whether particular activities are appropriate or desirable instead of examining broader questions about the whole enterprise: whether for example pupils have a sense of purpose and engagement in their learning.

Part of the process of preserving critical distance is not taking matters too much for granted, including the nature of English itself. There are various ways of 'coming to know' English as a subject: reflecting on how one was taught English, observing lessons, reading about practical and theoretical approaches. There is also no single correct way of acquiring a theoretical perspective. It should be explored from different angles and by taking different journeys, sometimes traversing the same place from different directions. Few writers can avoid reference to the analysis of English teaching given in the Cox Report (DES 1989) and the categories listed there will be examined in Chapter 1. Other common ways of gaining a perspective on English are through examining its history and the evolution of different schools of thought or by focusing on developing ideas in relation to language and learning, knowledge about language and critical theory.

## The development of English as a subject

It is beyond the scope of this Introduction to provide a detailed history of English as a subject but some familiarity with its development helps to provide a perspective on current assumptions and policies. It is sometimes easy to forget that there have been four versions of the National Curriculum for English in its relatively short history. This fact in itself suggests that thinking about the subject is constantly changing, whether one agrees with the changes or not. It is also salutary to discover that many 'progressive' ideas about the subject date back further than one might imagine. English had to struggle at the turn of the nineteenth century to replace classics as the main literary discipline, although it had existed as a low-status subject (mainly for girls) since the late sixteenth century. Two major landmarks in the teaching of English were the Newbolt Report (HMSO 1921) and *English for the English* (1921) written by George Sampson, one of the members of the Newbolt Committee. Both publications were in many ways very forward looking, arguing for the importance of a humane education which would be a preparation for 'life' not 'livelihood'. They can be seen as belonging to a tradition which owes much to the writing of Matthew Arnold with English standing as a bulwark against the dehumanising effects of the industrial revolution.

Educational thinkers who influenced English teaching at this time were reacting against the excesses of restrictive Victorian methods. Holmes, in 1911, argued that in contrast to 'the path of mechanical obedience' which prevailed in schools, teachers should follow 'the path of self-realisation'; rote learning and mechanical drills should give way to the development of creativity and imagination. The emphasis on individuality and self-expression owed much to the thinking of Rousseau and concepts of natural growth. Writers such as Caldwell Cook (who employed play and drama extensively in his teaching) and Hourd (*The Education of the Poetic Spirit*), although differing in emphasis in their thinking, belonged to what can be seen as a broadly humane and liberal approach to the teaching of English.

Even a brief examination of the history of English teaching puts paid to the popular notion that progressive ideas took hold in the mid- to late 1960s. Neither is it possible to make too many assumptions about the way ideas developed. Sampson, who questioned excessive attention to grammar and emphasised active approaches to the teaching of reading and writing, was nevertheless uncompromising about the need to teach standard English even at the risk of sacrificing differences in language: 'Even if the school tends to extinguish a local idiosyncrasy of speech, it is not necessarily doing evil' (1921: 63). The Newbolt Report referred to the 'evil habits of speech' acquired in the home and the need for pupils' language to be 'cleansed and purified'. In the work of the early writers on the subject can be found both romantic ideas about creative imagination and a lack of tolerance of diversification in language.

Historical accounts often tend to distort reality if they assume that a neat progression took place from one set of ideas to another. That is why thinking in terms of 'schools of thought' can provide a helpful way of representing the teaching of English because different strands of that thinking can be seen to persist through the decades. Abbs, writing in 1982, distinguished between three traditions in the subject and tried to identify strengths and weaknesses in each. The progressive school (identified with authors such as Holmes and Cook) recognised the importance of emotion and subjectivity in learning but erred in its view of art as undisciplined self-expression. What Abbs termed the Cambridge school (associated with such names as Sampson, and especially Leavis), although identifying the importance of tradition, criticism and the public element, which was ignored by the progressives, in their turn ignored the importance of subjectivity and creativity. The third tradition, which was described as the contemporary socio-linguistic school, had the virtue of recognising the importance of the active use of language and of allowing pupils to formulate their own responses but tended to reduce English to linguistics or social studies.

## What are the implications for practice in each of these broad views of the subject? Which of them is closest to your view of English teaching?

Abbs's analysis of English is helpful because one can associate the particular schools with characteristic descriptions of classroom practice: the free, creative writing lesson of the progressives; the practical criticism of the Cambridge school; and the discussion of issues of the socio-linguistic approach. It is important to note that this way of dissecting the subject is not necessarily 'correct'. Watson, for example, writing in 1981 distinguished between approaches to English which centred on 'literature', 'experience', 'language' and 'skills'. No analysis tells the whole story and all attempts are necessarily reductive in some way. For example, the descriptions of English as a subject offered in the early 1980s tended to take the concept of 'literature' for granted.

If 'literature' was taken for granted this was not true of language; different views of its role and development had a major influence on the teaching of English. The Bullock Report (DES 1975) is rightly seen as another major landmark and embodied much of the theory which had been coming to the fore in preceding years related to the role of language not just in communication but in thinking and making sense of the world. Writers such as Britton and Barnes had been emphasising the importance of the relationship between language and learning, which was a significant theme in the Report. An example of what this meant in practical terms was that more stress was to be placed on genuine exploratory talk in order to allow the expression and development of concepts. Attention was to be paid to the various functions of language instead of concentrating purely on form. A central idea which had a significant effect on English teaching was that language develops by its active use in meaningful contexts rather than by narrow instruction in skills. Current emphasis on the role of talk in learning and teaching is reflected in the idea of dialogic teaching, which is intended to exploit the potential of classroom talk for cognitive development (Alexander 2008).

An extreme 'language in use' view was one of two opposing positions described in the Kingman Report (DES 1988). The traditional error in teaching English was to concentrate on grammar exercises and skills at the expense of meaning; the progressive mistake was to concentrate exclusively on the use of language without taking opportunities to focus adequately on language itself. The important word here is 'adequately'. There is no evidence that writers or teachers advocated a complete neglect of language; it is difficult to imagine what that would look like in practice. The question was rather how much and what kind of attention it should receive. The Kingman view was to accept that the way we acquire language is to use it in all its forms but that in addition pupils should acquire specific knowledge about language. This issue will be explored in more depth in Chapter 3 but it is important to note here that the Report was not only concerned with knowledge of language forms. Also important was knowledge about the ways in which language is used in society, how language is affected by social contexts, appreciation of the value of dialect, knowledge that language changes, and factors affecting communication other than words spoken. Much of the debate at the time focused on whether knowledge about language is necessary for its effective use. This preoccupation sometimes obscured the fact that the change of emphasis was much wider and had to do with what can be described as a new 'self-consciousness' about language.

The importance of the Kingman Report as a landmark in the teaching of English is sometimes underestimated because the Cox Report (DES 1989) and the National Curriculum were published so soon afterwards. It was the Kingman Report, however, which, despite the ambiguity of its tone and the lack of clear practical direction for teachers, presented the broad divisions between 'language in use' and 'knowledge about language' so clearly and so significantly for English teaching.

The mistake made by advocates of an extreme version of 'language in use' was to assume that language develops simply by being used in a variety of contexts. Using language is a necessary but not sufficient aspect of learning English (the mistake made by exponents of traditional models was not to see using language in meaningful contexts as being essential). The error partly arises from treating 'language' as a single category, assuming that what is true of speaking can be applied equally to reading and writing.

## What are some of the key differences between the way we learn to use language in its spoken and written forms?

Pinker (1994: 18) (after Chomsky) has argued very convincingly that the acquisition of spoken language is an instinct, a natural process:

> Language is not a cultural artefact that we learn the way we learn to tell time or how the federal government works. Instead it is a distinct piece of the biological makeup of our brains. Language is a complex, specialised skill, which develops in the child spontaneously, without conscious effort or formal instruction, is deployed without awareness of its underlying logic, is qualitatively the same in every individual, and is distinct from more general abilities to process information or behave intelligently.

Language here of course refers to spoken language and the same is not true of writing and reading, both of which developed relatively recently in the history of the human race and have to be taught more explicitly and systematically. It is deceptive to speak of 'language' as a generic ability because this disguises very important differences in the approach needed to the different language modes. That language can be deceptive is a theme we shall return to elsewhere in this book. 'Literature' is not an easy category to demarcate or a straightforward concept to define because language does not operate with clear boundaries and is rarely transparent. To become effective users of language, in addition to acquiring specific skills, it is important to be able to see underlying meanings, connotations, subtleties, contradictions and 'colour'. Language does not lend itself to a constraining black and white, objectified logic or exactitude.

## Language and meaning

The 'language in use' view criticised in its extreme form by Kingman is an approach derived more from psychological theories of language acquisition rather than philosophical insights into how language has meaning. In order to develop as a reader it is necessary to read widely for pleasure, to be engaged by the ideas and to talk about them. This is supported by the 'language in use' view. But it is also helpful to be able to identify techniques authors use, to know about different genres, to use different strategies and, at a more basic level, to be able to decode text. Similarly, to develop as a writer one needs to use language in a variety of contexts with a sense of purpose. But it can also be helpful to have knowledge of some technical terms (adjective, verb, prefix). In other words explicit knowledge (including grammar) taught in a systematic, structured way helps to support the development of language. The mistake, however, is to go a step further and assume that it is the structures which determine meaning. This was a mistake made by the early Wittgenstein and structuralist thinkers, and is found implicitly in some aspects of the first version of the literacy strand of the secondary National Strategy. Viewed positively, the strategy provided a challenge to English teachers to review whether their work on language was sufficiently structured to ensure progression and systematic coverage, and whether there was enough explicit teaching in the classroom. It also provided some useful pedagogic ideas and support for teachers. However, the absence of a theoretical rationale goes some way to explaining the unevenness of the documents and training materials.

Take for instance the following example from the literacy progress units (an explanation of how the units fit in with the Strategy is given in Chapter 2). Pupils are expected to see the ambiguity in sentences such as 'A significant price is commanded in the market place by the polar bear's coat', 'This is the only bear found south of the equator' and 'Bears eat all kinds of food'. In order to see these sentences as ambiguous one has to interpret them in a bizarre, counter-intuitive way. For example, in the case of the first sentence the pupils are prompted by the teacher to ask 'Is the bear's coat talking?' The second sentence, in context, would hardly be ambiguous because the referent of 'this' would be clear. In the case of the third sentence the pupils are asked 'Do bears eat all kinds of food, including burgers?' But this question is a denial of the normal convention of assuming that 'all kinds of food' simply means 'many types of food'. This strange exercise is artificially generated to show that the passive rather than active sentences are more likely to create ambiguity. Ambiguity, however, is a function of use and context, not merely of form and structure. In the same exercise, the pupils are given an active sentence to compare with the first one but this is now totally different: 'Fur traders can ask a huge amount for a polar bear's coat.' Why this confusing change? Because the first sentence, rewritten as active – 'The polar bear's coat commands a significant price in the market place' – is neither more nor less ambiguous. The exercise becomes misleading and pointless.

Equally strange is an exercise which is intended to show pupils how to summarise a passage based on the way the Boy Scout movement helped with the war effort. The pupils are taught to do this by literally deleting words in the passage that are not relevant. The fact that the task is for low achievers does not make this activity any more convincing and there are pedagogic weaknesses here too. For example, instead of just reading the passage cold from an overhead, it might be more sensible to start a lesson like this asking the pupils if any of them is a scout or guide, what they know about scouts, and whether they think scouts might have been helpful during the war. More significant, however, is the implicit view of language in the activity. The assumption is that meaning is simply a function of the logical structure of the passage, and that a summary, instead of being a matter of condensing meaning in a different form of words, is just a matter of taking away bits that are irrelevant.

Many of the technical linguistic mistakes in the Literacy Strategy and accompanying documents derive from a desire to tame language unduly, to see uniform structure where there is none (Cajkler 1999; Cajkler and Hislam 2002). Many of these have now been corrected. Examples of words with the prefix 'auto', meaning 'self', include, rightly enough, 'autobiography' but also 'autopsy'. In the accompanying 'Spelling Banks' rules are suggested (e.g. that the words ending in –f change to –v when they become verbs) which do not in fact point to any patterns which are consistent enough to make them useful. The rule works for a word like 'half' but not for 'dwarf', 'loaf', 'brief', 'leaf', 'wolf'. The following sentence is, wrongly, given as an example of a passive: 'The butler was dead.' This mistake is likely only if we look at its structure without thinking about meaning.

In his early writing Wittgenstein thought the meaning of language could be explained in a precise, logical way by describing the way in which it relates to reality. His early account of language treats it as a kind of 'calculus'. His quest in his early writing sought for a form of 'logical purity' (Peters and Marshall 1999: 28). He later revised his thinking when he saw that meaning arises through use, through agreements in culture or 'forms of life' and not just by attaching names to objects or phenomena in the world. The idea that language has meaning in a form of life is in total contrast to the idea of language simply as a system of signs. It emphasises instead that language is embedded in the significant behaviour (including non-linguistic behaviour) of human beings. That does not mean that grammatical structures are not important – but the bedrock of meaning is in its use. Wittgenstein distinguished between 'surface' and 'deep' grammar. The surface grammar of 'I have a pain' and 'I have a pin' is the same but the two sentences function in very different ways; philosophical problems arise when the surface grammar leads us to wrong conclusions. The starting point for English teachers in the classroom must then be use of language, with technical terminology and study of the conventions of language playing a supportive rather than dominant role. What that means in practice will be explored in the rest of this book.

## Cross-curricular dimensions

The cross-curricular dimensions were developed to support the new secondary curriculum that was launched in 2007. The dimensions, intended to reflect some of the challenges that face individuals and society, and help provide curriculum links, are as follows: identity and cultural diversity, healthy lifestyles, community participation, enterprise, global dimension and sustainable development, technology and the media, creativity and critical thinking. It is intended that these themes should be seen as permeating across the curriculum, being therefore interdependent. All of them can be readily addressed in the English curriculum or in an integrated project of which English is part.

English as a subject is centrally concerned with values, personal identity and developing and expressing critical opinion and it is therefore particularly suited to these themes. It is, however, worth drawing attention to the way in which literature has a particularly significant role to play. Literature and art work at the level of the particular, and prompt pupils to see situations and relationships in subtle rather than simplistic ways. There is a paradox at work: literature simplifies situations because a closed world is created, but in doing so opens up complexity. In everyday life language is 'saturated'; it is full of resonance and subtleties that derive from the form of life in which the language is embedded. The creation of a fictional context, the effect of artistic form, strips away some of that complexity but in turn makes our perception more insightful. It is by studying a play such as Arthur Miller's *All My Sons* that the moral aspects of the conflict between family loyalty and duty to the wider community can be explored in depth.

## English and subjectivity

One of the themes which emerges in various forthcoming chapters is contrasting notions of 'subjectivity' and 'objectivity'. Such concepts are also not reducible to simple definitions. Traditional western philosophy has struggled with the question of how a human subject can come to know an objective world. The question formulated in that way assumes a dualism between an inner private self and external 'reality'. The problem arises from a particular conception of the way language works and is resolved by taking a different view. If language is seen not as a means of giving expression to inner thoughts and meanings which are somehow separate from it, but as itself the embodiment of meaning, the problem is dissolved. The 'private' (in the philosophical sense) inner subject disappears. Understanding and meaning through language need to be seen as taking place between, and not simply within, people.

The emphasis on collaboration in this book (both pupils' collaborative learning and that which takes place between teachers) is not simply a form of pragmatism. The process of sharing understanding and meaning is a *sine qua non* of a rich human existence. Nor is collaboration a denial of individuality. The writing of this book has been a collaborative venture but each author has taken the major responsibility for particular chapters. Michael Fleming has taken the main responsibility for this introduction and chapters on planning, assessment, drama, poetry, ICT, Key Stage 4, inclusion and research and writing; David Stevens for chapters on the National Curriculum, the Strategy, knowledge about language, speaking and listening, reading, writing, media and Post-16 English.

We have used the term 'subjectivity' in this book not in the philosophical sense of postulating an inner self nor in the more popular meaning referring to individual opinions or beliefs, where its use so often becomes redundant. How can opinions be other than subjective? The term 'subjectivity' has been used to denote a level of individual engagement and involvement in learning and coming to know the world.

Education has become increasingly dominated by ideas which have an 'objective' ring, suggesting a world of neat logic and rationality, systems and structures, objectives and targets. The danger is, however, that this world has no place for human complexity: it presents an arid context devoid of culture and spirituality. For some readers the last two sentences will have immediate profound meaning and will strike a chord with their experiences; for others the words will sound like empty rhetoric. The book as a whole is intended to be an exemplification of what is meant by those statements.

The fact that words written in this Introduction will have a different impact on different readers is precisely the point about language which is central to our view of the teaching of English. As suggested above, language has meaning not by any simple correspondence with reality or with ideas in someone's head but through shared, human contexts or 'forms of life'. It is in this sense that engaging 'subjectivity' is an essential element of good English teaching because without it pupils will merely be performing mechanical operations, with no sense of purpose or engagement. Once again it is worth emphasising that we refer here to a quality of participation rather than to the nature of specific tasks; it is possible to be disengaged when writing a dutiful poem or response to *Macbeth* just as it is possible to be really hooked by trying to get the use of speech marks right.

When using words such as 'engagement' we do not wish to appear to underestimate the challenge facing teachers when trying to teach large classes with limited resources. We have taught in secondary schools for a combined total of 30 years and each of us has worked as Head of English in two different secondary schools. A good deal of our professional lives is now spent visiting schools. Young people have in the last 20 years become increasingly independent, challenging and individualistic. The development of these 'qualities' could be seen as a laudable educational aim but they present more as problems when pupils come in groups of 30 or so at a time. Despite pressures on teachers to differentiate, identify and respond to individual needs, and use innovative methods and a variety of teaching and learning styles, schools are still resourced as if Victorian, authoritarian methods prevail. Such comments are made in order to strike a note of realism rather than to be defeatist. This book is intended to be optimistic but written with an awareness of practical constraints and with the knowledge that teaching today is often about compromise.

Many writers on the subject have argued for the importance of English as an art, asserting for example that experience is comprehended not only through linear, abstract thinking but through feeling and intuition, that the arts as sensitive instruments for self-awareness have importance in developing the emotional and imaginative energies of children. Abbs (1982: 7) had a vision of schools being committed to the 'inner life of the student'. Staples (1992: 9) identifies polarities between the 'cognitive' and 'affective' with aesthetic experience seeking to keep the polarities in unison. The problem with many approaches to English as an art is that emphasis is placed largely on the reading of literature and on expressive forms of language (with pupils' written poetry representing the pinnacle of achievement). Such arguments often do not speak to contemporary English teachers who are busy trying to fulfil the broad requirements of the National Curriculum. An alternative, more inclusive, view is that seeing English as an art is unavoidable if language is taken at all seriously.

Such a view becomes possible if, as suggested above, the rigid boundaries which separate the 'aesthetic' from other forms of experience are seen to dissolve. Language is both 'intelligible and sensuous' (Bowie 1990: 147). Even in its simplest form it is often subject to different interpretations; it invariably carries different levels of meaning. It allows us to engage with life but also to distance ourselves from experiences. There is much that we can learn about the way it works but its depths can never be fully explored and explained. It has meaning not simply by reference to something outside itself but by its occurrence in cultural contexts of human communities. Language itself has many of the characteristics which have been traditionally associated with art.

To summarise: the concept of 'subjectivity' as used in this book must not be seen in the traditional metaphysical sense as representing the private, inner world. Just as language has meaning only in public contexts, subjectivity makes sense only in a context of shared understandings. A defence of subjectivity is not an argument for individuality but is quite the opposite. Shared meanings which define the self are derived from collaboration and engagement in objective contexts.

The central aim of English teaching, 'to use language effectively', can be interpreted in different ways. It can imply that learning language is a logical, mechanical, individualistic, shallow process governed by rules. Or it can suggest that using language effectively is a rich, deep, communal activity bound by conventions which occur in cultural contexts. Only the latter view makes philosophical and human sense or can provide any proper rationale for the teaching of English.

## Further reading

The language policies section of the Council of Europe website provides a range of discussion papers on the languages of schooling and language as subject, available at http://www.coe.int/T/DG4/Linguistic/Default_en.asp.

Theoretical issues on teaching English are addressed in Pike (2004) *Teaching Secondary English*, Clarke, Dickinson and Westbrook (2004) *The Complete Guide to Becoming an English Teacher*, Davison and Moss (eds) (2000) *Issues in English Teaching* and Brindley (ed.) (1994) *Teaching English*, as well as in the journals *English in Education*, *Use of English* and *Changing English*. Useful chapters on the history of English teaching can be found in Jeffcoate (1992) *Starting English Teaching*, Davison and Dowson (1998) *Learning to Teach English in the Secondary School* and Williamson *et al.* (2001) *Meeting the Standards in Secondary English*. More detailed histories are by Shayer (1972) *The Teaching of English in Schools 1900–1970* and Michael (1992) *The Teaching of English from the Sixteenth Century to 1870*. Mathieson (1975) has written very interestingly on the changing role of English in the last two centuries in *The Preachers of Culture*.

# 1

# The English teacher and the National Curriculum

*Bring out number, weight and measure in a year of dearth.*

William Blake, *The Marriage of Heaven and Hell*

## Setting the scene

OVER THE PAST FEW YEARS – although to many it may seem more like an eternity, and not in the liberating Blakean sense either – English teachers in secondary schools have become increasingly used to living with number, weight and measure. The National Curriculum, ushered in by the 1988 Education Act and, for English, substantially revised since, has been largely responsible for the obsession with measurement. Not that 1988 was a year of dearth as far as most secondary English teachers were concerned: new examination syllabuses at 16 and 18, based largely on coursework, opened up exciting opportunities for effective and innovative teaching of both language and literature, increasingly integrated at all levels. At the same time pioneering work was going on in English departments in a range of other areas: speaking and listening; integration with drama; media education; active approaches to literature, including Shakespeare; awareness and knowledge of the workings of language; and collaboration with other curricular subjects. If there was dearth, it perhaps arrived as a result of and simultaneously with the fashion for 'objective' measurement, rather than pre-dating it, and this is of course precisely what I imagine Blake himself meant. As Knight (1996: 22) has it:

> the desire for an unattainable objectivity is the key to many of the difficulties we have faced in formulating an adequate version of National Curriculum English. The quest for objectives and certainties where none is to be found produces paradoxical results: that matters in which we (teachers and pupils) should trust our intuitive understanding are made both more complex and more shallow when we do not.

This is quite an indictment. But what English teachers have to do, and in many cases are doing, is to convert this threat into an opportunity: not only to live with the National Curriculum, but actually to make it work for us. The most thorough revision of the National Curriculum, for English as for the other school subjects, was from 2000 (DfEE/QCA 1999). This edition was firmly embedded in classroom practice, largely uncontroversially despite what D'Arcy (2000: 30) has described as 'the increasingly formalistic emphasis' and a rather more terse, instructional tone than that used previously. In fact its impact has been lessened somewhat by the introduction of the National Strategy (or National Literacy Strategy – NLS – as it once was and is still often known) at secondary level in 2001: English departments have been far more concerned with its wide-ranging and profound implications than with any changes in the National Curriculum itself. This preoccupation, of course, turned out to be prescient, as the latest manifestation of the National Curriculum, instrumental for Year 7 from 2008–9 and for subsequent Secondary year groups over the respective following 4 years, has in fact conflated the Strategy with the National Curriculum itself. This new curriculum is itself rather more fluid than its previous manifestations, a characteristic underlined by its availability only online, where any revisions or amendments are also publicised. The next chapter deals in more detail with the impact of the Strategy.

Fortunately the National Curriculum is not only about measurement but also about establishing a framework for teaching through specification of programmes of study. It has more broadly served to focus attention on the nature of English teaching: why the subject has such a prominent place within the curriculum, and what to do with it once it is there. This is not some esoteric debate undertaken solely by those professionally involved in the teaching of English: for better or for worse, education has been opened up to an unprecedented degree to the wider public – New Labour's battlecry during the 1997 General Election, 'Education! Education! Education!', for example, clearly struck a chord with the electorate; subsequent developments have borne this out, even when (or perhaps especially when) governmental policies have been contentious. Most people feel that they have something to contribute to the education debate; certainly most have an opinion to offer, based either on their own remembered education or on their children's continuing schooling, in a way unlikely to apply, say, to the processes and professions of law or medicine. The position of English is perhaps even more extreme, in that the English language is almost universally shared by the citizens of the UK and virtually everyone feels a degree of expertise. In a sense, of course, there is a great deal of truth in this – language is by its very nature owned by those who use it and the learning of spoken English is achieved without any formal teaching – but these same people would be less likely to pronounce upon the nature of art, geography or mathematics in education. The special position of English teachers in this context presents an opportunity both to influence opinion and to draw on existing views; but it is an elusive opportunity, all too easily missed.

In the reality of English teaching in a secondary school, one can expect huge diversity of opinions and expectations as expressed by parents, governing bodies, colleagues and many others, and it is part of the English teacher's function to integrate, discuss, deflect, confirm and argue the viewpoints as the case may be. In a world of flux, the National Curriculum must be seen as a reasonably broad church: it may appear – indeed it seeks to appear – as completely authoritative; in truth it offers a series of touchstones, and the real nature of the subject has to be discovered and invented ever anew by those most intensely involved.

This process requires a certain immersion in the subject, and at the same time an ability to see both wood and trees in formulating over-arching aims and values. It is all too easy, especially perhaps in the first year or two of teaching, to be drawn into thinking that mechanistic teaching of the National Curriculum is an end in itself, spawning its own self-justification. Following Rex Gibson (1986), we could term this position 'instrumental rationality': the dichotomous separation of fact from feeling, demanding an absence of thought about the consequences and context of one's actions in any profound sense. The process thus becomes its own legitimisation with its own particular – sometimes impenetrable – rationality. This, of course, is nothing new. The poet Thomas Traherne (1960: 132), for example, writing of his own Oxford education in the seventeenth century, having initially paid tribute to the breadth of learning possible there, went on to regret that:

> Nevertheless some things were defective too. There was never a tutor that did expressly teach Felicity, though that be the mistress of all other sciences. Nor did any of us study those things but as aliena, which we ought to have studied as our enjoyments. We studied to inform our knowledge, but knew not for what end we so studied. And for lack of aiming at a certain end we erred in the manner.

So in Traherne's view of the curriculum, felicity, for him the full and visionary enjoyment of life's possibilities, becomes the central tenet, the 'mistress', of all else. What was lacking in the Oxford education of the mid-seventeenth century is still perhaps avoided by the curriculum legislators of today. It is important to keep a broad sense of what is the purpose of education.

## Models of English teaching

In the version of the National Curriculum for English based on the Report of the Cox Committee (DES 1989), it was suggested that there were essentially five models of English teaching, and that most English teachers combined in their teaching several if not all of these. The types of English teaching posited by Cox were as follows:

- a personal growth view, which tends to emphasise the pupil as a creative and imaginative individual developing, in terms of the teaching and learning of English, primarily through an intensive engagement with literature and personal creative writing;

- a cross-curricular approach, stressing the distinctive nature of English as the language of learning for virtually all curriculum areas and implying a definition of service to these areas and to education in a generic sense;

- an adult needs emphasis, as essentially a preparation for the demands of life beyond school in terms of effective understanding of and communication through the English language in its many forms, including those vocationally based;

- a cultural heritage model, with the teaching based heavily on 'great' works of literature, generally drawn from the past;

■ a cultural analysis view, leading pupils to a critical understanding of the social and cultural context of English, particularly the value systems which are inevitably embedded in the ways language is used.

In many ways, these characteristics also underlie the subsequent versions of the National Curriculum (1995, 2000 and 2008) – but do they suffice as a statement of principle? In particular, it is worth considering whether the five 'versions' of English are as comfortably compatible as Cox implies in his accompanying gloss: 'they are not sharply distinguishable, and they are certainly not mutually exclusive'. Is there not rather something of a struggle for ascendancy between some, if not all, of these views? In what sense is the second formulation a view of English as a distinctive subject at all? Certainly, the subject English has been something of a battleground for years – since its comparatively recent inception, in fact – and it is all the more important to take a principled position with regard to its teaching, eschewing the temptations of a superficial compromise; as Goodwyn (1997a: 39) puts it:

> English teachers do not . . . recognise the cross-curricular model as a model of English . . . They are quite clear that this model belongs to the whole school and should not be identified with English . . . The other four models are acknowledged as a normal part of English, but they do not have a comfortable or neutral relationship with each other; neither are they politically or historically innocent, they are not simply 'there'.

There is some value in differentiating between views, if only as an aid to reflection about one's own practice. It may be possible – in the best tradition of teenage magazines – to undertake a self-analysing quiz to ascertain where you stand: asked to devise a scheme of work for a Year 8 mixed-ability group, is your first instinct to:

(a) plan alongside other departments in, for example, giving presentations and conducting library-based research, or

(b) examine advertising as an introduction to media education, focusing on the manipulation of language and images to boost product sales, or

(c) base the scheme on a celebration of character and plot in *Twelfth Night*, exploring also the development of English theatre during Shakespeare's period, or

(d) block-book the IT facilities with a view to examining the ways in which IT skills could be used in a range of vocational areas, including journalism, advertising and the promotion of tourism, or

(e) plan around the theme of the environment, aiming for the production of a series of colourful anthologies of creative writing celebrating personal relationships with aspects of the environment?

Clearly this is something of an artificial exercise, and the answer is not to be found on the back page, but it may well serve to illustrate how teachers of English will differ in the weight they give to different views of the subject. Before the National Curriculum an

English teacher (depending on the degree of autonomy given by a department or school) was able to follow individual strengths and preferences. This had clear advantages. It meant, however, that pupils' experiences could be very narrow and unbalanced.

## Tensions in the nature of English

It is also interesting to consider the name of the subject English. Clearly, as it stands, it carries many connotations (as does the term 'National Curriculum') beyond its definition as one subject in the curriculum: some, perhaps, of nationality and exclusivity which may not be entirely desirable. What's in a name? you may ask, but thinking about alternative possible names will focus on what precisely the subject is all about and where the thrust of its teaching should be situated. Possibilities are:

- the language arts (favoured by Abbs 1976 among others);
- rhetorical studies (implied by Eagleton 1983);
- literacy studies (certainly in line with the present government's concern);
- cultural studies;
- communications;
- discourse awareness;
- language and literature studies.

Examining English from the perspective of different people in society – parents, professionals, curriculum legislators, teachers of other subjects or phases, for example – can help us think about the name and nature of the subject, and may illustrate a wide diversity of thinking. A principled position is necessary but it is of course practicable to remain reasonably eclectic in approach, keeping an open mind not only to different philosophies – which assuredly will develop and change with time – but to the different needs and ideas as discerned in and expressed by the pupils themselves. It is perfectly feasible, for example, to cover all five of the hypothetical schemes of work designed for the Year 8 class within one year; indeed, this may be a very effective way of ensuring breadth of entitlement. What we need to do, above all, is to reflect on our own preferences and predilections, compensating when appropriate for any personal shortcomings through a conscious effort to adapt to new ways and areas of English teaching. The subject provides an extremely fertile field for exploration and experimentation, for differing relationships between theory and practice. It may be instructive here to examine some of the tensions involved in this complex interrelationship, and I should like to use Stead's theories of poetic creativity to draw one or two parallels with the subject English, before reappraising the National Curriculum in the light of the findings. Stead (1964: 11) had this to say about poetry:

> A poem may be said to exist in a triangle, the points of which are, first, the poet, second, the audience, and, third, the areas of experience which we call variously 'Reality', 'Truth', or 'Nature'. Between these points run lines of tension, and depending on the time, the place, the

poet, and the audience, these lines will lengthen or shorten . . . There are infinite variations, but . . . the finest poems are likely to be those which exist in an equilateral triangle, each point pulling equally in a moment of perfect tension.

It strikes me that there is a great deal of validity in this with reference to the whole process of writing, which will be explored in Chapter 6, and Stead develops his own argument through close textual analysis of the work of several poets; but in what sense might this taut or sagging triangle refer to the teaching of English?

A great deal depends on what goes into the triangle, and what exactly is represented by each of the three points. If we take the triangle to enclose and express the whole business of English teaching, which, like Stead's poem, is created, then it may follow that one point represents the English teacher; another, the audience of pupils (although this may not be the only possible audience); and the final point symbolises the context – the outer world, perhaps, which exerts so many often contradictory pressures on the processes of teaching. If we pursue the parallel further, we can see that effective teaching depends on the maintenance of a certain tension along the lines joining the points: if the points become too close to, or too distant from, either each other or the central project of teaching itself, there may well be a danger that the creative art of teaching could be damaged. This is in the end an argument for a dynamic combination of reflective distance and imaginative involvement – qualities which may seem like opposites, and perhaps they are; but to go back to Blake's *Marriage of Heaven and Hell*, 'without contraries is no progression'.

To aim for such a dynamic combination is to inform the totality of the experience of teaching English, not only in relation to the considerations outlined above but, perhaps more importantly and certainly more immediately, as affecting classroom practice. The principle of reflective distance combining with imaginative involvement must be a principle encouraged in pupils' attitudes towards their own experience of the subject as well as being embedded as a pedagogical cornerstone. We need, paradoxically, to be rigorous in creating the objective circumstances to allow our pupils' own subjectivities to take root. In addition to ensuring appropriate coverage of the National Curriculum requirements, the teacher must also be prepared to give space, to keep a distance, to allow for genuine and autonomous development. I am reminded of the Zen *koan* that the way to control a flock of sheep is to give them a wide pasture to wander in. Harrison (1994: 7), pursuing the apt metaphor of education as theatre, asks pertinently:

Could the theatre of education . . . be trying too hard to 'deliver the goods' to its clients, the learners, and leaving no space for them to create their own vision? Are we providing enough space for learners to bring their own minds and cultures into taking part in learning? Have we lost sight of essential qualities such as play, curiosity and friendship in learning? Whose 'production' is it, anyway?

Whose indeed? The question demands an affirmative answer: ours, both teacher's and pupils'. It is not simply a matter of standing back, of showing more tolerance – although these are often underrated virtues, particularly when teaching adolescent boys – but of being able at times to live with a Keatsian negative capability, 'that is when man is capable of being in uncertainties, Mysteries, doubts without any irritable reaching after fact and reason' (2002: 41).

## Practical dimensions

The teaching and learning of English needs adventurousness, but also must be accompanied by a positive effort to create the right conditions and provide the boundaries to ensure a sense of security for those involved: the shepherd of the Zen *koan* (and it is interesting how often the pastoral metaphor finds its way into education) would be less than wise if the ultimate boundary of the wide pasture was a cliff edge. One of the implications for practice is the need to create an appropriate environment for each other's learning, if possible as part of whole-school practice, and, more particularly for English, attending to such concerns as:

- the layout of the classroom;
- excellence and relevance of displays;
- provision of designated areas for reading, audio-visual work and other activities;
- class libraries;
- facilities for ICT and self-directed studies.

In many ways, secondary English teachers need to learn, indeed have learned already, from the best of primary school practice: it has often struck me that by Year 6 many youngsters have become significantly autonomous learners, only to take a step or two backwards on arrival in secondary school. The impact of the National Strategy has been considerable here, however, and has altered the relationship between primary and secondary school phases. Since 2001, when the Strategy was first implemented at Key Stage 3, initially for Year 7, secondary school English teachers have needed to acknowledge, far more so than in previous years, the work of primary school colleagues in fostering literacy-based learning in their incoming Year 7 pupils. Indeed this aim was made explicit in the original NLS Framework of 1997, applicable then only to the primary phase:

> Because it is vitally important to ensure that there is continuity between primary and secondary schools in the efforts to improve literacy, we recommend that in their strategy for literacy, local education authorities give deliberate attention to creating and maintaining co-operation between secondary schools and their feeder primary schools.
>
> (DfEE 1998: para 119)

In fact the shift in the balance of power and influence between primary and secondary schools has gone a great deal further than this 1997 pronouncement has suggested, so that it is now somewhat inappropriate to speak, perhaps patronisingly, of 'feeder' primary schools. In this context, Goodwyn and Findlay have coined the term 'phase-related role reversal', maintaining that the Strategy 'has broken the implicit belief that primary and secondary schools are actually different planets in an age when interplanetary travel for teachers themselves is just possible but not really very desirable' (2002: 50). Now, however, increasingly, secondary English teachers find the young aliens alarmingly knowledgeable and their teachers challengingly expert; as a result secondary teachers are discovering how to travel and are returning mightily impressed and not a little daunted at the task they face.

(ibid.: 50–1)

In the main this has been a positive change, bringing the two phases closer in a positive spirit of collaboration. During both primary and secondary phases, increasing collaboration has suggested that we need to safeguard principles of independence and creative English teaching against the onslaught of insistence from some quarters for more and more didactic teaching as narrow preparation for equally narrow SATs – essentially the policing mechanism for adherence to official policy. Although the KS3 SATs have now been abandoned – thanks in no small measure to the sustained opposition of the English teaching community – this policing is still very much in place through the inspection regime, stringent target setting and similar pressures.

Which brings us back to the National Curriculum. In the light of the considerations noted above, it may be helpful at this stage to take stock of the National Curriculum for English through conducting a Strengths/Weaknesses/Opportunities/Threats (SWOT) analysis. This is a convenient and widely used management tool effective in summarising ideas and potential conflicts about any topic; the idea is to convert the threats and weaknesses into opportunities and strengths – not always that easy! The eventual diagram may look something like Figure 1.1.

The particular strengths, weaknesses, opportunities and threats listed here are the result of PGCE students' reflections on fairly early acquaintance with the National Curriculum, and it is likely that no two groups would come up with the same list: what is important is achieving an appreciation both of balance and of conflict in order to make sense of the practicalities of actually teaching the English curriculum. The idea is to work collaboratively to convert the weaknesses into strengths, the threats into opportunities.

| STRENGTHS | WEAKNESSES |
|---|---|
| Clear basis for planning | Inflexibility: lack of scope |
| Criteria for assessment | Overcrowding of curriculum |
| Progress and continuity | Summative not formative assessment |
| Reasonably full idea of English | Focus on 'traditional values' |
| Speaking/listening given status | Scant regard for special needs |
| **OPPORTUNITIES** | **THREATS** |
| Scope to develop beyond the stated curriculum | Temptation to 'teach to the SATs' |
| Minimum entitlement established | Teachers reduced to 'technicians' |
| Collaborative possibilities within and outside | Undue pressure on scarce resources |
| English departments | Cultural bias: marginalisation of ethnic groups |

**FIGURE 1.1**

In order to illustrate the possibilities of working with the National Curriculum for English, consider the set of ideas based around an exploration of the world of traditional ballads for Year 7 through a broad range of activities shown in Figure 1.2.

You can see at a glance the wide range of different activities possible through study of one particular genre, and of course this sort of list of diverse activities could be replicated or extended for an endless variety of themes, texts or genres. Using the National Curriculum for English, it may be instructive at this point to 'map out' the activities, or their equivalent, using the official framework. This process can also provide a useful means of giving more direction to the teaching. The table in Figure 1.3 shows how each activity links to the Programmes of Study and the teaching focus which may result.

This process will be further developed in Chapter 7, but it may already be evident that planning in this way, in this order, helps to keep the National Curriculum's demands in perspective: good English teaching starts from what is desirable and possible in the reality of classroom engagement, with a 'best possible fit' into the detail of the National Curriculum. If at the end of a specific period of study the English teacher – or, better still, the English department working collaboratively – finds that certain areas have not been sufficiently covered, then is the time to extend or adapt the scheme of study.

---

## EXPLORATION OF THE WORLD OF TRADITIONAL BALLADS

**Resources** might include recorded versions of the following:

- 'Little Musgrave' or the variant 'Matty Groves' (Nic Jones/Planxty/Fairport Convention)
- 'Rosie Anderson' (Dave Burland)
- 'The House of the Rising Sun' (The Animals/Joan Baez)
- 'Dark Streets of London' (The Pogues)
- 'The Dark Eyed Sailor' (June Tabor/Steeleye Span/Kate Rusby)

**Activities**

- Drama: group interpretation of ballads for performance.
- Reading aloud, rehearsed, in pairs to the rest of the class.
- Arranging a coherent sequence from jumbled verse order as poetry.
- Discussion of and research into the importance of oral tradition, including modern equivalents of tales, urban myths, jokes, rhymes.
- Presentation through posters, book illustrations, comic strips, music.
- Writing a ballad version of a modern story based on press cuttings.
- Writing a modern prose version of a traditional ballad.
- Writing based on characters and plots in ballads.
- Newspaper account of ballad events.

Broader issues and extension work may include, through research, drama and discussion: study of dreams and the supernatural, the nature of the experiences often sensationally highlighted in ballads, the social and historical context of myths, the subsequent decline of the ballad form, and cross-curricular possibilities.

**FIGURE 1.2**

| Pupil activities | English curriculum area | Possible teaching focus |
|---|---|---|
| Group interpretation of ballads. | Analyse and engage with ideas, themes and language; analyse and discuss alternative interpretations; take notes from written and oral sources. | Pupils take notes and compare each other's performances in discussion. |
| Reading aloud, rehearsed, in pairs to the rest of the class. | Read aloud, telling and enacting stories and poems; adapt their presentations. | Teacher advises about intonation and expression. |
| Arranging a coherent sequence from jumbled verse order. | Analyse and engage with the ideas, themes and language in poetry. | Pupils asked to give reasons for their choices and decisions; pupils given guidance through language use, symbolism, conventions of the genre, poetic devices. |
| Discussion of and research into the importance of oral tradition, including modern equivalents of tales, urban myths, jokes, rhymes. | How usage, words and meaning change over time; current influences on spoken and written language; differences between speech and writing. | Pupils present research findings in terms of specific aspects of language change. |
| Presentation through posters, book illustrations, comic strips, music. | Analyse and evaluate the use of language in a variety of media; compare and synthesise information drawn from different texts. | Pupils compare and analyse the different versions after completion with reference to the original. |
| Writing a ballad version of a modern story based on press cuttings. | Write in a range of forms; read to select information. | Teacher draws attention to form and style of ballads; pupils shown how to select and adapt information for composition. |
| Writing a modern prose version of a traditional ballad. | Use knowledge of distinctive ways of organising and expressing ideas; examine discourse structure. | Teacher draws attention to use of paragraphs in prose. |
| Writing based on characters and plots in ballads. | Reflection on motivation and behaviour of characters, the development of plot and the overall impact of a text. | Pupils underline words and phrases which give insight into character before attempting their own writing. |
| Newspaper account of ballad events. | Use knowledge of the distinctive ways of organising and expressing ideas and information; evaluate how information is presented. | Comparison of use of headline and exaggeration in modern newspapers; media study based on comparison between sensational journalism and ballads. |

FIGURE 1.3

The example in Figure 1.3 is deliberately broad in its range, and clearly the English teacher should focus on specific needs and preferences in detail as appropriate. At other times, especially when addressing a particular 'gap' in pupils' coverage of the National Curriculum stipulations, the need for greater detail should inform planning from the start. The examples in Figures 1.4 and 1.5, both created by beginning teachers of English, are based on Janni Howker's short story 'Badger on the Barge' (1986) as taught to a Year 9 group; the first examines narrative structure and development; the second seeks a creative way to teach the skills of letter writing and appropriate register.

Again we can see how, with a little imagination, the requirements of the National Curriculum may be met through an organic rather than mechanistic approach. Indeed the introduction to the 2000 Orders, under the heading 'The Importance of English', suggested that English enables pupils 'to express themselves creatively and imaginatively

---

## A. Introductory lesson on 'Badger on the Barge' with a Year 9 English group

**Resources**

- the story 'Badger on the Barge': one copy for each pupil;
- sets of ten cards, each containing the following words: badger, wheelchair, geriatric ward, motorbike helmet, truant, brandy, earthworms.

**Development**

- Arrange the class into five friendship groups. Given the cards, each group has to invent a storyline using all the depicted words within ten minutes. Each group then presents its skeleton story, with all pupils taking some part (possibly using some dramatic role-play).
- Whole-class discussion ensues on the nature of narrative development and the significance of key words, the teacher using the whiteboard to summarise.
- During a subsequent lesson, the class is introduced to the short story itself, and, as the reading progresses, compares the original with the groups' ideas.
- A further possibility is to examine in detail the use Janni Howker makes of the key words in the narrative development.

**FIGURE 1.4**

---

## B. The skills of letter writing through study of 'Badger on the Barge'

After reading the short story, pupils are given the choice of writing a letter from the following list, and the whole class discusses the appropriate register and vocabulary for each, making notes if necessary:

- Helen's mother to the school, explaining Helen's absence;
- an interfering neighbour to the school's head teacher, complaining about truancy;
- a nursing sister to the old lady's daughter;
- Helen to a friend, telling her side of the story;
- a passerby to the local newspaper complaining about the state of the barge.

The letters could then be shared among the class, with each pupil writing a reply to a letter in a contrasting register to that sent originally.

**FIGURE 1.5**

and to communicate with others effectively' (DfEE/QCA 1999: 13). Thus the National Curriculum can be viewed not just as a set of individual syllabus requirements but as providing a broad conception of the way English should be realised as a subject in schools. Attention has tended to focus on the more controversial aspects such as the place of standard English (to be discussed in more detail in later chapters). However, the following selected quotations from the 1995 National Curriculum, still very much embedded in the current version, indicate that it can be judged to require a dynamic and varied approach:

- Pupils' abilities should be developed within an integrated programme of speaking and listening, reading and writing.
- Pupils should be given opportunities to talk for a range of purposes.
- Pupils should be given opportunities to read a wide variety of literature . . . to read widely and independently solely for enjoyment.
- The main emphasis should be on the encouragement of wider reading in order to develop independent, responsive and enthusiastic readers.
- Pupils should be encouraged to extend their confidence in writing for a variety of purposes and to develop their own distinctive and original styles.
- Pupils should be given opportunities to write for specific readers, for a large unknown readership and for themselves.

We can add to this list two quotations from the earliest formulation of the English Order:

- Working on tasks which they have chosen and which they direct for themselves.
- Working with teachers who are themselves involved in the processes, with special expertise, as talkers, listeners, readers and writers.

## Working collaboratively

A list of this kind can be used to evaluate how well the objectives are being achieved. Such aims are at best extremely difficult to achieve as a lone English teacher isolated in his or her classroom. This realisation opens the door for a spirit of collaboration, and the advent of the National Curriculum for English has ushered in a highly practical sense of working together – even at times sharpened by the sense of opposition to a common enemy in some of the more foolish aspects of this curriculum. Sometimes the only creative response to a threat is to fight back, as with the KS3 SATs, and this can serve to highlight common ground and shared ideals among English teachers. The need for collaboration has been sharpened further by the increasing – and generally very healthy – diversity of new entrants' degree backgrounds. Even among those whose degree is in some sense 'English', there are bound to be areas of knowledge and expertise in which practitioners feel less secure than others. Correspondingly, the scope and breadth of the subject English have increased enormously in recent years. With these factors in mind, mutual support among English teachers in a department or some other kind of network (for example a local authority inspired group of newly qualified teachers, or one convened through the National Association of Teachers of English, or a PGCE partnership) could be swiftly facilitated through completion and distribution of a simple form requesting information which can be shared (Figure 1.6).

This sort of questioning can indeed form a useful starting point, but the real work – and the real rewards – starts afterwards and must be sustained. In the sense that this is a vision-inspired process to be skilfully managed, all English teachers involved in it are both leaders, providing the vision, and managers, grappling with the means of attainment. This is in reality a process of professional development. It is a question of achieving some sort of balance between creative, individual autonomy (traditionally the hallmark of the English teacher) and the needs of the organisation in interpreting and teaching the National Curriculum. For Knight (1996: 1) it is precisely this curriculum which is the problem:

> Traditionally there has often been a healthy tension between the individualism invited by the subject and the systems within which it was obliged to work. Until the coming of the National Curriculum it was possible for many teachers of 'English' to reconcile the two: to teach the subject according to their best conscience and to ensure that their pupils were not thereby disabled when it came to public certification of their achievements.

The fundamental issue at stake here is whether the National Curriculum and its attendant policing mechanisms need be seen entirely as a threat, as Knight maintains; is there, even, an opportunity lurking there? Perhaps we have already demonstrated that there is one, for the taking, and English teachers, resilient as ever, are not slow on the uptake. Characteristics of positive collaboration, in practical terms, may include:

---

**AREAS OF EXPERTISE IN ENGLISH TEACHING**
**Mutual support for aspects of English in the secondary school curriculum**

Areas of particular interest or expertise:

Key English texts, used in schools, with which you are familiar:

Area(s) in which you'd welcome assistance:

Experience of cross-curricular possibilities:

Specific experience of such aspects as:

- drama
- media education
- ICT
- Special Educational Needs
- teaching of grammar
- post-16
- mixed ability/setting

---

**FIGURE 1.6**

- shared schemes of work, collaboratively formed;
- swapping of resources;
- regular meetings to share pedagogical ideas and practices;
- mutual observation of lessons;
- reaching out to other departments to examine cross-curricular potential;
- involvement in wider contexts such as NATE or PGCE partnerships;
- collaborative mentoring of new teachers;
- involvement of pupils in formulating and responding to practice;
- informal involvement in extra-curricular and social activities.

Collaboration without individual flair can be sterile, as Fullan and Hargreaves (1992: 14) note: 'People can find themselves collaborating for the sake of collaboration . . . and, contrary to popular opinion, it can reduce innovation and imaginative solutions to individual situations, as susceptibility to the latest chosen innovation and "groupthink" carry the day.' English teachers seem particularly well equipped to avoid pitfalls such as these, but it is a position that has been hard won and that will need to be defended with a watchful eye by those entering the profession. As we turn to look in more detail at the areas of experience involved in the teaching of English, whether stemming from the National Curriculum or bursting its boundaries, it is as well to keep this in mind. To conclude this chapter we could do worse than finish as we started with William Blake, who asserted through his character Los in *Jerusalem*:

> I must create a system or be enslaved by another man's.
> I will not reason or compare: my business is to create.

### Further reading

Two books by Cox – *Cox on Cox* (1991) and *Cox on the Battle for the English Curriculum* (1995) – give fascinating insights into the emergence of the English Order. Of the official documents, the Report of the Kingman Committee (DES 1988) and that of the Cox Committee (DES 1989) are still worth reading. Books by Goodson and Medway (1990) *Bringing English to Order*, Protherough and King (eds) (1995) *The Challenge of English in the National Curriculum*, Davies (1996) *What is English Teaching?*, Knight (1996) *Valuing English: Reflections on the National Curriculum* and Goodwyn (ed.) (1995) *English and Ability* contain critiques of the English Order. Many of the more recent books attempt to focus less on the National Curriculum itself and more on the National Strategy – see Further reading section in Chapter 2 for more details.

## Resources

Many educational publishers have attempted to ease the English teacher's burden of planning and implementing the National Curriculum. Some of the most effective in combining imaginative and rigorous approaches are to be found in *The English Pack* (Bates *et al.* 1994) (photocopiable) and *Key Stage 3 English Units* (ed. Broadbent 1995), English and Media Centre (photocopiable, and including detailed planning sections). As noted above, much recent publishing has been more concerned with implementation of the Strategy in practical terms – although all have to work on the basis of the National Curriculum. The website Teachit (www.teachit.co.uk) is a boon for many English teachers seeking resources and ideas for lessons, and the collection *The Full English* (Blake 2006), jointly published by Teachit and NATE, contains an inspiring sample of these ideas.

# 2

# The impact of the Strategy

*By words the mind is winged.*

Aristophanes

## Introduction: the context

THE MAJOR CHANGE to the secondary English curriculum since the first edition of this book has occurred at Key Stage 3 developing (some would add, with indecent haste) from the primary phase National Literacy Strategy and its centrally embedded Literacy Hour. The National Strategy: English Strand, as the National Literacy Strategy in so far as it affects English has become, now profoundly influences the entire English curriculum, as already noted, through its integration into the current National Curriculum. Perhaps 'influences' is too weak a word in this context, however: certainly all English departments are influenced, but in some schools and some local authorities the English curriculum as it has hitherto developed is in danger of being subsumed by the Strategy. Certainly there is something potentially all-encompassing about it, but the argument here – throughout the book and in this chapter particularly – is that it need not be so. Rather, I hope to show that, with flexible and positive interpretation, it is possible and desirable to implement the curricular changes inspired by the Strategy, and also to safeguard and develop all that is worth fighting for in the English curriculum. At the same time we need to be realistic, and directly critical when necessary, if this desirable flexibility is to be attained.

It could be argued that because the demands of literacy education are so fundamental to the teaching and learning of English, ideally so integrated into the practical curriculum, it would be mistaken to devote a chapter to it as a discrete entity in a book like this. Most English teachers could happily agree with Davies that:

> the first requirement of the English teacher has to be to ensure that students can read and write, to make them literate. Beyond that point I believe that students should be actively encouraged to read for pleasure and should be provided with an adequate timetable for personal reading.
>
> (1996: 135)

The Strategy, it could be argued, is simply there to facilitate such an aim. To a point, there is validity in this argument, but three important questions are begged: first, the nature of the literacy at the centre of the debate; second, the nature of the Strategy in place ostensibly at least to service the need; and, third, the perhaps inevitable tension between the ability to read and the desire to read for pleasure. It is precisely because these issues are so fundamental to the teaching of English in secondary schools that we feel it is appropriate to devote a single chapter to literacy – and the Strategy in particular.

The rich variety of the English curriculum as a whole, ever-shifting entity could not – certainly should not – be reduced to any one strategy, however laudable. And this would indeed be the danger if we failed to distinguish between the needs and recommendations of the Strategy, and those of the curriculum as a whole. Already there is a widely perceived issue here concerning the apparently all-pervasive, unquestioning – and all too often unquestioned – nature of the Strategy: what Goodwyn and Findlay (2002: 50) term 'the fundamentalist tendency in the strategy . . . its ubiquitous ability to make criticism almost unthinkable, the only question is how to implement this great good and to convert unbelievers'. It is in the spirit of this book precisely to open up the Strategy to critical – but practically orientated – appraisal, and here again we need to maintain the kind of sharp focus on its nature and implications which would be difficult to achieve if examination and discussion were to be diffused through its integration into other chapters.

The three questions outlined above – the nature of literacy, the Strategy itself, and the tension between ability and enjoyment – are the guiding issues of this chapter. I shall look in some detail at the first two questions shortly; the third suggests an immediate, and possibly very familiar, way in to the whole area of literacy and its relationship to the English curriculum. Interestingly in this context, recent research conducted by Marion Sainsbury for the National Foundation for Educational Research in 2003 (NFER; see www.nfer.ac.uk) has highlighted the tension. Findings from research on Year 4 and Year 6 children, conducted between 1998 and 2003, have suggested that 'children's enjoyment of reading has significantly declined since 1998', and, further, that 'boys' enjoyment of reading has declined more than girls', especially among the older children in this age range. However, the research also indicated that 'children's confidence and independence as readers have significantly improved since 1998'. Giving a broader context for these findings, Sainsbury infers that 'children in England are good at reading, and this finds a reflection in their confidence in themselves as readers. However, their enjoyment of reading is poor in comparison to other countries and has declined over recent years.' Although this survey was focused on primary phase pupils, and limited itself to the field of reading, arguably just one facet of literacy, the results and tentative conclusions are surely pertinent to English teaching in the secondary school. Indeed, anecdotal evidence suggests if anything an exacerbation of the problem as youngsters go through Key Stage 3 and beyond, continuing the trend already noted in the research evidence between Year 4 and Year 6. Many English teachers I have spoken to in recent years have commented on the apparent literacy proficiency of their Year 7 intake as well as a certain reluctance among those same pupils to actually read for pleasure. Clearly it would be unfair, at least on this evidence, to blame the Strategy, in any of the key stages, for demotivating children as readers. But on the other hand it seems to me that there is enough here to suggest a certain tension with which English teachers have to grapple, and one I shall return to in the context of this chapter. What indeed is the point of educating children to read ever more proficiently if the love of reading itself has not been successfully fostered?

The context and immediate history of the development of the Strategy is undoubtedly significant here – as is the nature of the word 'strategy' itself. Indeed we are encouraged as English teachers to emphasise word-level studies, and this word is especially interesting. It connotes, for me at least, a world of managerial directives and more or less willing civil servants slotting into some large-scale, centrally planned initiative; and by more or less the same token, I sense a military dimension here: an implied metaphor for military forces deployed, again centrally, by some military technician to destroy an enemy. Moreover, the etymology of the word tells me it derives from the Greek *strategia*, or 'generalship'. But maybe this is the wrong sort of word-level analysis; maybe I should instead be focusing on the spelling rules I could glean from such a word rather than on metaphorical suggestiveness, or on what preconceptions about the nature of teaching and learning the widespread use of the word might belie. Maybe I should not be straying into the field of critical literacy at all. Herein lies another tension – words and their joining together seem to me inherently fascinating, at least in the hands of good English teachers, and not just in their basic (whatever this word means) spelling or punctuation. Words are inextricably mixed up with implied and inferred meanings, and our aim as English teachers, I maintain, must be to explore literacy in this its fullest sense, harnessing the Strategy wherever appropriate with this aim in mind. This is of course quite a different conception of the role of the English teacher from that implied – however subjectively – by the word 'strategy': technicians simply enforcing, 'delivering', a pre-ordained plan. But the 'Rationale' of the Strategy itself reminds us that 'a shrewd and fluent independent reader', among other things, should be 'sensitive to the way meanings are made' and able to read 'in different ways for different purposes' (DfEE 2001: 10). Further, the reader (at text level in Year 9 at least) should be able to 'synthesise information from a range of sources, shaping the material to meet the reader's needs' (ibid.: 31). How apt indeed: this kind of shrewd sensitivity and expertise surely applies as much to English teachers in their relationship to the Strategy as it does to English learners with regard to any other text. After all it is our business to model good practice.

## The arrival of the Strategy

The immediate historical context of the Strategy has been the well-nigh universally implemented National Literacy Strategy at Key Stages 1 and 2 – successfully, at least according to official evaluations – and continuing fears about the nation's economic performance in relation to its competitors in so far as this may derive from the perceived literacy levels of the workforce. Thus the incoming Labour government of 1997 made improvement in literacy the cornerstone of its drive to raise achievement levels throughout the school age range and, after a brief pilot exercise at secondary level (DfEE 2000), quickly went on to establish the literacy Framework in virtually all secondary schools for the incoming Year 7 in 2001–2, and for Years 8 and 9 successively by 2003–4. Although never statutory (unlike the National Curriculum), the policing of Key Stage 3 teaching, especially through Ofsted (the Office for Standards in Education, Children's Services and Skills) inspections and through local education authority (LEA) literacy 'consultants', meant that the adoption of the Strategy has been pretty close to universal. It is possible, as with all such things, to 'read' this transformation – for transformation it certainly is – in different ways. It could be suggested, for example, that, not content with prescribing (and by extension proscribing too) the 'what' of the English curriculum through the implementation of the National Curriculum, the central government has been intent also on determining the pedagogical 'how'. Certainly the Strategy, in its bald documentary manifestations but far more through the work of its officials and consultants, is greatly concerned with deliberate intervention in pedagogical matters, and this is where its impact has been felt most strongly. The prescription of competencies for teaching, subsequently *Professional Standards for Qualified Teacher Status* (TTA 2002, substantially revised (TDA) in 2007), in initial teacher education as supervised officially by the Teacher Training Agency has perhaps, to a lesser extent, been part of the same broad intention.

Possibly in a more favourable light, however, the Strategy may be seen as something of a fulfilment of the far-sighted but only ever patchily implemented insights and recommendations of the 1975 official report *A Language for Life* (DES 1975 – widely known as the Bullock Report), which arose from the investigations and deliberations of a committee of enquiry chaired by Bullock. As such the Strategy seeks to influence the entire school curriculum, as did Bullock, in ways which focus consciously and rigorously on language as a tool for learning across all disciplines but with particular reference to English. But whereas adherence to Bullock's recommendations depended largely on the leanings of particular schools or LEAs, in the rather more laissez-faire climate of those times, the current Strategy is in effect the cornerstone of official education policy. Certainly its impact is being felt across the curriculum, but, perhaps inevitably, it is English departments that are most closely involved with its literacy dimensions. In the late 1990s HMI conducted exhaustive investigations into the literacy models then used in secondary education, including the pilot secondary literacy projects of 1998–9. The resulting 'agenda' provides an interesting list of 18 literacy issues to consider – pertinent now as then to secondary English teachers. They include (Hertrich 1999):

- What is meant by a literate secondary age pupil?
- What strategies and structures are necessary to sustain literary development beyond Year 7?
- Is literacy development for all? What are the particular needs of boys, EAL pupils and higher attainers?
- What is the relationship of literacy developments to English and to existing SEN work?
- What kind of guidance do schools need?
- To what extent can/does literacy development entail a 'dumbing down' of English?
- What level of knowledge about language do teachers need?

All these points deserve serious attention, and all are distinctly pertinent to the work of English teachers. It may well be that the general direction of the Strategy, following HMI's lead among others, has been in furthering the cross-curricular and adult needs approaches to the subject English (two of the five models for English suggested by Cox in 1989, as outlined in Chapter 1, and arguably the least popular of the five among English specialists). The introductory words of the resulting *Framework for Teaching English: Years 7, 8 and 9* (DfEE 2001: 1), for example, manage to avoid the subject (in both senses of this word) of English altogether, stating that 'The Key Stage 3 National Strategy is part of the government's commitment to raise standards in schools. Effective literacy is the key to raising standards across all subjects, and equipping pupils with the skills and knowledge they need for life beyond school.' This terse and uncompromising tone is typical of the official pronouncements we have become used to, and contrasts markedly with the language of Bullock, for example, or the language of persuasion English teachers habitually and effectively use in their teaching. However, putting this gripe aside, there does seem to be enough in Hertrich's original list of issues to enable English teachers to focus questioningly, realistically and creatively on the nature of their subject knowledge and pedagogy – especially in the penultimate bullet point quoted above.

## Issues of transition

In the light of such issues, and as mentioned previously in the context of changes in the National Curriculum, the relationship between primary and secondary phases has altered considerably with the implementation of the Strategy. A large part of the funding of the Strategy has gone towards easing the transition between phases, and guidance such as that offered in *Transition from Year 6 to Year 7 English* (DfES 2002a) is certainly helpful and practically orientated. Literacy is in many ways the key area as the foundation for all subsequent learning, particularly in terms of the transfer and subsequent use of pupil-based information, the continuity of the literacy curriculum, the introduction of Summer Literacy Schools as a means of raising standards in preparation for the secondary curriculum, and general cross-phase liaison. The impact of initiatives such as these has been significant, especially in those school-partnerships that have taken them seriously; as Beverton notes (2003: 219), there is an emerging consensus of opinion that social upheavals caused by moving to secondary school are so great that unless school intervenes in a positive way, to focus upon what Ruddock (1995) calls 'the seriousness of learning', students find learning difficult during the first year or longer of secondary education. Thus there is now growing evidence of the need for establishing at primary/secondary transfer sound academic bases for secondary students' future learning. However, as Beverton also finds, as do Goodwyn and Findlay (2002), such an emphasis in practice is far from universal. What is now certain is that, in order to do their job effectively, English teachers at secondary level need to address the issues of continuity and progression in a positive but realistic spirit. The nature of the subject will inevitably change as a result, and we as a profession must ensure that this change is positive.

## The nature of the Strategy

So, what exactly are the implications of all this for the teaching and learning of English in the secondary classroom? Essentially the Strategy, in terms of its recommended pedagogy, is based around what Harrison, in his officially sponsored appraisal (*The National Strategy for English at Key Stage 3: Roots and Research*) has approvingly called 'the five elements of the [then] proposed teaching sequence' (Harrison 2002: 3):

- identification of prior knowledge;
- teacher demonstration of process;
- shared exploration through activity;
- scaffolded pupil application of new learning;
- consolidation through discussion/activity.

Clearly there is little to take issue with here; indeed much of the thrust of this book's recommendations has been along these lines. Effective English teaching acknowledges students' immense linguistic experience and knowledge as its starting point, building collaboratively with appropriate leadership, modelling and scaffolding towards deep learning. If there is a devil at work at all here – and many would maintain there is, as we shall see – it must be in the interpretation of these five points for classroom activity. The main danger, it seems to me, is in too narrow or restrictive an interpretation of these laudable aims. If, for example, 'identification of prior knowledge' comes to mean simply 'ascertaining what's been previously taught', or, worse, 'what National Curriculum level has been attained', or if 'teacher demonstration of process' implies merely the teacher showing – teaching, in effect – just one way of conducting an activity according to the conventions of a particular genre, then a real opportunity to strengthen English pedagogy – in terms of both breadth and depth – will have been missed. Similarly, 'consolidation' could mean simply a rather mechanistic reinforcement of what the teacher thinks has been learned, as opposed to anything of a genuinely exploratory nature. If secondary English teachers are to learn anything from the more negative aspects of the Key Stage 1 and 2 experience of the Strategy during its often painful implementation in the latter half of the 1990s, it is that sensitive, reflective flexibility has to be at the centre of literacy teaching.

## Practical implications of the Strategy

Of course there is a great deal more to the Strategy as it affects secondary English than better cross-phase liaison and a pedagogy based on five key elements. English teachers are now required to have a far more rigorous and detailed knowledge of language, particularly in terms of grammar and spelling, than previously, both for textual analysis and for improving pupils' conscious awareness of their own writing. There is too a far greater emphasis on non-fiction, signalling a move away from cultural heritage and personal growth models of English towards more functionally orientated conceptions of the subject, as noted previously. Further, English teachers are now having to accept that the teaching of reading, often at quite a basic level, is not the responsibility only of primary phase teachers, and that it involves techniques previously seen only in Special Educational Needs departments in secondary schools, if indeed there. Again, in all three of these broad areas, there is a distinct opportunity to extend meaningfully (and sharpen) the English curriculum; but again, so much depends on enlightened interpretation of the possibilities.

This kind of interpretation has to be based on a clear and detailed knowledge and understanding of what exactly is in the Framework, in terms of both its potential and its limitations. I shall look shortly at the model of literacy at its core, and at some of the criticisms levelled at the Strategy; before this, however, an outline of the main concerns may be helpful. The essential structure is along the lines of three distinctive variations of language analysis: at word level, sentence level and text level. At text level especially the Framework seeks to influence all three National Curriculum facets (or Attainment Targets as National Curriculum-speak somewhat oddly has them) of English, namely reading, writing, and speaking and listening. A measure of integration is clearly intended:

> The list of objectives does not imply that teachers should approach them in isolation or teach them in a reductive way. Objectives benefit from being taught explicitly and from being identified and deployed in context. Planning should draw together objectives from Word, Sentence and Text level . . . Teachers are encouraged to find ways of clustering together complementary objectives.
>
> (DfES 2001: 11)

In terms of fostering pupils' writing practice, building on Key Stage 2 literacy experience, English teachers are advised to specify purpose above all, as defined in 'triplets': 'imagine, explore and entertain', 'inform, explain and describe', 'persuade, argue and advise', and 'analyse, review and comment'. The rest of the Framework document is really an exposition of how to implement this structure in some detail. Much of what is written emphasises good practice in English teaching – but there are some elements which for better or for worse have given, at least for some English departments, pause for thought. Among these could be included the emphasis on objectives-led planning, on teaching that is 'direct and explicit' and 'distinguished by a fast pace and strong focus' (ibid.: 16), and on the four-part lesson. The latter has for many teachers become something of a new orthodoxy, involving a short language-based starter activity, followed by first the introduction to the 'main teaching points' of the lesson, second the longer development phase, and finally, the culmination in the 'plenary to draw out learning'. Although recommended, this structure 'is not intended to become a straitjacket' (ibid.: 17). As ever, so much depends on taste in tailoring: 'Damn braces; bless relaxes', as Blake had it. All of these stipulations, among many others, can be challenged – indeed should be – even if in the end (flexibly) accepted. English teachers need to cultivate the confidence to do precisely that. Many learners, myself included, would indeed find a diet of fast-paced explicit four-part lessons, for which predetermined objectives are carefully signalled, monotonous in the extreme. The need is for a reflective, wide-ranging pedagogy that includes these elements when apt, but selectively and in the context of genuine concern for all kinds of teaching and learning.

There are several other elements of the Strategy, either embedded in the Framework or developed subsequently through subsidiary initiatives or through recommended practice. In many cases these developments have been accompanied by lavish handbooks and video resources of variable quality and usefulness. Shared reading or writing is recommended as the basis of the introductory part of the lesson, whereby 'the teacher demonstrates and models the process of comprehension or composition with the whole class' (ibid.) in what is usually a clearly focused session of up to about 15 minutes. Explicitness is the key here, and pace. Resources such as interactive whiteboards can be invaluable, but direct writing on to OHTs often suffices. Although intended to be interactive, this part of the lesson is frequently characterised by quick-fire closed questions and answers. The main part of the lesson, which should follow seamlessly from the introduction, often takes the form of guided reading or writing, sometimes accompanied by speaking and listening activity. Here there is greater autonomy for small groups of pupils, following the clear instructions given previously, allowing the teacher the opportunity to work closely and intensively with a particular group according to perceived need and, over time, ensuring that all pupils' requirements are similarly catered for. The plenary generally comes at the lesson's end, although this does not have to be the case, and is intended to be a short teacher-led (but interactive) summary of what has been learned and how, if possible referring back to the original explicit learning objectives. Pike (2004: 65–6) has described

the vigour, energy, dynamism and motivational impact that a good plenary should have. Children should be challenged and should know what, of real significance, has happened during the lesson. They should be aware of their learning experience and derive a real sense of purpose from it . . . The key to a good plenary is the start of the lesson where learning objectives are communicated. These are revisited in the plenary so that children know why they have done what they have done and what they have learned from it. They must know the rationale for and purpose of their time in the classroom.

Quite a tall order, in other words, but one that in practice is all too often reduced to a hurried rounding-off of the lesson before the school bell closes it down completely.

For those unfortunate pupils who have failed to match up to their no doubt explicitly made age-related level expectations, there were made available (again copiously resourced) units of work intended, through intensive small-group work, to remedy the situation. Although these units have officially been abandoned, the implications of this sort of remedial teaching are still very much apparent – not least in that much of the material is still used, albeit selectively, in some schools, and is thus worth considering. Specifically, the intention here was to enable all pupils to reach level 4 in National Curriculum terms, widely regarded as the basis of functional literacy and at the heart of much curricular development subsequently. These units were known as Literacy Progress Units (LPUs), and although their teaching generally took place outside the mainstream English class through withdrawal or at separate times, they related directly to the Strategy and thus to the responsibility of the English teacher. As an aside, it is interesting how the term 'progress', once euphemistically used as a label for special educational needs groups

– see for example Willy Russell's humorous, moving play *Our Day Out* – has found its time again. It sometimes seems that everything in education repeats itself ad infinitum. There were in all six LPUs, ranging from units on spelling and grammar through to information retrieval and 'reading between the lines'. Harrison, in the official review of the early years of the secondary Strategy, acknowledged that the list of specified 'critical features' to be taught through the LPUs

> sounds like a rather instrumental approach to literacy improvement, one that is based more on an artificial attempt to enhance pupils' scores on the government's own tests than on the need to motivate and enthuse those who have not made a good start in literacy, [although] the activities within the Literacy Progress Units seem to hold out more promise.

> (DfEE 2001: 32)

Implementation of the LPUs in schools was always patchy, both in quantitative and qualitative terms, but there are assuredly some good teaching ideas and plans contained in them for the determined skim-reading English teacher.

## Models of literacy and the Strategy

To understand more fully the implications of the Strategy for secondary English teachers we need to consider in greater detail the model of literacy teaching and learning upon which it is based, and other possible models. It is here perhaps that there is greatest controversy among English teachers and others concerned with English teaching – and by controversy I do not euphemistically mean simply opposition to the Strategy, for many of those directly or indirectly involved speak of it enthusiastically.

A helpful starting point here is that offered by Pat D'Arcy, characterising the teaching and assessment of writing (but extending into all forms of literacy) in terms of 'two contrasting paradigms'. The first possibility D'Arcy presents as

> a paradigm which focuses on writing largely as a matter of construction and correctness – at word level, sentence level and text level. This kind of linguistic analysis is mechanistic because it pays little or no attention to the meaning of any specific piece of writing. Instead it restricts itself to generalisations about aspects of composition such as structure, organisation, spelling and punctuation.

> (2000: 3)

On the other hand, the 'contrasting paradigm' is 'centred on a meaning-related approach both to how a text is constructed through the thoughts and feelings of the writer and also how a text is interpreted through the thoughts and feelings it evokes in the mind of a reader' (ibid.). Appropriately enough, this fundamental distinction between approaches brings us back to the tension between technical proficiency and enthusiastic willingness in reading I alluded to at the start of this chapter. As D'Arcy elaborates, 'these paradigms are not mutually exclusive' and any difference is 'crucially a matter of focus'.

However, although this particular paper was written before the Key Stage 3 Strategy's implementation, the author already feared that 'this second paradigm . . . has vanished without trace beneath the weight of a steady and relentless spate of official publications' (ibid.). Certainly there is a strong sense, in my reading at least, that the Strategy's theoretical base leans – perhaps alarmingly – towards the former conception of literacy: a model essentially based on analysis of generic form as the key to understanding any given text, rather than emphasising more subtle senses of meaning and value. All the more reason for English teachers to breathe meaning into (and inhale meaning from) any studied or created text – and this of course includes the Strategy itself.

Essentially, then, the Strategy's conception of literacy bases itself on textual analysis to answer questions of intended audience and basic purpose as the twin keys to understanding genre. Resulting insights into generic characteristics and conventions should apparently lead into full understanding, at word, sentence and text levels, and, if appropriate, should give pupils the tools needed for textual replication or emulation. This is basically the 'functional grammar' position as developed in the 1980s and 1990s by such linguists as Kress and Littlefair. Although in many ways persuasive, there are clearly lacking in this model elements of value and values, subjective voice (and ear), and critical literacy. I have elsewhere considered more fully these and other elements (Stevens and McGuinn 2004), suggesting that although they may not be readily evident in the Strategy's theoretical or practical bases, neither are they actually excluded. Given the will, indeed, classroom practice is already demonstrating, anecdotally at least, that secondary English teaching positively includes these facets of literacy, integrating them constructively with more generic considerations. The more enlightened guidance offered by some consultants and others concerned with interpretation and implementation of the Strategy actively bears this out – although there is scope here for much more rigorous research. This fuller sense of literacy is much closer to that offered, for example, by Margaret Meek (1991: 238):

> To be literate we have to be confident that the world of signs and print, in all the different mixtures of mode and meaning that surround us, is a world we can cope with, be at home in, contribute to and play with. If it is simply mysterious, threatening, unreliable or hostile, then we feel at a disadvantage, victimized and inadequate. There is no guarantee that literacy makes the world a more benign place, but it helps everyone to consider how it may be different.

There is evident here a humane quality perhaps understandably lacking in the more hard-nosed official pronouncements of the Strategy – and yet nothing in these communications actually precludes such an approach. Harrison, indeed, in the officially sanctioned *Roots and Research* investigation acknowledges that 'there may not be simple answers to complex questions' in this context, going on to quote approvingly Linda Flower:

> A literate act . . . is an attempt to create meaning, and in doing so, reflects – is itself shaped by – literate, social and cultural practices . . . At the same time, literacy is also a personal, intentional action, an attempt to understand, express, explore, communicate, or influence.
>
> (Flower 1994 in Harrison 2002: 7)

Seen in this light it is possible to place the Strategy itself in a broader, more meaningful (and ultimately more workable) context.

In a little more detail, the Strategy's approach to literacy, at least in terms of its preoccupation with non-literary texts, can be seen to be founded on the 'Extending Interactions with Texts' (EXIT) model. This model was developed by Lewis and Wray in the late 1990s through the Nuffield Extending Literacy (EXEL) Project. Simply stated, this model involves 10 elements, expounded in persuasive detail by Lewis and Wray (2000). The authors acknowledge the 'difficulty of representing a complex and essentially recursive set of processes in the two-dimensional space defined by print on paper' – a familiar issue for any writer – and explain that 'we do not intend the model to be read as a linear description of what happens when we interact with information texts' (2000: 17). Although 'information texts' are specified here, there is a sense that, whatever the text, the Strategy tends to view it as potentially informative rather than, say, primarily affective. I shall return to this issue, with regard to literary texts, later. The ten points of the EXIT model are (ibid.):

- eliciting previous knowledge;
- establishing purposes;
- locating information;
- adopting an appropriate strategy;
- interacting with text;
- monitoring understanding;
- making a record;
- evaluating information;
- assisting memory;
- communicating information.

Some of these approaches should already be familiar; all may be interpreted in different ways (the authors are keen for this to occur), as adventurously as the English teacher sees fit. It is vital also to be acutely sensitive to the particular characteristics and needs both of the audience in question – the nature of the class being taught, normally – and of the kind of text being studied. Selectivity and imaginative interpretation are the watchwords here, but, as long as this is understood, English teachers – along with colleagues from other disciplines, which is one of the main points – can benefit from using the EXIT model.

Issues of linearity and hierarchy in models of learning are problematic for English, which is essentially recursive by nature. Implicit or explicit in a great deal of what passes for literacy teaching is the assumption that the learner has to master 'basic' skills as a precondition of developing towards higher-order understanding. This model is embedded in the organisation of the Framework document, as it is in the National Curriculum with its progressively presented levels of attainment. Although there is clearly some validity in this view – not all ways of reading would be apt for all readers, or indeed for all texts – too rigid an adherence to it would be severely limiting and would risk demotivation for both learners and teachers. 'Basic' readers would be treated as this term suggests: in a basic, unimaginative way – at least until some point of take-off towards greater sophistication. Thus pupils in this category may miss out on creative – and critical – aspects of literacy. Again the English teacher needs to maintain a delicate balance between making literacy accessible to those pupils finding parts of it difficult, and creating exciting learning opportunities at all levels of textual engagement. Harrison (2002: 17) characterises the 'basic skills for basic readers' approach as essentially cognitive, maintaining that 'To take only a cognitive perspective, and to focus on teaching basic skills, therefore, and to ignore the wider rhetorical and social purposes of text, is to deny to the novice models of how to behave like an expert.' Literacy, in other words, needs to be involving, fascinating, challenging at all levels and ages and with all texts. Perhaps if it were, and it is after all in the hands of teachers, the disjunction between reading capability and the desire to read for pleasure would lessen. In effect, this means a literacy that is at base actively critical rather than passively received. As Comber makes clear, we need

> to question any suggestion that critical literacy is a developmental attainment rather than social practice which may be excluded or deliberately included in early literacy curriculum . . . in the early years of schooling, students learn what it means to read and write successfully in terms of school practices. They need opportunities to take on this text analysis role from the start, as part of how culture defines literacy, not as a special curriculum in the later years of schooling or in media studies.
>
> (Comber 2001 in Hunt 2002: 133)

Exactly the same could be said of 'basic literacy' teaching and learning in secondary schools. The use of book series such as 'Livewire Real Lives' (Hodder & Stoughton in association with The Basic Skills Agency 1997 onwards), for example, which attempt to deal with interestingly relevant topics (in this instance the lives of celebrities likely to appeal to the secondary age range), could focus critically on issues such as why exactly these celebrities have been chosen, how they are presented, which pictures have been included and why, the tone of the text, and the overall production. These areas, and many others, may be addressed as part of the reading – a critical part, indeed – even with (perhaps especially with) less confident readers.

## Criticism of the Strategy

There has been, and still is, considerable criticism of the Strategy from various quarters. Secondary English teachers need to be aware of the gist of the most prominent of these critical positions, if only to come to terms with them theoretically and practically. The most vehement criticism I have encountered has come from Richard Marshall, in his editorial for an edition of *English in Education* entitled – appropriately enough, given the force of the invective – 'Revolting Literacy'. Here, the Strategy is described as 'a half-baked set of reactionary prejudices overcooked by expensive PR' (Marshall 2002: 1). Marshall goes on to bemoan: 'What is most surprising is the number of English teachers who have been ready to help serve up this dish, thinking, . . . rather arrogant, this – they're good enough to add enough spice and flavour to make it palatable, even nourishing' (ibid.). For Marshall, 'the NLS is distorting English education', and English teachers have been – and are being – 'brow-beaten in many cases by heavy-handed local authority apparatchiks who seem hell-bent on making sure the wretched stuff happens' (ibid.: 4). The author Philip Pullman (2002: 14) is similarly savage in his criticism, maintaining, especially in the context of literacy assessment through the SATs, that:

> Of course we have to cheat. In a system that has nothing to do with true education, nothing to do with a deep, liberal, wise, tentative, rich response to literature, but everything to do with meeting targets and measuring performance levels, then the only way for honest people to survive is to cheat, and do so with a clear conscience.

Powerful criticism indeed, and well worth English teachers keeping in mind whenever confronted by yet another slick PowerPoint presentation celebrating the wonders of the Strategy. But ultimately we need to adopt a more conciliatory, reasoned and selectively adoptive approach if the subject English is to survive.

Richard Hoggart offers a critique of the theoretical base underpinning the Strategy (albeit written before the Key Stage 3 development) that is both profound and subtle, and one which, implicitly and explicitly, I have attempted to acknowledge positively throughout this chapter. Essentially, he argues, first, that 'literacy is not enough', and, as a direct corollary, that what we need is 'critical literacy for all'. Radically, he argues that:

> the level of literacy we accept for the bulk of the population, of literacy unrelated to the way language is misused in this kind of society, ensures that literacy becomes simply a way of further subordinating great numbers of people. We make them just literate enough to be conned by the mass persuaders.
>
> (1998: 59)

In many respects it is precisely the case, I am suggesting here, that Hoggart's twin aims have to be fundamental to English – literacy – teaching; and that the Strategy, if treated flexibly, reflectively and selectively, may be harnessed for such purposes. In a related context, we have already encountered the reasoned and well-grounded fears for the future of English expressed by Pat D'Arcy. Her concern stems from what she sees as a 'narrowly linguistic approach' in the Strategy:

> we are in danger of approaching the bond between semantics and linguistics from the wrong direction – assuming that if we teach children grammatical patterns at word, sentence and text levels, they will learn to think more extensively . . . we urgently need to rediscover . . . a concept of writing as a process grounded in the search for meaning. A mechanistic paradigm which focuses primarily on construction and correctness, lacks those seeds of growth which this second paradigm would apply.
>
> (2000: 4)

Essentially this is an argument for balance and synthesis in acknowledging the two paradigms – a quest to which I shall return below.

Goodwyn (2002: 1–2) maintains in his introduction that 'this monolithic policy is based on very little research evidence, that its evaluations seem to have been insignificant or disregarded and that the only measures of its success are narrowly focused tests that most teachers find of dubious validity'. Later in the same book, a practising English teacher is quoted with reference to the literacy training – again echoing the views of many others:

> You don't start by offending people by telling them they are not doing it well enough and then give them a whole load of jargon and a whole pile of paperwork that is so mammoth that even the most dedicated and organized person is going to shy away in horror and then expect people to welcome it.
>
> (Brookes 2002: 120)

This is clearly much more than a presentational issue, in that the cardinal lesson of all good English teaching – that we start positively from present experience and good practice – is in danger of being ignored. Neil Allen, another practising English teacher, makes the further observation that 'the NLS has inherent contradictions: between teaching discrete elements of language, working to tight objectives and the far more profound nature of teaching literature' (2002: 13). Hardman and colleagues have reported on research into the working of the Strategy at primary level, voicing concern that, despite explicit intentions, didactic teaching techniques are frequently employed instead of more interactive pedagogy – often precisely because of the weight of material to be somehow transmitted. They argue cogently that

> Such an emphasis on directive forms of teaching in the NLS goes against the widely accepted social constructivist theory of learning . . . which suggests that classroom discourse is not effective unless pupils play an active part in their learning . . . our findings suggest pupils are mainly expected to be passive and to recall, when asked, what they have learned and to report other people's thinking.
>
> (Hardman *et al*. 2003: 212–13)

A pertinent warning indeed for secondary English teachers. No doubt as the Strategy beds down so such issues may disappear from view: hopefully because English teachers continue in their best tradition to reflect on their pedagogy, to build on good practice and to discard what is worthless, and assuredly not because they simply accept what is dictated to them.

## Towards a synthesis: linking theory and practice

Three of the critics we have just encountered, Philip Pullman, Pat D'Arcy and Richard Hoggart, also offer interesting possibilities for resolving the disjunction between apparently opposing conceptions of literacy in education. As ever, so much depends on viewpoint. Pullman (2002: 22), for example, maintains that 'Education ought to be concerned with the basics. We just disagree about what the basics are.' He goes on to explain his idea of what is basic: 'the joy of discovery, wonder, excitement, pleasure . . . the whole attitude we express in our work, the attitude we express by working . . . that truly is basic. So I'm all for basics.' Pullman ends his paper (it was originally a speech given to English teachers at the NATE Conference of 2002): 'The one thing that sustains my hope about education is actually talking to teachers . . . Do what you know is right, ignore what you know is wrong, but carry on teaching' (ibid.: 23). Cue tumultuous applause – but in effect this is precisely what I recommend too. D'Arcy (2000: 38) quotes approvingly from David Moffet (1980):

> The process of writing cannot be realistically perceived and taught so long as we try to work from the outside in. The most fundamental and effective way to improve compositional 'decisions' about word choice, phrasing, sentence structure, and overall organisation is to clarify, enrich and harmonise the thinking that predetermines the student's initial choices of these.

Richard Hoggart (1998: 68), further, reminds us that

> All serious writing is about discrepancies, discordances and their possible resolution between the world outside as we would wish to see it and as we encounter it; between what others have made of it and what we are now making of it; between the world of relationships we inhabit and the world inside our selves.

There is a real suggestion in perceptions such as these of a genuinely full, humane and apt approach to literacy – and one that is in no way actually precluded or prevented by the Strategy. As English teachers we may need to shift our perspective a little, however, and glimpse both wood and trees, in order to play a real part in the transformation in literacy teaching centred on what actually happens in the classroom. Harrison, in the officially sponsored Roots and Research appraisal of Key Stage 3 literacy teaching, reinforces the point, arguing that professional development is crucial, and must 'recognise teachers as professionals and not as technicians' (Harrison 2002: 11). Harrison's research (ibid.: 13) highlighted literacy teachers who

> regarded theory as emancipating and professionally empowering – it was what enabled them to make confident and professionally informed decisions about their literacy teaching. It was what enabled them to move beyond the role of technician or educational paramedic and into the role of professional, to become teachers who could use the Strategy as a toolkit, not a script, and apply it with flexibility and confidence, rather than obedience.

Ultimately, as Harrison concludes, 'If we want to create skilled, confident, independent and adaptable pupils, they need to be taught by skilled, confident, independent and adaptable teachers' (ibid.: 34).

In practice we need to make constructive connections between critical, intercultural literacy, the best elements of what may be termed the Romantic tradition of English teaching (including such notions as personal growth and cultural heritage), and the most appropriate aspects of functional literacy. Nicholas McGuinn and I have argued in more depth for such a synthesis elsewhere (Stevens and McGuinn 2004); here I need to focus on the practical relevance to the Strategy. As ever there is a need for critical clarity and breadth in our conception of literacy; as Goodwyn and Findlay (2002: 22) remind us, teachers need to be

> sensitive to the literacy practices and events pupils experience outside school and the relationship between home and school literacies . . . beyond a simplistic . . . model of literacy to recognize that some literacies are more powerful than others and all are inherently ideological . . . The ideological effects of literacy are transparent but nowhere are they more powerful than in educational settings.

Again the *Roots and Research* document is helpful, and runs counter to the way the Strategy is often viewed by practising teachers; the four bullet points quoted below should go quite a way to allaying some of these fears, focusing as they do on the conditions of successful literacy teaching:

- There must be a central emphasis on language, particularly that related to understanding and managing the activity;
- Teaching should be grounded in *culturally meaningful experiences* that help pupils to be able to transfer learning to new contexts;
- Effective teaching and learning occur in *collaborative activities*, with active learning in contexts in which individual differences are respected;
- *The basic form of teaching is dialogue* that leads to an integrated approach to listening, speaking, reading and writing, with an emphasis on pupils increasingly directing their own learning.

(Harrison 2002: 18; emphasis as in the original)

If principles like these really can be made the basis of good literacy teaching, and English teachers above all should be in a position to ensure they can, then some of the manacles heard in the classroom may be more 'mind forg'd' than real.

## Two examples of literacy teaching

I have chosen two examples of what I consider to be effective, challenging literacy teaching, both drawn from recent classroom experience, and in both cases relating to particular foci from the Strategy Key Stage 3 Framework. The first of these is the opening page of Margaret Mahy's novel *The Haunting*, as taught to a Year 7 class. The second illustration is an excerpt from a guitar magazine (*Total Guitar*) article on JJ72, apparently a new rock band, as taught to a Year 9 group:

From *The Haunting* (Margaret Mahy)

Chapter 1

'Barnaby's Dead'

When, suddenly, on an ordinary Wednesday, it seemed to Barney that the world tilted and ran downhill in all directions, he knew he was about to be haunted again. It had happened when he was younger but he had thought that being haunted was a babyish thing that you grew out of, like crying when you fell over, or not having a bike.

'Remember Barney's imaginary friends, Mantis, Bigbuzz and Ghost?' Claire – his stepmother – sometimes said. 'The garden seems empty now that they've gone. I quite miss them.'

But she was really pleased perhaps because, being so very real to Barney, they had become too real for her to laugh over. Barney had been sorry to lose them, but he wanted Claire to feel comfortable living with him. He could not remember his own mother and Claire had come as a wonderful surprise, giving him a hug when he came home from school, asking him about his day, telling him about hers, arranging picnics and unexpected parties and helping him with hard homework. It seemed worth losing Mantis, Bigbuzz and Ghost and the other kind phantoms that had been his friends for so many days before Claire came.

Yet here it was beginning again . . .

This is the opening lesson from a scheme of work based on class reading of the novel in question, and one of the prime purposes was simply to whet pupils' appetites to read on. In this context, fostering the desire to read texts-as-literature may be successfully married to a literacy-based approach. For all the apparent tensions between these approaches, as noted previously, they need not be contradictory or mutually exclusive – especially if the literacy dimension is handled in ways sensitive to the nature of the text itself. I was acutely aware of the danger of seeing any text – literature perhaps especially – as a mere vehicle for study of language features divorced from meaning, engagement or imagination. David Almond, for example, has been rightly scathing about some attempts to reduce his novel *Skellig* in such a way. My other aim was to introduce pupils to aspects of language used by Mahy in this extract: both literary and literacy-based elements in so far as they can be separated. So, the twin objectives as displayed to the class were:

- to introduce the novel and explore some possible themes;
- to examine closely some aspects of the language used.

Here again I was careful not to close down possible responses through the nature of objectives, and the Strategy pedagogy, I suggest, may fit this exploratory mode.

The first stage was to split the class into five 'home' groups, as established previously on more or less mixed-ability lines. The 'warm-up' for the first few minutes was simply to look at the book's cover and title and then report back briefly with any ideas or predictions; this worked well enough to open up tentative interpretive possibilities, reinforcing the notion that meaning is fluid and open to suggestion. I myself then read the passage aloud to the group, but did not follow up with any whole-class discussion, despite some enthusiasm for this; I preferred rather to funnel this readiness to talk about the book into the ensuing group work. Thus the next stage was to move into 'jigsaw' mode, a way of learning with which the class was already familiar, resulting in five new groups each comprising one pupil from each of the 'home' groups. Each 'new' group was then given a particular aspect of the text to examine, based on a range of the teaching objectives from the Framework and represented in brief summarising prompt sheets. The areas/tasks given to the groups were as follows (Framework for Year 7 references in brackets):

- Look at sentence structure, use of tenses, and active/passive voice to see how the author creates a particular effect. (sentence level 1, 4, 5)

- Think about who is speaking and what we learn of the speaker – What clues are there? Are there other voices too? (sentence level 7; text level 8, 9)

- What is the overall tone of the passage? Think about choice of words, differences in spoken/written English, names. (text level 12, 14)

- Consider how you think this story might continue – What possibilities does the author have so early in the narrative? Are there any clues? (text level 7, 15)

- What do we learn about the characters either present or mentioned? Do we get enough information to really picture any of them at this stage? (text level 9, 16)

Interestingly, with some explanation, all pupils in this mixed-ability class were able to engage fruitfully with the questions posed, building on their previous literacy (including literature-based) work. The English teachers present (there were two of us) were able to participate in each group's activity – a form of sensitively guided reading. Either at group discussion or whole-class plenary stages, the sort of points emerging included:

- the possible ambiguity of the title 'Barnaby's Dead', hinging on the two plausible uses of the apostrophe (and incidentally raising questions of authorial intent/'reading meanings into text');

- the relationship between main and subordinate clauses in the first sentence, and how the structure of this sentence reflects and amplifies meaning;

- the dramatic effect of the interrupting (remembered) speech – and the use of speech punctuation and attendant conventions;

- the nature of the 'voice' of the passage: third-person narrative, yet first-person familiarity and sympathy;

- variations in use of past tenses and relationship to the imagined 'present';

- the informal, familiar, even perhaps confidential, tone of the passage;

- textual pointers to future narrative directions, including use of punctuation (. . .) and key words such as 'again';

- opening of sentences/paragraphs with words such as 'But' and 'Yet', flouting traditional grammatical conventions, again suggestive of a certain tone;

- the use of commas for parenthesising words, distinguishing between clauses within sentences, and separating listed items.

As ever, a list like this does scant justice to the quality of discussions and analysis, but it may serve to suggest just how stimulating a literacy lesson, focused on literature, can be.

From *Total Guitar* (March 2002 edition)

Dublin 1997. After getting their teenage kicks from early-period Manics, *Siamese Dream* era Pumpkins and just, like, all of Nirvana, Mark Greaney (guitar, Buckley-inspired vocals), Hillary Woods (bass and total babe) plus Fergal Matthews (drums, joined the band because Mark 'had a jacket that was really nice') decided to form their own band. 'You shoulda been there' gigs soon followed and by August 2000 their self-titled debut was out: angsty Nirvana-isms colliding with a guitar sound that conjured up the spirit of early Manic Street Preachers and Joy Division.

Greaney . . . is definitely in the 'less is more' school of guitar playing. But that's certainly not a polite way of saying he's a slouch in the guitar department: his richly evocative guitar harmonies on I to Sky weave a web of melodies that help bring to life the spiritual themes of the album's lyrics. Now, how cool is *that*?

I looked at this text with a post-SATs Year 9 English class (significantly, the abandonment of the KS3 SATs has now enabled English teachers to do more of this kind of work), with a view to analysing the genre and its implied characteristics as a prelude to the pupils themselves experimenting with writing some similarly lucid, knowing, somewhat ironic pieces about music (or other broadly cultural artefacts – but they all chose music) liked by the pupils themselves. This time the groups were friendship based, and the questions posed were uniform throughout the class. At sentence level I focused on three objectives from the Year 9 Framework: use of the full range of punctuation (2) – I was especially looking at the use of the colon here; different ways of opening paragraphs (6); and analysis of the stylistic conventions of this genre (7). At text level, for the reading strand I was concerned principally with how media texts influence and are influenced by readers (8) – in other words the kind of intimate complicity implied in this writing. Each group was able to report back on all of these areas, arriving at interesting insights gained through their own cultural literacy in an area I certainly knew very little about. I too was becoming more literate, as I freely acknowledge. Following this up with writing at text level we explored three areas: pupils' ability to write for a range of audiences and purposes (1); exploiting the creative and aesthetic features of language in non-literary texts (6); and exploring how non-fiction texts can convey information or ideas in amusing or entertaining ways. In a subsequent lesson each group presented their piece of writing aloud, having first played a section of the music they had chosen as their particular focus. Ensuing discussion centred on the nature of the cultural artefact of rock/pop music, its attempted manipulation by commercial interests, and its continuing ability to escape such interests – at least momentarily. Or maybe that last point represents my own thinking rather than theirs – but then as literacy teacher I too am entitled to explore my (Romantic) point of view.

## Further reading

As indicated in the body of the chapter, Brian Cox's (edited) collection of articles on the nature of literacy *Literacy is not Enough* (1998) gives a helpful and critical background to the issues and tensions. Also stimulating are two short booklets: Pat D'Arcy's *Two Contrasting Paradigms for the Teaching and Assessment of Writing* (2000) and the transcript of Philip Pullman's closing address to the 2002 NATE Conference, *Perverse, all monstrous, all prodigious things* (2002). Mark Pike's *Teaching Secondary English* has a useful chapter summarising literacy developments at KS3. Geoff Dean has also written two helpful and practically orientated books: *Teaching Reading in Secondary Schools* (2000) and *Teaching English in the Key Stage 3 Literacy Strategy: A Practical Guide* (2002). There are also available two 'readers' containing many valuable insights: *Language, Literacy and Education: A Reader* (Goodman, Lillis, Maybin and Mercer 2003) and *Literacy in the Secondary School* (ed. Lewis and Wray 2000), which is especially helpful in providing a whole-school inter-disciplinary perspective. Andrew Goodwyn's (edited) *Improving Literacy at KS2 and KS3* and the book I have written with Nicholas McGuinn (*The Art of English Teaching* 2004) attempt to give a broader, critical perspective; Colin Harrison's *Understanding Reading Development* (2003) fills many gaps in most secondary English teachers' knowledge of this central area. Four more books have proved helpful in exploring further the implications of literacy teaching and learning in the English curriculum in a range of contexts: *Literacy Moves On* (ed. J. Evans 2005), *Literacy through Creativity* (P. Goodwin 2004), *The Routledge-Falmer Reader in Language and Literacy* (ed. T. Grainger 2004) – a particularly valuable collection of papers – and *Teaching Secondary School Literacies with ICT* (ed. M. Monteith 2005).

## Resources

Predictably – and quite rightly – educational publishers great and small have attempted to service teachers' need for effective and imaginative literacy materials, and there is now a wide range available. The Cambridge University Press *Literacy in Context for KS3* series is broad in its conception and attractively presented, offering a good basis for literacy teaching and including both pupils' texts and 'teacher's portfolios'. NATE has produce two impressive collections too: *Guided Reading Packs* and *KS3 Strategy Group Reading* (in conjunction with the National Strategy). Also available and helpful from NATE, despite its 7–11 age range focus, is Trevor Millum's *ICT and Literacy*. Hodder Murray's *English Works*, *Hodder English Starters* and *New Hodder English* series, Heinemann's *Edges*, *Skills in English* and *Progress English*, Nelson-Thorne's *Level Best*, Collins' *English Frameworking*, and Longman's *Literacy through Texts* series are among the most helpful and well presented published materials for classroom literacy approaches.

# 3

# Knowledge about language

*You taught me language, and my profit on't*
*Is I know how to curse. The red plague rid you*
*For learning me your language!*

Caliban in Shakespeare's *The Tempest*

## The context

AS INDICATED IN THE INTRODUCTION, one of the central questions in English is how far should we as teachers seek to decontextualise language, to make it in itself an object of study. The question, as we have already seen in Chapter 2 and will seek to explore further, has very real implications for the practice of English teaching: we may endanger the spontaneity of language through over analysis, in the sense that Wordsworth protested, 'We murder to dissect.' We must also keep our eye on exactly what language is being used for; and Caliban's lament, quoted above, should serve as a timely warning – for Prospero, appropriately both his captor and his teacher, has indeed, wittingly or not, sown the seeds of Caliban's curse. The very term 'knowledge about language' has become for some rather outdated, replaced in effect by the more directed emphasis on literacy through the Key Stage 3 Strategy and beyond, including that strangely misleading term 'functional literacy'. The preceding chapter has indeed sought to place the impact of the Strategy within a broader context of English teaching – and that context must by definition include knowledge (with awareness and understanding) of language. In effect, the Strategy presents a particular model of knowledge about language, but it is far from being the only model, in theoretical or practical terms; thus the necessity of a separate chapter dealing explicitly, and unapologetically, with these issues.

To use the analogy of learning to ride a bicycle, it may well be necessary for the learner to know something of the principles of balancing one's entire body weight on two narrow strips of rubber, but effectively expertise only comes with practice – with cycling, in fact, the teacher having 'let go'. Perhaps it is the same with acquiring and developing language. Indeed it may well be that too great a knowledge and constant awareness of the laws of gravity – improbable as they seem – may simply cause anxiety, wobbling, and ultimately falling off. On the other hand, if our cyclist is to improve, especially when the terrain gets rough and the competition hots up, some knowledge of the theories and techniques of effective cycling is surely helpful. Perhaps here, if we finally abandon the cycling metaphor, is the clue to what constitutes genuinely useful knowledge about language: the need to improve language capability for ever more sophisticated purposes and contexts in a complex and demanding – not to mention highly competitive – world. A fundamental tension does remain, between on the one hand the need to perceive the manipulative effects of language in society in order no longer to fall victim to them, and, on the other hand, the understandable but rather less laudable desire to increase one's own manipulative powers of language.

The point is really that effective and interesting knowledge about language is centrally concerned with the integration of analysis with practice. This is not the place to rehearse the well-documented demise of what Mittins (1988) critically termed the 'Naming of Parts' philosophy of teaching about language, for so long the dominant school practice, based on decontextualised exercises and drills. The subsequent abandonment, in the 1960s and 1970s, of this sort of approach did leave something of a vacuum in language teaching, although far less of one than certain commentators would have us believe. An integrated, more holistic and practical approach is now much commoner, despite a politically motivated rearguard action which saw the disgraceful undermining of the recommendations of the Language in the National Curriculum (LINC) working group and constant sniping at any innovative approaches to language teaching. English departments are now able to evaluate pedagogies and accompanying resources forged in the heat of the ideological battles of the 1980s and early 1990s rather more dispassionately than was possible at the time, with a view to implementing a truly holistic teaching of knowledge about language. However, we must also be conscious of the limitations. Towards the end of Brian Friel's play *Translations* (1981) – a marvellous study of language and power which we shall revisit in Chapter 14 – the disconsolate and disillusioned Hugh explains to his pupil Maire, anxious as she is to learn English, 'don't expect too much. I will provide you with the available words and the available grammar. But will that help you to interpret between privacies? I have no idea. But it's all we have' (1981: 90). Ultimately this may well be the case; but 'all we have' may be considerably more than the tragic Hugh realises.

English teachers have an invaluable ally here in what seems to be the intrinsically fascinating nature of language, precisely because it denotes so many things and is open to so many interpretations. It is at once intensely personally subjective in how it feels, and dynamically social in its communicative uses. Class, age, personal identity, peer group membership, locality and nationality all contribute to this fascination, and all of these provide excellent starting points for the examination of language in the English classroom. Such is the overwhelming power of the human feel for language that it may be described as instinctive (although this word itself is problematic in meaning). Pinker (1994: 21) suggests:

The workings of language are as far from our awareness as the rationale for egg-laying is from the fly's. Our thoughts come out of our mouths so effortlessly that they often embarrass us, having eluded our mental censors. When we are comprehending sentences, the stream of words is transparent; we see through to the meaning so automatically that we can forget that a movie is in a foreign language and subtitled . . . The effortlessness, the transparency, the automaticity are illusions, masking a system of great richness and beauty.

Knowledge about language should be geared towards uncovering this 'system of great richness and beauty', while at the same time enhancing celebratory spontaneity. This is no easy task, and requires great skill: and here 'skill' does not refer to some blandly reductive going-through-the-motions activity. We are talking rather about the professional expertise, no less, of an English teacher.

## Varieties of English

To speak of knowledge about language is in some respects misleading, for we all use, and know about, many different languages. English activities, some of which we shall look at below, can explore these different forms of English, depending as they do on context and purpose, and even without the aid of good teaching children are impressively adept at functioning in a vast range of linguistic circumstances and switching painlessly from one to another. We need to build on this 'natural' ability, and we need to pay particular attention to formal and informal modes – to describe them somewhat simplistically. As with so much else, there is nothing especially new in this. Consider Hardy's 1891 presentation of his heroine Tess, in part at least the product of the new national education system, in contrast to her relatively unschooled mother:

> Mrs Durbeyfield habitually spoke the dialect; her daughter, who had passed the Sixth Standard in the National School under a London-trained mistress, spoke two languages; the dialect at home, more or less; ordinary English abroad and to persons of quality.

(1985: 58)

Hardy, presumably, intends irony here: Tess's ability to converse in standard English opens the way to two 'persons of quality' in particular, who between them destroy her. Interestingly, Hardy, in his first edition of the novel, wrote of Tess using the local dialect form of English not merely 'at home, more or less' but 'only when excited by joy, surprise, or grief'.

On one level, of course, we need as teachers to ensure that our pupils can function and flourish in the full range of language forms manifested in a pluralist society – a drive towards equality of opportunity. But the reality is far more complex than this: potentially liberating, certainly; but also, as Tess found to her cost, potentially dangerous. The relationship between language, emotions ('joy, surprise, or grief') and social reality is complex and often problematic, and any worthwhile attempt to educate our children in knowledge about language must fully acknowledge this. Neither should the relationship be conceived as static, but rather as dynamic and dialectical, with social opportunities and constraints both influencing and in turn being influenced by the nature of the language(s) involved. In practical terms, as in so much else concerned with English teaching, this is an argument for a fully integrated curriculum both within the subject itself and in relationship with other curricular areas, all of which assuredly deal with manifestations of social reality. One of the strengths of English, however, is its potential use of literature as language in action and in this sense all literature, including *Tess of the D'Urbervilles*, is centrally concerned with (and of course expressed through) language, whatever else it may be about.

With this in mind, a useful practical exercise for an English department could be to consider the texts used as the basis for the curriculum, asking how each lends itself specifically to the teaching of knowledge about language. If the department is large enough, individual or paired teachers could report back to colleagues on their findings, highlighting such possibilities as:

- variety of sentence structure and syntax, including passive and active forms;
- use of connectives and other ways of combining phrases and clauses;
- use of semicolons, dashes and colons as subtle ways of breaking up language;
- paragraphing and other ways of splitting up text;
- adverbial and adjectival modifiers;
- presentation of dialogue, including its punctuation;
- varieties of dialect, and even accent;
- uses and limitations of standard English;
- departures from generally conceived 'correctness' in presentation;
- how characters' language changes in different contexts;
- distinctions between American – and other national forms of – English and our own 'British' English;
- issues of class, race and gender as referring to the nature of language;
- language change over time, and exploration of why changes occur and whether we can apply labels of progress or deterioration to such changes.

A great deal can be achieved through this sort of exploration of literature, and in an increasingly overcrowded English curriculum making full and varied use of any resources is utterly sensible – perhaps essential. The list of possible approaches is very far from exhaustive, but one can see in it a development from what might be termed the formal, presentational aspects of written language towards a consideration of some of the underlying questions about its use. The important point – and an important qualification, perhaps – is that language features should be related to the purpose and context of the literature rather than simply extracted from it in some sort of disjointed fashion. In this respect, pupils may of course be invited to evaluate the effectiveness of language as used by authors, thus further accentuating fresh responses to literature.

## Language study in the English curriculum

Language study based on what is read is but one 'way in'. We need now to consider in more general terms what shape the integration of language knowledge into the English curriculum could begin to take. There are a number of questions to answer, all of which revolve around the central tensions of knowledge about language outlined above:

- How exactly can knowledge about language be integrated into the other aspects of the English curriculum, for example those dealing with literature?

- How may we respect, and encourage respect for, pupils' linguistic experience while preparing them for the realities of language in society?

- How do we deal with the tension between 'correctness' in terms of standard English and 'appropriateness' as preferred by most linguists?

- In seeking to improve pupils' language use, either written or spoken, should we rely principally on a 'remedial' approach, tackling faults and shortcomings as they arise naturally in English activities?

- Should we rather be 'proactive' in teaching methodically aspects of language which we know through experience often give problems, such as speech punctuation, certain spellings, the use of semicolons, or sentence structure?

- Whichever of the last two approaches is used – and they are not, of course, entirely mutually exclusive – what sort of meta-linguistic vocabulary is needed in order to teach effectively about language?

- How should this meta-linguistic vocabulary itself be taught?

- What opportunities are there for cross-curricular collaboration in terms of language in society (the humanities), expressive forms of language (the arts), language as a communication system (modern foreign languages), etc.?

- What opportunities are there also for cross-phase collaboration, so that the often impressive knowledge about language developed in primary schools may be further built on in the secondary phase, and any omissions made good?

These questions must inform our practice, and like the most useful questions in teaching itself they are intended to be open, suggestive of ways forward rather than implying 'correct' answers given by us or anyone else. Brian Cox's descriptions of his Committee's investigations into English teaching as they worked on the original National Curriculum in the mid-1980s are useful here. He noted that although there was often little formal teaching of knowledge about language in English classrooms, meta-linguistic terms such as 'sentence', 'verb' or 'full stop' were constantly and unavoidably being used. This, of course, relates to two of the key questions posed above concerning meta-linguistic terminology, with some implications for other points also. This is just one rather narrow aspect of knowledge about language, but a vital one which may provide a very practical focus for explicit planning of language teaching. To help in contextualising it into English teaching practice a worthwhile exercise may be to consider and list, with colleagues if possible:

- the meta-linguistic terms commonly used;

- whether there is likely to be a shared or widespread understanding of them;

- how they are used (orally, in marking, remedially, prescriptively, descriptively, etc.);

- how these terms are taught or explained;

- which, if any, may be discarded;

- which other terms may be usefully added to the list.

The resulting list should provide a useful starting point for development, but it is the process through which it is arrived at that may well throw up differences in approach. Cox (1991: 57) is again helpful in providing a broader context here:

> Two justifications for teaching pupils explicitly about language are, first, the positive effect on aspects of their use of language and, secondly, the general value of such knowledge as an important part of their understanding of their social and cultural environment, since language has vital functions in the life of the individual and of society . . . Language is not merely a neutral medium for the conveying of information; it can trigger emotional responses which may spring from prejudice, stereotyping or misunderstanding. Such attitudes need to be laid open to examination and discussion.

In practical terms, this suggests that the sort of language analysis we are concerned with developing in the classroom, and the attendant terminology, should not be conceived as neutral, decontextualised or static. Whatever the results of your list, the next stage is rather more time-consuming: the planned implementation of knowledge about language through the curriculum in an integrated and interesting way, bearing in mind the considerations quoted above.

To help further in this process it may be useful to go back a little further, to the Kingman Report (DES 1988), which was intended to provide the theoretical framework for the teaching of language but, because it failed to provide a narrowly prescriptive model, never really gained the official approval it deserved. Perhaps this has been its strength: certainly there is a great deal of value in it and it is well worth referring back to a couple of decades on. Selective quotations give a flavour of the Report:

> We believe that for children not to be taught anything about their language is seriously to their disadvantage . . . pupils need to have their attention drawn to what they are doing and why they are doing it because this is helpful to their language ability.
>
> (p. 12)

> Awareness of the forms of language is an entirely natural development.
>
> (p. 13)

> Teaching language must involve talking about language since learning without that activity is slow, inefficient and inequitable (in that it favours those whose ability enables them to generalise without tuition).
>
> (p. 3)

> Nor do we see it as part of our task to plead for a return to old fashioned grammar teaching and learning by rote.
>
> (p. 3)

> We reject the belief that any notion of correct or incorrect use of language is an affront to personal liberty. We also reject the belief that knowing how to use terminology in which to speak of

language is undesirable. There is no positive advantage in such ignorance. It is just as important to teach about our language environment. The skills, perceptions and knowledge that we are advocating will be of value to all pupils, and should in no way be the exclusive privilege of the more able.

(p. 3)

We have met some of these arguments before, particularly those implying an entitlement curriculum, and they – like language itself – may remain somewhat contentious. A further valuable reflective exercise, again conducted collaboratively if possible, might be to consider the validity or otherwise of these statements and how they could be implemented or modified in practical terms of English teaching. One of the explicit recommendations of the Kingman Committee was that knowledge about language should inform teacher education; there has already been significant legislation in this area, and new 'standards' (replacing 'competences', now almost a term of disparagement!) have been developed in initial and continuing teacher education. For English teachers these contain detailed areas of subject knowledge concerning the workings of language, so the practically reflective exercise recommended above has a very real significance in the development of English teaching and should be accorded a high priority. It is essentially a matter of exploring the possibilities of legitimising and subsequently developing the fascination for and considerable knowledge of language brought into any English classroom by the pupils – and, for that matter, their teacher (lest we forget!). This development requires conscious decision making about language use; and as Davies (1996: 52) has pointed out:

> This is what English teaching should provide especially well: opportunities for learning about the choices that can and must be made in the use of language, and help for learners in developing explicit understandings and vision of what they can make language do for their own varied and complex needs.

In this context of making informed choices we do need some sort of structure within which to develop the teaching of language. Kingman's four-part model for the consideration of language – its forms; communication and comprehension; its acquisition; its variation – makes a great deal of sense and has been used, in its more detailed form as presented in the Report itself, by some English departments as a convenient model to ensure entitlement.

## Language awareness beyond the secondary English classroom

As with other aspects of the English curriculum, we should as English teachers be ready to look around us as well as examining closely the detail of our own subject teaching. Particularly, we have in mind here the possibilities for cross-phase and cross-curricular cooperation, both of which should serve to emphasise the nature of knowledge about language. For the former, there is a wealth of excellent practice going on in primary schools about which secondary colleagues are sometimes only dimly aware. Pressures of time and curriculum crowding, together with the shrinking of In-Service Education and Training (INSET) courses, have made it more difficult to share ideas and practices, although the current literacy initiative and the emphasis the National Association for the Teaching of English (NATE) is placing on attracting primary-based English teachers may do something to alleviate the worst effects in our subject. Successful cross-phase partnerships depend on the willingness of whole school staffs, with the impetus often coming from senior management, but there is still a fair amount achievable by English teachers to build bridges to enhance language teaching. Some possibilities specifically on knowledge about language include:

- cross-phase meetings to discuss which aspects of knowledge about language are taught – including the appropriate terminology – and when;

- projects involving research and interviews on aspects of language, perhaps focusing particularly on acquisition, development and variation;

- teaching specific lessons across the phase divide, perhaps for secondary teachers as 'tasters' of what is to come, and for primary colleagues addressing areas of expertise relevant to a secondary English curriculum such as early years language development;

- primary and secondary pupils using IT programs such as 'Success Maker', probably sited for logistical reasons in the secondary school, to enhance language 'skills';

- sharing of relevant resources, many of which are deliberately cross-phase in nature (see resources list at the end of this chapter);

- the keeping by pupils of a language scrap-book or journal to be carried on from the primary school into the secondary phase;

- pupils in both phases using each other as audiences for language-based activities, such as code making and breaking;

- mutual project study of language as used in either phase, such as teachers' language (a sensitive one, this!) or the language of school brochures and publicity material.

Often it takes the efforts of just one teacher to set the ball rolling, and the advantages, clearly, go well beyond the enhancement of knowledge about language – as the leadership of any school will be quick to realise.

The opportunities for cross-curricular collaboration in this field may seem more readily available; in practice they are often difficult to achieve. Teachers from different curriculum areas often work in quite distinct ways – this in itself can be an opportunity for professional investigation into language use – which are not always easily compatible. English and modern foreign language departments are both centrally concerned with knowledge about language, for example, but often approach it in very different ways with different pedagogical stances. Nevertheless, it is certainly worth attempting to cooperate in establishing a coherent language awareness course across both curriculum areas, perhaps in the early years of Key Stage 3 before the pressure of assessment targets and second foreign languages becomes too intense, focusing on the common requirements. Cross-fertilisation such as this must have positive outcomes, and an important one, paradoxically, may well be to raise awareness of the differences in style and content across the curriculum – often the first stage in finding common ground. Modern foreign languages may be the obvious first choice for cooperation, but there are other possibilities: special educational needs staff, for example, dealing with learning support and (hopefully) extension may well usefully focus on knowledge about language – feasibly at either end of the academic spectrum – and often in any case work closely with English departments. Consider too the potential of history teachers to collaborate in teaching about language change and its connections with social history; geography for language diversity across the world and, perhaps, the increasing dominance of (American) English today; science and mathematics for the language of precision and for symbolic systems; and music for a non-verbal system of communication and expression. These are just a few of the opportunities available once colleagues start working and thinking together: in fact, virtually any area of learning involves some sort of knowledge about some sort of language. We simply need to make the connections. At a professional development level, such collaboration can make for enterprising opportunities to consider the nature of language used in teaching and learning with a view to formulating a coherent language for learning policy. Often a dynamic starting point for this sort of process is to invite an authority to speak to the whole staff about the nature of language in schools.

## Practical implications

Recent publications on English teaching and those aimed at classroom use have positively bristled with imaginative ideas for the teaching of knowledge about language within English. Davies (1996), for example, offers a very useful overview of recommended topics intended as a programme of study that would last the whole of compulsory secondary education at least:

> The history of the English language:
>     the development of dialects of English
>     the development of standard English
>     language change
> Language structures:
>     an introduction to descriptive linguistics
> The nature of language variation:
>     variation according to user: social class and locality
>     variation according to use: register (discourse analysis)
>     attitudes to language variation
> Language development and learning
> Language and power: gender, race, class and education.

(1996: 70)

This appears to be a comprehensive framework, and could easily be adapted for specific school circumstances – not least for the kinds of activities outlined in the rest of this chapter. Resources are many and varied, and we have attempted to present a selection from those available. Language is all around us, and the English teacher needs to cultivate a 'magpie' attitude towards collecting linguistic resources: junk mail, instruction booklets, tourist guides, health information leaflets, fliers and the like.

As hinted previously, however, the most important resource may be ourselves: teachers and pupils. With this in mind, an appropriate starting point for learning about language, and one to be revisited throughout a course, could be a language autobiography. The sort of experiences and issues which may arise from such an enterprise could each provide a useful stimulus for further, directed, language investigation. They may include, if past experience is a guide:

- 'telling' of language to younger brothers and sisters – learning through teaching;
- experience of early school/nursery language;
- experience of languages other than English, in a vast range of circumstances;
- use of nursery rhymes, games, sayings, proverbs and other examples of the oral language tradition;
- discovery of different accents and dialects – social and geographical mobility;
- trends in language – 'in' words, 'slang' and jargon;
- the influence of the media on language, particularly television, popular music and certain radio stations;
- early experiences of the power of reading and writing;
- memories of parents' use of 'childish' language;
- the impact of 'formal' language requirements and standard English;
- growing awareness of the power of language to express emotions and desires;
- simultaneous, often linked, awareness of the manipulative possibilities in language;
- diverse, often exclusive, 'private languages'.

In planning and realising any language awareness within the English curriculum, the language autobiography may be seen as central, converting itself into something of a journalistic enterprise. It is also worth undertaking as a team of English teachers, not only modelling good practice but, more profoundly, uncovering some of the links between language and experience. Some of these, clearly, may be painful, and a word of warning is apposite here: as language and identity are so closely intertwined, the English teacher needs great sensitivity and humour to bring some aspects of both to consciousness. It may be that some areas are best left uncovered.

The language autobiography, properly introduced and sustained, should give rise to many valuable starting points and resources. To broaden your range of material it may not be necessary to look beyond the staffroom for good examples of diverse accents and dialects, experiences of different languages, and histories of language in use. Again, with sensitivity, here is a wealth of valuable language resources. The guiding principle in all this enterprise must be one of respect for each other's languages, and this is not always easily achieved. Many people feel quite ashamed of their own accent, dialect or command of standard English and, predictably enough, this sense of shame may all too easily be projected into disparagement of others' languages. If knowledge about language is to achieve anything significant, there must be a concerted effort to confront such issues; the general suggestions for activities listed below are intended to be used in this context, and can of course be adapted and extended for particular purposes:

- interviews with older/younger people about language issues and experiences – particularly concerned with acquisition and development;

- subsequent writing of transcripts from taped interviews as a way of exploring the distinctions between written and spoken (standard) English;

- activities based on past examples of language, including the literary, to investigate language change through such activities as cloze and adaptation;

- activities on accent and dialect, including standard English itself, to emphasise the distinction between the two, using local and media examples;

- exploration of language and stereotyping, using comic strip examples (perhaps with blanked out speech bubbles) and characters from TV soaps;

- study of the relationship between gender and language, making use of resources such as advertisements, adapted fairy tales and gender-specific magazines;

- role-plays presenting appropriate and inappropriate language (spanning such facets as dialect, register and vocabulary) in a range of situations;

- research into and exploration of the connotations of names, including personal names, nicknames, brand names, logos, school names;

- invention of new names along similar lines, perhaps extending into logos, crests, mottoes, names for new soaps or other media products;

- invention of new language systems, codes, sign languages and creoles;

- investigation into animal 'languages' and other non-verbal forms of communication including the apparently endlessly fascinating language of the body and gestures;

- extension of the language autobiography to include a linguistic family tree and, possibly, maps to place variants of language geographically;

- activities based on foreign language instructions with translations withheld (as they often seem to be in any case) to explore the similarities between languages and attempt a translation;

- exploration of jargons, including those around education, and such manifestations as acronyms (no shortage here either);

- investigation of euphemisms and double standards, especially as used in the media (with death of civilians becoming 'collateral damage');

- playing with language through the formation of puns, anagrams, limericks, ambiguous headlines and signs, unlikely name combinations and rhyming slang;

- study of the 'invented' languages of literature, such as those presented in 'Jabberwocky', *Nineteen Eighty-Four*, *The Hobbit*, *A Clockwork Orange* and many others.

The study of language is endlessly fascinating, not least because it is so important in defining whatever to be human really is. We should perhaps bear in mind the words of T. S. Eliot in 'Little Gidding' as we undertake the study:

We shall not cease from exploration
And the end of all our exploring
Will be to arrive where we started
And know the place for the first time.

## Further reading

Perera (1987) *Understanding Language* is succinct and provocative. Carter (1995) *Key Words in Language and Literature* is a handy reference guide which focuses on language in education, and the same author's *Knowledge About Language and the Curriculum: The LINC Reader* (1991) summarises the excellent work undertaken by the LINC project. Mittins (1990) *Language Awareness for Teachers* and (1988) *English: Not the Naming of Parts* are both humane and de-mystifying texts. Crystal (ed.) *The Cambridge Encyclopaedia of Language* (1987) and *The Cambridge Encyclopaedia of the English Language* (1995) are useful reference texts. Another title which refers more directly to the practicalities of the English classroom is Bain *et al.* (1992) *Looking into Language: Classroom Approaches to Knowledge about Language*. For refreshment and extension of subject knowledge, the Penguin English – Applied Linguistics series (eds Carter and Nunan) is excellent, providing insight into a range of language areas such as Woods (1995) *Introducing Grammar* and Wilkinson (1995) *Introducing Standard English*. Crystal's *Rediscover Grammar* (1986), O'Connor's *The Pocket Guide to English Language* (Cambridge UP 2004), and Williamson's chapters 'What Do We Mean by Standard English and Language Study' and 'What Do We Mean by Grammar' (in Williamson *et al.* 2001) offer pertinent and clear summaries of the level of language knowledge required for secondary English teaching. *Use of Language across the Secondary Curriculum* (ed. Bearne 1999), chapters on 'Language Study' and 'Investigating Grammar' (in Haworth *et al.* 2004), and Davies' chapter 'Correct or Appropriate?' (in Davison and Moss eds 2000) are all very useful guides to the continuing debate about language in the English curriculum and beyond. David Crystal has recently revised his perennially popular *Rediscover Grammar* (Pearson Longman, 3rd edn 2004), and added another helpful guide (2004) *Making Sense of Grammar*. Geoff Dean's (2003) *Grammar for Improving Reading and Writing in the Secondary School* and Deborah Cameron's (2007) *The Teacher's Guide to Grammar* are further useful explorations, and Alison Ross's (2006) *Language Knowledge for Secondary Teachers* is excellent.

## Resources

The Exploring Language series (ed. Bain, Cambridge University Press) is a lively, colourful set of texts for Key Stage 3. Also impressive is the Critical Language Awareness series, Hodder & Stoughton, consisting of six short books on different aspects of language and society. Through Framework Press, NATE has provided excellent resources in photocopiable loose-leaf binders: *The Language Awareness Project, Years 7–9, An Introduction to the Nature and Functions of Language*. For the broad connections between different forms and contexts of language Sweetman's series *Language Links (1,2,3)* (Collins) is well presented and stimulating. *The Grammar Book* and *The Grammar Book Supplement* (NATE) are innovative in approach and cover the full 11–16 age range with photocopiable activities. *The Cheshire Cat's Guide to English Grammar*, available from Cheshire County Council Education Services, is a similarly adventurous collection of materials, focusing on Key Stages 2 and 3.

# 4

# Speaking and listening

*He gave men speech, and speech created thought,*
*Which is the measure of the universe.*

Percy Bysshe Shelley, *Prometheus Unbound*

## The background

NEED WE DROWN IN A SEA OF HUMAN VOICES? English teachers are faced with a bewildering array of practical and theoretical possibilities – many of which are alluded to in this book – and it does certainly seem sometimes like drowning. In dealing with speaking and listening, we have at once the oldest, most deeply rooted aspect of human communication and the most recently opened up to adventurous pedagogical possibilities. We have already noted the imposed hegemony of reading and writing over the older, less formal oral tradition of learning with the development of organised schooling; traditionally, this process has relied on the restriction of speaking and listening – especially if in any way spontaneous. This has not escaped the notice of the more astute educational commentators; take, for example, this ironic observation from a near-60-year-old handbook (Lewis 1946: 52):

> Before the teacher enters the classroom there is a buzz of conversation; he puts his nose through the door and it stops. The lesson is 'oral composition'; the teacher laboriously squeezes a few reluctant, formal, and stilted sentences from an otherwise dumb class. At length the lesson is over. The teacher has barely closed the door behind him before unauthorised oral composition is again in full swing.

Hopefully, this scenario is not quite as familiar to today's English teachers, but it may well still strike a chord. I remember a colleague explaining to me in my early days of teaching that the reason why teachers feel so tired so often is that they are in fact engaged in damming up and holding back a powerful torrent of youthful energy all their working lives. I have often reflected on this, and clearly such energy is unlikely to be expressed in reading or writing: its principal 'voice' is oral. The idea of education – or more specifically schooling – as a form of control, even opposition, has always been contested too, of course, and increasingly so. 'Energy is eternal delight' wrote Blake: the challenge is to make positive use of this energy and power in our English classrooms.

To return to another of the writers whose words have informed this book, Thomas Traherne, we need more than ever to know for what end we study with matters of speaking and listening, for it is such a vast area, and so deeply personal, that we will surely err in the manner if we do not. By the same token that has reading and writing as formally taught, oral development is the most 'naturally' accomplished of language feats; in this we are presented, as so often, with both an opportunity and a threat. A worthwhile question to pose to a new teaching group is, 'what do you consider to be the point of English lessons in speaking and listening, when you have all become fluent speakers without the need of school?' The responses will vary, but may polarise along the lines of two possibilities:

- to broaden the scope of and opportunities for speaking and listening activities;
- to teach and reinforce 'correct' spoken English, rectifying habitual errors of speech.

The former suggests an enlightened opportunity; the latter, perhaps, is more of a threat and may well reflect a belief among fluent speakers of English that they in fact speak badly or, even worse, that their speech is somehow 'common'. But we have to work with what we have, to start from a realistic appraisal, and maybe even this sort of threat can be converted into something of an opportunity.

Any such realistic appraisal must acknowledge the absolute centrality of speech to language in general, embedded in the very words we use to reflect on practice. For example: we speak of helping pupils find a personal voice in response to literature, perhaps even to discern an authorial voice in the text; but in reality I am here writing about what is likely to be a written response to reading. This is more than just a stylistic nicety: the metaphor of speech brings a suggestion of freshness and spontaneity to language. Surely these are the qualities that we wish to characterise the English classroom? In some ways it may be apt to see each individual pupil as a microcosm of the linguistic development of society as a whole, with a personal reservoir of oral experience pre-dating acquisition of reading and writing: an oral tradition at once social and intensely individual which lays the foundations of all linguistic achievement, and, however sophisticated formal literacy skills may become, continues to give language its 'flavour'. Further, language and thought itself are intrinsically bound up – as Shelley, quoted above, knew full well.

## Some defining voices

The work of Vygotsky has done much to inform the philosophy and practice of English teaching in this context (see, for example, Britton's illuminating chapter in Brindley 1994, or Daniels' more broadly based *Vygotsky and Pedagogy* 2001). If, following Vygotsky, we see thought as a development of 'interior speech', literally spoken aloud during infancy, then we ignore the delicate relationship between thought and speech at our peril. This is particularly important at adolescence for this is the time of continuing, often accelerating, experimentation: sometimes pupils will 'think before speaking', sometimes not; sometimes we need to go with the spontaneous flow, sometimes intervene to focus on the need to reflect before – or even without – speech. The latter is fundamental to listening, in practice often the neglected partner in the combination of speaking and listening.

Carlyle, writing in his highly personal treatise *Sartor Resartus* (1834), realised the intimate relationship between thought and language: 'Language is called the garment of thought; however, it should rather be, language is the flesh-garment, the body, of thought' (1834: 57).

The responsibility of English teachers is enormous and challenging, then, but simultaneously exciting and invigorating. As Quirk and Stein (1990: 19) put it:

> Not all of us depend to the same extent on words when we are thinking to ourselves, but it is certain that, in general, thinking and decision-making are vastly supported and facilitated by language, even though we may be using the language silently. Most of us can grasp a distinction better when we have the linguistic apparatus to identify it amid the flux and chaos of raw experience around us.

This fusion of language and thought clearly includes reading and writing as well as speaking and listening, but it is the latter facets of language which remain absolutely basic to the process throughout our, and our pupils', development as language users and thinkers.

Quotations from the likes of Shelley and Carlyle testify to the long acknowledged depth of this relationship, but educational practice does not always act accordingly. There can be, for example, a debilitating reliance on 'exercises' in oral 'skills' with the implication that appropriate 'training' will achieve the desired results. It is easy to look back at Tomkinson (1921) and imagine we have left his recommended exercises far behind – 'exercises for beauty of tone', for example, or 'for clear articulation and facility' leading up to the skills of debating for which involvement in the subject matter or personal opinion count for nothing in favour of 'pure' technique. Decontextualised and superficial such activity might be, but the 'presentational skills' demanded by modern oral assessment may in the end amount to much the same thing. The huge interest in speaking and listening during the 1980s gave rise to words such as 'oracy' and 'aural' (which, ironically, nobody was quite sure how to pronounce) and accompanying assessment exercises. A clipboard mentality of 'if it speaks, assess it' swept the English classrooms of the day, often leaving little room for sanity. The National Curriculum served to reinforce this approach, with the lowest attainment level demanding that pupils should be able to communicate a 'simple' message effectively: colleagues I worked with at the time were ready with clipboards to see how quickly a pupil shouting 'Fire!' could empty a school. However, through all this – and perhaps despite much of it – a great deal has been achieved in raising the profile of speaking and listening. Excellent practice is steadily broadening its base, developing an English curriculum in which speaking and listening are fully integrated with the other facets of the subject.

## Tensions in speaking and listening

Tensions remain, nevertheless, and it is time to examine them in greater depth. An effective method to use here is to consider nine statements and arrange them into a diamond pattern – either with the most important or agreeable at the top and the others in descending order of priority, or with the most vital statement in the centre and the others around it. This 'Diamond Nine' exercise models good teaching practice, and is most effectively used as a focus for discussion, perhaps for an English department. The statements are as follows:

- A pupil's spoken English should never be 'corrected' by the teacher.
- All classroom talk may be legitimately assessed by the English teacher.
- Pupils should be taught that non-standard dialect is inappropriate in some speaking situations.
- Speaking and listening should underpin as many English activities as possible.
- Pupils should always be made aware of when and how their speaking and listening are being assessed.
- Oral English can be broken down into specific skills and taught accordingly.
- Formal speaking situations, such as debates and public speaking, should be highly valued in English.
- Anything really valuable in speaking and listening cannot be formally assessed.
- Sloppy oral expression reflects and/or influences sloppy thought.

You are unlikely to find it easy to fit the statements into a neat pattern, and this in itself testifies to the problematic nature of speaking and listening. Again, some of the statements are mutually exclusive whereas others are compatible, and it is quite possible to have all of them agreed with by different members of an English department. What matters is that the issues should be openly debated and what matters in this debate is substance rather than style.

On close examination many of the tensions in oral English may be reduced to a basic concern for the nature of its assessment. This is considered in Chapter 8. English teachers face something of a quandary here, for in today's educational world formal assessment assigns significance to speaking and listening – but at what cost to any real value? Certainly, even if we agree that giving oral performance some sort of accreditation is welcome (and it is still proportionally far less than that given to reading or writing), this is an aspect of English calling for great sensitivity. Some aspects of oral work may demand a detailed and relatively objective set of assessment criteria well known to both pupils and teacher; for example, the delivery of a talk to the rest of the class or the chairing of a small-group discussion. At other times, such a public awareness of and concern for the minutiae of assessment may actually hinder the free flow of orally expressed ideas by emphasising the how, the means of delivery, at the expense of the what, the content, the ideas struggling for adequate expression but worth expressing even if imperfectly. In this sort of instance it should be enough for the pupil (and teacher) to be only half consciously aware that oral performance is in the long term assessed. Whole-class discussions, for example, often spontaneous by nature, are generally best assessed in this way. Assessment, then, should match the nature of the activity and should, where possible, involve pupils and teacher in partnership – designing assessment criteria, perhaps, to help each other in the enhancement of the quality of talk. The method of assessment used will arise from the nature of the activity and the logistics involved. Cassette recorders and video cameras can be useful, as can clipboards and checklists – used sparingly. It is of course vital that a clear record is kept over the full range of activities so that a 'snapshot' judgement of a particular pupil may be given if required and so that continuity may be eased between teacher and teacher, year and year.

The dangers of compartmentalisation of speaking and listening into various 'skills' – 'presentational skills', 'listening skills' and so on – for apparent ease of assessment go much further than immediate classroom practice. As with other aspects of education, day-to-day practice both reflects and informs the wider philosophical and cultural context – the English classroom as a microcosm – which is why we have to be so careful. There is a real tension here: we want our pupils to speak confidently, fluently and effectively in the real world of social interaction and work, but do we want to help usher in the Disney Store 'have a nice day!' view of talk according to which customer-friendly performance is all and serves a sophisticated profit motive? Hornbrook (1988: 156) warned us of the insidious nature of curriculum changes along these lines:

> The worried liberal-left in the teaching profession has been perhaps too easily persuaded to connive at these seemingly beneficient manipulations of the curriculum . . . The smartly turned out hotel receptionists and hypermarket cashiers of TVEI and CPVE and YTS are the compliant service class of tomorrow, non-unionised and badly paid, trained for the telephone and the till, and as doomed in their subordination as the mute congregations of the Middle Ages.

The initials of the initiatives may have changed in 15 years, like the names of nuclear power stations, but the dangers are just as real. English teachers need to be fully aware of the implications of what happens in their classrooms; they need to integrate the content with the style of speaking and listening so that values such as honesty, sincerity and respect for others' views are combined with increasing oral lucidity and effectiveness. Indeed, as Harrison (1994) asks, what learning can take place without interaction through talk? It may well be that in a democratic and pluralist society confidently and fluently expressed public opinion is increasingly heard, in interactive radio programmes, for example; and it just might have something to do with the effective teaching of speaking and listening as a major priority in schools over the past three decades. We as English teachers cannot make the agenda, for we operate in the context of powerful social and cultural forces, but we can perhaps offer opportunities and encourage genuine expression.

## Elements of good practice: towards resolution

Harrison (1994: 135) offers us an extremely useful summary of the nature of good oral English teaching. Learners need confidence and expertise in talk, he maintains, so that they can:

- listen to, convey and share ideas and feelings;
- listen to, convey and share information;

- understand, convey and share the 'story' (their own and others');
- listen to, present, defend and interrogate points of view;
- consider questions, raise questions, work towards answers;
- understand accounts of processes, be able to describe and evaluate processes;
- be sensitive (as listener and as speaker) to appropriate tone and rhythms of voice – for example, sometimes reflective and exploratory, at other times assertive and persuasive;
- be aware (as listener and as speaker) of the need for clear expression;
- know when to be tolerant, when to support and when to challenge in talk with others;
- be confident in providing a personal presence in talking, without letting self-consciousness intrude on what you want to say – and accept the personal presence of others, while respecting what they have to say (rather than how they say it).

This list reflects a holistic and exhaustive view of the nature of speaking and listening in the English classroom with both subtlety and rigour.

The role of the audience for talk is a vital one. It is an active role too, for the audience provides the other half of the speaking and listening combination. To fulfil the full range of oral possibilities alluded to above, pupils should be given every opportunity to experience a variety of audiences involving:

- their classmates, as a whole class or as individuals or small groups;
- other pupils of different ages and interests;
- pupils from different schools, particularly cross-phase partnership schools;
- teachers – and not only their English teacher, if feasible opportunities can be found;
- other adults from different walks of life with particularly relevant interests;
- imagined audiences through role-play and media-based oral projects;
- real audiences through the media of audio- and video-taping, and even, as the facility becomes more widely available, video-conferencing.

For listeners too there should be a wide range of meaningful experiences, many of which will be integrated into the sort of activities noted above; we could add, with a specific focus on listening, the use of:

- the teacher as lecturer (let us not forget Ofsted's advice to teachers to rediscover the didactic approach);
- outside speakers, especially if relevant to the particular theme studied, such as representatives from pressure groups, societies, the press, charities, the media and political organisations;

■ writers, poets, theatre groups and story-tellers; teachers from different curricular areas with particular information on the topic studied – be aware of the wealth of under-used knowledge and oral expertise in any school.

Throughout all this resourcefulness, the English teacher's own role, as always, is crucial. Apart from creating the conditions of encouragement and stimulation, we too must above all listen attentively and sympathetically. Not all of us are natural listeners, and we are unlikely to be trained counsellors (neither should we be); but we can, nevertheless, 'heal ourselves' in the arts of listening through the focusing of attention on the utterance itself without prejudice. Social intercourse consisting of Pinteresque interrupted monologues is all too common, not least in the classroom, and it may well take a real effort of will to clear one's mind sufficiently of such issues as 'how to respond' or 'what is my view?' to really hear what is being said. If we are to model good practice, however, this is precisely what we need to do. As a practical aid to such reflective learning, it is worth taping an orally based lesson and analysing the results critically to see how much genuine listening took place and what it resulted in. We as teachers need to learn from our classrooms as do our pupils, and good listening is the key to a great deal of effective teaching right across the curriculum.

Much oral activity will be spontaneous, and quite rightly so. However, the drafting of oral work, where appropriate and with the same provisos we noted for the drafting of written English, should also be actively encouraged. Although, as we argue elsewhere, learning to speak is largely a natural process, the English teacher needs to understand just when drafting may be appropriate as a means of actively teaching speaking and listening as opposed to simply facilitating their occurrence. Oral drafting may well be most apt in different types of planned performance, and the potential and power of the voice to celebrate and accomplish should never be under-estimated or under-taught. As for written drafting, the teacher's judicious intervention is vital, and the use of peer support. Thus the stages of drafting should be geared towards effective communication through a polished product, and may well involve, in the process:

■ alteration and adaptation of spoken content;

■ increased sophistication of delivery;

■ greater awareness of the specific audience in mind;

■ changes in register, perhaps achieved through reflective use of taping;

■ increasing awareness of the precise function of the particular performance – is it, for example, to persuade, to entertain, to instruct, to report, to clarify, to narrate or to describe (to name but a few)?

The nature of the drafting strategy used is dependent upon the type of activity, its context, and its projected audience. In essence, it is the formalisation of preparation, and, as all teachers know full well through their own professional work, many spoken performances require a great deal of painstaking preparation; it would be unfair to expect otherwise of our pupils.

We have already seen just how much scope there is for English teachers to make judgements about the nature of oral activities, audiences, assessment and so on. In the sense that we are concerned to teach children to become better oral practitioners, the making of these judgements begs the question of exactly what constitutes progress in speaking and listening. We have looked at some of the tensions involved in assessment, and much of what actually occurs seems to be based on differentiation by outcome rather than by task. The National Curriculum generally follows this model, and although the levels of attainment are couched in rather generalised terms this may be their saving grace: the only realistic way of assessing oral performance. However, we need also to recognise that different oral tasks will demand in themselves different levels of expertise, without becoming too hidebound by the notion of hierarchical 'skills'. Anderson *et al.* (1984: 51) put the case strongly:

> We have found that different types of tasks elicit different types of language and pose different communicative problems for the speaker . . . we have found that there is an ascending scale of difficulty among different task types. Tasks which involve the speaker in describing static relationships among objects are fairly easy to communicate to a hearer, if there are relatively few objects and the relationships between them are fairly simple. Tasks which involve dynamic relationships among people or objects, where a speaker has to describe events which change over time and space, are more difficult. Tasks which require the speaker to communicate abstract notions, for instance in argument or justifications, are more difficult again, for most young speakers.

Some of the terms used here seem to me problematic when they are intended to be taken at face value: when are relationships 'simple' or 'dynamic', for example? Nevertheless, as a reminder that not all oral activities are equally challenging, and that in planning the oral dimension of the English curriculum we have to take this into account, there is a degree of validity in what is expressed here. The issue is further complicated by the realisation that different pupils will have different strengths and weaknesses in different stages of their development and in different social combinations. Variables such as this need careful acknowledgement, and it may be that differentiation by outcome is, in the final analysis, the most feasible method. But variety of approach and activity is fundamental. It may be that a non-hierarchical model of oral interaction in the English classroom has greater relevance, such as Howe's 'oracy map' (1994: 47).

Another potentially problematic area, especially relevant in any sort of hierarchical notion of oral 'skills' and deliberately foregrounded in the National Curriculum, is that of standard spoken English. Looking back again to Lewis (1946: 51) we find a genuinely humane and egalitarian hope that the spread of standard spoken English might alleviate and erode social class inequalities:

> if it can be shown that it is necessary for the health of our society that there shall be a truly common speech, then we may perhaps hope to bring this about by an appeal to feeling; by fostering a pride in nothing less than spoken English, speech common to all who live in these islands . . . It is a fantastic transposition of values to wish to preserve 'picturesque' dialects at the expense of the social health of our community.

There is a world of difference in tone between these words, with their understandable post-war optimism, and Rhodes Boyson's hectoring reaction to the debate on National Curriculum English in the late 1980s (originally in *The Sun*, subsequently in Moon 1996: 44):

> Teachers should be putting across proper English and expect to be spoken to in the same way by children. Grammar has to be taught. It is not something children are born with . . . Standard English is the passport to mobility. Sloppiness in speech rules you out for a job.

Taking this notion still further, David Pascall, then chair of the National Curriculum Council (NCC), suggested in 1992 that teachers should not be content to insist on 'correct' expression in their classrooms but should infiltrate the playground, intervening in pupils' speech to enforce standard English. The point is that for all the differences in tone, the ultimate message amounts to much the same. And there is some validity in it, if of rather a simplistic nature, for if a pupil could speak only in a local dialect of English this would undoubtedly close down many vocational and social opportunities. Even if we regret this, we have, among many other things, to prepare our pupils for the realities of adult life, and none is harsher.

In reality, the situation is not as grim, neither need it be as polarised. People – adults and children alike – are adept at speaking many different forms of English according to the context, purpose and audience. For writing, perhaps, the difficulties are fewer, in that writing is a skill learned in a relatively formal fashion and implies in any case a more formal grammar. This is perhaps the root of the confusion, in that it is written English that has largely determined what most regard as 'correct' spoken English – and even a cursory glance over virtually any transcript of spoken English will show the falsehood of a direct correlation. Indeed, any attempt to transfer from one to the other is fraught with problems: the speech sounds stilted, and writing, except in the most informal circumstances, seems imprecise. What matters is the richness of language, whether spoken or written, as Knight (1996) makes abundantly clear in his illuminating chapter entitled 'Standard English and the Spoken Word'. With talk, it is difficult to disentangle the speaker from the spoken: an attack on the nature of a person's speech is an attack on that person's being. Nevertheless, as in writing, it is important that pupils realise that spoken standard English is required for formal situations, such as job interviews, and where necessary the teacher may have to intervene. Any intervention should be carried out with the greatest sensitivity, most effectively through role-play and subsequent open discussion. Other pupils' perceptions may be useful to start debate on the nature of appropriate speech, but the teacher needs to be all the more wary lest prejudice replace realistic appraisal. It is worth noting here the distinction between accent and dialect: a pupil's accent should in no circumstances be tutored or criticised, as it is perfectly possible to speak the standard form of English in any accent, and, indeed, impossible to speak it without one. Effective English teaching thrives on the richness of oral experience, spoken and listened to, and this should be the guiding principle.

## The practical dimension

So what would this sort of effective English teaching look – or, rather, sound – like? In the context of an integrated English curriculum, we might expect to find a stimulating range of activities and approaches; it would be likely that, whatever the emphasis on reading or writing in any given assignment, some part of it would entail speaking and listening. In fact it would be hard to think up an English activity not involving them, and in this we have an important starting point. Since the advent of the Key Stage 3 Strategy, with its insistence on rather more didactic than facilitative approaches to English teaching, there has been greater emphasis on the active teaching of speaking and listening as opposed to simply stimulating and resourcing the activity. Pedagogical tools such as teacher-led direction, demonstration, modelling and scaffolding are now intended to apply to speaking and listening as much as the rather more obvious activities of reading and writing. As with so much of the Strategy, the key to success here is in flexibility and selectivity, and it is now all the more important to avoid the trap of destroying spontaneity by over-teaching – particularly with regard to speaking and listening. Pre-dating the Strategy, but perhaps all the more significant for that, Harrison (1994: 239) advised the following safeguards on behalf of all learners:

- Encourage *flexibility* among all speakers, in mediating between non-standard (usually colloquial) and standard (usually written) forms of the mother tongue.
- *Empower* all speakers to range over the whole universe of discourse – intellectual and affective.
- Encourage a full sense of *ownership* of all the versions of language that may be required by speakers.
- Instil *confidence* in the use of these versions of language.
- Encourage *respect* for the variant versions of language that may be used by other individuals and other communities, for their own particular needs.

To which I would add:

- Enjoy and celebrate the many possibilities of language use as absolutely fundamental to oral English.

With these principles in mind, the attentive listener in a thriving English classroom may hear some of the following going on:

- Jigsaw technique for group-based research and reporting work: four separate roles, each role combining with pupils from other groups fulfilling the same role to conduct research/discuss a given aspect of a topic for a set period of time, then reporting back to the original 'home' group. Endless variations of context, method, purpose, audience and roles played.
- Fruitbowl method of small-group formation: the teacher assigns each pupil a 'fruit', and then forms groups for effective oral work accordingly – each group usually forming a mixed fruit salad, sweetened to taste.

- Pair combinations: friendship pairs, working and talking well together for the first part of any activity, are then combined with compatible other pairs to broaden the base of discussion, perhaps mixing genders.

- Rainbow groups: 'random' group formation based on colour combinations, or allocation of numbers to each pupil with all 'ones' and so on then congregating.

- Envoy technique: groups send envoys (or vary to become gossip columnists) to other groups working on the same topic to glean information/gossip and/or be quizzed on their own group's deliberations, with time limits for each stage.

- Goldfish-bowl method: one group member passively observes the group's effectiveness and reports back on the nature of the findings.

- Eavesdropping session: class focuses on the workings of one particular small group's discussion as a model of good practice, perhaps then offering constructive ideas, guided by the teacher.

- Buzz-session: 30-second (or vary) pair discussions on a given topic before teacher-selected individuals report back to whole class – a good opening for class discussion, ensuring some sort of preparation from all.

- Storytelling: groups of four tell each other autobiographical/fictional stories; each group selects their favourite; another member of the group then relates the tale in first person to the rest of the class, who try to guess the identity of the original teller.

- Just a minute: the teacher picks an unlikely topic (e.g. 'the common housefly') and selects a pupil to speak uninterrupted for one minute, with no repetition or hesitation. An elaboration is to insist on the next pupil making a coherent link to the next unlikely topic ('hot-water bottles').

- Statement-arrangement: statements on cards distributed as a stimulus for group discussion on a given theme or issue, as in the 'Diamond Nine' activity.

- Drama-based techniques such as:
  - □ monologues;
  - □ back-to-back alter-ego dialogues;
  - □ hot-seating of pupils (or teacher) in role;
  - □ mock trials;
  - □ role-play, perhaps with assigned characteristics or 'status numbers';
  - □ deliberately inappropriate role-play such as aggressively conducting an interview.

- Chinese whispers: using the whole class to illustrate how oral transmission can change messages/stories/jokes, etc.

- Formal oral activities: such as debates and public speaking sessions – some pupils respond very well to formal structures for oral performance.

- Use of media resources: not merely as an aid to assessment, in which they have a use, but as aids to effective oral performance.

- Listening activities: often neglected, but easy to set up, for example asking pupils to remember what the salient points were from a taped speech sequence.

- Celebratory performances: for example, prepared story telling, choral presentation of poetry learned by heart.

- Predictive activities, through which pupils listen to or invent one half of a conversation, implying the other speaker's words, as in the common experience of overhearing one side of a telephone conversation. Wole Soyinka's poem 'Telephone Coversation' is an excellent starting point for this sort of work, as are some of the radio sketches of the American comedian Bob Newhart ('The Driving Instructor' or 'Bringing Tobacco to England').

The list of enterprising activities and approaches is endless, and endlessly adaptable. It may well be that the human voice is an imperfect medium – 'human speech is like a cracked kettle on which we strum out tunes to make a bear dance, when we would move the stars to pity' (Flaubert, in *Madame Bovary*) – but it is all we have and should be celebrated and cherished. Oral work lies at the very heart of the English curriculum, and the resulting pulse should be the sign of good health.

## Further reading

Integrated views of speaking and listening can be found in Jones (1988) *Lipservice: The Story of Talk in Schools*, Tarleton (1988) *Learning and Talking* and Wilkinson *et al.* (1990) *Spoken English Illuminated*. Alan Howe's study in the 'Papers in Education' series, *Making Talk Work* (NATE 1997) combines theoretical insights with practical activities; the same author has also contributed a stimulating chapter in Goodwyn (1995) *English and Ability*, summarising recent developments in oral English. NATE publish four booklets, *Teaching, Talking and Learning*, one for each Key Stage; they have a practical orientation and interesting cross-curricular ideas, drawing positively on the work of the National Oracy Project. Also useful is Holderness and Lalljee (1997) *An Introduction to Oracy: Frameworks for Talk*, and the 'Speaking and Listening' section of Brindley (ed.) (1994) *Teaching English*. More recently Andrews (2001) has included a helpful chapter on developments and research into speaking and listening, and Grainger's chapter, 'The current status of oracy: a cause of (dis)satisfaction?', in Davison and Moss (2000) is also thought-provoking. Haworth, Turner and Whiteley (2004) include a more practically-focused chapter on oracy in their book too. Goodwin's (edited) *The Articulate Classroom* (2001), although focused on primary practice, has many interesting and relevant things to say for secondary English teachers.

## Resources

Speaking and listening activity is promoted in virtually all educational publishers' English materials, explicitly and implicitly, although rarely as a separate strand in the way reading and writing are presented. However, NATE publishes materials through Framework Press in the familiar form of ring-bound photocopiable sheets: *Speaking and Listening: Activities at Key Stage 3* (Kilpatrick) and *Speaking and Listening: Integrated Activities for Pupils at Key Stage 4* (Phillips) are up to date and inventive. *Exploring Spoken English* (Carter and McCarthy), Cambridge University Press, focuses imaginatively on oral activities, and has the additional benefit of an accompanying cassette. In so far as speaking and listening need to be assessed, the examination boards have produced helpful video guides (vastly improved since the early days of GCSE oral assessment), and SCAA (now QCA) have performed much the same function at Key Stage 3. Rather more distantly, the Assessment of Performance Unit published a still useful audio cassette in 1986, entitled *Speaking and Listening: Assessment at Age 11* (NFER-Nelson).

# 5

# Reading

*A book is like a garden carried in the pocket.*

Chinese proverb

## The nature of reading in the English curriculum

READING, traditionally the first of the three Rs, is currently the focus of hugely energetic enterprise as the central facet of the drive to improve basic literacy. Although the Key Stage 3 Strategy has put out its feelers to all aspects and stages of the English curriculum, it is essentially founded on a project to improve pupils' functional reading. In the 'Rationale' introducing the Strategy (DfEE 1998: 9–19), for instance, reading is always placed before writing and speaking and listening, in a perhaps significant shift away from the order established in the National Curriculum. Clearly then, much of Chapter 2 is relevant to the present subject matter. Indeed, for many within and outside the world of education reading has become synonymous with literacy, and there is a good deal of semantic confusion and vagueness on this score. Whether such attention will prove energising rather than energy-draining remains to be seen, but it is against this background that we need to examine the teaching of reading within English in the secondary school. Looking back 50 years, we find one of the standard guides on the teaching of English (Smith 1954: 36) offering the following advice to student teachers:

> Perhaps the most important, and certainly the most dangerous thing we attempt to do with a child in school is to try to teach him [sic] to read. On his ability to read, in the widest sense, will depend the ultimate success or failure of all our attempts to educate him. We cannot even proceed far with instruction until we have taught him to do something more than bark at print. Whatever our definition of an educated person might include, we could not omit the requirement that he should be able to make sense of what others write. Most would, one hopes, add the further qualification that he should also find pleasure and inspiration on the printed page.

We could pertinently ask: what has changed since 1954? Certainly some interesting, and still timely, issues arise from the passage:

- Why exactly is reading so important, and what implications does this have on its position in the secondary school?

- In what sense might the teaching of reading be dangerous?

- The use of the masculine form of the personal pronoun is, presumably, a conventional sign of the times; but is there a more significant question lurking here, to do with the question of gender and reading?

- Why does reading predicate all other learning, and, if indeed it does, what does this imply about its specific position as part of the secondary English curriculum?

- What other, perhaps less tangible, aspects of reading are there apart from the ability to 'bark at print', and how do we know if anything else significant is happening in the reading process?

- 'To make sense of what others write' sounds pretty uncontroversial, but one person's (pupil's?) sense may be another's (the teacher's?) nonsense: how far should we give free rein to subjectivity in interpretation?

- What place exactly do 'pleasure and inspiration' have in the reading curriculum in view of the pressure to meet basic literacy targets and achieve examination success at all levels of secondary education?

- What other forms of reading are there – and might there be – apart from the printed page?

The temporal distance of the quotation serves to illustrate both a sense of continuity of concern about reading – some would say déjà vu – and, hopefully, a certain progress in our understanding of its nature as a teachable activity. Discussion of these issues will inform our consideration of reading throughout this chapter.

Of course reading can be conducted for a vast range of different purposes and takes a number of different forms. Consider the qualitative difference between reading, say, a railway timetable for specific information, a guidebook for an art exhibition, a magazine read casually while waiting to meet an appointment, and a complex novel read for pleasure. Both in life generally and in school particularly the act of reading decodes and interprets virtually without cease, and is often seamlessly connected to oral and writing activity: consider, for example, the early-morning staffroom routine in many schools of the discovery of lesson supervision – the list is read and talked about (with despair or jubilation as the case may be) and reminder notes and / or complaints are hastily written. Here, as in so much else, the act of reading is primary, and on the initial understanding gained other forms of activity are predicated. In this sense, reading is basic to literacy, but not synonymous with it: literacy implies the ability to use language effectively and appropriately across a wide range of forms. The responsibility of the secondary English teacher is to secure, develop and extend the reading repertoire, including reading for specific information, skim-reading and inference. This can be achieved only through teaching a fully integrated curriculum, not only within English itself but as part of whole-school language practice, with each subject being clear about the types of reading demanded for progress to be made. As we have seen in the appraisal of the impact of the literacy-driven curriculum in Chapter 2, a significant part of the English teacher's repertoire – to put a positive gloss on this development – has now to do with the impact of the Strategy and its subsequent integration into the National Curriculum.

Recommended pedagogy involving shared and group-reading techniques, for example, with implications for the role of the English teacher in terms of modelled and guided reading strategies, for example, is very much part and parcel of English classroom life. If such approaches are employed flexibly and are creatively integrated into the broader context of teaching reading, they may be welcomed.

The Strategy has also pushed reading high up on the whole-school curriculum agenda, and here again the implications are considerable for English teachers in terms of offering particular expertise to colleagues from other subjects. Clearly reading goes well beyond the confines of English, and well beyond the preoccupation with written text. English idiomatic usage of the word 'reading' itself suggests this. In the same way as we speak of 'reading a situation', so do many of life's experiences require some sort of reading: reading someone's face, for example, or reading a game of football. Fascinatingly, common vernacular frequently suggests perceptive and subtle truths. In the context of schooling, each curricular area presents its own situations to be read, and not always through the medium of written English; consider, for example, the reading of musical notation, scientific symbols or works of art.

## Breadth in the reading curriculum

Reading is at once a highly focused activity and one rooted in an extremely broad cultural context, with the potential to take one or several of many different forms. Focusing with concentration on a text is, for many children, difficult – but that is precisely what effective reading demands and it is hard indeed to imagine paying attention simultaneously to other activities. At the same time, reader response theory, developed largely since the above-quoted advice to student teachers, has shown that there are in fact as many different possible readings of text as there are readers, and that each reader brings to the text a wealth of lived and read experience, including the ability or otherwise to focus with concentration on text. Taking account of and successfully fostering this multiplicity of readings of a fast increasing range of texts, including those based on the media and ICT, is the business of education. As already stated, there can be no escaping the responsibility of the whole school here, especially since each curricular subject demands its own ways of reading, but it is the particular responsibility of the English teacher to teach reading in and for itself. This is taken for granted in the primary phase, when the basic ability to read – that is, to make some sort of sense of marks on a page or elsewhere – is taught; we are, though, less familiar and perhaps less comfortable about the responsibility of the secondary English teacher to ensure progress in reading. And this does not simply mean, although it may include, the improvement of a pupil's reading age. The peculiar position of English in this respect is something we shall return to continually in this chapter; however, reading is cross-curricular, the foundation of a good deal of what is learned in school, and this may be the best place to start. Assuming that few secondary colleagues from other disciplines are likely to approach English departments with ideas for collaborative teaching of reading, mutually beneficial though this may be, it is in practice likely to be up to the English teacher to be pro-active here. As an example of good practice, consider the scheme of study in Figure 5.1; it is based on reading both of

---

**INTRODUCTION TO WORDSWORTH AND THE LAKE DISTRICT LANDSCAPE: KEY STAGE 4**

**Resources**

- Large-scale, detailed map of Lake District, with contours and shading;
- pictures/photographs of the Lakes – past and present, industrial and agrarian, 'realistic' and 'romanticised';
- extracts from biography of Wordsworth, and portraits;
- extracts from his poetry (particularly from *The Prelude*);
- extracts from Dorothy Wordsworth's *Journals*, to match subject matter of the verse;
- tourist information 'literature' on the Lakes, taken if possible from different periods and reflecting contrasting presentational styles;
- other written or pictorial records, such as newspaper articles, National Park information, or planning documents (on keeping the appropriate balance between tourism and employment or housing interests, for example).

**Activities**

- Whole-class work: general discussion on the nature of the different resources used, emphasising the different types of 'reading' involved and the contrasting messages conveyed by the various materials. The stress should also be on the purpose and context of a range of readings, and on similarities and dissimilarities between readers.
- Pairs would examine and then report back briefly on one particular resource in the light of this discussion.
- Small-group activity: to re-present group-chosen information from the above list in a specific form (for example, a magazine article in *Country Living*, a programme for local radio or a guidebook for American visitors) for a specific audience. There must be evidence of a wide range of source materials.

**FIGURE 5.1**

text and of landscape – and the practised eye does read landscape – devised through the collaboration of English and geography teachers to introduce the topic of Wordsworth and the Lake District landscape.

Important here is the realisation that shared good practice is possible and desirable even within the discrete subject-based curriculum underlined by the structure of the National Curriculum, not simply because it gets people working together in a common cause, but because it concentrates teaching on the range of reading styles to be experienced and developed – taught, in fact – as fundamental to the whole business of learning.

Most people would grant the importance of reading in education – but might balk at the idea of reading as dangerous. But reading, as a fundamental part of literacy, is about power; and power, as this century has surely demonstrated, is potentially dangerous. Just as interpretation through reading is subjective, so too is the notion of power: one person's idea of unjustifiable wielding of power is another's vaunted liberation. Consider these viewpoints:

Learn the ABC, it's not enough, but learn it. Don't let it get you down! . . . You who are starving, grab hold of the book: it's a weapon. You must take over the leadership.

Bertolt Brecht, 'In Praise of Learning' in Hoyles (1977: 78)

or:

Having created universal literacy, the next task of education is to counter the forces which would make the literate more ignorant than the illiterate by virtue of their (the literate) acquired susceptibility.

T. Merriam, 'The Consumer Society' Education and Survival in Tract 10, quoted in Abbs (1976: 8)

Brecht suggests that literacy empowers in a Marxist sense, and of course that is likely to be perceived as dangerous to those holding power: his poem is a call to arms born of the class struggle. We do not need to go as far, or indeed to share the revolutionary politics, to see the validity of literacy as empowering; even a cursory examination of classroom activity will show how valuable is the ability to read in gaining control – power – over one's learning and thus one's life. It is a fully democratic force in this sense, and good English teaching fosters its growth in a spirit of open learning. But the very effectiveness of the modern education system in bringing about widespread literacy may have its attendant dangers in that aesthetic and even moral considerations may be neglected. The teaching and learning of reading need to be fully conscious, nurturing a fully social creativity which confronts existential situations and attempts the evaluation and, if appropriate, the transcendence of any received position. Reid (1985: 135) makes the pertinent point:

The learning of, and in, any 'subject' whatsoever, should be a personal learning experience, an engagement, an involvement in whatever is being learnt. If, instead, it is as it too often is, merely the 'getting up' of 'knowledge' . . . the educational value of 'learning' that subject has been minimal.

This is indeed a challenge, and it would be ludicrously presumptuous to suggest that the teaching of English – specifically reading – could single-handedly meet it. But it may play a part. It is the process towards full aptitude for words and images which is so vital here, the process of linguistic consciousness described by Dorothy Owen as long ago as 1920 (quoted in Abbs 1976: 39):

Words must first be made the servants of images and the mastery will not be complete until subconscious thought becomes articulate. The word will then hold in itself the experience and be pregnant with the meaning which it, instead of the images, now encases.

## Practical implications and critical approaches

We need now to move on to some of the practicalities in this movement towards articulation through reading: an adventurous and exciting enterprise in response to the challenge noted above – not in the sense of living vicariously through books but, rather, through a full engagement with reading all sorts of formally and informally arranged texts as part of life itself. In formulating some sort of unifying frame of reference for the Cambridge Literature series, the editor, Judith Baxter, and the editorial team came up with five guiding questions, themselves an adaptation of six questions posed in the LINC training manual (Carter 1991) referred to earlier. The Cambridge Literature questions are, with minor variations depending on the text and author referred to:

■ Who has written this text and why?

■ What type of text is it?

■ How was it produced?

■ How does this text present its subject?

■ Who reads this text, and how do they interpret it?

These are pertinent questions to ask, and open up any text to interpretative possibilities both personal and collaborative. The very form of this sort of introduction to a text, as questions rather than statements, implies discovery and invention. Baxter (1995 and subsequently) elaborates, in her general introduction to any one of the series:

> This study edition invites you to think about what happens when you read . . . and it suggests that you are not passively responding to words on the page which have only one agreed interpretation, but that you are actively exploring and making new sense of what you read. Your 'reading' will stem partly from you as an individual, from your own experiences and point of view, and to this extent your interpretation will be distinctively your own. But your reading will also stem from the fact that you belong to a culture and a community, rooted in a particular time and place. So, your understanding may have much in common with that of others in your class or study group.
>
> (1995: 1)

The very fact that a major series intended for use in schools is centred around questions such as these suggests that reading can empower, through developing young readers' interpretative tools. The success of the series, and the consultation process with teachers involved, implies that the editorial 'way in' is in tune with good practice, and the range of approaches possible on these premises is liberating. Of course English teachers – and educational series editors – are not so naive as to believe that simply asking the appropriate questions will unlock genuine originality of interpretation, if indeed such a thing exists at all. Rather, the important principle is in the process of discovery and making of meaning. In this context, subjectivity (the intensely personal) and objectivity (the social and cultural context which enables meaning to be found) may be complementary rather than mutually exclusive as often supposed. Traherne, to return for a moment to the seventeenth century, celebrated his own subjectivity all the more for realising that everyone could possess this gift:

> You never enjoy the world aright, till the sea itself floweth in your veins, till you are clothed with the heavens, and crowned with the stars: and perceive yourself to be the sole heir of the whole world, and more than so, because men are in it *who are every one sole heirs as well as you*.
>
> (1960: 5, my emphasis)

Some may consider that we have wandered some way from the reality of English in the secondary classroom, but it is precisely this sort of celebration which must give reading its particular flavour and appeal as part of a specifically English curriculum – in other words, as an end in itself as well as a means to other kinds of investigation and learning.

To speak of the act of reading in an English classroom is somewhat misleading, for there are likely to be many different activities, including some or all of these:

- the whole-class reader, with each pupil having a text, read aloud
  - ☐ by the teacher;
  - ☐ by pupils 'in turn';
  - ☐ by pupils reading the dialogue 'in role';
  - ☐ by pupils having prepared passages beforehand;
  - ☐ if a drama text, by pupils playing the parts;
  - ☐ in some combination of these styles of reading;
- paired reading, known also as reading partnerships, whereby fluent readers help other pupils less advanced in their reading skills;
- reading text in small groups, generally with a view to presenting findings in some sort of appropriate form, which may include drama;
- guided reading for research, within and outside the classroom, with either the discovery of specific information in mind or a more open-ended intention;
- sustained silent reading on an individual basis, with the English teacher modelling good practice;
- reading of a particular textbook or worksheet, either individually or collaboratively, in order to carry out a specified task;
- involvement in one or more of the huge variety of text-related activities, rooted in reading but conceivably developing a range of quite different forms of learning: drama, music, interviews, writing, art, speaking and listening, for example;
- reading of data generated by ICT and the media;
- reading of written text in conjunction with other forms of presentation such as illustrations, maps, diagrams, tables and charts;
- detailed work on inferential comprehension conducted as part of an integrated English scheme of study.

As in so much else, the task of the English teacher is to balance, connect and integrate. There is room for all the forms of reading listed above, and many more, but there is an attendant danger that we become victims of our own success in formulating ever more adventurous ways of reading enacted for their own sake. We need to be all the more acutely focused on the primary requirement that we develop pupils' reading; in this context, we may select appropriately from the repertoire of activities, recognising each for its own particular value and limitations.

The integration of reading into the full English curriculum implies a blurring of the edges between different types of English activity. Take, for example, the plan (Figure 5.2) for connecting a drama sequence to the reading of Penelope Lively's novel *The Whispering Knights* (1971) for a mixed-ability Year 7 group. Clearly reading here is a springboard for diverse activities, including drama, speaking and listening, and writing. Possible extensions are numerous, such as media-based reporting of the controversy and the meeting itself and research-based work on local issues of genuine concern. The two points made at the end of the sequence description are vital, however, if reading is to remain the focus: first, that the group be returned to the text itself for enhanced understanding; and second, that subsequent discussion concentrate on how reading relates to its contexts and purposes. Combing the text for evidence of a particular pressure group's view, for example, is a different sort of reading from tracing the narrative to find out what happens next.

---

**DRAMA SEQUENCE: THE WHISPERING KNIGHTS (YEAR 7)**

**Background:** the novel centres around three children who arouse the malevolent spirit of Morgan le Fay, who then mischievously causes changes to a motorway building project so that it will go through the children's home village, Steeple Hampden, and some beautiful countryside to boot.

**Lesson focus:** to increase involvement with and understanding of the text, the pupils role-play a public meeting, chaired by the teacher in role, to discuss the motorway's proposed route. In previous lessons, alternative routes, based where possible on textual information, had been drawn up and a map devised. The class then divided into pressure groups for particular views and enacted propaganda campaigns and the collection of signatures in petitions.

In a subsequent lesson, pupils were given role cards, including one representative from each pressure group, for characters from the novel and other teacher-invented characters to enliven the debate. A preparatory lesson was spent making notes on the characters, culminating in a brief introduction from each to the rest of the group, and discussing the nature of public meetings (if possible using the experience of any real local issues).

For the public meeting role-play lesson itself, skilful chairing is required to ensure that each voice is heard, and that the evidence from the text itself is adhered to. The latter consideration may be returned to in future lessons focusing more directly on the novel again, teasing out what new perceptions had been gathered from the entire exercise.

**FIGURE 5.2**

Let us continue examining the widely used form of classroom-based reading, that of the shared reading of a text held in common – the 'class reader'. 'Reading around the class' has attracted considerable criticism over the years, and many of us remember, perhaps painfully, desperately trying to work out where our part in a text would fall so that we would not stumble quite as incoherently as some of our classmates. Any meaning tended to get lost, either through sheer boredom of hearing unprepared reading aloud, or through anticipatory panic. In a mixed-ability context these sorts of problems would be exacerbated, and no doubt the first person's patience to snap would be the teacher's. Consider this example, used with teachers by a Special Educational Needs Coordinator to illustrate the potential pitfalls (Soloman 1990):

CAN YOU READ THIS?

The boys' arrows were nearly gone so they sat down on the grass and stopped hunting. Over the edge of the wood they saw Henry making a bow to a small girl who was coming down the road. She had tears in her dress and tears in her eyes. She gave Henry a note which he brought over to the group of young hunters. Read to the boys it caused great excitement. After a minute but rapid examination of their weapons they ran down to the valley. Does were standing at the edge of the lake, making an excellent target.

At the very least, reading aloud needs some time for rehearsal: a fluent reader may recover very quickly from hesitation and stumbling in a passage like that above, but how much more difficult might it be for an inexperienced reader? This is not to deny, however, the many positive benefits to a class of sharing a common text and a collaborative reading – benefits which go well beyond the need to give some practice in reading aloud (which, in itself, may be seen as mere 'barking at print' to use the expression of the 1954 handbook, *English in the Modern School*; Smith 1954: 36). For one of the early NATE-inspired books dedicated to invigorating English teaching, Calthrop (1971: 23) interviewed English teachers who

felt that the shared experience of reading a common book was something of great value to themselves and to their classes. They regarded it as something quite different from the pleasure to be gained from individual reading and took the view that the feeling of sharing something worth while, the common sense of enjoyment, and the resulting sense of community was a deeply educative process . . . a reciprocal process . . . akin to the experience of a theatre audience . . . The whole process involved a performance by the teacher, a collective, but enjoyed and shared, response from the audience, together with a fair amount of audience participation.

This is reading in a celebratory sense, and requires that we 'awaken our faith' in the possibilities of performance and inspiration as central to English teaching. And like any performance, it needs preparation and rehearsal, not least on the part of the teacher. The rewards, however, can be immense, and more or less distinctive to the English classroom. Neither need the performance stop with the reading, and the use of drama here can be apposite, paradoxically, to halt the narrative in order that reflection may occur. As Grainger (1998: 32) points out:

In reading fiction, the power of the narrative can drive the reader relentlessly onwards, and unless opportunities to pause, consider and reflect upon the text are created and valued, their reading of it may only scratch the surface. Drama is not plot-driven, nor restricted by living time since techniques such as flashbacks, flash forwards and interior monologues provide opportunities to investigate the present moment further, as well as examine precursors and long-term consequences.

Such reflective interruptions need not necessarily take the form of fully fledged dramatic enterprises, such as hot-seating of characters or a 'talking heads' activity, and are most effective when rooted in reading and response. An English teacher may, for example, choosing the moment carefully, halt the reading to focus on one character in a way similar to that recommended in the chapter on writing, with the instruction to the class to stop reading, close their eyes, and imagine the textual scene just recounted. The teacher could then develop understanding by asking pupils to describe aloud, in first or third person, the character's thoughts and feelings. Alternatively, we may wish to concentrate on the reader as author of interpretation, again interrupting the reading to ask 'if you were writing this, what would you have happening next?' The empathetic and predictive possibilities are infinite, and could easily be explored further through writing, thus cementing the bond between reading, speaking and listening, and writing. The important point is always to return to the text, and this principle is worth bearing in mind whatever is being read, by whom, and however the imaginative nature of the activity is devised.

An approach to shared reading widely and successfully used in the primary phase is that instigated by Aidan Chambers, himself a highly accomplished children's author: the 'Tell Me' method. Chambers (1993) has developed his ideas from W. H. Auden's desire, presented in 'Reading' in *The Dyer's Hand and Other Essays* (1963), that literary critics

1   introduce me to authors or works of which I was hitherto unaware;

2   convince me that I have undervalued an author or a work because I had not read them carefully enough;

3   show me relations between works of different ages and cultures which I could never have seen for myself because I do not know enough and never shall;

4   give a 'reading' of a work which increases my understanding of it;

5   throw light upon the process of artistic 'Making';

6   throw light upon the relation of art to life, to science, economics, ethics, religion, etc.

(1993: 30)

As guidance for teachers of English, let alone literary critics, this seems excellent advice. Chambers asserts, on these secure foundations, that children can with guidance become judicious critics dedicated to the understanding and enjoyment of texts. The approach is essentially collaborative, and centres on a series of pertinent questions about the experience of books, with the initial warning that the 'Tell Me' approach is not a mechanical textbook programme – it is not meant to be slavishly followed. The basic 'Tell Me' questions are listed below; many others, in a variety of permutations, follow on from them:

- Was there anything you liked about this book?
- What especially caught your attention?
- What would you have liked more of?
- Was there anything you disliked?
- Were there parts that bored you?
- Did you skip parts? Which ones?
- If you gave up, where did you stop and what stopped you?
- Was there anything that puzzled you?
- Was there anything you thought strange?
- Was there anything you'd never found in a book before?
- Was there anything that took you completely by surprise?
- Did you notice any apparent inconsistencies?
- Were there any patterns – any connections – that you noticed?

The details of the subsequent questions are well worth looking up, but we can already see how pertinent is the framework. It may of course need adapting – that is, after all, its purpose – and the questions could be reinterpreted with specific readings in mind for worksheets and long-term schemes of work as well as for more immediate discussions. The reading itself, clearly, does not need to be a shared experience, and some of the questions imply otherwise; but the opening up of interpretative possibilities using the approach must be in some sense social, whether with a whole class, small group (perhaps set a particular book to read with a view to presenting it to the rest of the class), or between the teacher and a single pupil. This flexibility is particularly appropriate to the secondary, 'workshop'-based English classroom. The last of the 'basic questions' may be the most fruitful for interpretation in depth, bringing to mind E. M. Forster's aphoristic 'only connect', within English and in the cross-curricular dimension.

## Further practical implications

Innovative and detailed approaches to reading texts in school have been well documented elsewhere, most notably in the Cox version of the National Curriculum (Cox 1991), which helpfully contained a detailed appendix entitled 'Approaches to the Class Novel', and in the work of Lunzer and Gardner (1984), who pioneered the 'Directed Activities Related to Texts' (DARTS) approach to reading and comprehension. In the years since, published editions of texts for school use (some of which we have looked at), photocopiable ring-binders of accompanying resource materials, influential texts intended for English teachers, INSET workshops led by NATE, LEAs and others, and a rapidly increasing wealth of CD-ROM and media-based stimuli have all inspired excellent English teaching. There is also the possibility that, despite (or perhaps because of) this impressive array of materials, not a little confusion has been inspired. English teachers need to keep a clear sight of the wood of the text among all these magnificent trees, and the best way to do this is to share ideas with colleagues. English departments need to work together, gathering evidence about what works well with whom and when, and adapting resources continually. In such a context, a policy for reading within secondary English will be something of a working document, perpetually under review. Central to such a document would be issues such as these:

- coherent schemes of work to ensure both breadth and depth of reading;
- the use of the school library as a resource for fiction and for text-based and IT/media research;
- the teaching of study skills through reading, including the practical use of the library;
- the development and maintenance of class libraries;
- the continual review of English departmental stock, including multi-cultural authors and titles, non-fiction, women writers, books appealing to boys, questions of suitability of subject matter for age groups;
- the development of resources to aid teaching of reading, including those focused on improving 'basic literacy' in conjunction with SEN staff, pre-reading activities for class texts focusing on expectation, genre and context, activities to teach during the reading of texts, post-reading activities, integrated comprehension materials;
- the assessment of reading, including what Jill Pirrie terms 'the twin spectres of accountability and evidence' (Pirrie 1987);
- humane forms of reading recording such as reading journals, shared and displayed reviews and class folders;
- celebratory reading 'events', perhaps centred on the library, such as teachers talking about favourite childhood books, a book-based 'Blind Date', and visiting authors;
- cross-curricular possibilities for different types of reading;
- the balance of different types of reading within the English curriculum, given the constraints of time and resources;
- reading as an integral part of examination syllabuses;
- INSET and professional development in reading-focused pedagogy.

Presented in this sort of format, the list might appear daunting. In reality it need not be, and some of the best English departmental meetings could take the form of colleagues presenting favourite books and then discussing feasible teaching ideas. As an extension of this, teachers may wish to form their own 'reading circles'; certainly this is an invigorating way of keeping up with personal reading and could of course involve colleagues from other departments.

Some of the thornier issues to do with the place of reading in the English curriculum are concerned with assessment, progress, and what amounts to dictation and even censorship of reading matter. The three are in fact closely related: progress in reading depends on an appropriate assessment of a pupil's current position and can in any case be ascertained only if we use some sort of method of assessment; similarly, progress is likely to mean more demanding texts to read, and the English teacher's intervention here may be crucial. The assessment of reading is problematic, probably more so than either speaking and listening or writing, because it is personal and to a large extent invisible. We can approach assessment of reading only through listening to what pupils say, or looking at their writing – in other words, through some other medium than reading itself. Reading aloud may be merely 'barking at print' and is no guarantee of meaning: it is perfectly possible, in my teaching experience, for a pupil to appear to read aloud fluently but, on questioning, show only scant understanding. The converse may also hold true, and unfortunately has sometimes relegated pupils to low sets and even low achievement. Written comprehension tests may, in the same way, show up more of a pupil's ability to write cleverly formulaic answers – perhaps to what is assumed to be the teacher's expectation of a 'valid' response – than the ability to read with any sensitivity or depth. There are of course many reading tests and great store is set by them, but the fundamental problems remain. In a sense, we need something to grasp hold of, particularly in progress over the key stages, and it may not matter too much which method is used as long as the same format of test is used at the various levels. Even this, however, is hardly universal among partner schools. In practice, assessment of reading takes a great deal of sensitive observation of a pupil's reading across a range of reading activities, and the will to accumulate and record written insights.

In the final analysis the way to achieve progress in reading is to build on enthusiasm – not only for the pleasure of imaginative (generally fiction) reading, but for unlocking the secrets of text because one wants to find out what is there. In the reality of the classroom this means suggesting more demanding, stimulating texts to be read in more sophisticated ways: many of us will remember an English teacher some time in our various educations who took the trouble to recommend a book which changed our experience of reading for the better or revealed an alternative way of reading a favourite which challenged and stretched our understanding. It is precisely this sort of personal touch that can make all the difference, but it needs to be practised in a way which is methodical and rigorous, not merely haphazard. And sometimes, of course, a pupil is best left alone with yet another Judy Blume or Point Horror: it is a matter of judgement and, even more importantly, recognition and respect for the pupil's own needs. Concern about the quality and subject matter of what children read is important, and Tomkinson's (1921: 78) sympathy for English teachers shows it to be nothing new:

> Some of the titles will undoubtedly distress the earnest teacher who is anxious that his children should read good literature; but it is not to be expected that the young who have their reading synthesis still before them, should exercise a nice discrimination in their choice of books. If the teacher has a sense of humour, he may divert himself and do his class no harm, by publicly criticising one of the blood and thunder paper-backs which the reading boy usually conceals about his person.

There is indeed something comical about this scenario involving that strange creature 'the reading boy' (all too strange, all too often). There are times when the English teacher will need to intervene with reading matter, using 'a nice discrimination'; but there are others, rather more often in my experience, when humour is more appropriate. After all, we tend to forget that reading is meant to be for pleasure.

## Further reading

Geoff Dean's *Teaching Reading in Secondary Schools* (2000) is an apt reminder of the secondary English teacher's responsibilities here, and also extends into other subject teachers' work. *Tales, Tellers and Texts* (Cliff-Hodges *et al.* eds) is an excellent anthology of various writers' views of the reading curriculum, inventively broad in scope. Martin Blocksidge's (edited) *Teaching Literature 11–18* contains many very helpful suggestions; the practical dimension is uppermost here, as it is in my chapter 'What Do We Mean by Teaching Literature in Secondary English' (in Williamson *et al.*, Routledge Falmer 2001). Bearne and Cliff-Hodges' chapter 'Reading Rights and Responsibilities' (in Davison and Moss (eds) 2000) and Andrews' chapter 'Reading' (in Andrews 2001) offer perceptive theoretical contextualisation. A focused curricular perspective can be found in two publications from the English and Media Centre: *The English Curriculum: Reading 1* and *Comprehension and The English Curriculum: Reading 2, Slow Readers*. Chambers (1993), *Tell Me*, although aimed primarily at the primary age range, is very useful. Several publications have sought to adapt recent critical theories to the secondary English classroom and to children's reading generally; among the more accessible are Hunt (1991) *Criticism, Theory and Children's Literature*, and, aimed rather more at university level but still highly relevant, Green and LeBihan (1996) *Critical Theory and Practice – A Coursebook*. Stibbs (1991) *Reading Narrative as Literature: Signs of Life* is a lively, readable and inventive study. Three thoroughly enjoyable, stimulating books by Styles *et al.* provide insights into the ever-expanding world of fiction for children and young people; they are *The Prose and the Passion* (1994), *After Alice* (1992) and *Voices Off* (1996). The United Kingdom Literacy Association (UKLA; formerly UK Reading Association) does impressive work fostering good reading practices in education, including publication of the journal *Reading*. Colin Harrison's (2004) *Understanding Reading Development* is a helpful contextual discussion, and both Francis Spufford's (2002) *The Child that Books Built* and James Wood's (2009) *How Fiction Works* are fascinating, readily accessible books; from an ICT perspective, *Children's Literature and Computer-Based Teaching* (Unsworth *et al.* 2005).

## Resources

The widest ranging series of 'educational' fiction is undoubtedly the Heinemann New Windmill series, all of which are hard-wearing hardbacks and represent excellent value for money, but it is worth investigating other publishers' catalogues also, for series such as Collins Cascades, Macmillan M Books, and the low-priced Wordsworth Classics. Accompanying the larger series are ring-bound photocopiable further information and activities. The Cambridge Literature series (Cambridge University Press) offers a good range of texts intended for the 14–18 age range containing impressive resource notes and activities which take into account recent insights in critical theory. Longman also publishes a wide range of useful reading resources in its New Longman Literature series, including 11–18 non-fiction and stories from other culture. There is also impressive choice when it comes to imaginative literary study material and creative approaches. Texts from the English and Media Centre, for Key Stage 3, include *Making Stories*, *Changing Stories* and *Investigating Texts*, all providing excellent stimuli for inventive close reading. (See Chapter 8 for Key Stage 4 suggestions.) The *Figures in a Landscape: Writing from around the World* series (general editor Hayhoe, Cambridge University Press) and two Hodder Murray texts, *Diverse Cultures* and *Pre-Twentieth Century Short Stories* serve a very useful function in broadening the reading repertoire, as do *True or False? Non-Fiction for Secondary English* (ed. Ellison), also Hodder Murray, and *Pair and Compare 1 and 2* (Bousted and Barton), Collins, – the latter looking at imaginative inter-textual readings. Three excellent, if necessarily quite expensive, titles from Hodder Murray – *Double Vision*, *Painting with Words* and *Picture Poems* (each by Benton and Benton) explore the possibilities of parallel readings of paintings and texts, and are beautifully illustrated accordingly. The National Association of Writers in Education (NAWE) at www.nawe.co.uk offers excellent advice on bringing writers into schools, and publishes an interesting journal *Writing in Education*. The National Association for the Teaching of English (NATE) publishes exciting school-based texts and series, such as *Classic Reading 11–16* (ed. Protherough), and also markets innovative Australian texts published by the St Clair Press.

# 6 Writing

*How can I know what I think until I see what I write?*

E. M. Forster, *Aspects of the Novel*

## The development of writing in education

THE PROCESS OF WRITING AS undertaken by pupils in schools is the focus of a number of important characteristics, which must at least be acknowledged by teachers – especially English teachers – if effective teaching and learning is to take place. These sometimes contradictory insights could be summarised as follows:

- Writing is often the most painfully and formally learned of the three areas of English (misleadingly termed) 'attainment targets' in the National Curriculum.

- At the same time, as E. M. Forster's observation intimates, writing is perhaps the most important and reflective tool of all learning.

- Writing is the most obviously visible aspect of a pupil's learning, which is presumably why it has such central importance in virtually all examinations of attainment.

- Writing is a powerful means of self- and social expression, potentially communicating to an increasingly wide audience through formal or informal publication, easy and quick copying, and information and communication technology.

- Writing is an important controlling mechanism, a means of achieving orderly discipline, in many lessons.

- Perhaps because of this, across the curriculum pupils undergo a huge quantity of directed writing for a large proportion of their time in schools.

- Much of this writing has no particular or specified readership in mind, apart from the teacher or the pupil him/herself, and in practice not always even these audiences.

- Compared when the volume of writing completed during school years, most adults write little, and then mostly short, informal pieces.

- Perhaps for a combination of some or all of these reasons, writing is not generally liked by most pupils in secondary schools.

Much of this may read as quite an indictment of the practice of writing in secondary schools, although some of the observations are positive in nature. The list as a whole will inform this discussion on the role of writing as part of the English curriculum. Writing needs to be considered in the context of other aspects of English and of teaching and learning as a whole process, and in relationship to reading on the one hand and speaking and listening on the other. It is also helpful to cast an eye at the same time on the historical conditions which have given rise to the current situation. Monaghan and Saul (1987: 91) distinguish writing in schools from reading, characterising the former, potentially at least, as the more active:

> However variously reading and writing have been defined, it still remains the case that reading, even when oral, is the receptive skill . . . while writing is the productive skill. The question is relevant when the question of control is considered. The curriculum is, at least in part, the formal statement of what society believes is important for students to know. Society has focused on children as readers because, historically, it has been much more interested in children as receptors than producers of the written word.

Many writers would question whether it is appropriate to view reading purely as a receptive skill but writing is without doubt a potentially liberating, active force: centrally concerned with production as opposed to reception. And yet . . . we keep coming back to this word 'potential'. The reality 'on the ground', as some of the observations on writing listed above suggest, may be quite different, and certainly not liberating. If we compare writing in education to speaking and listening, again with the historical development of the curriculum in mind, a contrasting picture emerges. Green (1993: 213), while tracing the imposition of formal schooling and a curriculum based heavily on reading and writing on a centuries-old, all too often unrecognised, oral tradition of learning, shows this process to have been in part at least a means of maintaining social control. He alludes to

> the general shift from 'speech' to 'writing' as the basis of formal education, which needs to be seen as crucial to the emergence and consolidation of modern schooling. The shift went together historically with a new valuation of silence in education and, increasingly, an official emphasis on reading and writing, rather than speaking and listening.

The central tension concerning the role of writing in the classroom is inescapable: a means of control inflicted on a more or less unwilling pupil population, as against a liberating and creative means of expression. The reality of school life may serve to disguise this tension, and indeed the actual experience of most pupils most of the time may lie somewhere between the two poles. It may be instructive, given the opportunity (and it frequently is given, especially to student and beginning teachers), to shadow a group of pupils and observe just how much writing is asked of them, and the nature of the writing activities. This is not to criticise teachers and their curricula, and there is no doubt that writing takes many forms appropriate to different types of learning, as we shall see, but rather to begin to argue for a distinctive role for the English teacher in fostering effective writing.

That role has altered over the years. Writing in English has changed both in the way it has been conceptualised and in the way it has been taught, from a very simple to a more complex formulation and practice. In the traditional classroom, writing tended to take one form (the essay or composition) and had one intended reader (the teacher as evaluator and corrector). The emphasis was largely on a finished product and there was little relationship in practice of writing to reading or speaking and listening. As indicated in Chapter 7 on planning it is not possible to give a precise historical account of the development of English but in broad terms the increase in thematic teaching in the 1960s corresponded to a greater attention to the importance of integrating writing with other language modes. Sometimes the connection was fairly superficial but a fuller form of integration took place when writing arose very specifically from oral activities or reading (for example, writing in role as a character from a novel or using the original text as a model). More attention also started to be paid to the importance of writing for different purposes and in different forms for a variety of audiences (letters, reports, diaries, etc.). Such ideas were clearly embodied in the Bullock Report of 1975, and, interestingly, have returned to pre-eminence with the National Strategy, including emphasis on interdisciplinary and cross-phase writing practices. There was also a growing emphasis on the writing process and the role of the teacher intervening on content, presentation, style and accuracy through dialogue with the pupil.

## Categories of writing

As the conception and practice developed so also did methods of categorising writing. Some authors drew attention to the importance of 'writing to learn' as well as 'learning to write'. Official reports often used the term 'secretarial' to distinguish formal aspects from content; others separated 'compositional' from 'presentational' skills. It was common in the 1970s to distinguish between 'transactional', 'expressive' and 'poetic' forms. The 1995 National Curriculum used three categories, suggesting that pupils should be encouraged to write for aesthetic and imaginative purposes, to inform others and to develop thinking. The last English Order states that

> during key stages 3 and 4 pupils develop confidence in writing for a range of purposes. They develop their own distinctive styles and recognise the importance of writing with commitment and vitality. They learn to write correctly, using different formats, layouts and ways of presenting their work

> (DfES/QCA 1999: 37)

and this emphasis has been retained for the unfolding new National Curriculum for English. Leaving aside the deterministic tone of such pronouncements – after all, if all these things happen, why are teachers needed? – there is a positive meaning to be inferred, especially in the insistence on 'commitment and vitality'. The writing processes of the English classroom are then grouped in four 'triplets': 'writing to imagine, explore, entertain'; ' to inform, explain, describe'; 'to persuade, argue, advise'; ' to analyse, review, comment' (ibid.). This structure has become embedded in practice, reflected as it is both in Key Stage 3 Strategy and in GCSE syllabuses. As with all such attempts to organise an essentially creative, boundary-stretching act, English teachers need to be careful: there is no reason why an effective piece of writing should not combine aspects of all four elements, and good teaching may indeed inspire positive connections.

Various authors have preferred different ways of describing different types of writing and criticised others' attempts (the further reading section provides various examples). The important point here, as stated earlier in the Introduction when discussing broad categories of English, is that there is nothing intrinsically correct or wrong with any one form of categorisation. It is necessary, however, to be alert to possible limitations on practice to which different ways of thinking about writing may contribute. It may have been the category of 'creative writing' in the 1960s which encouraged some teachers to instruct pupils not to worry about aspects of punctuation and spelling on the grounds that this would somehow distract from the creative process. It is hardly helpful for pupils who are learning to write and need to acquire positive habits to receive confusing messages of this kind (experienced writers can afford to be more experimental). Distinguishing an 'aesthetic' or 'expressive' category from more functional forms makes obvious sense but may limit the manner in which certain written tasks are set. In Chapter 1 (p. 23) the example from 'Badger on the Barge' illustrated how letter writing can be taught from a literary text in a way which focuses on different registers but also gives depth to the writing. When pupils are asked to use language to inform, persuade, argue, give instructions, such tasks do not need to be set in any more narrow a way than when asking them to write a short story. With functional writing sometimes the task is invented purely for the sake of the language use, such as writing instructions for replacing the cover on a table tennis bat (one of the tasks on a sample SAT paper at Key Stage 3).

Despite this warning about categorisation, it is clearly helpful to distinguish different purposes for writing. It is best to start with the most positive of the listed characteristics: the ideas of writing as a reflective tool of learning, and as a powerful means of personal and social expression. In order to learn more, let us examine the insights of some accomplished writers from a range of backgrounds and periods.

## Inspirations of writing

The story of the genesis of Mary Shelley's *Frankenstein* is probably as well known as the novel itself – if not as popularly infamous as the central idea of the deliberate creation of human life going disastrously wrong. Mary Shelley herself, looking back some years later, recounted, in the introduction to *Frankenstein*, the events of the Byron-inspired competition to write a terrifying ghost story to while away the time beside Lake Geneva, and recalled how for several days she tried hard to 'think of a story' without success. Until one night, not sleeping,

> my imagination, unbidden, possessed and guided me, gifting the successive images that arose in my mind with a vividness far beyond the usual bounds of reverie. I saw . . . the pale student of unhallowed arts kneeling beside the thing he had put together. I saw the hideous phantasm

of a man stretched out, and then, on the working of some powerful engine, show signs of life, and stir with an uneasy, half vital motion.

(1969: 9)

This was the image around which the novel was to crystallise, and it is possible and perhaps helpful to see in this vivid picture a metaphor for the process of writing itself. Mary Shelley was able to announce that she had 'thought of a story' – but the extract suggests that her words are ironic: the story was in a sense thinking its own medium, its writer.

Such an experience is not unusual in human creativity: musicians, artists, sportspeople and others testify to the power of the unconscious to perform brilliantly once the conditions are right and it is given space. John Fowles in *The French Lieutenant's Woman* (1969) says much the same thing, as does Ian McEwan (1989: xxv), writing about the inspiration for *The Child in Time* (1987). He relates his experience of daydreaming, when

my thoughts were narrowed and intensified. I was haunted by the memory of a dream, of a footpath that emerges into a bend on a country road . . . A figure who is me and not me is walking . . . certain that he is about to witness something of overwhelming importance. Writing *The Child in Time* . . . was about the discovery of what that man saw.

A writer more familiar to the secondary English classroom, Nigel Hinton, visiting the school I was then teaching in, explained to an enthralled audience of 15-year-olds how he had begun professional writing. He had himself been an English teacher, and, on his disparaging dismissal of a particular class reader, had been challenged by his class to do better. That night he settled down to try just that, and by the morning his first novel, *Collision Course* (1976), had been virtually written, while he himself remained largely unconscious of what had happened. *Collision Course* remains a favourite in many English classrooms. Clearly, these experiences of writing do not suggest that the images and ideas come from nothing; Mary Shelley realised that 'invention . . . does not consist in creating out of a void, but out of chaos' and that the creative mind must allow Coleridge's 'shaping spirit of the imagination' to do its work (1969: 8).

But where does all this leave the English teacher and his or her perhaps reluctant youthful writers? We must be aware that the sort of writing processes outlined here may not always be appropriate to the realities of the English classroom, and that the insights of the quoted writers refer to a particular type of writing and to themselves as committed, ambitious writers. Nevertheless, despite these caveats, there is a great deal we can learn. Let us try first to summarise some of the conditions which appear to need to be in place for the creative process to begin and be sustained, although there are differences between the accounts and not all of these conditions apply to all of them:

- a sense of convivial, social engagement as an inspiration;
- an implied contextualising background in reading and in speaking and listening;
- the time and space for the writing process to proceed;
- the incentive of a particular occasion, which may even be competitively challenging;

- the appropriate environment to inspire ideas;
- a provisional sense of audience.

Within the limits and constraints of the classroom and the organisation of the curriculum, there is a great deal that the teacher of English can do to provide conditions which at least approximate to these areas, and we shall look more closely at some of these shortly. The overall intention must be to facilitate pupils' writing by creating the atmosphere of a purposeful workshop, perhaps borrowing on occasion from the traditional apprenticeship model; it is indeed interesting that Nigel Hinton's pupils had some expectation of their English teacher being able to write well, as this would not be as widespread as similar expectations of expertise in teachers of other expressive curricular subjects such as art, music or PE. Maybe English teachers should learn something from these models of frequently good practice: leading by example, practising what we teach.

With this firmly in mind, we may return now to Stead's triangular model of the tensions involved in poetry, which in its original form seems apposite to all forms of writing, and in our adaptation outlined in Chapter 1 (pp. 17–18) particularly apt for the teaching of writing in secondary English classrooms. It may be best at this stage to express this multi-layered series of meanings, closely interrelated, in diagrammatic form – at the risk, as always with such things, of gross oversimplification (Figure 6.1).

**FIGURE 6.1**

Again, the points of the triangle must not approach each other too closely, neither must they drift too far apart. Visualising the process – and the product – in this form enables us to see more clearly the relationships between the teaching and learning of writing and the broader aspects of education, as well as showing the originally intended highly specialised focus on the nature of poetic creation. The English classroom at its most effective should be characterised by the atmosphere of a workshop, in which subjectivity is allowed to operate within the tensions of the carefully established objective setting. And arguably the most important element in this setting is the English teacher who establishes and sustains it. If used sensitively, as I hope I have suggested in Chapter 2, the Key Stage 3 Strategy and its pedagogical recommendations may be helpful in this context: teacher modelling of writing processes, shared-writing and group-writing teaching techniques, for example, may all play a part in developing a workshop-style writing classroom.

## Forms of writing

Writing, of course, takes many different forms. The curriculum for secondary English has to take this into account, but, to return to the cross-curricular nature of literacy development alluded to in our examination of the English curriculum, it may well be the responsibility of certain other subject areas to cultivate particular types of writing appropriate to their particular purposes. This is not to excuse the English teacher of responsibility, but it may be a different kind of responsibility: one of involvement in teacher education in the context of whole-school professional development and curriculum organisation rather than attempting actually to teach everything. We need to bear in mind also another of Cox's models of English teaching, that of preparation for adult life, in order to decide precisely which types of writing need to appear in the secondary curriculum and where. It may be helpful to construct a list of types of writing practised in life generally and in school in particular; the one which follows is not intended to be definitive, and you may wish to add to it or take issue with certain parts:

- letter writing, formal or informal;
- poetry composition;
- spider and other types of diagrammatic representation;
- reminder notes: for example, in homework diaries or as lists of tasks / items;
- dialogue and playscript writing;
- assessment sheets – for self or others;
- writing as an aid to presentations: for example, flip charts and OHP slides;
- notes from texts, lectures and other sources;
- narrative, descriptive and discursive writing, including formal essays;
- analytical and empathetic writing based on literature;
- surveys and questionnaires, at all stages of the process and as both creator and respondent;
- mass media-based writing, such as newspapers, magazines and scripts;

- basic transactional writing: requests, memos, reminders, messages;
- diary and journal writing;
- writing distinctively using ICT: word processing, desktop publishing, email, etc.;
- collaborative writing in a number of possible forms.

To follow up a list such as this, try to work out – if possible with colleagues from both within and outside the English department – where you consider other curriculum areas have responsibility and where the English teacher has a distinctive role to play either as teacher or as a consultant to colleagues. It may well be that the more collaboratively this task is undertaken, the more contentious and contested it will be; certainly this has been our experience of formulating policies and practices for writing in schools. Whatever variations arise, it is often the discussion itself that is most valuable in raising consciousness of what writing is all about, and, where appropriate, challenging its often habitual operation in schools. The English teacher will inevitably wish to safeguard the value of writing in learning and its potential for productive enjoyment; for example, it may be necessary to argue against the all too common practice of using writing as a form of punishment in detention or otherwise, lest the art of writing itself be brought into disrepute. In seeking a guide for what sort of writing should characterise English lessons as distinctive, Kress (1995: 90) offers a useful starting point:

> In a view of English as central in the making of a culture of innovation the production of subjectivity is at the centre, between social and cultural possibilities and forces on the one hand – available resources, structures of power – and the individual's action in the making of signs on the other . . . [the child's] interest in the making of signs may range from dispositions called 'conformity' to those called 'resistance' . . . Whether in solidarity or subversion, the child's own production of her representational resources is intimately connected, in a relation of reciprocity, with her production of her subjectivity.

The detail, clearly, is a matter for English teachers' judgement, in the context of whole-school policy and practice. However, Kress's phrase 'production of subjectivity' implies forms of writing which set out to achieve precisely that: the expressive, poetic, formative, evaluative, argumentative and imaginatively responsive.

We need now to consider the creation of the appropriate classroom conditions for such writing expertise to develop. Some or all of the following may be in evidence in the teaching of English based on these principles:

- English lessons where it is possible for pupils to take some genuine responsibility for their writing, with different resources designated for different types and stages of writing; for example, ICT, collaborative ventures, silent writing, research, drafting, proof reading and performance. If space allows, it may be that some of these activities could be based in specific areas within and beyond the classroom.
- A sense that, within the inevitable constraints of the curriculum, deadlines and good discipline, pupils may take negotiated responsibility for when and where writing takes place, in recognition of personal preferences.

- An atmosphere where pupils feel secure in trying out new ideas and means of expression through their writing, knowing that it is through experimentation and errors that learning and the development of a distinctive style take place.

- A purposeful attention to the details of accuracy in writing, whether undertaken collaboratively or individually, using available resources and positive, formative responses by the English teacher.

- Constructive but judicial use of drafting as a tool for the development of writing, recognising that it may not always be appropriate, and that for some pupils it may become a tedious chore.

- A sense that creativity through writing is something to be persevered with, celebrated and shared; for example, through attention to:

    □ completed written assignments;

    □ performed readings with a range of audiences;

    □ the English teacher modelling good practice by writing with the rest of the class; frequently renewed displays;

    □ involvement of published writers in a variety of genres.

Before moving on to consider further the sorts of stimuli which could serve to inspire good writing in such conditions, it seems timely to follow our own advice and involve one of the most successful of contemporary writers for children and young people, Anne Fine, in a plea for flexibility. In an interview for the National Association for Writers in Education (1996), she had this to say:

> I think there is a little bit too much over-confidence on the part of educationists that they know the way to do it [writing]. I feel extremely distressed at the moment about watching some children being expected to draft and re-draft on the grounds, the very spurious grounds, that that is what a real writer does. That is not what this real writer did when she was young. When this real writer was young she was allowed to sit down, write it, hand it in, get a mark, and never come back to it again. And if she had been going back to it, she would have hated re-drafting it more than I can say . . . I hope this fashion for re-drafting will die out very fast because it's putting an awful lot of really bright, cheerful, happy children off English.

Of course this is but one point of view, albeit one based on successful and influential experience of writing, and there are plenty of other writers who one could use to demonstrate the opposite view: William Blake or Wilfred Owen, for example, wrote poems which improved immeasurably through their painstaking drafting. Anne Fine may have been adept at producing excellent writing at first shot; others may need more target practice and particular expectations may be counter-productive. George (1971) noted that

> the teacher and the pupil enter into a true adventure in the exploration of ideas and the language necessary to express these ideas. He [sic] cannot do this if he is expected to produce immediate results in the shape of 'creative efforts' worthy of public inspection.

And this is precisely the point: the English teacher needs to be attuned to the specific writing needs of each individual pupil for, to return once more to Blake, 'One law for the lion and the ox is oppression.'

## Practical considerations in the teaching of writing

It is, of course, not simply a matter of creating the right conditions, along the lines described above, and then just 'letting it happen'. Indeed, perhaps the most important component of these conditions is the encouragement and stimulation offered by the English teacher in very practical terms, for what good is a 'workshop' when the participants have little idea of how to proceed? Some ideas follow, gleaned from personal experience and observation; they are intended not as 'useful tips' but as possible practical implications of the theoretical context outlined.

Consider accumulating a collection of resources for the stimulation of writing, which should be readily available to pupils. Particularly useful are:

- art postcards available from art galleries (and 'spent' calendars);
- old postcards, perhaps with messages inscribed;
- evocative music, playable, if conditions permit, in 'listening booths';
- fascinating natural objects such as pine cones, shells and curious stones;
- brief magazine articles to inspire discursive writing;
- mounted pictures, advertisements and even 'personal ads'.

The list of possible materials is endless, as are the potential uses, including unlikely combinations woven into writing and empathetic insights.

Vary the audiences for writing, making use of ready readerships such as local primary school children, interest groups within the school (for example, adult visitors or members of particular societies) or, through the use of ICT, pupils in other, perhaps contrasting, schools.

Looking back to the list of possible occasions for writing, it can be interesting to experiment with different genres:

- combining letters, journals and narrative in a particular story;
- challenging the expectations of a particular genre, such as the fairy tale or the detective story, by subverting the normal sequence of events or deliberately mixing apparently incompatible genres;
- using a particular 'class theme', ask pupils to tackle it for a range of contrasting genres, comparing the results and discussing the implications;
- using ICT as a facilitating tool, experiment with moving text around, possibly using published fiction as a model (as with so much writing in English);
- constructing 'choice' fiction in which, at appropriate points, the reader must make arbitrary (using dice, for example) or reasoned choices as to where in the text to go next;

- 'cutting up' text, arbitrarily or otherwise, to discover various patterns of sequence in writing;

- trying out different possibilities with the passage of time, from the relatively conventional use of 'flashbacks' to more experimental ideas such as tracing a narrative backwards, as in Martin Amis's disturbing *Time's Arrow* (1991);

- adapting writing for media presentation, using cassette taping to accompany the book (a familiar technique to children's publishers), or writing specifically for the visual image by using storyboards;

- using whole-class or small-group collaborative writing, which could be initially inspired by games such as 'consequences' (using a fold in the paper to hide each individual's entry, except for the last word or two, before passing it around the group), or 'imagining' (for want of a better title), when the teacher, having got the whole class to close their eyes, asks, with carefully directed questions, specific pupils in turn to picture and express what happens next in a narrative sequence.

The point of all these activities is not to entertain with an attractive set of one-off lessons but to vary the inspiration, form and outcome of writing activities in an integrated scheme of work, coherently planned to involve – as most writing activities inevitably do at some point – both reading and oral dimensions also. It is often helpful to provide pupils with templates to help them when they get down to the nitty gritty of what exactly is going to go into a piece of writing: the planning stages. They might be helped to use a story planning sheet as follows:

| | |
|---|---|
| Setting: | Where does your story take place? |
| Characters: | Who are your main characters? |
| | Why are they at a particular place? |
| Plot: | Where are your characters at the beginning of the story? |
| | What are they doing there? |
| | Are there any minor characters who play a part in the story? |
| | Who are they and what role do they play? |
| | What happens and why? |

More detailed planning specifically on character can also sometimes help pupils get started:

- Give your character a name.

- Explain where they are in some detail, using place names, street names, etc.

- What exactly are they doing? Write down the date and day this is happening.

- What is the weather like?

- What sort of mood are they in?

- What are they thinking about?

- Write down three things they can see, smell, feel, hear.

- Write down one detail of their appearance, item of clothing, etc.
- What are they going to do next?

The English teacher must, of course, keep a clear view of what is actually being achieved through writing activities and must also ensure that each pupil cultivates different forms in the creation of meaning. The diagram in Figure 6.2, from the ill-fated original *LINC Reader* (Carter 1990), may be a helpful reminder of what exactly is going on: easily forgotten as the detail and entertainment of the activity gather their own momentum.

It may seem sometimes that the art of effective English teaching is a little like juggling – keeping several balls in the air simultaneously, concentrating hard on the activity while not becoming too conscious of any one ball or part of the process lest the smooth operation of the whole collapses – and the teaching of writing is no exception. In this context, a plan such as that illustrated above may be very useful, almost as a checklist, to ensure that different aspects of writing are sufficiently covered. Not every part, of course, will apply to every stage of each pupil's development or, indeed, to every facet of the teaching of writing: here, as in so much else, the English teacher's professional judgement must remain paramount.

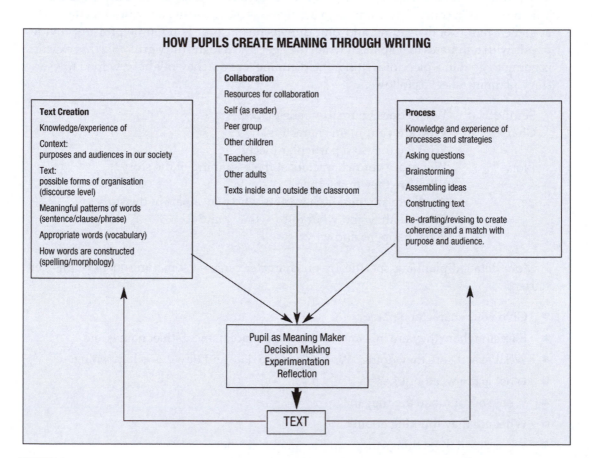

**FIGURE 6.2**

We need now to turn to the English teacher's response to pupils' writing, both during the process and as recognition of the final product, for it is one thing to inspire writing to happen but quite another to sustain, develop and complete it. HMI, incidentally, in conducting English inspections, were keen on examining the range of pupils' completed written assignments, together with evidence of the process such as worked up notes and drafts; such good practice has frequently found its way into local authority and Ofsted inspections, and into the coursework requirements of GCSE examinations. We need to examine in particular how the English teacher may, by judicious response to pupils' writing, guarantee that good progress is made. We need to ensure that learning takes place not only through the writing (as in writing about a particular text or, in other curricular areas, about a certain scientific experiment or historical epoch), but in the quality of the writing itself. Here, surely, lies the special role of the English teacher.

Subsequent chapters on knowledge about language and teaching across the ability range will deal in more detail with the sort of meta-language required in order to have pupils understand more clearly what exactly is going on when written text is created, and we shall examine which linguistic or semi-linguistic terms are appropriate, at different stages, to bring about a shared, common understanding of text. At this stage, though, we must look at possible approaches that are simultaneously more general, in that they refer to the broad sweep of classroom strategy, and more specific, in that they focus on the particular requirement to improve pupils' expertise in one aspect of English: writing. Again, the work of the Language in the National Curriculum Project proves useful in providing a template for the English teacher to lay against pupils' writing, in the form of a number of questions to ask either with the writer while the task is being undertaken, or as a guide for eventual marking and commenting on the finished piece (Figure 6.3).

As we have suggested, the use of a series of questions like this in the classroom must remain flexible, and there are of course adaptations and additions that could be made for specific purposes. It is worth noting here, however, the concentration on the verb as the engine of the piece of writing in the central series of questions. And, of course, the nature of the verb is infinitely variable and by no means peculiar to narrative writing – although it is in this broad genre that its role is perhaps most obvious. On the practical level of operation, one particularly useful adaptation could be for use by pupils themselves, working either collaboratively or individually, in ways such as these:

- The development of writing partners in the context of the classroom, helping each other with the processes. As Sawyer *et al.* (1989: 234) point out, this approach can be very successful 'provided the partners are empathetic and positive in their response to each other's writing. There needs to be a sense of co-operative relationship between the partners. In the classroom it may take some time for writers to develop the constructive responsiveness necessary for the method's effectiveness.'

- Through the use of ICT (or, more traditionally, the Royal Mail), the extension of writing partnerships beyond the confines of the classroom.

- The deployment of older pupils and other adults as collaborators in the writing and responding processes.

---

## A FRAMEWORK FOR LOOKING AT WRITING

What do you feel is the writer's purpose or goal? How can you tell?

How is the text structured or organised? What specific features of language show this?

What is the text about?
  e.g. people or things? individuals or groups? concrete or abstract?

What kinds of actions or processes are there?
Are verbs concerned with:

  physical actions?
  ways of behaving?
  thoughts and feelings?
  processes of communication?
  describing things – by what they are? (definition)
                    – by what they have? (attribution)

What tenses are used?

Are verbs concerned with:
  future possibilities? (e.g. might, could, ought)
  certainties? (e.g. shall, will, must)

What is the relationship between reader and writer? How is this shown?

Does the text read as a coherent whole? What helps it hang together?
  e.g. vocabulary; references forward and back; linking of clauses and sentences.

What kind of text is this?

---

**FIGURE 6.3**

- The encouragement of a writing journal, which is likely to be an individual (and possibly private) enterprise, and, of course, is a way in itself of extending pupils' writing repertoires.

One possible pitfall in the concentration on the form of the writing, implied by many of these guidelines for constructive response, is that the content may be neglected. The two should be inseparable, and, ideally, complement each other: certainly it is this happy union that should be aimed for in the guidance and reception of pupils' writing. One particular question posed in the LINC framework above – 'what tenses are used?' – will serve to remind us of the sort of disastrous situation which may arise if form and content are viewed discretely. Hopefully we have moved a long way since this example occurred, as recounted by the HMI Edward Wilkinson in 1966, but the warning remains apposite:

A class had been set to write on 'My Father', and one nine-year-old boy entitled his work 'My Real Father', something to be alerted by in itself. This is what he wrote: 'My father is on the broad side and tall side. My father was a hard working man and he had a lot of money. He was not fat or thin . . . His age was about thirty years when he died, he has a good reputation, he is a married man. When he was in hospital I went to see him every Sunday afternoon . . . He likes doing woodwork, my father, for me, and he likes a little game of cards now and then; or a game of darts. He chops the wood and saws the planks and he is a handsome man but he is dead. He worked at the rubber works before he died.

(1966: 25)

On this intensely moving piece the teacher commented: 'Tenses. You keep mixing past and present.' This might be the comment of an utterly insensitive teacher, but perhaps it is the comment of an utterly committed one – or an utterly bewildered one, not knowing what he wanted to say, taking refuge in 'grammar'.

This is a timely warning indeed, with the current drive to improve 'basic' literacy, but what exactly do we do when confronted by work like this? The example shows how the process of writing can unleash all sorts of personally painful experiences and, often, fantasies in a way in which oral activities, say, may not. The English teacher is in a highly privileged position – but this privilege carries its own burden of responsibility in terms of sensitivity. The apparent preoccupation with formal characteristics of writing according to the perceived characteristics and conventions of any particular genre at the expense of meaning and value, which many practitioners ascribe to the Key Stage 3 Strategy, for example, makes this warning all the more apposite.

In the final analysis we can agree with Cox that pupils should be praised for writing that is vigorous, committed, honest and interesting, and assert that the proper response to writing should encourage such qualities. Different English departments have developed different marking policies, but it must surely be basic that any marking should be formative, supportive, critical in a positive sense, and unobtrusive. If we summarise the fundamental stages of the writing process to involve:

- assembling strategies;
- developing the text;
- editing and proof reading;

then judicious intervention may be appropriate at any one of them, provided the teacher remains true to the principle that pupils should be able to maintain ultimate control over their own writing. Certainly there is some evidence that more writing – of the genuinely vigorous, committed, honest and interesting variety – is being done with the development of ICT opportunities, both within and outside the classroom. Internet chatrooms, text-messages on mobile phones, and interactive websites are used enthusiastically by people, often men, who would probably have written very little otherwise. Football websites, for instance, offer opportunities and examples of this kind of writing, frequently of high quality. It is good to think that effective English teaching has undoubtedly played its part in opening up writing, through ICT and otherwise, as a pleasurable and useful activity in this context; English teachers need now to ensure that the many opportunities available – some of which are mentioned in Chapter 12 – become part of habitual classroom life.

## Further reading

Publications by Styles (ed.) (1989) *Collaboration and Writing* and Arnold (1991) *Writing Development* are especially useful for teachers anxious to ensure pupils' progress in writing without hampering spontaneity. Also helpful are Harrison (1983) *Learning through Writing* and Foggin (1992) *Real Writing*. Brindley (ed.) (1994) *Teaching English* contains succinct chapters on several facets of writing in the English curriculum. The English and Media Centre publishes a wide-ranging collection of articles and activities on writing entitled *The English Curriculum: Writing – Material for Discussion*. Pat D'Arcy's succinct *Two Contrasting Paradigms for the Teaching and Assessment of Writing* (NATE 2000) is very thought-provoking, as I hope I have already demonstrated. These titles are also helpful: *Writing: The Drafting Process* (Dawes 1995), *Learning about Punctuation* (Hall and Robinson 1996) and *Words and Images on the Page* (Johnson 1996), the last of which is cross-phase in its subject matter. Millard and Walsh have published an invaluable practically orientated guide, intended for KS2 but with a wealth of suggestions for KS3 and beyond, entitled *Improving Writing at KS2* (Kirklees LEA 2001). Carole King's chapter 'Can Teachers Empower Pupils as Writers?' (in Davison and Moss 2000) is both succinct and perceptive, as is Richard Andrews' survey of research and developments in the teaching of writing, 'Learning to Write' in *Teaching and Learning English* (Continuum 2001). The following four books give excellent practical advice to English (and other) teachers concerning the teaching of writing, underpinned by coherent theoretical exploration: Evans (2002) *How to Teach Non-fiction Writing*, Macrae (2002) *How to Teach Fiction Writing*, Myhill (2001) *Better Writers*, and Williams (ed.) (2002) *Unlocking Writing: A Guide for Teachers*.

## Resources

Framework Press publish a most helpful classroom guide, with photocopiable material: *Key Stage 3 Writing: A Language Approach* (Armstrong and Goddard, 1996). Folens Press publish an excellent series, each with accompanying CD-ROM – 'English Writing Frames' – to provide support for pupils' writing at various levels and for various genres: *Inform, Explain, Describe* (Machin); *Persuade, Argue, Advise*; *Imagine, Explore, Entertain* (both Gould); and *Analyse, Review, Comment* (Green). Hodder Murray publish a very useful and comprehensive range of classroom texts to help stimulate and develop pupils' writing at various levels: the 'Fast Forward Writing', 'English Works' and 'Writing: Steps to Success' series. Musical and artistic resources are particularly useful, and many art galleries, including the Tate, the National and the National Portrait offer educational services for visits. Two books by Richard Palmer – *The Good Grammar Guide* and *Write in Style* (Routledge 2003 and 2002 respectively) – offer good practical advice on the writing process for both pupils and teachers.

# 7

# Planning

*Misce stultitiam consiliis brevem*
*Dulce est desipere in loco.*
*(Mix a little levity in your plans*
*It is good to unbend at the proper time.)*

Horace, *Ars Poetica*

## Introduction

THIS CHAPTER WILL EXAMINE PRACTICAL approaches to planning individual lessons and schemes of work. It will also explore some of the tensions and difficulties involved in planning work in English. As described earlier, the teaching of the subject needs to be sufficiently centred on the National Curriculum and the National Strategy Framework for secondary English to provide coverage, continuity and appropriate progression while at the same time sufficiently pupil-centred to ensure engagement in learning at a rich level.

The need to fulfil the competing demands of 'systematic coverage' and 'rich subjective engagement' can be translated in practical terms into different conceptions of the planning process. These can be more vividly described if presented as caricatures. If planning is seen as something akin to a military operation with very precise targets, rigid structures and exact timings, the secure semblance of order may conceal a lack of involvement and ownership by those involved. At the other extreme, a laissez faire 'happening' which may appear on the surface to be affording room for creativity and personal expression may amount to no more than an aimless and empty experience with no significant outcome. Finding an appropriate balance between these two extremes is the obvious but by no means straightforward task.

As described in the Introduction and Chapter 2, the first version of the English strand of the National Strategy had some trenchant criticisms and when first published was associated in some people's minds with the kind of military model described above. However, its attempts to bring clearer outcomes and formulate a framework for progression could be seen as well intentioned. The revised Framework fulfils this goal in a far more sensible way. Newcomers to teaching are sometimes told that the key to teaching the National Curriculum and Framework well is to operate them flexibly. This is self-evident but also, by itself, rather feeble advice. It is important to consider in more specific ways how planning can support teaching without constraining it unduly.

# Preserving flexibility

In recent years there has been a tendency to elevate some useful practical ideas about planning to the status of universal principles. There are many approaches to planning which have value but only if used sensibly and selectively:

- It is often helpful to tell the pupils what the purpose of the learning is at the beginning of the lesson. In the past pupils were often given what seemed to them arbitrary instructions without any overall sense of context and purpose. However, it is sometimes desirable to deviate from this approach when, for example, a topic is being introduced in an oblique way.

- Similarly it is sometimes a good idea to plan lessons using objectives phrased as clear learning outcomes: 'by the end of the lesson pupils will be able to . . .' However, this approach is not appropriate for every lesson. It can be appropriate on those occasions when specific language learning outcomes are being addressed but it can easily close down exploratory approaches to text.

- It is a good idea not to have too many objectives for any one lesson but it is unhelpful to try to work with a rigid number of objectives per lesson.

- It is not always appropriate that pupils should be able to say at the end of a lesson what they have learned. Not all learning in English is of that kind.

- Beginning a lesson with 'starters' can have value but, when conceived as discrete language exercises, they do not always engage with meaning, and often do not lead on to the central theme. The concept of 'ways in' was more to the fore in English teaching in the 1980s and needs to be borne in mind as an alternative method (some books include 'ways in' as a form of starter: the principle is more important than the terminology).

- Lessons can take a variety of structures – it is not necessary to stick slavishly to three- or four-part lessons.

- Pace has quite appropriately been lauded as an important aspect of effective teaching. This feature along with some whole-class teaching is an important corrective to the tendency to see English teaching only in terms of setting tasks, a consequence of a misdirected 'creative', 'language in use' approach. At its worst this involved pupils writing endlessly (often the same piece of work for numerous lessons) without teacher intervention. However, an obsession with pace can make lessons too teacher-centred. It is widely recognised for example that real understanding of challenging poetry is impossible without reflection and familiarity that deepens over time.

As with other aspects of teaching English considered in this book the message then is that particular methodologies should be neither rejected nor adopted wholesale. Particular lesson structures with pre-determined plenaries that were almost obligatory a few years ago are now sometimes the subject of derision. Neither stance is sensible. Thinking about how best to break a lesson up into sections can help bring variety. Decisions about what is appropriate for a particular context need to be employed on the basis of a sound rationale. The rest of this chapter will explore how theoretical perspectives can inform the choices a teacher makes when planning.

## Working with objectives

Newcomers to the teaching of English may be forgiven for being confused as they sometimes receive conflicting messages about the setting of objectives and how precisely and clearly these should be defined. The whole notion of objectives can seem very constraining and in direct opposition to the nature of English as an art, privileging logical modes of thought over the aesthetic. It is after all easier to be more specific about the teaching of punctuation skills than it is to describe precisely what is to be gained by reading a poem. Trainee teachers are expected to be able to identify clear objectives. It is also a criterion of teaching quality used by Ofsted inspectors. Objectives are central to the National Strategy Framework. Yet these directives have to be reconciled with an increasing emphasis on creativity and flexible planning.

When discussing the place and purpose of objectives in English teaching, much depends on what is meant by the term 'objectives' itself, whether it is being used in a general sense to describe the purpose of a lesson (small group discussions and feedback on . . . ) or whether it refers more specifically to precise learning outcomes (pupils will be able to . . . ). Frequently in the educational literature of the 1970s, battle lines were drawn between those who adhered to a model of rational curriculum planning by behavioural objectives and those who felt that such an approach was too narrow and reductive. Much of the recent writing on the development of teaching skills reduces lesson planning to a simple, mechanical process (what headings to use, importance of timings, etc.). It will be argued here that in order to plan well it is necessary to have a deeper understanding of the tensions involved. In order to be able to make use of objectives in English teaching to further learning, it is necessary to have an insight into their limitations.

Most accounts of planning in the literature on teaching (whether concerned with generic teaching skills or specific subjects) distinguish between long-term planning of schemes of work and the planning of individual lessons. Frequently the advice is that a logical approach should be adopted whereby the teacher will decide on the learning objectives, choose the appropriate means which will be used to achieve those ends and devise a method for evaluating whether the objectives have been achieved.

The problem with this account is not so much that it is wrong but that it is not the whole story; the way people learn and consequently the way people plan for learning are both rather more complex than this model implies. The setting of clear outcomes even for individual chapters in books has become de rigueur in writing about education, particularly in books addressed to newly qualified teachers or students. The style will be familiar, 'By the end of reading this chapter you will be able to . . . ' Imagine the same formula applied to a reading of *King Lear*:

By the end of reading Shakespeare's *King Lear* you should be able to:

(a) manage relationships with parents or children more productively;

(b) understand the difference between 'man' and 'nature';

(c) identify and use animal imagery effectively;

(d) recognise fools by the way they speak.

The absurdity of the formula in this context is fairly self-evident. The type of learning which occurs through experience of great art is not easily expressed in discursive propositions. Of course, it may be thought that the argument is a false one, that there is a considerable difference between reading a training manual and reading a great work of art. However, much can be gained from drawing parallels with engagement in making and responding to art and learning in other contexts. At the very least, recognition of the inappropriateness of formulating objectives in this way in relation to the reading of a Shakespeare play will urge caution in applying the formula in an unthinking fashion to other contexts.

Reading a book or chapter of any kind is likely to work more effectively as a potential source of learning if it sets up associations, patterns of thought, lines of enquiry – if it engages the passions and attention of the reader in a very real, active, creative sense. The way humans learn in any rich sense is rather more messy and complex than the rational model implies. The setting of clear outcomes or objectives has an orderly, clinical appeal but the reality is rarely that simple.

It is not uncommon for newcomers to the teaching of English to find it more natural to specify tasks rather than learning objectives. For example, it is often easier to describe the purpose of a lesson as being the reading and study of a particular poem than to offer any more specific information about the intended learning outcomes. This arises not necessarily from lazy or imprecise thinking but from an intuitive recognition that in any teaching encounter several different levels of learning may be taking place at once. A lesson which has as its purpose the reading and understanding of a poem is likely to have a variety of implicit intended outcomes such as: expressing a personal response to the poem; recognising stylistic and poetic devices; describing the content or theme of the poem; learning the meaning of unfamiliar words. Identifying just one or two objectives may serve to exclude others in the teaching process: one can easily imagine a teacher trying to teach 'similes and metaphors' in a single-minded way which destroys any interest in language or poetry. The specification of precise learning outcomes (e.g. identifying different sonnet structures) may neglect important questions of value (developing a love of poetry). How one teaches (the means) is likely to have a very significant effect on what children learn.

This may be illustrated by a concrete example. Imagine the passage from *David Copperfield* on p. 110 being used to teach a class 'to make good use of the full range of punctuation, including colons and semicolons' or 'to explore the impact of a variety of sentence structures'. In both cases, the potential for engaging personally with a vivid and evocative piece of writing could easily be circumscribed by the narrowness of the focus. Being very precise about what one is trying to teach in an English lesson is not just a pedagogical question but relates to wider theoretical issues. How, for example, does one reconcile the narrow model with post-structuralist writing (including reader-response theory) which places emphasis on the active role of the reader in the creation of meaning? The argument can be extended to the very language used to describe objectives because there is an implicit assumption that the meaning will be clear and transparent, rather than ambiguous.

Pupils do not learn how to use paragraphs, set out a letter, use visual aids when doing a presentation simply by being given 'opportunities' to perform these tasks but nor do they necessarily acquire these skills purely by direct instruction. Trying to teach pupils to use 'gesture' when giving a talk (whether this be through feedback, modelling, specific instruction) could lead to embarrassing artificiality. Knowing when to be directive and explicit and when not to is quite a subtle teaching skill. All teachers will be familiar with the fact that even when learning objectives are specified in advance of a lesson, outcomes are often different from those intended. Actively involving pupils in the lesson may serve to change its direction. Moreover, individual pupils may bring their own meanings and understanding to what is going on. Alternative outcomes may be the sign of effective rather than ineffective teaching. If we agree with Curtis (1993: 33) that the teacher 'needs to encourage her students to play their full part in shaping the English curriculum' then a rigid objectives model is unlikely to allow that to happen. Many of the insights into pupils' learning in the last 100 years through the work of such writers as Dewey, Vygotsky and Bruner have stressed the importance of pupils' taking ownership, being actively engaged in the learning process and the formation of ideas. It is possible, then, to summarise why the setting of clear learning objectives in English can be problematic:

■ learning outcomes sometimes differ for individual pupils;

■ learning in English is not easily separated into discrete units;

■ pupils must be actively involved in the creation of meaning;

■ the learner is often involved in determining the learning outcome;

■ setting predetermined learning outcomes may run the risk of setting unhelpful limitations;

■ language is more ambiguous than an objectives model implies;

■ the separation of means from ends is not always desirable.

The problem with objectives is that they are precisely that, 'objective', and may be employed in such a way that they do not acknowledge the importance of subjectivity in learning. However, an excessive reliance on subjectivity brings its own dangers and it is necessary to examine when and how objectives may be usefully employed in teaching English.

It was suggested above that it is not uncommon for newcomers to the teaching of English to find it more natural to specify tasks rather than learning objectives because the intended learning is implicit in the task. However, there may be a fine line between what is implicit and what is in fact non-existent. Unless objectives actually influence the way a lesson is structured and taught, they are of little value and often 'implicit' objectives are of that kind. Quite often lessons which are based simply on the specification of tasks lack sufficient direction and focus. This can be illustrated by reference to the following extract from *David Copperfield*:

> Looking back, as I was saying, into the blank of my infancy, the first objects I can remember as standing out by themselves from a confusion of things are my mother and Peggotty. What else do I remember? Let me see.
>
> There comes out of the cloud, our house – not new to me, but quite familiar, in its earliest remembrance. On the ground-floor is Peggoty's kitchen, opening into the back yard; with a pigeon-house on a pole, in the centre, without any pigeons in it; a great dog-kennel in a corner, without any dog; and a quantity of fowls that look terribly tall to me, walking about, in a menacing and ferocious manner. There is one cock who gets upon a post to crow, and seems to take particular notice of me as I look at him through the kitchen-window, who makes me shiver, he is so fierce. Of the geese outside the side-gate who come waddling after me with their long necks stretched out when I go that way, I dream at night: as a man environed by wild beasts might dream of lions.
>
> Here is a long passage – what an enormous perspective I make of it! – leading from Peggoty's kitchen to the front-door. A dark store-room opens out if it, and that is a place to be run past at night; for I don't know what may be among those tubs and jars and old tea-chests, when there is nobody in there with a dimly-burning light, letting a mouldy air come out at the door, in which there is the smell of soap, pickles, pepper, candles, and coffee, all at one whiff.

Imagine a simply structured lesson based on this text. Having read the extract, the teacher leads a whole-class discussion/question and answer session which ranges over the writer's feelings, the meanings of particular words, the clues which tell us that the scene is set in the past, the wider context of the story, and the interpretation of the information. The class are then given the task of writing about their own earliest memories. The problem here is that the oral work on the extract, whatever intrinsic value it may have had, has not been sufficiently linked with the writing task. An even more disjointed lesson might proceed as follows: reading of extract; pupils identify aspects of the content and style which tell us that this was written in the past; pupils asked to write about a time when they were afraid. In both cases the task was to read the extract and do some writing of their own but the lack of focus could be attributed to an absence of clear objectives.

Another approach after reading the extract might be to ask the class to recall their early memories of childhood so that they have ideas to use in their writing. Pupils tend to enjoy this kind of sharing of experience and again there is nothing intrinsically wrong with the task. However, the Dickens extract has become somewhat redundant except as a very mild (and somewhat inappropriate) stimulus. For this particular activity, a contemporary extract or even just a brainstorm of ideas would serve the purpose better.

The choice of appropriate objectives would of course depend on the particular class and the overall context of the scheme of work. The extract could be used as a 'way in' to the novel (in which case speculation on who the characters are and what might happen would be appropriate), as a way of examining the way language is used to convey feeling and mood (analysis of the words which have negative connotations) or to explore style and sentence structure. As a preparation for pupils' own writing, analysis of the writer's techniques and in particular the way he uses size to evoke childhood memories of the past could be the focus. Specification of objectives will give focus to the lesson without necessarily narrowing the teaching approach and excluding the children's personal experiences. Depending on their age and experience, pupils might be asked to:

- recall and share their very earliest memories;
- think about the way early memories are often 'blank', hazy or distorted;
- underline all the phrases in the extract associated with size and then words or phrases which convey the writer's feelings;
- think of objects (possibly from personal experience) which might frighten a young child because of their perceived size;
- share any similar experiences;
- try a similar paragraph of their own in which size is a key ingredient using the original extract as a model.

Objectives can be a very useful planning device as long as meaning is kept to the fore when teaching the lesson. This passage lends itself to an exploration of 'the effects of changes in tense' (using the present tense to evoke the past vividly). Notice however that it would be easy to teach a lesson in which pupils happily circle all present tense verbs and use the term 'present tense' (all this with impressive pace) without any real appreciation of the effect it has in this passage.

Lessons sometimes lack sufficient focus when no objectives are specified. This also happens when too many are identified, partly as a result of trying to link the plan to the National Curriculum. Many English lessons contain some element of speaking and listening, reading and writing but it is far more helpful to identify the key focus of the lesson rather than to describe all the links with the National Curriculum in a 'scatter gun' fashion.

To summarise then: the fact that the specification of objectives in English is a complex process does not mean that they have no value at all. Without objectives, lessons may have insufficient focus and clarity; unless pupils know what the purpose of a lesson is, the whole enterprise may be bewildering to them. Merely describing tasks may not give enough direction to the teaching. Objectives can help the teacher have a better sense of the intended progression in a scheme of work. It is not uncommon for beginning teachers to feel uncertainty about what they are trying to achieve and for the lesson to lose direction or lack coherence. On the other hand not all lessons lend themselves to the specification of clear learning outcomes and flexibility needs to be adopted in the planning process. Learning objectives are more likely to be employed positively in English if the following considerations are kept in mind:

- All lessons must have a purpose which is clearly identified.
- Lessons take different forms and have different purposes (introductory lessons, continuation lessons).

- Some lessons require 'soft' objectives and others require more specific learning outcomes.

- The scheme of work will be a key element in giving a broad framework of aims and ensuring balance and progression.

- The specification of precise objectives will not necessarily restrict the teaching and learning if the broader aims of the scheme of work are borne in mind.

- The specification of too many objectives may prevent a sufficiently sharp focus.

- The evaluation of outcomes to monitor coverage after the completion of lessons and schemes of work will preserve flexibility.

## Schemes of work

The National Curriculum does not dictate how the teaching of English should be organised and structured, nor does it specify, except implicitly, particular teaching methods. It is still up to departments and teachers to plan their own schemes of work.

There are a number of broad approaches to the teaching of English, each of which has its disadvantages and dangers. These days departments are likely to plan their schemes of work using a mixture of the methods which will be described in this section rather than by focusing on one approach alone. It is, however, useful to consider the advantages and disadvantages of the different ways of organising the teaching in order to be aware of the dangers and drawbacks of each one. They can be very loosely identified with particular eras and ideologies but the degree to which a historical or theoretical interpretation can be imposed on the different models should not be exaggerated.

The traditional approach to teaching English dominant in most schools up to the mid-1960s was one which divided the subject into discrete lessons and activities: Monday would be comprehension, Tuesday the class reader, Wednesday composition and so on. The approach had the advantage of offering a comforting predictability and a degree of flexibility which could allow an imaginative teacher to exploit serendipitous opportunities which presented themselves. This type of structure tended to coincide with a narrow approach to the subject, focusing on comprehensions, compositions and class debates rather than a wider range of reading, writing and oral activities. There is nothing endemic to this way of working which makes it narrow; a balanced curriculum is possible provided the range of activities is wide enough. Such an approach, however, fragmented the subject and offered few opportunities for integrating the language modes of speaking, reading and writing.

This was precisely the advantage of a thematic approach which came to the fore in the late 1960s and early 1970s. The approach is still prevalent and is becoming more popular with a renewed emphasis on curriculum integration. Pupils saw themselves as not so much developing skills in English as studying particular topics, such as the family, life in the city or crime. Personal growth was a strong underpinning aim and a 'language in use' conception of language development tended to prevail. The approach has the laudable aim of giving unity and meaning to the pupils' experiences but runs the risk of circumscribing the meaning of literature by using it in the service of a theme.

An exclusively thematic approach leaves little room for the teaching of specific language skills. On the surface this seems to be the most pupil-centred method of English teaching but in fact it runs the risk of robbing pupils of any opportunities for genuinely free and open responses to literature. It can offer a spurious kind of integration because the content of every lesson is related to a theme but that integration may not be at a very deep level.

Text-centred approaches to English meant that the central play or novel being studied became the focal point for all the related language as well as literature work. This way of teaching had been popular for some time but perhaps it gained ground with the advent of 16+ and GCSE, which endorsed creative responses to literature as being suitable methods of assessment. There was a burgeoning of published support texts with ideas for 'things to do with literature'. At its worst English started to look like maths with pie charts, timelines, graphs of emotions. There were times when it felt as if pupils could not read a book without having to draw 'wanted' posters or write journals and diaries in role. The advantage of the approach was that the varied activities related to the text helped to ensure that pupils of all abilities in the class were able to understand and respond to its content and themes.

Whereas thematic and text-centred approaches are commonly referred to in the literature on English teaching, the concept of a project-based approach is less well established. It is being used here to refer to specific work on language or other extended work which is not related to a single theme. After the publication of the Kingman Report there was an increased emphasis on broad knowledge about language. This meant the development of more units of work specifically related to language, focusing on language change, accent, dialect, etc.

Few departments are likely to structure their English teaching around skills because one would simply not be fulfilling the programmes of study in the National Curriculum. However, it does raise the question whether the teaching of specific skills should arise in context or be the subject of a systematic programme. Some course books are structured not around themes or literature extracts but according to the types of writing which are being taught and practised; for example, descriptive, factual, argumentative. Spelling, which would in a pure 'language in use' approach be taught entirely in context, is increasingly receiving particular attention in schools.

The different approaches are summarised in Figure 7.1. It should be emphasised that the disadvantages apply if any one approach is used exclusively. Possible related theoretical positions are suggested but they are not definitive and other connections could just as easily be described. As suggested, any department is likely to use a mixture of approaches but the advantages and disadvantages of each illustrate the tensions involved in broad planning. It is possible to guarantee coverage by planning in a highly systematic way but the engagement of subjectivity, which is essential to rich learning, is more likely to take place with a less rigid approach.

Schemes of work are often seen merely as organising devices, as collections of resources and ideas as opposed to lesson plans which deal with educational purposes and the structuring of learning experiences. This is unfortunate because thinking about the aims of a unit of work is important not only to give it direction, breadth and balance but to retain a sense of broad purpose and values which underpin every lesson plan.

| Approach | Advantages | Disadvantages | Related theoretical underpinning |
|---|---|---|---|
| Discrete | allows teaching to be spontaneous; flexibility; | offers fragmented experiences; language modes not integrated; | cultural heritage; new criticism; |
| Text at centre | active approaches to text and reading; ensures understanding of texts; integrates language and literature; | may exclude specific work on language; | reader response; |
| Thematic | emphasis on meaning; integrates language modes; | concentration on extracts; meaning of literature circumscribed; distinct nature of English as a subject easily lost; focus may be on content rather than language; | personal growth; language in use; |
| Project-based | systematic; learning focus is clear; | context may lack meaning; | adult needs; |
| Skills-based | systematic; inclusive; objectives clear. | may exclude sufficient use of language in context. | adult needs. |

**FIGURE 7.1**

After all, learning in English is more likely to accrue over a period of time than in a single lesson. For example, being able to 'identify the ways implied and explicit meanings are conveyed in a text' as a general skill is not something which happens in a single lesson. That is why ticking off objectives in a mechanical way and always expecting pupils to identify the precise learning at the end of every lesson is questionable. Much of the literature on planning stresses the need to give much thought to the shape and structure of a lesson without acknowledging that it is important to give the same level and type of attention to planning a scheme of work. The importance of structuring schemes of work will also be considered in Chapter 15 in the context of a discussion on differentiation.

I have reserved the term 'aims' for use with schemes of work and 'objectives' for specific lessons. This is an arbitrary decision. Trying to distinguish 'aims' from 'objectives' (a common pursuit of the rational planning literature of the 1970s) in some essentialist way is fairly pointless. The important issue is that schemes of work and lesson plans need to have specific purposes, whatever terms are used.

All English departments will have syllabuses for English, although these will vary in the degree of detail they contain and the amount of flexibility given to individual teachers to decide the content of lessons. They are likely to be structured around themes, texts or projects as described earlier and are likely to specify the type of speaking and listening, reading and writing activities which need to be set in order to ensure coverage and balance over a year. Many departments have adapted their schemes to incorporate the National Strategy Framework objectives because these are now more closely linked to the programmes of study. No matter how much detail is prescribed by a department syllabus, the individual teacher needs to translate the prescribed content into a scheme of work which has a structure, content, tasks and inbuilt flexibility appropriate to the class for which it is designed.

When planning schemes of work it is often easier to think initially at the level of resources and tasks rather than aims, despite the rhetoric of advocates of the rational planning model. Teachers are more likely to approach the initial stages of planning by choosing activities which will 'go down well' or which will 'work'. These terms can be seen as shorthand ways of recognising that the material and activities must engage the pupils, and there is no reason to feel apologetic for thinking in those terms. The subsequent establishment of aims, assessment tasks, and coverage of the National Curriculum (using the new Framework objectives) serve to provide the necessary external structures and systems which are equally important. The following example will illustrate how the initial ideas need to be shaped and developed. A brainstorm on a topic entitled 'autobiographies' might generate the thoughts in Figure 7.2.

The brainstorm is presented here in a deliberately random fashion to illustrate the degree to which thinking about tasks and possible reading material may also be

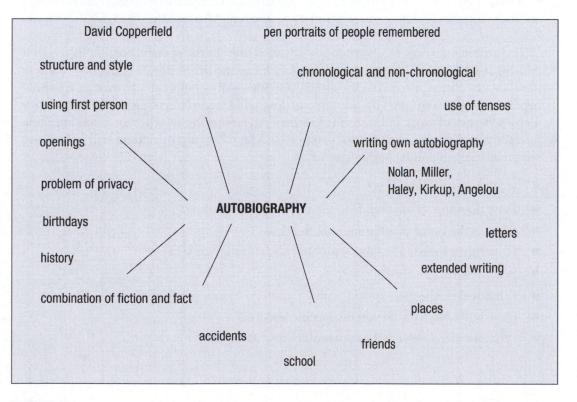

**FIGURE 7.2**

accompanied by anticipation of possible difficulties (pupils might see the writing of their own autobiography as an intrusion into their privacy), associated material/topics (autobiographies as insight into history), specific aspects of language (tenses, first person) and ways of deepening the topic (Dickens's view that autobiography is always a combination of fiction and fact). Attention is also given to ways of providing a central focus; for example, a piece of extended writing, a possible series of letters. The activities range from the very accessible (drawing on personal experience by remembering details of their own life) to the reading of fairly challenging material and grappling with demanding concepts. This suggests a structure which will move pupils from the subjective and personal to the objective, giving form and expression to personal thoughts, feelings and ideas through reading other examples.

It is easy to see how the scheme of work can be justified in relation to the National Curriculum but it is also possible to see how checking against the programmes of study or Framework objectives might also inform and extend the type of work undertaken. The initial brainstorm has less emphasis on speaking and listening activities and, depending on the broad balance of the curriculum, the teacher might choose to include drama activities related to some of the reading.

If the extended task will be to write an autobiography (perhaps allowing the pupils to use an invented character as author if they choose) the preliminary work could aim to give pupils insight into the techniques writers use to structure and present personal experience. Another focus might be to understand the difference between fact and fiction and how these boundaries can sometimes be blurred. An example is provided in Figure 7.3.

The scheme of work can be properly planned only in the specific context in which it will be taught and will depend on such factors as the achievement/range of levels in the class, the likely interests of the group, previous work completed. Particular attention needs to be given to the way the topic or text will be introduced; a useful pattern for many schemes of work in English is to start with a fairly tight structure, allowing more flexibility and choice as the work progresses. The following questions will help bring structure to the planning of the scheme:

- What are the broad aims?
- How does the scheme relate to the pupils' prior learning?
- What is the range of attainment in the class?
- How much time is available – number and duration of lessons?
- What resources are available?
- What will be the major pupil tasks?
- How will objectives be met on specific lessons?
- What are the assessment opportunities and strategies?

| SUMMARY OF ACTIVITY | RELATED OBJECTIVES |
|---|---|
| Pupils make notes on early childhood memories (favourite toy, accidents, first day at school, arguments, special place); creation of a timeline presenting life as a journey. | This lesson is designed to introduce the unit of work in an accessible way which will engage pupils of all abilities. |
| Teacher models the telling of an anecdote from early childhood in two ways: one in a monotonous voice with slow delivery, the other with more pace and vigour. Pupils choose a particular event from their life and shape into a short oral account for the rest of the class. | Speaking and Listening: tell a story, recount an experience, choosing and changing the mood, tone and pace of delivery for particular effect. |
| Linking with any childhood anecdotes based on frightening situations, shared reading of *David Copperfield* extract; analysis of extract – in particular use of punctuation and tenses and writing based on the model. | Make good use of the full range of punctuation, including colons and semicolons. Explore the effects of changes in tense. Understand and use key terms that help to describe and analyse language. |
| Reading of John Wain's 'Message From the Pigman'. Oral sharing of childhood fears, times when felt excluded, times when adult world not understood followed by questions. Short written paragraphs how things might have been different. | Recognise and exploit the use of conditionals and modal verbs. Speaking and Listening: ask questions to clarify understanding and refine ideas. |
| Reading of opening of Arthur Miller's *Timebends* (use of present tense, first person, child's perspective); examination of other openings – analyse and list devices: use of third person, direct speech, flashback, child's viewpoint, direct address of reader, way paragraphs are structured. | Develop different ways of linking paragraphs, using a range of strategies to improve cohesion and coherence. |
| Reading a variety of extracts from published autobiographies which evoke different themes, times and cultures; analyse different structures and contexts. | Reading: analyse the overall structure of a text to see how key ideas are developed. Reading: investigate the way familiar themes are explored and presented by different writers; compare treatment of same theme. Text level, Reading: recognise how texts refer to and reflect the culture in which they were produced. |
| Completion of a language autobiography after a class examination/discussion of the ways children acquire language. | Speaking and Listening: reflect on the development of their abilities as speakers in a range of different languages. |
| Reading vivid portraits of people from the work of Dylan Thomas, James Kirkup, Laurie Lee, with analysis of stylistic devices. | Writing: experiment with figurative language in conveying a sense of character and setting. Writing: develop the use of commentary and description in narrative. |
| Tableaux and dramatic presentations based on one of the extracts. | Speaking and Listening: collaborate in and evaluate the presentation of dramatic performances. |
| Drafting of own autobiography using devices studied. | Assessed piece focused on a range of objectives addressed in the unit. |

FIGURE 7.3

The following suggested headings could be used to write up the final version of the scheme:

- Topic/title;
- Aims;
- Links with National Curriculum;
- Resources;
- Major pupil tasks;
- Assessment;
- Outline plan (introduction of topic, number of lessons, possible sequence which will be adapted as lessons are taught, main objectives).

## Individual lesson plans

There are different preferred methods for setting out a lesson plan; the actual headings employed are less important than thinking about the dynamics of the teaching and learning context. It is clearly important to have a systematic approach to planning lessons simply to save time but it should be remembered that the written plan is not an end in itself and should support rather than distract from the teaching.

After the first introduction of the National Strategy the terms 'starter' and 'plenary' came into very wide use. Thinking about a lesson as a four-part structure is a useful reminder that quite often a lesson is a long time for some pupils to concentrate and variety and pace can be key elements. However, starters and plenaries should be seen as useful pedagogic devices and not as universal principles, as they tended to be viewed when first introduced.

When devising a scheme of work it is often quite difficult to integrate specific work on language with the particular theme or text being studied. To argue that everything should be fully integrated would be as dogmatic and inflexible as the view that every single lesson should begin in an identical way. Starters are often best used when related to the rest of the lesson but they can operate as ten-minute stand-alone exercises on aspects of English such as spelling rules and vocabulary.

The concept of a 'plenary' is a useful reminder that a lesson is almost always improved by making time to draw together the main features of the lesson. Often this is a matter of reinforcing the central learning related to objectives. However, as discussed above, it is not always appropriate to try to pin down the precise learning in a single lesson. In such cases the plenary acts more as a summary or drawing together of the central points which have emerged, for example in an exploratory discussion of a poem.

The following headings are among those commonly recommended for beginning teachers. With more experience the headings can be reduced and the content shortened but at the start it is a good idea to plan in detail:

- Information about class, date, lesson time, etc.

    Apart from the need to keep plans organised, the information here may be a useful reminder to the beginning teacher (e.g. is the lesson the right one for a Friday afternoon?).

- Main objective(s)/purpose

    This heading may seem somewhat clumsy but it is intended as a reminder that whereas some lessons require focused objectives (in the sense of learning outcomes), others do not.

- Resources

    It is a matter for individuals to decide whether a reminder of this kind is necessary but in the early days of planning it is easy to forget some vital item needed for the lesson.

- Special considerations

    A catch-all heading of this kind can be useful to make notes about special needs pupils, differentiation, room changes, reminders about homework, etc.

- Way in/starter

    A starter is a useful device for addressing work at the specific word level but at the beginning of a new topic a 'way in' may be more appropriate.

- Development of lesson

    In the early stages of teaching it is highly advisable to include rough estimates of timings for each stage of the lesson. Some writers like to distinguish between teacher and pupil activities. Whatever the approach taken, the stages of the lesson should be identified clearly.

- Plenary/conclusion

    Identifying time for a plenary at the end of the lesson is a useful reminder that the lesson should not just drift away (plenary sessions can of course also take place during a lesson).

- Evaluation

    Reflection on the degree to which the lesson has been successful or not is a useful way of improving practice. A systematic record of what has been achieved in the lesson is also a way of preserving flexibility and avoids the obsessive need to fulfil intentions every lesson, which can make for poor teaching.

Training courses and schools will have different policies and preferences as will individual teachers; there is no one correct way of setting out a plan. In these days of accountability and external scrutiny, lesson plans are not just aids to teaching but are also ways of demonstrating competence and proving compliance with standards. Other headings (differentiation, assessment, homework, special needs) could also be included but it is wise not to make the plan too cluttered. The intention here is to stimulate thinking about the process rather than to argue for one particular approach.

This chapter will end with a critical discussion of three lesson plans as a way of examining some of the general observations in more specific contexts.

## Lesson Plan A

**Lesson objective:**  Spelling of multi-syllable words.

**Starter:**  Using white boards pupils practise spelling multi-syllable words.

**Introduction:**  Read aloud first four chapters of *Holes* – pupils listen and follow in their books.

**Development:**  In pairs ask pupils to predict what will happen in the novel.

**Plenary:**  Pupils choose their main prediction and write on a piece of paper to be pinned to the board. Class choose the prediction they think is the most likely.

## Commentary

The plan for Lesson A has a varied structure but it might have benefited from rough timings for each activity. This level of detail is fine as an aide-memoire for an experienced teacher but for a beginner more detail would help. The lesson objective is clear but it relates only to the starter and not to the rest of the lesson. In fact it is questionable whether a separate starter is appropriate for a lesson which is introducing a new novel. The first four chapters of *Holes* are compelling. Even so, with some classes an introductory task might be helpful (e.g. consider what the book might be about on the basis of the title and cover). The prediction task is a good one but an opportunity is lost to get the pupils to think about the clues in the text which prompted the pupils to make their choices. A clearer objective related to the narrative clues might have kept this more to the fore. The idea of writing up one prediction for display provides a concrete goal. The mechanics of choosing the favourite idea is more complex than suggested in the plan as it requires pupils to read a large number of extracts and compare them. Simply sharing and discussing the choices, and starting to categorise them, might have been more appropriate for this lesson.

## Lesson Plan B

**Class**: Year 9 mixed ability

**Objectives:**  To read the short story 'The Mysteries of the Heart' by Nigel Hinton. To complete a written task in response to the story.

**Resources:**  Copies of short story
Rough paper for drafts
Exercise books

**Special considerations:**  John and Paul very poor readers.
Write extract on board before start of lesson.

**Pupil tasks:**  Class discussion
Letter in role from one character in the story to another

**Lesson development:**

**Starter/way in:**  Extract from story written on the board to engage their interest.
Ask pupils to guess what is in box. What is the story likely to be about? Pupils write a brief note in rough on their ideas, share with partner and then some sharing with the whole class. (10 mins)

Read story. (15 mins)

Class discussion of central ideas and themes. (5 mins)

**Pupil task:**  To choose a character from the story and write a letter in role as that character to someone else. Pupils may invent characters if they wish (e.g. a friend or relative). Rough drafts to be completed first. (15 mins)

**Conclusion:** Volunteers to read out letters or beginnings of letters. (5 mins)

**Relationship to National Curriculum:** ATs 1, 2 and 3.

**Evaluation**

The pupils seemed to enjoy the initial task of trying to guess what was going on in the extract and the activity did create interest in knowing what the story was about. I was disappointed with the class discussion which did not seem to get anywhere. They did say they liked the story which was encouraging and they settled down to the written work quite well.

## Commentary

The plan for Lesson B has a clear structure and the teacher has thought of a simple, controlled method of introducing the story and trying to capture the interest of the class. The use of approximate timings is a helpful guide. However, there are three related ways in which the plan could be given more focus: by defining objectives more clearly, by making the relationship to the National Curriculum more precise and by planning in more detail what is meant by 'class discussion'. The latter mistake is not uncommon amongst beginning teachers because to plan a discussion in advance can seem very mechanistic and inflexible. However, without some sense of purpose and direction it is easy to flounder and ask vague questions ('what did you think of it?') or ones which are not sufficiently challenging ('what did he find in the box?'). Linking more closely with the programmes of study for reading, an appropriate objective for this particular story might have been either 'to reflect on the motivation and behaviour of characters' or 'to examine the narrative structure'. The story is not written very densely and a focus on language and style would have been less relevant. A more precise objective might have informed the planning of the discussion in more detail; for example, requiring pupils to think about why the mother chose not to tell her son about the identity of his real father (one of the themes of the story). The pupils could then have been given clearer criteria for the written work requirements and the lesson evaluation could have focused on the pupils' fulfilment of the objectives. The fact that two pupils have difficulties with reading is identified in the plan but there is no indication of what the practical consequences are for this lesson.

## Lesson Plan C

**Class:** Year 9 top set

**Objectives:** To comment on interpretations of text in same media (Reading 10) to assess AT1.

To establish working groups.

To extend pupils' understanding of drama in performance.

To further understanding of *Romeo and Juliet* Act 3, Scene 1.

Continuity with previous work.

Pupils know the plot of the play and are familiar with Act 3, Scene 1.

**Resources:** Copies of *Romeo and Juliet*

DVD of *Romeo and Juliet* and DVD player

**Starter:** Brief recap of plot of scene through question and answer quiz establishing that Mercutio was killed by Tybalt (under Romeo's arm) and Romeo took revenge by killing Tybalt.

**Lesson Content:**

Divide class into groups of four or five.

Reread the first thirty-three lines of the scene and give groups five minutes to work out how they would film the introduction to the scene. Prompt questions: where would they set the scene? what actions might accompany the lines? how would they establish that it is a hot day?

Show class the relevant section based on the opening thirty-three lines from the Zeffirelli film and compare with their versions.

Ask class to continue working in groups deciding how the scene might be filmed (up to death of Tybalt) with a view to giving a brief oral presentation on their ideas at the end of the lesson.

Presentations.

**Plenary:** Show class entire scene from film and inform them that next lesson the Zeffirelli version will be compared to the Luhrmann film which has a modern setting.

## Commentary

The structure of Lesson C is well conceived because it seeks to generate ideas for the subsequent group work by showing an initial extract from the relevant film. The objectives however are more complex than necessary. Assessing pupils may be a purpose of the lesson (although it does not seem to appear in the rest of the plan) but it does not in itself count as a learning outcome. Considering 'how texts are changed when adapted to different media' seems less appropriate than 'understanding of drama in performance' because the focus of the lesson as presented in the plan is more on interpretation than change. Establishing working groups is part of the methodology rather than an objective.

What the plan seems to lack is clear guidance for the pupils on how they are to record and present the results of their discussion, which might be in the form of a story board, director's notes added to the text or their own summaries. The plan attempts to cram a great deal into one lesson. 'Brief oral presentation' is vague and giving the pupils more time would also allow the teacher to give them more direction.

Planning lessons and schemes of work, like so many aspects of teaching English, is not a simple mechanical process but requires sensitivity to contexts, an understanding of one's own preferred ways of working as a teacher and a capacity to reflect on and learn from previous experiences. There is now a great deal of support for teachers with planning. However, the proliferation of pre-formed lesson plans in books and websites is a mixed blessing. They can be a useful source of ideas and structures but they can easily lead to dull routine or even disaster if not adapted sensibly.

## Further reading

Evans *et al.* (2009) *Teaching English* has a chapter on 'Planning for Learning'. General advice on lesson planning (not just in English) can be found in Pollard (2002) *Reflective Teaching*, Capel *et al.* (1995) *Learning to Teach in the Secondary School* and Kyriacou (1991) *Essential Teaching Skills*. Readers interested in pursuing the earlier, more theoretical discussion of objectives and rational planning might consult Stenhouse (1975) *An Introduction to Curriculum Research and Development* and Sockett (1976) *Designing the Curriculum*. For an accessible text on cognitive styles see Riding (2002) *School Learning and Cognitive Styles*. For a general overview of learning see the chapter by Cox in Nicholls (1991) *Learning to Teach*.

## Resources

Schemes of work and lessons plans for English (which should of course be used with discrimination) can be found at the following websites: www.english-teaching.co.uk/freeresources.htm and www.teachit.co.uk. A template for pupils to write an 'Autobiography of Intercultural Encounters' is available on the Council of Europe website, www.coe.int/t/dg4/linguistic%5CAutobiogrWeb_EN.asp.

# 8

# Assessment

*The new system of weights and measures will be a stumbling block
and the source of difficulties for several generations . . . It's just
tormenting the people with trivia.*

Napoleon, *Mémoires*

## Thinking about assessment

READERS WHO HAVE WORKED their way through this book systematically will already be
familiar with a number of themes and polarities which have emerged in the first seven
chapters: deep and surface learning, feeling and cognition, mechanical systems and
dynamic processes, to name just a few. The likelihood, however, is that not everyone will
have necessarily read the book in a systematic way, chapter by chapter, but some will have
dipped into sections as the mood has taken them or as the need has arisen. Just as people
do not always read books in the logical, linear sequence that one expects them to, neither
do they necessarily learn in neat, predictable stages. The system of formal assessment
introduced with the National Curriculum was an attempt to impose an external structure
of predetermined stages on complex, dynamic, idiosyncratic learning processes and this
inevitably led to difficulties. For almost 20 years the national approach to assessment has
had a largely negative impact on the curriculum. The abolition of standard attainment
tests at the end of Key Stage 3 therefore has to be welcomed as a positive development.
That does not mean that assessment is unimportant; on the contrary it is a key element
in successful teaching and learning. It is important therefore for new teachers to have a
grasp of the tensions and difficulties involved in assessment.

One consequence of the emphasis on external systems of assessment designed for
accountability is that it can distract from the more important role of assessment in
informing and improving teaching and learning ('assessment for learning' or 'assessment
for pupil progress'). It is often claimed that the different purposes for assessment should
be kept in mind and reconciled in practice but this is more difficult than is often assumed.
Preparation of pupils for external examinations can easily distract from the need to give
wide-ranging feedback to pupils to improve their general achievement in the subject. It
is as if a driving instructor decides to conduct a driving lesson by waiting at a given
destination to which the pupil has been told to drive. The instructor proceeds to look at
the time it took, checks the vehicle for any bumps and scratches and then provides the

pupil with a report which gives a simple grade and includes comments such as 'could do better', 'go a bit faster next time' or 'watch your steering'. For a teacher to use assessment effectively it is necessary to be thoroughly 'beside the wheel' and involved in the process of learning.

It is easy to get so submerged in the language of assessment (summative/formative; normative/criterion referenced; validity/reliability) that one loses any real insight into the tensions and issues at the heart of the process. Similarly, close involvement with the mechanics of assessment may distract from a real sense of educational purpose. I begin this chapter therefore not with a consideration of technicalities but with a discussion of a sample of a pupil's writing which raises a number of general issues. This is followed by a brief description of a traditional, narrow approach to assessment in English before considering contemporary developments.

The piece was written by a 14-year-old pupil in response to the Wilfred Owen poem, 'Dulce et Decorum Est'. As a 'way in' the class were presented with the final Latin phrase from which the poem gets its title ('it is good and noble to die for your country') and set about translating it which they did by various guesses and prompts from the teacher. The poem was read twice aloud and then, with no discussion or analysis, the class were asked to respond in writing to what they had read in any way they wished; they were given no other instructions. This is a revised version of the pupil's work:

'Dulce et Decorum est'

*Flopping down dragging their bodies along the mud and sludge, many half starved with not enough strength to pull the trigger on the gun and half naked and trampling over bodies lying in the trenches and watching people. I heard a shout, 'Help! Help!' I looked down. Just then a plane came. We dived to the ground and as I got up I heard a cry. As the blood was pouring from him, one of the other men began to shout and become hysterical. I slapped him and when he stopped I said, 'Thank your god that that was not you lying there dead'. We began to trample on as a bomb landed nearby. We began to run but it was too late – we lost half our men. Many others had wounds. Some had arms and legs missing. As we sat there in the slum and muck waiting for help we slowly deteriorated into dead bodies. As I was the last one to survive the filth and muck even now I regret joining the army to serve my country.*

This is what the original version looked like:

*flopping down draging there bodys along the mud and slut, meny harf starved and not enough strenth to pul the trigger on the gun and harf naked and trampling over bodys lying in the trenches and waching people dye and I heard a shout HELP HELP I looked down gust then a playn come we dived to the ground as I got up I heard a cry as the blud was poring from him one of the uther men began to shout and go hiserikal I slaped him one and when he stop I sed thank your god that hat was not you lying ther ded we began to trammel on as one of the men klapst as a bom landed right near him we began to run but it was to larte we lost harf our men meny others with woonds as the bodys lyed ola over sum wuth arms and legs misson as we sat there in the slum and muick wating four help as we slaoly detereated into ded bodys as is was the last one to surive the filth and muck even now I regret goyning the army to serve my contry*

The piece was written many years ago and it has served well in countless in-service and training sessions since, raising questions about approaches to marking, assessment policies and how to deal with special needs pupils, among others. Reading the piece aloud draws attention to the sensitivity and effectiveness of the writing which can easily be missed by concentrating on the surface features. One of the most dramatic responses given by a teacher in one of those very early courses was a red line through the work with 'see me' at the end. Not that mere recognition of its qualities necessarily means that the writing is easy to assess in any formal sense. The achievement can be acknowledged, the piece can be corrected and published, but judging according to predetermined criteria may mean that it has to receive a low grade, percentage or level.

The performance on this piece of work may not be representative of the pupil's overall standard because the creative effort could well have detracted from the accuracy of the writing. In order to make a proper judgement, a range of pieces would need to be considered. If the writing here is viewed as an initial draft, the judgement may need to be reserved until a final version is seen. Nor is it by any means straightforward how the piece should be corrected. Improving the spelling is reasonably uncontroversial but other matters are open to dispute. Notice in the corrected version the teacher has retained some aspects of the writing which technically are mistakes; the first sentence does not have a main clause. Paradoxically, the stylistic effectiveness of the writing is partly achieved by the limitation of the technical aspects; the absence of punctuation, the repetition of the word 'and' gives the writing a momentum and pace which would be impressive if it had been intended. The question of intention becomes relevant if the piece is used to assess reading rather than writing. There seems to be a genuine, intuitive response to the content and form of the original but whether that counts as 'understanding' is another matter; for that one might argue that an analytic, more cognitive, discursive response is needed.

In the context of a traditional, simple system whereby, for the sake of argument, every written piece was awarded a mark out of ten, a teacher would find some difficulty in knowing how to deal with this piece. At its worst a system of that kind did not give any clear indication of what the mark was for, or any indication of the strengths and weaknesses of the work. What it did give was a sense of how the individual had performed in relation to other pupils in the class (normative assessment). It is easy to understand why pupils were so concerned to ask each other 'what did you get?' (and often admonished for doing so) because in the absence of any clear criteria to accompany the mark, the only touchstone would be their performance in relation to others in the class. Of course, marks would frequently be accompanied by verbal or written comments but these were more often than not bland or predictable; a seven would qualify for a 'very good', a six for 'good' and so on.

The absence of clear criteria meant that pupils were often not significantly motivated by the assessment system to improve performance. In order to achieve a higher grade it is necessary to know what aspects of the work need improvement; if the judgements appear arbitrary then such extrinsic motivation is likely to be minimal. The lack of transparency meant that there was a corresponding lack of useful information for various interested parties: telling a parent that a pupil received a B+ is rather less helpful than telling them what the pupil is able to do and how they can improve performance. The same is true of giving marks to pupils; the emphasis was more on providing judgements than on using the assessment system to provide feedback to pupils of a formative kind.

Through the 1960s and early 1970s positive approaches to marking emerged. The hissing and spitting red pen was in many instances replaced by what was judged to be a more positive and comforting green. Not everyone went for the change of colour but many departments developed enlightened marking policies, recommending that teachers should not be obsessed with grading but should celebrate achievement, respond to content, and be selective when correcting mistakes. Such positive approaches were a considerable improvement and are still central tenets of many assessment policies but there was often a lack of detailed evidence of achievement or detailed feedback on how pupils might make progress.

The limitations of the more traditional model then indicate some of the requirements of a more enlightened system which should:

- motivate pupils;

- provide clear information for pupils, parents and other interested parties;

- provide a diagnosis of pupils' learning needs and support for how they might improve.

## Assessment in the National Curriculum

In the light of those demands the emergence of the national system at first looked promising. Specification of eight (or in the original version, ten) levels with specific criteria for each appears to solve the problem at a stroke. Pupils and parents know exactly what needs to be done in order to move from one level to another; the system thus provides formative feedback but also allows more formal, summative judgements to be made at specific times. The approach seems logical enough in theory, until the specific details are examined. Consider, for example, what needs to happen for a pupil to make progress from level 5 to level 6 in reading:

---

**Reading level 5**

Pupils show understanding of a range of texts, selecting essential points and using inference and deduction where appropriate. In their responses, they identify key features, themes and characters and select sentences, phrases and relevant information to support their views. *They understand that texts fit into historical and literary traditions.* They retrieve and collate information from a range of sources.

**Reading level 6**

In reading and discussing a range of texts, pupils identify different layers of meaning and comment on their significance and effect. They give personal responses to literary texts, referring to aspects of language, structure and themes in justifying their views, *and making connections between texts from different times and cultures and their own experiences.* They summarise a range of information from different sources.

---

**FIGURE 8.1**

In each of the attainment targets, the language used to distinguish one level from another is often vague and indeterminate, sometimes depending on a particular phrase. The sentences in italics were added when the 1999 version of the curriculum was amended for implementation in 2007. One solution for teachers is to provide examples of what counts as a particular level. The exemplification materials with levels and commentary provided by QCA serve that purpose and in my view are a more important resource than the lesson plans (although the latter are no doubt consulted more frequently). Exemplification, however, does not necessarily help the pupil for whom the system is meant to be transparent. Nor is the answer to make the statements more specific because that in turn would be a betrayal of the nature of English as a subject and a failure to recognise that language development does not take place in simple, linear fashion. The current broad level descriptors (of which examples are given above), which operate by teachers making 'best fit' judgements, are a vast improvement on the original statements published in 1989, which were broken into strands and led teachers into ticking endless boxes.

Despite the vagueness of the statements, another problem is that the range of attainment being described at any one level is broad. Pupils are expected to move through the levels fairly slowly (just over one a year) and using them to mark progress may prove to be demotivating. A further difficulty is that because the statements of attainment are intended to be objective, measurable indicators of what pupils have achieved, they tend to place more emphasis on surface features of performance. This was acknowledged by Cox (1991: 147) in relation to pupils' writing: 'The best writing is vigorous, committed, honest and interesting. We did not include these qualities in our statements of attainment because they cannot be mapped on to levels.'

It is possible to summarise why the (apparently promising) national system of assessing pupils by levels offers only limited help to teachers in their assessment of pupils' progress as follows:

- the language used to describe the levels does not help to differentiate them (although exemplification helps);
- the range of achievement at any one level is very broad;
- pupils' learning in English does not develop in a simple linear fashion;
- use of levels may be demotivating for pupils;
- there is a tendency for the statements to be reductive.

What the system does offer is a crude method of accountability by comparing the performance of one individual, class, school or local authority with another. In order to compare levels of achievement pupils need to be assessed in a way which produces consistent results or is 'reliable'. Reliability has to do with the degree to which the form of assessment is likely to yield the same results if repeated on different occasions and judged by different people. A multiple choice test tends to be very reliable because its objectivity is such that it can be marked by a computer.

Imagine trying to produce a highly reliable test for speaking and listening. It would need to be capable of being replicated throughout the country and marked according to a clear scheme so that comparing results would be fair. There would be little point in asking for group discussions or conversations with an examiner (along the lines of traditional CSE and O level oral exams) because the outcomes would be too unpredictable. The closest one might come to a reliable test would be to ask all pupils to read the same passage aloud and award marks for accuracy and expression. Even so, the room for individual interpretation is vast and a considerable degree of moderation would be required.

However, the problem with the construction of the test is that in order to make it as reliable as possible it has ceased to be an appropriate or valid test of speaking and listening. As an assessment of English the test has very little validity. Reliability and validity are key concepts in understanding the tension at the heart of assessing English for they tend to pull in opposite directions. Speaking and listening is extremely difficult to assess because, even more than other aspects of English, performance varies with subject, context and level of motivation. In Barry Hines's novel *Kes* Billy Casper's ability with language seems to be transformed when he speaks about his kestrel. Poor performance in oral work is often to do with the nature of the task which has been devised, the atmosphere of the classroom and the dynamics of the group rather than the ability of the pupils; to provide a valid assessment of speaking and listening, evidence needs to be drawn from a variety of situations.

Of course what is true of speaking and listening is also true of reading and writing. A valid test of reading cannot be based on a single set of questions on one passage. A portfolio of evidence with writing for different purposes on a variety of subjects, which shows evidence of process as well as product, is likely to provide a better indication of an individual's aptitude than a narrow paper and pencil test taken under examination conditions.

This history of the English SATs prior to their abolition is informative. The boycott of the tests, which came to a head in the summer of 1993, was precipitated because of the highly reductive conception of the subject embodied in them. In order to form reasonably valid judgements of pupils' achievements in English it is necessary to consider a variety of different information drawn from different sources.

The controversy surrounding the English Key Stage 3 SATs throughout their history can be understood in terms of the competing requirements of validity and reliability. It is not surprising that so many results were questioned by schools and subsequently changed after a re-mark. Questions which leave no room for a marker's individual interpretation would be far too narrow as a test of a pupil's achievement in English. Curiously, the way the Shakespeare question in the SATs paper was changed in 2003 (asking pupils to write creatively in response to Shakespeare) was neither reliable nor valid and succeeded in alienating almost everyone.

The quest for 'objective' and reliable methods of assessment driven by notions of accountability brings with it a number of dangers. So called 'teaching to the test' may not be a problem if the tests are sophisticated and wide-ranging but there may be practical difficulties in administering those that are (the original English SATs at Key Stage 3 took the form of extended projects). The demand for schemes which will standardise marking has a tendency to place more emphasis on the testing of superficial knowledge with a consequent narrowing of the curriculum. Most significantly, there is a danger that the emphasis on summative assessment will distract attention from the important day-to-day monitoring and feedback which is an essential part of the teacher's role.

The word 'monitoring' tends to be used to refer to the less formal checking of pupils' understanding and progress. It is sometimes used synonymously with 'formative assessment' but if anything the term 'monitoring' implies an even less formal approach. Effective monitoring means being alert to all the signs which may give some indication of pupils' achievement or lack of success. It also carries connotations of a process which extends over time. However, the use of terminology is less important than an appreciation of the fact that effective teaching requires being alert to all of the indicators which provide information about understanding, whether or not more formal assessments are taking place: contributions to group discussions; individual, informal conversations; reading aloud; drama presentations; drawings and diagrams; answering questions in the class; responses to short tasks not necessarily designed for assessment purposes (e.g. sequencing a text, choosing a favourite extract, commenting on a video).

## Setting targets

Target setting has in recent years become a feature of many aspects of public life, not just education. The combination of harsh targets and penalties can be counter-productive, leading to the adoption of strategies to meet targets in meaningless ways: hospital waiting lists can be reduced by having patients seen (not treated) as soon as they arrive and then keeping them waiting; targets for train punctuality can be improved by increasing journey times. Nor is education immune from similar practices. Targets for passes at GCSE A to C or equivalent can be increased by changing the Key Stage 4 curriculum and adding extra subjects thought to have a higher pass rate. The indicator then changes to 'GCSE A to C including maths and English', thus reinforcing the sense of game-playing. Some schools change exam boards if a higher pass rate can be expected elsewhere. The percentage of pupils passing at GCSE A to G can often be improved considerably by controlling a school's intake.

It is unlikely that many schools have been forced into such transparently cynical measures to meet targets. There are more ambiguous strategies which are less drastic. The A to C pass rate is considered such a central indicator that many schools give particular attention to borderline C/D candidates. There are perhaps ethical issues at stake here if this means providing undue support to one cohort of pupils and neglecting others. External targets can also result in a loss of educational judgement. In an effort to improve scores, for example, it is tempting to resort to a narrow curriculum of practice papers, drills and mechanical coaching resulting in pupils who are bored, lacking in motivation and unlikely to achieve. If the various artificial short-term measures to boost scores do happen to work, this can have a negative effect at the next key stage when pupils appear to regress.

'Value added' test scores are used to show how much progress an individual class or school has made in comparison to what they achieved in a previous test (this could be a similar type of test or a non-verbal cognitive test). This is different from comparing one cohort of pupils to another simply on the basis of raw scores. A school in a leafy suburb may have a high percentage of pupils achieving A to C grades at GCSE but may be judged on a 'value-added' basis not to be having as much positive impact on the pupils as a neighbouring school with a lower raw score.

Governing bodies and head teachers now have a statutory duty to set annual targets which are related to Local Authority and national targets. Individual class teachers need to be aware of this wider political and educational context but target setting for individual pupils is more likely to have immediate relevance in day-to-day teaching. As with other aspects of English teaching sensitive judgement is required rather than the application of a mechanical formula. Setting targets can at best be seen as a useful antidote to the bland and uninformative 'could do better' comment on pupils' work. The word 'target' suggests clarity and precision; it selects one or two central areas for improvement and thus provides focus for pupils' efforts. It is more explicit about the action needed which may be only implicit in the notion of 'feedback'. This kind of precision, however, if used in an unthinking way, can make little room for dialogue for the sort of more exploratory response captured in such formulations as 'have you ever thought of . . . ?', 'is there any way in which you could . . . ?', 'what do you think of . . . ?'. Responses of this kind are important in helping the pupil become reflective and self-managing as a learner. Targets and test data need to be used in a thoughtful rather than mechanistic manner.

## Assessment for learning

It was always the intention of the Task Group on Assessment and Testing Report on which the original National Curriculum system of testing was based that assessment should be 'an integral part of teaching and learning' rather than a 'bolt-on addition'. The statement is often quoted but the implications of what it might mean in practice need exploration. It may seem fairly obvious to say that teachers are assessing pupils' work and progress all the time but, as indicated above, opportunities for making valuable use of these judgements may be missed if there is too much emphasis on formal assessment and record keeping. Integrated, informal, formative assessment in its widest sense will take the form of advising, giving critical feedback, encouraging peer group evaluation and so on. It is important therefore to recognise that integrated assessment will inform teaching as much as it will provide information about pupils' progress. It is also necessary to recognise that the components of English, speaking and listening, reading and writing, cannot be treated identically.

Speaking develops largely naturally, whereas reading and writing have to be taught and learned. The extreme version of a 'language in use' approach to English arose because of a failure to distinguish sufficiently between the language modes; it was assumed that reading and writing, like speaking, would develop simply by exposure to language. A policy of providing critical feedback and setting targets is less appropriate in the context of oral work for the same reason. As for the assessment of listening, there is a strong argument that this should be conducted only in a doctor's surgery. Once it is established that people can hear, whether they listen or not will depend on what they are being told. In the National Curriculum what is called 'listening' can more appropriately be described as 'understanding'.

Phrased that bluntly, the argument seems a little crude because it appears not to recognise that speaking takes place in a range of formal as well as informal contexts. Whereas it would look crass to offer advice on how to conduct a conversation with a friend, it may be more appropriate to give formative feedback on how a pupil has delivered a speech. But even in more formal contexts, caution needs to be exercised. Most teachers will be familiar with pupils who have been over-coached as public speakers, who are more interested in style than content, who strive too hard for effect, who are just plain embarrassing. Interviewees who have been 'trained' by over-zealous advisers appear devoid of personality and detached from themselves. It is no surprise that we refer to such people as appearing 'unnatural'.

Planning rich contexts for talk will have more effect on pupils' confidence and performance than assessing and giving feedback. That does not mean that there will not be times when specific instruction and evaluation by peer group, self or teacher are required (for example, how to structure a talk, making use of notes, techniques for conducting an interview), but these should be thought through carefully.

Writing, however, is a different matter because it relies for its development partly on the quality of formative assessment and feedback which pupils receive. It is a very salutary experience to ask a group of English teachers to discuss what advice they would give to pupils about a particular piece of writing. More often than not agreement only extends to matters of punctuation and spelling (even paragraphing can be controversial). Advice on content, style, effectiveness of opening and structure can all be matters for disagreement. That is why entering into a dialogue with pupils about their writing is a more appropriate approach than passing authoritative judgements. The National Writing Project offered a useful set of categories for responding to writing which may feature in formative feedback:

- surface features (spelling, punctuation, handwriting);
- style and structure (appropriateness of language to purpose);
- ideas and content (coherence of and reflection on facts, opinions, action, thoughts);
- writer as writer (comment on process/pupil's understanding and reflection on this);
- writer as person (response to personal content, encouragement, further personal dialogue stemming from the text).

One of the problems in assessing the 'Dulce et Decorum Est' piece has to do with the way the task was set. The main criteria for evaluation were not clear in advance, nor was it obvious what the piece was intended to achieve. Although the writing as it stands is effective, the approach in setting the task, which emphasised free self-expression, caused problems when it came to assessment. Another difficulty is that by the time the piece was submitted for assessment it was almost too late; the teacher needed the opportunity to offer help by intervening in the process.

It was suggested above that it might be difficult to use the 'Dulce et Decorum Est' piece as a formal assessment of reading. But the pupil's writing does suggest that there has been quite a significant aesthetic response to the form and content of the poem which might well have been easily articulated either orally or in more analytic writing. Assessment of understanding at a deep rather than surface level is not easy and is achieved in the classroom by the teacher being alert to signs and clues from a variety of sources. The classroom activities listed below give opportunities for assessment of reading other than simply setting written questions on a passage:

- class and group discussion;
- individual conversations;
- creative responses;
- drawings;
- active approaches to text (choosing favourite lines);
- dramatic presentations;
- representing texts in different forms of media (e.g. narrative to drama; poem to newspaper article).

The following is an example of a nonsense comprehension; the task is to read the passage and answer the questions which follow:

The blonke was maily, like all the others. Unlike the others, however, it had spiss crinet completely covering its fairney cloots concealing, just below one of them, a small wam. It was quite drumly – lennow, almost samded in fact. When yerden it did not winx, like the other blonkes or even flerk. The other blonkes, which had not been given the same nesh, were by no means lennow or samded. They winxed readily enough. The nesh was quite kexy, had a strong shawk, and was probably venenated. There was only one thing to do with it – gevel in the wong and gaff it in. This would be much better than to sparple it in the flosh as the blonkes that were not drumly could iswonk in the wong but not in the flosh. And in any case, it might not be wise to venenate the flosh.

- What is drumly?
- Why were the other blonkes not lennow and samded?
- In what ways was the blonke like/unlike the others?
- If nesh is venenated, is it wise to gaff it in the wong?

The syntax makes it possible to answer the questions without having very much understanding of what the passage is about. A pupil might be able to 'read' the passage out loud by sounding out the words but this would hardly count as reading in any rich sense of the term. Some of the early reading tests which were simply based on word recognition did little to assess response to meaning. That does not mean that standardised reading tests have no place or value at all as long as they are used with caution and with some insight into their limitations. More sophisticated tests than those which merely asked pupils to articulate words out loud involve pupils in answering comprehension questions, completing sentences from multiple choice alternatives or inserting missing words in a passage (cloze procedure). Such tests can be useful when screening an intake of pupils or in seeking to establish some broad diagnosis of reading ability. It is important, however, as with any form of assessment, not to make too many inferences about pupils' abilities or potential on limited evidence.

To return to the 'blonkes' passage, the questions which can be easily answered need not be confined to the literal. It would not be inconceivable to write some sort of reply to the question, 'Are the main ideas in the passage put across clearly and succinctly?' The point is that it is possible to manipulate objective language and concepts at some distance from the self without real engagement or understanding. For some pupils, writing 'It says at the beginning of the play that Romeo and Juliet are a pair of star cross'd lovers' may be no different from answering questions about blonkes.

A key to having a real appreciation of the complexities of assessment is to have a rich notion of 'understanding', a consideration which is often ignored in the debate about assessment. According to Midgley (1979: 18), understanding 'is relating; it is fitting things into a context'.

We can easily be deceived into thinking that someone has understood something by their use of language. If in answer to the question 'what is the capital of France?' they answer 'Paris' we might be tempted to draw conclusions which would have to be revised if in answer to 'what is the capital of Spain?' they also answered 'Paris'. Understanding, moreover, is not an 'all or nothing' affair. It can, like learning, take a deep or surface form. When a teacher asks, 'Do you understand or not?' this can be a misleading form of words. It is perhaps worth reiterating that this does not mean that all sorts of tests (even ones which are very simple and focused) do not have their place. It does mean that some caution and humility is required when exercising judgements.

The themes of objectivity and subjectivity, which are continuing strands in this book, are particularly relevant to assessment. A number of concepts and terms have been used in the course of this chapter and they can be very roughly grouped in the following way:

| | | |
|---|---|---|
| objective | | subjective |
| summative | | formative |
| mark schemes | | feedback |
| formal tests | moderated teacher assessment | dialogue |
| reliability | | validity |
| grading | | teacher assessment |
| surface | | deep |

The two columns on the right and left indicate a tendency towards polarities. The whole quasi-scientific edifice of mark schemes, calculations, percentages and grades can obscure the fact that assessment invariably involves flawed human beings making personal judgements. The myth of measurement, as Broadfoot (1996: 218) has described it, is that educational assessment can never be fully objective:

> Belief in the possibility of educational measurement is part of the more general culture in which the salience of the interpersonal and of individual idiosyncrasies is excluded. By the same token

it may be that as the significance of chaos theory and of 'fuzzy logic' in particular becomes increasingly influential in scientific thinking, so the inevitably 'fuzzy' character of assessment will also be both recognised and accepted.

On the other hand, the need for some form of accountability means that assessment has to be seen as a reasonably reliable process and not based purely on individual whims. The two columns are somewhat reconciled by the use of moderated teacher assessment. In this approach (exemplified at one time in the 1980s by the so-called 100 per cent coursework schemes at Key Stage 4) individual teachers make judgements on pupils' progress but these are constantly compared and adjusted by a process of negotiation and consideration of differences of opinion. Agreeing standards in this way allows teacher judgements to be used for other purposes, including certification and accountability. The whole process can be taken to very sophisticated levels (see Chapter 13) and the benefits are considerable in terms of teachers' own professional development.

The use of moderated teacher assessment means that summative and formative assessments coincide more readily and that records can serve the purposes both of providing feedback to pupils and more public information. The importance of formative assessment is emphasised by Black and Wiliam (1998) in a report based on an extensive survey of the research evidence on assessment. They argue very convincingly that the initiatives of the last 10 years designed to raise standards have not taken sufficient account of the fact that 'learning is driven by what teachers and pupils do in the classroom' (1998: 1); the changes in policy with regard to National Curriculum testing, GCSE, league tables, management initiatives, target setting and school inspection do not provide enough help and support for teachers in their day-to-day work.

Their view that formative assessment is 'at the heart of effective teaching' (ibid.: 2)is based on a detailed research review which suggests that there is evidence that improving formative assessment raises standards. They suggest improvement can be achieved if formative assessment is used to raise the self-esteem of pupils:

> What is needed is a culture of success, backed by a belief that all can achieve. Formative assessment can be a powerful weapon here if it is communicated in the right way. Whilst it can help all pupils, it gives particularly good results with low achievers where it concentrates on specific problems with their work, and gives them both a clear understanding of what is wrong and achievable targets for putting it right.
>
> (1998: 141)

Black and Wiliam's (1998) report included the following recommendations:

- Feedback to pupils should concentrate on the qualities of the individual's work rather than fostering comparison with others.

- This is a key factor in improving self-esteem. The research evidence suggests that if the prevailing ethos concentrates too much on extrinsic rewards pupils avoid tasks which are too difficult and constantly look for the 'right answer'. In the English classroom it is difficult to foster genuine responses to texts if there is an undue emphasis on comparison with other pupils.

- Pupils should be trained in self-assessment.

- Many teachers find that pupils' attempts at self-assessment are not very satisfactory, amounting often to a perfunctory statement that they should 'do better at punctuation and spelling' or 'try harder'. The problem is that self-assessment is often treated as an added extra to the whole teaching and learning enterprise. Pupils need an awareness of what they are trying to achieve instead of receiving classroom teaching as 'an arbitrary sequence of exercises with no over-arching rationale'.

- Opportunities for pupils to express their understanding should be designed into the teaching.

- As suggested earlier in this chapter, a wide variety of methods can be used in the classroom to evaluate pupils' progress, which can then form a basis for feedback. This includes observation of tasks and activities (e.g. sequencing a poem) as well as pupils' oral and written contributions.

- Dialogue between pupils and teacher should be thoughtful, reflective and focused.

- A common method of assessing pupils' understanding has traditionally been through whole-class questioning by the teacher. The limitations of restricting classroom talk in English in this way was well documented in the 1970s through the work of writers such as Barnes (1976) who argued for the importance of exploratory talk. The report by Black and Wiliam (1998) extends the argument by applying it to assessment. In whole-class questioning it is often only a few pupils who respond and the level of questions is frequently low. Alternative methods of assessing understanding need to be found (for example, asking pupils to jot down answers and read them aloud).

- Tests and homework exercises must be clear and relevant to learning aims.

- The conclusion here from the analysis of the research is that 'Feedback has been shown to improve learning when it gives each pupil specific guidance on strengths and weaknesses, preferably without any overall marks' (Black and Wiliam 1998: 12). The use of formative assessment does not necessarily exclude the use of simple (such as spelling) tests but these are employed for very specific purposes.

The approach recommended by Black and Wiliam based on their review of research has been endorsed by the QCA through publication of a leaflet giving principles of 'Assessment for Learning' and is embodied in the notion of assessment of pupil progress'. Assessment for learning should:

- be part of effective planning of teaching and learning;
- focus on how students learn;
- be recognised as central to classroom practice;
- be regarded as a key professional skill for teachers;
- be sensitive and constructive because any assessment has an emotional impact;
- take account of the importance of learner motivation;

- promote commitment to learning goals and a shared understanding of the criteria by which they are assessed.

In addition:

- Learners should receive constructive guidance about how to improve.
- Assessment for learning develops learners' capacity for self-assessment so that they can become reflective and self-managing.

## Assessing pupils' progress (APP)

APP is the name given to the structured approach to teacher assessment, developed by QCA in partnership with the National Strategies. It is intended to support teachers to make judgements on pupils' progress, to fine-tune their understanding of learners' needs and to tailor their planning and teaching accordingly. The approach draws on the thinking on formative asssessment developed in the last 20 years. It aims to use diagnostic information about pupils' strengths and weaknesses to improve teaching, learning and pupils' progress. The assessment of pupils' progress could be greatly facilitated nationally with the provision of more resources (especially time) to allow teachers to engage in moderation exercises, both within their own schools and with other schools.

Moderated teacher assessment provides an indication of the appropriate kind of recording system which might best serve teaching and learning. Time is too precious in schools to duplicate effort. This tended to happen after the first version of the National Curriculum was published. For the purpose of accountability, checklists were needed to record pupils' progress through each strand of each attainment target. These bore little relationship to the kind of day-to-day marking and feedback which was necessary within the classroom. With the revised National Curriculum, portfolios of written work which include the formative feedback given to pupils provide a more detailed record of achievement than separate marks or comments. Records of reading should include details of pupils' preferences, personal responses to plays, poems and novels, and information about their ability to analyse a wide variety of texts; again a portfolio of evidence accompanied by pupils' own self-assessment and peer assessment is an appropriate format. The type of proformas used by GCSE examination boards can be adapted for use at Key Stage 3 showing performance across a range of contexts. As with assessment, recording should serve teaching and learning rather than provide a distraction from it. This chapter concludes with a summary of some features of a successful assessment and recording policy for English:

- Pupils' work is assessed in a range of contexts using a variety of methods.
- The approach to pupils' work is one which recognises achievement and identifies limitations in order to avoid a situation in which high achievers only receive bland praise and low achievers receive little encouragement.

- Criteria for assessment are shared with pupils to give them a sense of overall purpose and direction in their learning.
- Pupils are given specific help and guidance about their progress.
- The reporting system translates easily into reports for parents to avoid duplication of work.

## Further reading

A chapter by Midgley in Evans *et al. Teaching English* (2009) provides information on 'Monitoring Performance and Securing Progress'. A chapter which provides a general overview of 'Monitoring, Assessment, Recording, Reporting and Accountability' can be found in Beck and Earl (eds) (2000). For other background reading on assessment the following texts are helpful: Black *et al.* (2003) *Assessment for Learning: Putting it into Practice;* Black (1998) *Testing: Friend or Foe? Theory and Practice of Assessment and Testing;* Broadfoot (1996) *Education, Assessment and Society;* Gipps (1994) *Beyond Testing.* Stobart and Gibbs (1990) have produced a teacher's guide with a clear explanation of the issues; a revised edition was published in 1997.

For books specifically related to assessment in English see Barrs (1990) *Words Not Numbers: Assessment in English* and Johnstone (1987) *Assessing English: Helping Students to Reflect on Their Work.* Staples (1992) and Protherough and King (eds) (1995) both have a chapter on teaching and assessment. For exploration of the complexities involved in the assessment of reading, see Harrison's chapter 'The Assessment of Response to Reading: Developing a Post-Modern Perspective' in Goodwyn (1995).

## Resources

QCA have recently published materials to support APP: www.qca.org.uk.

Videos of oral work are also available. Examination boards produce similar materials for Key Stage 4: AQA www.aqa.org.uk; EDEXCEL www.edexcel.org.uk; OCR www.ocr.org.uk.

# 9

# Drama

*Art, though it must have the effect of nature,*
*is art because it is not nature . . .*

W. B. Yeats, *Advice to Playwrights*

## Drama and English

THE RELATIONSHIP BETWEEN ENGLISH AND DRAMA has rarely been straightforward. This is partly because the term 'drama' has been used in education to mean different things to different people. The study of plays has invariably been part of the English curriculum but the term 'drama' was more often used to refer to some form of improvised play-making. In the early days of child drama this usually meant having the pupils make up plays in groups to perform for each other at the end of the lesson. In the 1970s and 1980s, as the practice of drama in education became more sophisticated with the teacher intervening in the process to elevate the quality of the work, many English teachers saw the potential for a greater level of integration, using drama to increase pupils' understanding of literature (including scripted plays curiously enough), as a stimulus for writing or to explore a theme in greater depth.

It is not the intention to provide a detailed history of drama teaching in this chapter but some understanding of the debates and tensions which have been associated with the subject will provide a firmer basis for exploring its practical value. The main difference of opinion centred on the distinction made between 'theatre', which was thought to be largely concerned with communication between actors and an audience, and 'drama', which was seen as having more to do with the experience of the participants (Way 1967). Teachers who were familiar with the negative aspects of performance (pupils showing off and mouthing lines with no sense of purpose) were eager to embrace the new experiential approach, which sought to engage pupils in meaningful contexts demanding real thinking and feeling. Rather than seek to educate people in and about drama, the emphasis was on developing understanding *through* drama.

Instead of teaching pupils how to act, project their voices, design sets and use lights, the emphasis was on the content of the drama, on how to develop insight into human situations through active participation in play-making. Advocates of one or other approach tended to advance their argument by criticising the worst excesses of their opponents. Traditional theatre practice in schools was thought to be superficial, authoritarian and devoid of educational purpose; 'drama' was accused of being excessively indulgent, undisciplined and devoid of artistic form.

These extreme positions have now largely given way to a more inclusive view of drama which recognises that previous arguments were based on false polarities. Performing in the school play, sharing prepared sketches in the classroom and participating in spontaneous improvised work without an audience can be seen as different manifestations of drama which all have the same 'family resemblance'. Activities of this kind were not always grouped together. Whereas performing to an audience and working from a scripted play belonged in a separate category called 'theatre', improvised drama was more associated with play and dramatic playing. The change of emphasis in categorisation is so fundamental to this chapter that it is worth representing it in diagrammatic form to reinforce the point (Figure 9.1).

Early advocates of drama in education tended to draw on theoretical writings on child play and psychology rather than on the theatre. The emphasis was on the personal growth of the individual through creative self-expression and much less on coming to know an external world through its depiction in the art form. It is very easy to see why children's drama was more associated with playing than theatre because of surface appearances. Make-believe play in the home corner of the infant classroom and a small group of Year 8 pupils improvising a play about a bank robbery seem to have more in common with each other than with a performance of *King Lear*. However, the consequences of the conceptual realignment are far-reaching and will inform all the specific practical suggestions in the rest of this chapter. The change in the framework for categorising drama has the following consequences:

- All manifestations of drama in the classroom no matter how simple can draw on insights provided by the nature of drama as art, as in the examples below. Often drama (in the classroom or when used on training courses) is reduced to mere role-play or simulation and fails to exploit the full potential of the art form.

- Although drama appears to come naturally to pupils it should not be assumed they do not have to be taught techniques and conventions. It is reasonable enough to

From:

| | |
|---|---|
| theatre | improvised drama and role-play |
| scripted plays | play |
| dramatic art | dramatic playing |

To:

| | |
|---|---|
| theatre | play |
| scripted plays | dramatic playing |
| dramatic art | |
| improvised drama and role-play | |

**FIGURE 9.1**

argue that the motivation to engage in drama is part of human nature (a similar argument will be advanced in relation to poetry in Chapter 10) but drama as art is not as 'natural' as play.

■ The frequently quoted line from *Hamlet* that the purpose of drama is 'to hold a mirror up to nature', although partially true, is potentially misleading if taken too literally. It is self-evidently true in that drama draws on the human condition and is 'grounded in reality' (States 1994) but as an art form it is not entirely representational. Teachers sometimes assume that the purpose of pupils' drama is to replicate real life as far as possible whereas its value in understanding human situations often derives from the way in which it differs from real-life situations.

■ Whether drama is taught as a separate subject or incorporated into English it makes sense to include the study of plays, including Shakespeare, as part of the drama curriculum. The drama curriculum, which at one time was only concerned with creating and making plays, needs to include responding to dramatic art as well.

The term 'family resemblance' was used above to indicate that certain concepts resemble each other rather than share one or more identical characteristics. A minority of writers still persist in arguing that only performing scripted plays to an audience counts as 'dramatic art'. The effect of this type of argument is to view other types of classroom drama in a very reductive way, as mere 'role-play', which is very limiting. Common sense dictates that if a teacher is concerned to use drama in the classroom to explore a poem or short story, placing too much emphasis on performance may limit the involvement of some pupils, change the nature of the experience and simply be a waste of energy. It is a bit like arguing that every piece of writing a pupil produces in school must go on the wall or be published in a magazine instead of being shared informally.

The more experiential and improvised approach gave rise to a particular genre of 'process drama', which involves the workshop leader or teacher leading the group through the active creation of a fictional context using various drama techniques. The concept of 'applied theatre' is increasingly used to refer to active drama projects undertaken outside the traditional theatre context. Both developments have been heavily influenced by drama in education practice.

## Drama in the National Curriculum

The inclusion of drama in the National Curriculum for English is something of a mixed blessing. It does ensure that some participation in drama is now every pupil's entitlement; and in many schools it continues to flourish as a separate subject and is popular at GCSE and A level. In other schools, however, drama has ceased to be taught as a specialism and is subsumed under English. The purpose of this chapter will be to provide an insight into the way drama as an art form can function in English, while recognising at the same time that the educational potential for drama is considerably enhanced when it is given separate curriculum provision.

It is easy to understand why drama in school became associated more with the play of young children than with scripted plays and the theatre. As stated above, child drama often resembles dramatic playing and draws its popularity partly from that association. Some pupils find it embarrassing to participate in drama but in general it is a very popular activity in schools. For young adolescents, if they can overcome initial inhibitions, it provides an opportunity to experiment with roles and identities, which is arguably a developmental need at this stage (see Chapter 13). Drama is a very concrete activity involving intellect, body and emotions, which derives its power from the fact that it occurs in the present. If, instead of talking about the fight scene in *Romeo and Juliet*, the teacher starts to interview an eyewitness 'where were you standing at the time? . . . how did Mercutio get stabbed? . . . are you trying to hide something?' – the mood in the classroom and the level of attention and motivation will often increase dramatically.

It was suggested above that it is rather curious that 'drama' was sometimes used in the course of the English lesson in order to study plays. It can be seen now how this situation arose because the term 'drama' tended to refer exclusively to active play-making. As well as including work on scripted plays as a central aspect of the drama curriculum, active drama approaches can also be used in English in the following ways:

- as a 'way in' to a novel or short story;
- to develop understanding of themes and character in literature;
- in order to engage with a poem prior to or instead of analysis;
- as a stimulus for writing;
- as a means of developing language in all its forms by providing appropriate contexts for different uses, including standard English;
- as a way of exploring genre by transposing from one to another.

The revised National Curriculum places emphasis on the notion of 'compelling learning experiences', which involves the creation of relevant contexts for learning in order to engender genuine engagement. Drama is particularly well placed to meet these goals and one of the purposes of this chapter is to explain why that is the case. The drama strand has been strengthened in successive versions of the English National Curriculum. Currently it appears in each of the attainment targets at all key stages and as a significant strand in speaking and listening. A separate strand for 'drama, role-play and performance' is identified in the National Strategy Framework, with a worthy attempt to describe progression (Figure 9.2). The different level descriptors illustrate the challenge: the objectives for Year 9 are precisely the type of work that drama pioneers such as Heathcote and Bolton would have been pursuing with Key Stage 2 pupils.

| Year 7 | Year 8 | Year 9 | Year 10 | Year 11 |
|--------|--------|--------|---------|---------|
| explore ideas, texts and issues through a variety of dramatic approaches and conventions | use specific dramatic approaches and conventions in structured ways for effective exploration of ideas, texts, issues and themes | use a wide variety of dramatic approaches and conventions to analyse complex and challenging ideas, issues, themes and texts | compare, question and analyse complex and challenging ideas, texts, issues and themes by using a wide variety of dramatic approaches and conventions | draw on a repertoire of dramatic approaches and conventions to pursue original and inventive lines of thought when exploring ideas, texts and issues, and transfer them to other ideas and texts |

FIGURE 9.2

## Recognising drama at its best

In much of the contemporary literature on drama teaching there are often few grounds for discriminating between one sort of practice and another. At one time this was provided by a distinction between 'drama' (with its emphasis on engagement and quality of experience) and 'theatre' (with its emphasis on acting and performance) but, as suggested above, those divisions are simply not tenable. With the increased publication of lesson schemes on websites and from bodies such as the QCA it is useful to have some criteria for discriminating between one sort of practice and another.

The three concepts 'dramatic play', 'drama as art' and 'role-play/simulation' provide a helpful means of making a critical distinction between drama practices and understanding why drama teaching can be difficult. Drama has its origins in the dramatic play of young children – that is part of its appeal. Pupils are always liable to revert to having fun and playing in their drama, much to the frustration of teachers who are looking for serious commitment: the shipwreck culminates in a hilarious fight with sharks; the bank robbery descends into a chaotic shooting battle; the confrontation between friends ends in an unconvincing fist fight. This sort of reaction is often misinterpreted as bad behaviour. Sometimes it is, but more often it arises because the pupils do not know what else to do. This type of pupil reaction, which is not uncommon because it is 'natural', is not acknowledged often enough in the books on drama.

There is another type of practice in drama which could be termed 'role-play or simulation'. There is nothing wrong with role-play and many teachers who have witnessed pupils engage in the kind of dramatic playing described above would be delighted if pupils settled down to engage in some role-play in the classroom. As with all language and concepts there is no clear-cut distinction here – simple definitions are not helpful. However, role-play tends to be simple and two-dimensional (as opposed to drama as art, which has more depth). It involves the surface imitation of real-life situations such as a client asking for a loan from a bank manager. It is a very useful device in teaching – hence the title of this section 'recognising drama at its best' not 'recognising good drama'. The term 'simulation' is being used here to refer to activities which require participants to 'go through the motions' without any sense of complexity or depth. Thus a meeting in a town hall discussing a new bypass can be set up by giving pupils role cards: 'you are the shopkeeper and you object to the bypass because it will take business away'.

In contrast 'drama as art' seeks to weave in a greater level of depth and nuances of meaning. Suppose the client and bank manager knew each other when they were younger and one used to bully the other or stole his girlfriend – the acting now has a hidden dimension. The shopkeeper arguing against the bypass does not want to appear selfish so his argument is actually based on children's safety – although others in the meeting are suspicious of his real motives. Drama as art looks for 'multi-levels' and sub-texts whereas role-play and simulation tends to operate on surface levels of meaning. A tableau can operate as a form of simulation ('create a wedding photograph') or can

| Dramatic playing | Drama as art | Drama as role-play and simulation |
|---|---|---|
| Pupils have little sense of the consequences of their actions (people die and come alive easily). | Pupils are aware of the consequences of their actions. | The teacher tends to have more awareness of consequences of actions, structure and focus than the pupils. |
| There is little structure and goal (a drama about ghosts turns into a game of chase). | The activity has a structure and focus which works toward fulfilment. | Drama activities are more like 'exercises' which have some value but are limited in scope. |
| There may be absorption in the activity but no sense of dramatic form – it is often hectic (pupils may enjoy chasing and catching rats in a play based on the Pied Piper). | Dramatic focus and form serve to slow the action down to explore layers of meaning (e.g. pupils act out a scripted extract with real feeling in different ways to explore meanings). | Lesson plans tend to be mechanistic and there is limited room for negotiation with pupils or ownership by them. |
| The narrative, such as there is, develops according to the whim of the participants and is not constrained (the bank robbery moves quickly to chase and shoot out without any proper development). | Non-naturalistic techniques are used deliberately to explore situations in ways which are not possible in real life. | Pupils act out scripts rather woodenly without a sense of the complexity of meaning. |
| The 'drama' is superficially fun – it is about 'having a laugh'. | Pupils are aware of the constructed nature of drama. | The drama is largely seen as replicating real experience. |
| The value of the drama is related more to personal development than learning outcomes. | Pupils are engaged by the work and feel that they have some control over its content and direction. | Pupils do what they are told but they have no sense of how drama works. |
| | The learning outcomes with regard to the content are more exploratory and open-ended. | The drama can appear orderly but it is flat and feels to the pupils like going through the motions; they sometimes turn it into dramatic playing to liven it up. |
| | | The learning outcomes with regard to the content are clear-cut. |

**FIGURE 9.3**

tend more towards drama ('create a wedding photograph which shows a truth about the relationships', e.g. the best man and bride were former lovers).

The point here is not to create a sense of drama as something rarefied and elitist. This happened far too often in the 1970s and 1980s when demonstration drama lessons which were intensely moving were very hard to recreate in the classroom. Writing about drama should not make the subject too remote nor should its challenges be unacknowledged. The teaching point is that pupils can often find role-play and simulation activities dull, and they can become lacking in motivation. Dramatic playing can be superficially fun but in the end unrewarding. When evaluating suggestions for drama lessons it is a good idea to avoid recommendations which are likely to lead pupils too readily towards dramatic playing, such as when they are told to get into groups and act something out without sufficient support, focus and direction. It is also wise to avoid lessons which are unlikely to engage pupils' interest because they operate too mechanically and too much on the surface. Figure 9.3 provides a summary of the three concepts that should be interpreted as indicating tendencies rather than clear-cut categories. It is not the precise use of a term which is important but the underlying principles. Notice also that a sequence of lessons is likely to have some elements of role-play and even of dramatic playing; it is when these approaches dominate that the drama is not likely to reach its full potential.

## Exploring text through drama

Before the influence of drama in education in the 1970s and 1980s it was assumed that the only way of approaching literature in the context of drama was to act it out, whether it was a play, short story or extract from a novel. Some writers began to argue that this was the least useful way of working because it did no more than reinforce superficial knowledge of the text (working at the level of simulation). Much, however, depends on how successfully the dramatised version is realised. The value of acting out a plot well was sometimes underestimated; translating a text from one medium to another demands considerable understanding of content and form. It is important, however, to acknowledge that acting out the story is not the only way of using drama to approach a text and it is often desirable to work more obliquely in order to explore character, themes and aspects of the language.

No matter how uncomplicated the outer form of the drama (a simple piece of improvised dialogue in pairs or work on a few lines of script) the work can usually be given more depth by seeking to highlight or inject below the surface possible different levels of meaning.

### Tableau

Tableau or freeze frame is one of the most common conventions used in the classroom because it is so controlled. Asking pupils to use their bodies to depict a situation, a scene from a short story, an abstract concept or a moment from a play as a still image culminates in a moment of welcome stillness and silence. The technique also has other advantages: pupils are encouraged to think about the way meaning is conveyed through gesture and expression; it can be a useful way of depicting scenes which would otherwise be too difficult or sensitive to act; it slows the drama down and prevents the superficial onward rush of plot which tends to inhibit thinking.

Sometimes the full potential of tableau is not realised because the possibilities of exploring different levels of meaning is not fully exploited. The topic of bullying is one which lends itself to tableau because the approach avoids physical confrontation between pupils. Instead of or in addition to asking pupils to present a scene depicting bullying, their work on tableau might include:

- a scene in which the bullying would not at first be obvious to a casual observer;
- two scenes in which the bully in one is the victim in the other;
- a scene which shows on close inspection that one of the bullies is not comfortable with the role;
- a scene in which one of the bullies is a former friend;
- two scenes, one of which shows the consequences of the bullying;
- a scene which is accompanied by characters' thoughts which show that what is happening is different from the way things first appear.

In these cases drama is being used to probe below external appearances. As such it can provide a useful preliminary to reading a short story or a poem such as John Walsh's 'The Bully Asleep'. Tableau can be a valuable activity when reading in class because it demands that pupils' translate their understanding of the text into a concrete form. It can therefore consolidate pupils' grasp of plot and character. The search for different levels of meaning in drama can take place either through looking below the surface or through looking at different interpretations. Asking pupils to create a still image of a moment from the fight scene between Mercutio and Tybalt in Act 3, Scene 3 of *Romeo and Juliet* will require some understanding of the scene as a whole. However, asking them to depict the moment in both a serious and a light-hearted way will also focus their thinking on different interpretations and prepare them for contrasting theatre and film representations.

## Sub-text

Adding sub-text to lines of dialogue is another means of probing hidden meanings either with invented texts or extracts from scripts or novels. Pupils are asked to read the dialogue aloud with the thoughts of the characters included. This technique is used by Brian Friel in *Philadelphia, Here I Come*, in which the author has written two parts for the central character, one of which gives voice to his private thoughts throughout the play. A similar technique can be used with dialogue from a novel. In the following extract, adapted from Jane Austen's *Emma*, the characters are discussing their first meeting with Mrs Elton, whose truly odious character has yet to be revealed; Emma has her misgivings, in contrast to the more naïve Harriet. Attempting to supply Emma's accompanying thoughts is not straightforward and is likely to provoke discussion about her character:

| | |
|---|---|
| HARRIET: | Well, Miss Woodhouse, what do you think of her? – Is she not charming? |
| EMMA: | Oh! yes – very – a very pleasing young woman. |
| HARRIET: | I think her beautiful, quite beautiful. |
| EMMA: | Very nicely dressed, indeed; a remarkably elegant gown. |
| HARRIET: | I am not at all surprised that he should have fallen in love. |
| EMMA: | Oh! No – there is nothing to surprise one at all. A pretty fortune; and she came in his way. |

Sometimes sub-text can refer not just to the characters' private thoughts but to the intended meaning. Emma's final sentence, which gives an unromantic view of Elton's motives, is not likely to be picked up by Harriet although the meaning is clear to the reader. Asking pupils to create a sub-text which highlights intended meaning provides a complex view of language rather than seeing it as simple and transparent. The following example of a conversation between husband and wife (Fleming 1997) includes a possible intended meaning in brackets:

None of these shirts is ironed. (*Why aren't you doing your proper job as a wife?*)

It's still plugged in downstairs. (*Do it yourself – I'm not a slave.*)

I've got a really important meeting today. (*I'm the one who brings the money in – the least you can do is help.*)

I'll probably tidy another cupboard. (*I wish I had some fulfilment and interest in my life.*)

I'll be late tonight. (*I'm annoyed with you.*)

Fine. (*I'm annoyed with you.*)

Pupils can experiment with the way different interpretations of meanings and sub-text affect the acting and the way lines are delivered. The above would have to be acted very differently if the sub-text changed to convey good humour and affection.

Creating sub-text for a few lines of dialogue may also be a useful 'way in' to a scripted play. Pinter's play *Betrayal* opens with the following lines:

| | |
|---|---|
| JERRY: | Well . . . |
| EMMA: | How are you? |
| JERRY: | All right. |
| EMMA: | You look well. |
| JERRY: | Well, I'm not all that well really. |
| EMMA: | Why? What's the matter? |
| JERRY: | Hangover. |

The dialogue seems innocent and straightforward enough until we learn that Jerry and Emma have had an affair some time in the past and that Emma's husband was Jerry's best friend. Again, pupils can experiment with different ways of reading and acting just a few lines of dialogue (particularly in the case of this play using pauses) to convey different sub-texts.

Arthur Miller's *The Crucible* contains the following exchange near the beginning of the second act:

PROCTOR: If the crop is good I'll buy George Jacob's heifer. How would that please you?

ELIZABETH: Aye, it would.

PROCTOR (*with a grin*): I mean to please you, Elizabeth.

ELIZABETH (*it is hard to say*): I know it, John. (*He gets up, goes to her, kisses her. She receives it. With a certain disappointment, he returns to the table.*)

PROCTOR (*as gently as he can*): Cider?

ELIZABETH (*with a sense of reprimanding herself for having forgot*): Aye!

The play contains many scenes which are more obviously dramatic; the previous act culminated in hysteria caused by the 'discovery' of witchcraft in the village. However this simple domestic scene contains much tension below the surface of the words. This is the first time the audience has seen Elizabeth and Proctor together and both of them are living under the strain of his previous affair with the servant girl. Creating a sub-text for the characters' lines raises questions about the precise nature of their relationship at this point: there seems to be an excessive politeness, a straining after authenticity.

## Hot-seating

*Questioning in role* (or hot-seating) is an example of working obliquely on a text and is popular because, like tableau, it gives the teacher a considerable degree of control and is a fairly straightforward way of introducing role to a class. The simplest form of the technique involves one pupil or the teacher being questioned as a character from a play or novel. They can be asked about their motivation, attitude, relationships, etc. The approach can be made more oblique by questioning a minor rather than a main character, which is helpful when the pupils' knowledge is not sufficiently developed to allow them to be subjected to a full questioning in role. Thus, questioning the guards who lead Cordelia and King Lear away to prison near the end of the play or the servants who wait at the feast at which Banquo appears (*Macbeth*) does not assume a full knowledge of events and understanding of characters' motivation.

Using a teacher to play the role tends to work more successfully in a team-teaching context with the other teacher free to organise the questioning. Sometimes pupils are unable to get beyond the stage of asking very literal questions ('What were you wearing at the time of the murder?') instead of probing deeper issues. Teacher intervention may help to indicate some of the possibilities. Sometimes pupils become confused about the identity of the questioners and this is something which may need to be clarified at the start. Whether they are other characters, newspaper reporters or simply 'readers' of the text who do not have any other clearly defined role will influence the level of knowledge they are supposed to have. For example, are the characters from *Lord of the Flies* being questioned by someone who knows what happened on the island?

## Creating distance

Using an oblique approach in drama is one way of creating *aesthetic distance* and can be a useful way of approaching content which for some classes is too emotionally charged to be handled in a naturalistic way: mime, narration, tableau, ritual, reported action and using the perspective of minor characters are all ways of representing a funeral in drama (the scene at Juliet's grave, for example) other than simply acting it out. The objective of creating distance is contrary to the way drama in education was often conceived in the 1970s and 1980s when 'real' feeling and belief were often seen to be the central objects. Examples of indirect approaches include: holding a press conference given by Mark Antony after Caesar's death; tribunal investigating the deaths of Romeo and Juliet.

Working through *analogy* is another way of approaching a topic or text obliquely. Orwell's *Nineteen Eighty-Four* might be introduced by a whole-class improvisation designed to capture the sense of a repressive futuristic society. This could happen in the form of a meeting with teacher in role addressing a group of teenagers who have been arrested for holding an illegal meeting.

Juxtaposition refers to the technique of creating meaning by placing two or more dramatic scenes side by side or combining drama with text (poem, letter, novel extract) in a way which provides insight into both. If text is used, the stimulus for the work becomes incorporated into the final product to give it more aesthetic impact, as in the following examples:

- A newspaper article is contrasted with an improvised scene which provides an insight into the truth of what happened; for example, an article (and headline) which takes a high moral tone in condemning a young woman for shoplifting is contrasted with a scene which shows the domestic pressures which were part of the cause. Notice that placing the article and drama side by side avoids too much heavy didactic moralising; the meaning of the total 'performance' retains some ambiguity.

- A poem is set against a tableau, short piece of scripted dialogue or improvised scene suggested by one of the lines. Alternatively, a long narrative poem or ballad may be represented in tableaux with each group presenting one of the verses.

- Pupils present short scenes based on and incorporating the line, 'Telling lies to the young is wrong' (or other similar expression). The expression (or quotation) acts as more than just a stimulus. Incorporating it into the finished product will give more impact and influence the overall meaning.

- A paragraph from a police list of 'missing persons' is followed by a dramatised version of what might have caused the individual to leave home.

- A diary entry is accompanied by an enacted scene which shows a change (obvious or subtle) in the way it was remembered from the way it was recorded; for example, a new teacher writes self-deceptively about the first day spent in a new school.

The possibilities and limitations of using drama to explore a short story can be illustrated by the following example. Doris Lessing's 'Through the Tunnel' (which is often read at Key Stage 4) deals with the 'rite of passage' of an 11-year-old when he plucks up the courage to swim through an underground tunnel while on holiday with his mother. The story does not lend itself immediately to interpretation through drama; there are very few characters and much of the writing consists of intricate descriptions of the beach environment, the sea and the boy's efforts under the water. The density of the description, however, can make it difficult for some pupils to concentrate and engage with the text. Drama could be used to open up the theme rather than to act out the story, as in the following suggestions:

■ Before reading the story write the following extract from it on the board:

He was an only child, 11 years old. She was a widow. She was determined to be neither possessive nor lacking in devotion.

Ask the pupils to say what they understand by the phrases 'possessive' and 'lacking in devotion'. In pairs, pupils create short scenarios (either improvised or scripted) between parent and 11-year-old child which show examples of each.

■ Volunteers perform one of their short sketches and the parent in each case is hot-seated to determine more about his/her attitude to their child. The other pupils are asked to say whether the behaviour was reasonable or not. The discussion is directed towards the difficulties for parents of getting the right balance.

■ Pupils are given lines of dialogue from the end of the story and are asked to create a context, deciding what might have happened. They then read the lines in different ways to create different meanings, and include a sub-text. They explore different possible interpretations; for example, the parent intends to be caring while the child reacts to the concerns as being over protective:

'Have a nice morning?'
'Oh, yes, thank you.'
'You look a bit pale. How did you bang your head?'
'Oh, just banged it.'

The class are then given two extra lines of dialogue from the story and asked to speculate further about the context with this new information:

'I can stay under water for two minutes – three minutes at least.'
'Can you darling? Well I shouldn't overdo it. I don't think you ought to swim any more today.'

■ Pupils read the story. A selection could then be made from the following possible questions and tasks:

What kind of person is the mother? Is she too possessive?
To what degree might the mother's attitude be determined by the fact that she is a single parent?
Why is swimming through the tunnel so important to Jerry?
Underline any phrases which suggest that the boy has mixed feelings about his mother.
Underline any phrases from the descriptive passages which give a feeling that the environment is threatening.
Draw a sketch of the underground tunnel from the description.

■ Pupils ask questions of the teacher in role as first the mother and then the boy.

- Pupils create a collage of sounds and words (some derived from the actual text) which represent the boy's dream that night as he sleeps.

- The extract in which Jerry wants to join the older boys is re-read. Groups each create a tableau of a scene not related to this story which shows a young boy trying to join the company of an older crowd. Pupils share the tableaux and say what might be going though the younger boy's mind at that moment in time.

## Speaking and listening

Almost all uses of drama (apart from techniques such as mime) support speaking and listening. Arguments for its use to support this attainment target can be summarised as follows:

- It provides rich and varied contexts both formal and informal for using language.

- It can provide contexts for language use which are outside the normal sphere of reference of the pupils' lives.

- The contexts it provides are embedded with real feeling, intention and motivation.

- It can protect participants and offer contexts for experimenting with language. Without the use of drama the pupils by definition can only speak as themselves. In a fictitious context pupils can speak as politician, doctor, prisoner, young child or pensioner.

### Pairs work

It is easy to extol the value of drama but it is not always easy to translate theory into practical ideas. For the newcomer to drama the use of pairs work can be valuable.

Using pairs work effectively in the classroom means that the teacher must understand the way drama works. It also prevents some of the misunderstandings about how best to start drama with a class. Experience of the theatre can lead to assumptions that in order to initiate drama one always needs to cast characters, plan a scenario and direct the action but the structures can be much simpler than that:

- Get pairs to decide at the start who is A and who is B. It helps to assign roles without argument.

- Whatever the central exercise is (e.g. interviewing an eyewitness to a crash, questioning a character from a novel) use warm-up exercises before the main task. For example, in the case of the interview try having them interview someone who does not want to get involved first.

- When planning try to imagine what the pupils will actually do and say when they attempt the task. This is a good way of avoiding tasks which are too difficult. For example asking two pupils to discover a discarded jacket (as a way of recreating a character from the contents of the pockets) does not give enough tension. A scene in which one pupil is nervous about picking it up and tries to persuade the partner not to do so gives them more to work on.

- Mixing improvisation and script can help pupils get started. They can be asked to continue improvising after a few lines of dialogue or condense their improvisation into script.

- Remember that pupils find it easier to adopt roles which are close to their experience. Although it is important that the subject matter for drama is wide, it is often helpful to use familiar situations as starting points: a pupil is late for school and has a good reason but is reluctant to tell; one pupil is trying to persuade another to go to a concert which clashes with a family outing; a reporter is interviewing a parent about the failure to place speed bumps outside the school.

- When starting with pairs work 'explaining' and 'telling' are less appropriate than 'persuading' and 'finding out' because they tend to contain less tension.

- It helps to supply intention and motivation to the characters to move the exercise from role-play toward dramatic art. In the case of an interview: 'This job is important to you – if you don't get it you will have to cancel the holiday which your family has been expecting.'

- It often helps to supply an action to support the dialogue. 'The parent is washing the dishes while the child is trying to persuade them'; 'The teacher is marking while the pupil is trying to convince her that he did not do it'; 'The sergeant is cleaning his rifle while the soldier is trying to tell him he does not want to go on the mission'.

- Many pupils who are new to drama simply do not know how to get started. Try giving them the first line: 'I know you don't want to talk about this but I think we have to . . .' (Head of Year to pupil). 'Could I take a little of your time to ask you some questions – it is very important' (policeman on a house-to-house enquiry).

- Straightforward conflict situations tend to lead pupils to shallow, confrontational scenes. Try a 'no physical contact' rule or use telephone conversations.

- Share work in a non-threatening way by using an 'open door' or 'eavesdropping' technique whereby just a 30-second snatch of conversation is heard.

- Use modelling to demonstrate what is required. It sometimes helps to have the class watch the work of a particularly successful pair or for the teacher to demonstrate with a pupil in the class.

- When pupils are writing script (in pairs or in larger groups) it is often a good idea to restrict them to a specific number of lines to bring more focus to the work.

## Small-group drama

Instructing a class to get into groups in order to prepare and deliver a performance can lead to disaster if pupils do not know how to structure their work. A key to success is often providing sufficient focus:

- Trying to locate a drama in too many places may make it too complex for beginners. Instead place and time can be restricted. For example, a drama based on a prison can be limited to a five-minute scene taking place in the visitor's room.

- It can also help to give precise parameters for the work: restrict the use of physical space, give a time limit for preparation, ask for the scene to be enacted without words, without physical contact.

- Use a drafting and feedback approach to preparing the work. Pupils can also be encouraged to share 'rough drafts' which can be subject to critical advice using a style of 'forum theatre' in which the audience make suggestions and direct the actors.

- Using media contexts (often incongruous ones) can be useful for facilitating speaking and listening activities because the structures are ready-made; for example, a blind date representation of Bathsheba and the suitors from *Far from the Madding Crowd*; a documentary account of the events of the Pied Piper with reconstructions, interviews and studio discussions. Press conferences, chat shows, reality TV shows are all formats with which pupils tend to be familiar.

- Encourage pupils to work out exactly how the drama will begin and end. When pupils perform their planned improvisations they often are unable to bring them to a conclusion.

- A prepared scene can be placed side by side with a piece of text (provided for them or written by them) to enhance meaning; the reading of a negative school report is set against a scene from the pupil's home life.

## Monologues

Monologues are more challenging for pupils but they are a useful focus for speaking and listening assessment purposes because by definition they are delivered by one individual. It helps for pupils to read and study examples of monologues (e.g. those by Alan Bennett) to understand the potential for monologues to convey subtle nuances of meaning. It is worth pointing out that the term 'monologue' is often used within dramas whenever a character has an extended speech (e.g. Lucky's speech in *Waiting for Godot*) or when they are alone on stage (as in the delivery of soliloquy). Here I am confining the term 'monologue' to refer to moments when the drama is delivered by just one person.

It is easier for monologues to be scripted in advance because improvising an extended piece is difficult. However, the monologue should not be seen as just a matter of reading aloud. The monologue can gain more dramatic impact in the following ways:

- Actions are included (e.g. teenager packing her case to leave home; prisoner in a cell reflecting on the events which got him there; old person in a home).

- Attempts are made to convey the emotional content through tone and volume.

- Direct speech by other characters is enacted.

- The monologue is embedded in a context (e.g. the diary of a bully's victim).

Notice that the monologue embodies the device widely used in Greek tragedy of reporting off-stage action. It can be useful therefore when dealing with themes that might be difficult to enact directly, for example the theme of war is addressed through one soldier's monologue; an account of a riot is given by one eyewitness.

## Meetings

*Conducting meetings* in a dramatic context provides another common method of taking an indirect approach to a theme or text. Often the technique appears to replace action with mere discussion: instead of becoming ghosts or prisoners, the pupils take the roles of investigators of the supernatural who are planning their next mission or guards who are planning how to increase security. This sort of work limits the potential for dramatic action and should not be overused but may provide a useful starting point for a drama project or a useful initial stage for a teacher who is introducing role-play for the first time. Creating an opportunity for talk in a make-believe context (as opposed to having a discussion or debate) can be liberating for pupils because it allows them the protection of the role to express views which are not necessarily their own. Artificial conflicts can be injected rather than relying simply on pupils' own opinions. In order to elevate such meetings from a simple role-play or simulation it helps to inject an element of dramatic tension; for example, some people at the meeting have hidden motives for their point of view which are not immediately made public.

## Drama and integrated planning

The revised National Curriculum provides more scope for innovative planning. Drama is particularly well-placed to support links between subjects because it can operate with any content. For example a project with a Year 7 based on the history of a local church might involve ICT, History, RE and English but could be framed with a 'mantle of the expert approach'.

## Mantle of the expert

This technique was created by Heathcote, who uses it in quite complex ways (Heathcote and Bolton 1995). It involves having the pupils take the role of 'experts' who are engaged in an enterprise, for example running a factory or an advisory service for some distant clients who never actually appear in the drama but communicate by letter or messenger. The curriculum learning takes place through the expert role when the pupils are called on to solve some problem or offer some advice to the clients. However, the key to this technique, as used by Heathcote, is that the expertise of the participants is established in detail and at great length before the engagement in the central focus of the work. Thus in the case of the history of the church project the pupils would be established in their fictitious roles (perhaps as architects, builders or explorers from outer space) before they are set to work on the church itself.

## Writing plays

An oblique approach is also a useful way of introducing *playwrighting*. Without constraints pupils are often too ambitious in what they try to achieve or are simply overwhelmed by the task. Working within clear guidelines may be liberating rather than the reverse; using reported action rather than trying to create intensely dramatic scenes may be more manageable, as in the following three examples (Fleming 1997: 153). The intention here is that the pupils are given the scenario and the first few lines of dialogue to get them started:

■ A family are at breakfast when a letter arrives. The person who receives the letter tries at first to conceal its contents from the others. When the contents are finally revealed the consequences for the whole family are considerable.

> MRS JONES: That sounds like the postman – could you see what it is?
> (*John leaves and returns moments later.*)
> JOHN: It's for Julie (*handing over a letter*).
> JULIE: Oh, thanks. I'll open it later.

■ A group of young people have planned for a bet to stay in a 'haunted house' overnight. One of the party has left the room where they are planning to sleep in order to go to the toilet. The scene begins with the return of the character who is very obviously shaken and ends with the group deciding to leave the house.

> BEN: She's been ages.
> ANGELA: She's got more courage than me staying out that long.
> (*The door opens and Jackie comes in obviously upset and frightened.*)
> MIKE: What's the matter with you?

■ The arrival of a stranger in a small village pub shatters the tranquillity of the village because of the news which he gradually reveals in the course of the scene.

> GEORGE: Not many strangers find their way to this pub when they first come here, it's so out of the way.
> STRANGER: It's not my first time here.
> GEORGE: I don't think I've met you before, have I?
> STRANGER: We never actually met but I remember you very well.

■ A monologue or soliloquy is spoken while the rest of the group present a tableau which throws light on its content. The monologue may be one written by the pupils themselves or taken from published works (e.g. by Alan Bennett).

■ Different groups are given a few lines of script and they invent and present different possible contexts and interpretations.

■ Different groups are given a few lines of script and the same context but each group gives the words a different meaning by changing the tone.

## Teaching Shakespeare

It is odd to think that some years ago the standard (often only) way of teaching Shakespeare was reading aloud in class with pauses for teacher explanation of meaning. The fact that so many people developed a love of Shakespeare even with uninspired teaching says something about the power of the work itself. Techniques derived from drama in education, theatre and voice training can be used to build up a variety of approaches to Shakespeare texts which are active and accessible to pupils of all ages and abilities. Some new teachers who have been inspired by the rarefied atmosphere of an adult workshop or by reading practical suggestions in one of the many books on the subject become disappointed when the ideas fall flat in the classroom. It is important, however, not to lose faith. Sometimes it helps to explain the purpose of the approach in general terms to pupils so that they do not feel they are just being asked to jump from one rather strange activity to another with little sense of meaning or direction. New teachers sometimes inadvertently send signals that they are not sure about what they are asking pupils to do for the obvious reason that they have not as yet experienced personal success in using the techniques. It is important to try to have confidence and be firm in giving directions and tasks.

Approaches to Shakespeare teaching use familiar drama techniques such as tableau and hot-seating but also incorporate elements such as choral speaking. One of the central aims is often to familiarise pupils with the language of the plays and for them to respond to its rhythms and images prior to any detailed attempt at understanding and analysis of its content. The pupils therefore need to be prepared to engage in tasks without necessarily having a full sense of the context, which is contrary to the way drama usually works.

### Choral speaking

A typical workshop designed to work on Juliet's soliloquy in *Romeo and Juliet* Act 4, Scene 3 might take the following form:

- The speech is broken up and different lines distributed to individual members of the class.

- The extract breaks up naturally into small sections of a line or two, for example:

  What if it be a poison which the friar
  Subtly hath minist'red to have me dead.

- It is a good idea to identify the lines in sequence by placing a number on the back.

- Pupils are asked to speak their lines in different ways (loudly, softly, quickly, slowly) to thoroughly familiarise themselves with the words. They all speak at once.

- They divide into pairs and use the two extracts as if they make sense as part of a conversation. This is continuing to make the lines familiar but it is also helping the pupils to savour the language and experiment with tone without worrying about meaning.

- The pupils stand in a circle and speak the lines in order several times (e.g. starting softly and getting progressively louder).

- They form groups of three and try to create one or more still images to go with particular lines, for example:

Come, vial.
What if this mixture do not work at all. (*Juliet holds a cup in front of her and looks at it intensely.*)
And, in this rage, with some great kinsman's bone
As with a club, dash out my desp'rate brains.
(*An angry figure makes to strike Juliet as she lies on the ground.*)

- The teacher explains any meanings which are not clear and the class discuss how difficult images could be conveyed. The context is explained: before taking the sleeping draught Juliet has terrifying images of what might happen when she is placed alive in the vault.

- One pupil as Juliet is placed at the centre of a group while the other group members start to move closer and closer to her, whispering selected phrases from the speech: 'fest'ring in his shroud . . . loathsome smells . . . bloody Tybalt'. The figure in the centre shouts Juliet's line 'This do I drink to thee' in different ways to symbolise her determination to overcome her fears.

- The class read the speech through again, this time from memory, with atmospheric music introducing the speech and playing softly in the background.

## Acting out sections of the play

It can be quite demanding for pupils at Key Stage 3 to act out large sections of Shakespeare. Books or scripts get in the way and teachers often do not feel they have enough time for pupils to memorise lines. Sometimes the acting demands are too much and the results are unconvincing, although the play within a play from *A Midsummer Night's Dream* is an exception because it lends itself to burlesque. An alternative is to condense a scene into a few lines (this is a valuable exercise in itself) in much the way a film director might edit the script (the animated version is a good example). Thus the scene in *Romeo and Juliet* (towards the end of Act 3, Scene 5) in which Juliet refuses to marry might be condensed into the following lines which are easy to learn and can then be acted out more convincingly:

| CAPULET: | Have you delivered to her our decree? |
| LADY CAPULET: | Ay sir but she will none. I would the fool were married to her grave. |
| CAPULET: | Go with Paris to St Peter's church |
| | Or I will drag thee on a hurdle thither. |
| JULIET: | Good father I beseech thee on my knees. |
| CAPULET: | Young baggage. My fingers itch. |
| NURSE: | God in heaven bless her! |

## Mime or exaggerated physical actions

Mime is useful for helping pupils get to grips with long speeches or for visualising how scenes might be staged. Pupils are given an extract which has a fair amount of implied or explicit physical action. They are asked to think of actions to go with each sentence or even phrase. The pupils experiment with the actions using them in different combinations: saying and doing the action as well as saying the text; doing the action and saying the text; say the text without saying the action or physically doing it. Pupils have to be prepared to throw themselves into this activity without feeling self-conscious or silly. Mercutio's Queen Mab speech is a good example of one which lends itself to this treatment; on stage or on film the actor often uses actions when delivering the speech.

## Identifying implicit stage directions

Shakespeare's plays largely embedded the actions in the dialogue. Full stage directions developed only in the nineteenth century. Asking pupils to identify stage directions in the dialogue is a reminder that the meaning does not just reside in the language spoken and that plays were written for performance. It can be helpful to distinguish between essential and probable directions. For example, 'Do you bite your thumb sir?' is fairly unambiguous. The scene in which Katherina has tied up Bianca in *The Taming of the Shrew* is a good one for identifying the implied action.

## Acting out dialogue in different ways

Groups are given a short sequence of simple dialogue and asked to try out different ways of acting it out. They do not change the actual words but can change the tone, pace and actions which accompany the words to change the meaning in subtle ways. The exchange between Macbeth and Banquo after the witches have appeared for the first time can be changed in the way it is read to provide different interpretations of their state of mind at this stage in the play.

## Creating the sub-text

In the exchange between Macbeth and Banquo, Shakespeare supplies the thoughts of the characters in the form of asides. Pupils can be asked to supply the 'asides' to go with other sections of dialogue. This is best done in groups of four with two people articulating the words spoken and two more providing the thoughts which accompany the words. This highlights the way in which meaning is not 'present' simply in the words spoken but is a function of the context and non-verbal signs.

## Further reading

For an overview of theory and practice in drama see Fleming (2003) *Starting Drama Teaching* and the further reading sections in that book. Contrasting perspectives on teaching drama can be found in Hornbrook (1989) *Education and Dramatic Art* and Bolton (1992) *New Perspectives on Classroom Drama*; the latter includes examples of lessons. For books on teaching Shakespeare see Reynolds (1991) *Practical Approaches to Teaching Shakespeare* and Gibson (1990) *Secondary School Shakespeare*. There is a section on 'Drama and Shakespeare' in Clarke, Dickinson and Westbrook (2004).

## Resources

Neelands (1990) *Structuring Drama Work* contains a comprehensive guide to conventions used in drama teaching. Fleming (1997) *The Art of Drama Teaching* discusses numerous drama techniques, each illustrated by an extract from a scripted play. For examples of sequences of lessons see Kempe and Ashwell (2000) *Progression in Secondary Drama* and Bennathan (2000) *Developing Drama Skills*. Kempe (1990) *The GCSE Drama Coursebook* is helpful for approaching scripted plays. The Cambridge School Shakespeare editions contain many practical ideas for teaching Shakespeare. The English and Media Centre publishes a range of useful resources for drama, for example *The Drama Book and Videos* and *Twelfth Night Video Pack*.

# 10

# Poetry

*Poetry's unnat'ral; no man ever talked poetry
'cept a beadle on boxin' day*

Mr Weller in Charles Dickens's *Pickwick Papers*

## The concept of 'poetry'

**THERE IS AN ARGUMENT** for saying that of all the different forms and uses of language, it is poetry which is the most natural. This may seem to be a strange and controversial claim because one of the characteristic features of poetry, that it is language at its most dense and aesthetically crafted, seems to suggest the opposite view. However, our earliest experiences of language as children could be said to be primarily poetic. A child takes a delight in sounds, rhythms, rhymes, images and textures without being particularly concerned with propositional meaning. The point is made convincingly by Mattenklott (1996: 13):

> Hans Magnus Enznesberger, the editor of an anthology of children's verse, *Allerleirauh* published in the 1960s, refers to children's verse as *prima poesis*, the first poetry in an individual's life. It accompanies the child from birth, with verses for nappy-changing, bathing and finger games, to the later counting rhymes, word rhymes and jingles which are all part of the independent games of older children. Common to all these forms of poetry is their direct relationship to the body, to movement and gesticulation . . . Other common characteristics of this poetry lie in the predominance of rhythm, alliteration, rhyme and euphony over meaning. In most cases the verses are sheer nonsense.

Young children, without being obsessed by rationality or logic, find pleasure in repetitions, the articulation of sounds and the way words create powerful images; they are not too concerned why it is that the little boy down the lane should need a bag of wool, nor why the dish decided to run away with the spoon. As Preen (1999) has pointed out, children do not ask, in response to 'Humpty Dumpty', why on a wall, why not a fence? They respond implicitly to the 'paired contrasts . . . the rise of the first line opposed to the cadence and anticlimax of the second; the galloping third line balanced by the braking to a halt of the heavily stressed last line' (ibid.: 1). It is a delicate pedagogical challenge to ensure that explicit knowledge enhances rather then detracts from enjoyment and appreciation. This is as true of poetry teaching as it is of other aspects of English.

Even if there are objections to the notion that poetry is 'natural', it is difficult to deny that poetry has very strong affinities with the child's earliest experiences of the spoken word. For this reason, the frequently quoted view that poetry tends to be unpopular in schools is somewhat surprising. In her article Mattenklott states that in Germany 'young people, adolescents and students at universities, even those who study literature, tend to reject poetry. They find that they cannot relate to poetic form and language, and even at times find them tiresome' (1996: 13). In England in the 1980s similar views were expressed in various reports (by the Assessment of Performance Unit and HMI), books and research papers. Whether the same is true now is difficult to judge. There are many reasons for a greater level of optimism: there has been a steady stream of appealing, modern anthologies for schools; innovative methods for teaching poetry have been developed and widely disseminated; there is a more accepting cultural climate which makes poetry seem less élite (poems on the underground, public performances, publication of the nation's favourite poems, etc.). The erosion of barriers between high art and popular culture is reflected in the increasing recognition of such items as song lyrics, especially rap, as poetry. Many pupils do enjoy the relative freedom of expression and response offered by poetry but many also find this the most 'difficult' aspect of the English curriculum.

A traditional approach to teaching poetry involved the teacher reading the poem aloud and then, through a question and answer session, leading the pupils to an appropriate understanding of the 'meaning' of the work and an appreciation of the formal poetic devices used to create effect. The method is described in the following extract:

> Such a stance dictates that a teacher's role is to conduct the reading of the poem, and hope somehow that his or her reading will be appropriated by pupils. It dictates a classroom procedure which operates primarily through a process of inductive questioning by the teacher and a corresponding developing sense of the poem by the pupils. The teacher is in charge of the meaning that evolves, and the text, rather than the readers' generally unverifiable (it seems) impressions and intuitions, must be adduced in support of the meaning that is 'unlocked' through the teacher's questioning.
>
> (Dias and Hayhoe 1988: 7)

This approach was widely criticised in the literature of the 1970s and 1980s because such methods emphasised analysis at the expense of response, and did not give pupils enough responsibility for creating their own meanings. Instead, teachers were advised to use methods such as encouraging pupils to discuss poems in small groups and reading poems aloud without too much analysis in order to emphasise pure enjoyment. Active, directed approaches to reading, such as cloze exercises, sequencing a cut-up text, inventing a title for the poem, were also frequently employed. Ideas of this kind did much to enliven the poetry lesson but in the wrong context these methods could be just as alienating and bewildering for pupils as the method of inductive questioning so readily condemned.

The problem with the concept 'poetry' is that it does not describe one simple category of text; it is not possible to offer necessary and sufficient conditions for saying exactly what is to count as 'poetry'. A less philosophical way of making the same point is to say that it is difficult to say very much that claims to be true of all poems for which exceptions cannot be found.

Some modern poems, such as William Carlos Williams' 'This Is Just to Say' with its simple 'prosaic' language and lack of imagery, rhythm and rhyme, appear to flout normal expectations of what poetry should be. Sometimes it is difficult to say to which category particular texts should be assigned. For example, which of the following can be said to count as 'poems': nursery rhymes, song lyrics, acrostics, raps, ballads, limericks? In what category should we place 'poetic prose'? Should concrete poetry really count as poetry? Deceived by language into assuming that there is an entity called 'poetry' which has a single essence, writers often give practical advice about ways of teaching poetry which is not universally applicable to all poems. For example, whereas it is often true that readers need time to respond to poems, this is not always the case; many poems are appropriate for reading aloud and responding with instant reactions (many of the humorous, lighter poems in contemporary anthologies for schools are of this kind). It is also not helpful to place too much emphasis on a relativist view (i.e. that readers can never be wrong in their reading of a poem), for this line of argument does not apply to all poems. Take the opening of Donne's 'The Extasie' as an example:

> Where, like a pillow on a bed,
> A pregnant banke swel'd up, to rest
> The violet's reclining head,
> Sat we two, one anothers best.
> Our hands were firmly cimented
> With a fast balme, which thence did spring,
> Our eye beams twisted, and did thread
> Our eyes upon one double string.

Once the reader gets past the slightly unfamiliar syntax, it is not difficult to grasp the context that one lover is addressing another while sitting on a river bank (not for example on a bed). That context is not a matter of opinion. On the other hand it is not necessary to have knowledge of all the references and conceits in the poem to respond to its impact. It is not necessarily that difficult, particularly for an adolescent, to grasp the significance of the phrase 'our hands were firmly cimented with a fast balme' without notes on the associations of the words 'cimented' and 'balme' in alchemy (in fact notes often appropriately just give the latter as meaning 'sweat').

Faced with a poem like 'The Extasie' it is easy to understand, while not necessarily agreeing with, the inductive question and answer ('guess what is in teacher's head') method of teaching because there seems so much that the pupils need to know. A teacher has to decide how much social and contextual background is needed when approaching a new author. In this case knowledge of ideas related to cosmology, alchemy, chemistry and beliefs about the soul may extend appreciation of this poem but are not essential. The concept of 'guided reading' is appropriate for a poem of this kind when paradoxically some direction is needed to facilitate a free and genuine response. That guidance could begin before the initial reading with a brief introduction which explains the simple context that this is a love poem about two lovers on a river bank. It is also appropriate to let pupils know that the poem sounds more complex than it is and that they will be able to get some sense of the meaning and get a feel for the rhythms and tone without understanding every word and allusion. After a powerful reading aloud by the teacher the directed reading tasks could then ask pupils in pairs to highlight lines and images within categories such as:

- key lines – those which are central to its meaning;
- lines or images which suggest union (these can then be categorised into spiritual and physical union);
- contrasts to which reference is directly made or implied in the poem;
- lines which suggest an argument is being presented;
- sections of the poem which indicate any change of tone.

The discussion prompted by pupils' findings will mean that in practice these categories will overlap and some flexibility will be necessary for them to flow from one to the other. The poem could then be performed by pairs as a dialogue between two lovers, first in its entirety and then condensed into a small number of lines. It is at this point when the poem is starting to become familiar and resonant that more detailed work on the text may be appropriate. Each pair of pupils can be given two or three lines of the poem to research in textual notes and report back, expanding the notes by their own thoughts on the images and associations. This poem with its ideas about union, love, sex and its celebration of human physicality has the potential to move young people profoundly.

There have been notable definitions of poetry such as Coleridge's 'the best words in the best order' or Eliot's view that it is not 'a turning loose of emotion but an escape from emotion'. Genuine poetry is 'conceived and composed in the soul' (Gray) and consists of 'noble grounds for noble emotions' (Ruskin). Poetry 'says one thing and means another' (Riffaterre 1978).

These aphorisms and descriptions provide useful insights into the genre but do not provide any definitive means of saying what is to count as poetry. Some poems are primarily concerned with structure, narrative or ideas rather than the texture of language. A 'found' poem is made up of snippets of language (bits of conversation, graffiti, notices) which are not necessarily 'poetic'. We might want to agree with Johnson, who said of poetry that 'it is much easier to say what it is not. We all know what light is but it is not easy to tell what it is' (Boswell 1953: 76).

The somewhat misguided search for a simple definition becomes more complicated because sometimes the term 'poetry' is used in an evaluative way. To say of a piece of text that it is 'not poetry' is simply to state that in the opinion of the reader it is not 'good' poetry. This approach may serve to banish all sorts of doggerel, valentine's verses, slogans and maudlin rhyming couplets from the category but does not help when disagreements occur about the quality of individual texts. The danger in restricting the definition in this way is that pupils' attempts to write poetry may need to be subject to unreasonable criteria.

An alternative approach to defining poetry is to place emphasis on the reader rather than on the text. The idea here is that any text could be read as poetry, depending on the stance the reader takes towards it.

Simply laying a piece of prose out in the form of a poem may change the way the reader approaches the text. Take for example an ordinary statement about a city that might be found in a guide book. If these lines are set out not as prose but as poetry the effect on the reader (particularly the experienced reader who understands at least implicitly the different genres) is likely to change. The reader will bring different expectations to the text and will not necessarily take its meaning at face value. The change in form may invite the reader to think differently about the meaning:

> This is a city
> For all seasons.
> Though
> The best time
> Is no doubt the summer.
> The days are short
> In the autumn,
> And the cold descends
> In the winter.

This is unlikely to strike the reader as very impressive poetry but if the words are encountered in this way, as poetry rather than prose, they are more likely to invite speculation about meaning and the poet's intention. Is this meant to be a metaphor for life? Is it an invitation to 'seize the day' because life is so brief? Perhaps this interpretation is reflected in the form of the poem with its short, staccato lines. The meaning is not inherent in the words themselves but is a function of the context, the form and the stance of the reader.

A shopping list may take on more meaning and significance if it is read as a poem, if the reader sees in it an ironic comment on domesticity. As part of a research project on perceptions of poetry, pupils were asked to say whether a number of texts could be described as poetry or not (Fleming 1992). The chosen texts included three versions of a shopping list (Figure 10.1).

Ninety-two per cent of the pupils identified the rhyming shopping list as a poem as opposed to the 32 per cent who thought 'A Woman's Work' could also be described in that way; they seemed to be more influenced by form than content (a result which was replicated elsewhere in the research). In view of this, it was somewhat surprising that as many as 10 per cent were prepared to say that the simple non-rhyming shopping list was a poem. It is likely however that their responses were influenced by having read 'A Woman's Work' first; if they were presented with the simple list first it is unlikely that any of them would have described it as a poem. The view that determining what counts as poetry has more to do with the stance which the reader takes towards the text than any intrinsic characteristics of the text itself is persuasive, but the argument is in danger of being circular for the reader's stance is partly determined by whether the text is seen

| | A Woman's Work | |
|---|---|---|
| Two pounds of sugar<br>A packet of PG Tips<br>A pint of milk<br>Twenty Players<br>Box of matches<br>A packet of Daz<br>Light bulbs<br>Tissues<br>Half a pound of mince | Two pounds of sugar<br>A packet of PG Tips<br>A pint of milk<br>Twenty Players<br>Box of matches<br>A packet of Daz<br>Light bulbs<br>Tissues<br>Half a pound of mince | Two pounds of sugar<br>A pint of milk, some tea<br>If you buy two packets<br>You get another free.<br>Half a dozen eggs<br>And a cotton reel of thread<br>Half a pound of butter<br>And a crusty loaf of bread. |

FIGURE 10.1

as a poem. The question still remains as to why a particular individual would read a text in this way other than the fact that it appeared in a poetry anthology or that the lines 'do not go to the end of the line'.

The difficulty of describing precise categories is true not just of the concept of 'poetry' but of language in general. It was a central aspect of Wittgenstein's later philosophy (and a tenet of much twentieth-century thought) that words acquire their meaning by use rather than by any simple relationship with reality. Words such as 'art' and 'poetry' may appear to describe discrete categories but their relationship with reality is not fixed and determined. All of this discussion may seem purely academic unless the practical implications are explored. These can be summarised as follows:

- It is a mistake to recommend practical methods of teaching poetry which may be only appropriate for particular poems or types of poems.

- Acceptance of a broad category may mean that the teaching of poetry can usefully be extended to include advertising jingles, song lyrics, headlines, snippets of conversation, etc.

- It is not necessary to provide pupils with a narrow definition of poetry – this is a misguided approach to language and will not lead to helpful conclusions.

- It is on the other hand useful to examine the concept of 'poetry', which may be a source of bewilderment or difficulty for pupils unless the term itself is subject to some discussion.

There has been a change of emphasis in the academic writing about the teaching of poetry in the last 10 years, with less concern about the neglect of poetry and more about its assessment (Benton 2000). Examination boards have been quick to support teachers in helping to fulfil National Curriculum requirements, particularly in the use of pre-release anthologies that obviate some of the negative impact of examinations in literature. The increased tendency to assess poetry in examinations is a cause for concern for many teachers. As Dymoke (2003: 170) has argued, 'poetry is becoming increasingly, even deadeningly, linked with critical responses on terminal examination papers'. She also suggests that in order for poetry assessment to be both viable and of value for the young writer, pupils should be writing poetry on a regular basis, developing poetry portfolios, experimenting with models making their own choices and reflecting on their work and that of others (ibid.).

Although there has been a change of emphasis from neglect of poetry and more concern with the negative effects of terminal examinations, one issue that has remained constant has been the view that pupils continue to find poetry difficult.

## Poetry does not have to be difficult

It will be worth examining why poetry is often described by pupils as being the aspect of English they find most difficult, before looking at approaches to teaching poetry in the classroom. Steiner (1978) identified several types of difficulties which can be encountered when reading poetry. These may be adapted to make more appropriate links with the practicalities of secondary school teaching.

Some texts present difficulties for pupils simply because they do not understand the vocabulary, allusions or references in them. That does not mean that pupils need to be able to understand every word before making a response to a poem but their lack of comprehension may present barriers which prevent further engagement with the work. This may seem to be a fairly obvious point but can easily be forgotten in the classroom. As described above, the emphasis, derived from reader response theory, on the role of the pupils in creating meaning meant that small-group discussion without teacher intervention was recommended in preference to traditional question and answer sessions. *Young Readers Responding to Poems* (Benton *et al.* 1988) contains some very convincing examples of the value of this methodology. However, without an appropriate choice of poem and without supplying necessary background information which will allow pupils' discussions to operate within appropriate parameters, they may set off on completely the wrong track. Consider the poem 'Mary, Mary Magdalene' by Charles Causley, which begins:

> Mary, Mary Magdalene
> Lying on the wall,
> I throw a pebble on your back.
> Will it lie or fall?

It helps us to know that on the wall of a church in Launceston in Cornwall is a figure of the saint and that the children of the town say that a stone lodged on the figure's back will bring good luck. This simple example is chosen because it is so easy to imagine ingenious pupils thinking up possible explanations without the introductory information. Some readers might argue that their suggestions are as valid as any others. However, there is a pragmatic rather than simply theoretical dimension which needs to be considered. It is not enough to argue that their subjective response should be respected if the pupils themselves are likely to recognise later that they were wrong. In that case the hidden message then becomes for the pupils that poems are problems or puzzles to which someone else usually has the key. Much modern poetry is deliberately ambiguous and invites the reader to speculate about meaning but not all poems are of that kind. When pupils are invited to exercise 'free play' in relation to the meaning and interpretations of poems, appropriate choices of text need to be made.

When choosing a poem for small-group discussion the teacher also needs to decide what kind of background and textual information is necessary. New Criticism may have marginalised the importance of historical and social contexts in relation to literature but reader response theory is in danger of doing the same if it is wrongly interpreted as meaning that pupils should be given no guidance at all. The Cambridge Poetry Workshop has some useful examples of ways in which pupils can be given information about particular poems while still leaving room for personal response. For example, they are told that the theme of the poem 'In Memory of God' by Jenny Joseph is 'conservation' before reading it, but are given room for personal response. All of the poems in the anthology are preceded by activities which are intended to engage the reader in the theme, content or 'emotional territory' of the work prior to reading.

Finding a 'way in' to a poem is sometimes important because the emotional content of the poem does not strike a chord with the reader; this represents another type of 'difficulty'. There may be a surface grasp of objective, semantic meaning but there is no subjective engagement with its deeper significance. This may be true of all readers, not just pupils in school. Response to any text is partly determined by the personal experiences which are brought to bear on the meaning: a reading of a poem about death will have more impact after a recent bereavement. Auden's poem which begins 'Stop all the clocks, cut off the telephone' had considerable impact in the film *Four Weddings and a Funeral* because of the creation of a context which determined the response. It is little wonder then that poems based on such themes as cruelty to animals, school and friendship are common in anthologies for pupils because the content is readily accessible. Yeats's 'Lake Isle of Innisfree' has few contingent difficulties (words and allusions which have to be explained) but it may have little impact unless the reader can relate to its central theme: the yearning to return to a place of tranquillity, peace and harmony (perhaps teachers will relate more readily to the poem than pupils):

> And I will have some peace there, for peace comes dropping slow,
> Dropping from the veils of the morning to where the cricket sings.

(1994: 57)

Notice this is not just a matter of relating to the content; only if one can engage with the emotional impact of the idea can one respond to the falling cadence of the line, the repetition of 'dropping' and the images suggesting peace. Of course pupils may readily write objectively about these features in an assignment or for examination purposes but that is a different matter.

Being 'grabbed' by a poem is not the same as writing technically about its impact but it is important not to think that the two are necessarily in opposition. Nor is the message here that there are any simple, modern teaching devices which can guarantee that all pupils will respond in a genuine way. One virtue of the traditional O level literature examination was that the rote learning of lengthy quotations and revision notes sometimes brought a level of familiarity which resulted in a deep response to the text almost in spite of, rather than because of, the teaching. In *Angela's Ashes* (McCourt 1996: 223) the naive but authentic response by the young boy Frank to Alfred Noyes's 'The Highwayman' is captured in a poignant account. A verse is recited each day to him while he is in hospital by a young girl, Patricia, who dies before she reaches the end of the poem.

> Every day I can't wait for the doctors and nurses to leave me alone so I can learn a new verse from Patricia and find out what's happening to the highwayman and the landlord's red-lipped daughter. I love the poem because it's exciting and almost as good as my two lines of Shakespeare. The redcoats are after the highwayman because they know he told her, I'll come to thee by moonlight, though hell should bar the way.

Learning by heart is less common in schools than it was years ago because of its association with mindless drilling. As Blake *et al.* (1998: 145) point out, rote learning is often associated in people's minds with surface rather than deep learning. Surface learning is associated with memorising bits of unconnected, rootless information without any response or understanding, without any real 'anchorage'. But sometimes the contrast between 'surface' and 'depth' learning is emphasised too strongly. With poetry as with other aspects of English, surface acquaintance may be but a first and necessary step on a route to a deeper familiarity and response. If something is learned 'by heart' (an appropriate metaphor), it becomes familiar. An obsession with 'complete' understanding which contains a misguided view of the way language has meaning may prevent us from using and enjoying the text. The resonance of language can haunt us and continue to unfold before we grasp its full meaning. Even the concept of 'full' meaning may be suspect because understanding can usually be enriched in some way.

This is not to argue that pupils should be drilled into learning lines by heart in an authoritarian fashion. It does however suggest that memorising lines through workshop activities and choral reading has more educational potential than has often been assumed.

Some poems are more easily understood in the wider context of a poet's entire work and with some knowledge of biographical details. As suggested above, New Criticism, on which the teaching of poetry has traditionally been based in schools, tended to marginalise the relevance of background details in favour of a focused concentration on the actual words of the text. Many poems are understood only in the context of the general corpus of the poet's work and most are illuminated by experience of reading beyond the particular text which is the object of study. The example of the shopping list above provides a very modest example of intertexuality – the way in which reading of one text influences the reading of another. Awareness of this type of difficulty will help the teacher decentre when choosing and presenting poems to pupils.

Another type of difficulty relates to poetry as a genre. Readers are likely to have problems if they approach poetry with inappropriate expectations derived from their experience of reading other texts: many poems, particularly those chosen for study in school, need successive readings before they can be properly experienced; form is as important and often more important in evoking response; trying to understand a poem line by line may not be appropriate. If pupils approach the reading of a poem expecting it to yield up meaning in the same way that prose does, it is not surprising that they find the genre difficult. Tolerance of ambiguity and a readiness to accept plurality of meaning are more necessary when reading poetry than other literary genres. The strong contrast between reading poetry and other utilitarian and functional uses of language in the English classroom (to instruct, report, inform, etc.) may be a source of difficulty if poetry only appears at irregular intervals in the classroom. Conversely we do children a disservice if we treat transactional language as straightforward and transparent.

It was suggested earlier that the broad category which the concept 'poetry' embraces may also be a source of bewilderment for pupils. The early delight in the aesthetics of language which the child experiences may rapidly be replaced by an imperative to analyse and interpret. The family resemblance between writing acrostics, enjoying humorous ditties, joining in with group readings and dissecting for examination purposes may be hard to discern. The argument here is not that poems should never be analysed; it is after all a key means of developing sensitivity to language; appropriate analysis can inform emotional and aesthetic response. The point is that the teacher needs to be aware of the difficulties which may arise and take steps to ensure that they do not become an insurmountable barrier.

It is perhaps more appropriate to think of poetry as being potentially 'bewildering' rather than 'difficult' because the barriers to understanding are more to do with having inappropriate expectations or not quite knowing the 'rules' which apply. Pupils therefore will be helped by some attention to the genre itself, not to pursue strict definitions of poetry but to examine the way different texts require different types of reading. Indeed they are likely to be able to make progress as readers by turning some explicit attention to the particular reading requirements of different discourses. Questions to do with the relevance of the author's intentions and such concepts as ambiguity and plurality of meaning can be addressed in the context of the pupils' own reading and response. Different types of poems can be examined in relation to each other as well as poetry in comparison with other types of written language, such as headlines, posters and advertising. A valuable starting point for such discussion is to give pupils a variety of different types of texts (riddles, jokes, rhymes, etc.) and ask them to say which can be described as poems, as in the research project described above. Alternatively, a modern minimalist poem, for example Stevie Smith's 'Croft' or Williams's 'This Is Just to Say', can be presented in prose and poetry form in order to examine the way in which the poetic form affects the reading and meaning of the text.

Poetry is likely to be bewildering for pupils if it only crops up periodically to fulfil external requirements. A discussion of practical approaches then needs to address not just the teaching of individual poems but the ways in which an appropriate poetry environment can be created in the classroom. The following suggestions are ways of working towards fulfilling that aim:

- include poetry in the classroom library;
- display a 'poem of the week' on a notice board;

- class display of 'our favourite poems';
- have pupils create their own anthologies;
- allow pupils to choose poems to read aloud;
- explore song lyrics with pupils;
- invite poets into the classroom;
- organise poetry festivals with other classes and schools;
- conduct poetry readings;
- publish poetry wall displays and magazines;
- create a supply of audio and video recordings of poems;
- tape-record pupils' discussions of poems for them to review later;
- organise a competition in which pupils have to match poems to titles;
- choose music to accompany the reading of poems;
- create poetry posters of favourite poems;
- pupils learn poems by heart.

Not all poetry requires close analysis and study. A classroom collection of accessible, entertaining anthologies with poems from different cultures will provide a valuable resource for some of the above activities. Whereas some poetry, particularly much of the humorous modern poetry written for children, works at a first reading, much poetry needs to be savoured and read closely in order to experience it.

The problem with the traditional inductive question and answer approach to poetry is that it rarely made enough room for pupils to engage with the text. The emphasis was on 'comprehension and criticism' rather than 'reading and response' (Benton *et al.* 1988: ix). Trying to answer questions which have been set by someone else immediately limits one's own response (Dias and Hayhoe 1988: 7):

> To borrow an analogy that Graves (1981) has used in speaking of how writing is often taught, the teacher, the keeper of the poem, 'owns' the poem, the children merely 'rent it'. They live so to speak in the poem on the owner's terms; for the poem is not theirs to 'mess around in'.

Fox and Merrick's 'Thirty-Six Things to do with a Poem' contains useful suggestions. The value of such activities is not only that they help pupils to become familiar with texts before premature analysis; they also encourage pupils to take a 'playful' approach to language. Figure 10.2 provides examples of activities which allow pupils to become familiar with texts prior to a close reading and analysis; sometimes the activity (or combined activities) may be sufficient in themselves as an alternative to analysis.

The final 'activity' listed is developed in an interesting way in *The Poetry Pack* (Bleiman 1995). It resembles the game of consequences in that the dramatic monologue 'My Last Duchess' is given in fragments to groups of students so that they can try to work out the speaker, the person being talked about, the listener, the context. They are also asked to note down any questions they would like answered. As they receive other fragments they

| Activity | Purpose | Suitable poems |
|---|---|---|
| Invent a title for a poem before being told the actual title. | Allows pupils to respond intuitively to totality of poem prior to analysis. Highlights possible ambiguities. | 'Mushrooms' by Sylvia Plath; 'In The Microscope' by Miroslav Holub; 'space Shot' by Gareth Owen. |
| Read the poem apart from the final stanza and attempt to write a version before reading the original. | Draws attention to style of writing. Invites pupils to speculate about meaning. | 'Meditation on the A30' by John Betjeman; 'My Grandmother' by Elizabeth Jennings. |
| Restore line lengths and endings to a poem which has been distributed as prose. | Prompts pupils to think about difference between prose and poetry. | 'The World is a Beautiful Place' by Lawrence Ferlinghetti; 'Orchids' by Theodore Roethke. |
| Place stanzas of poem in order. | Draws attention to structure of poem. | 'First Blood' by Jon Stallworthy; 'Ballad of the Bread Man' by Charles Causley. |
| Prepare imaginative readings of poems in groups. | Emphasises importance of reading poems aloud – tone. | 'Daniel Jazz' by Vachel Lindsay; 'First Men on Mercury', Edwin Morgan. |
| Make a collage using pictures, postcards, etc. juxtaposing with words of poem. | Draws attention to visual aspects of poem. May provide new interpretations. | 'A Martian Sends a Postcard Home' by Craig Raine; |
| Create a group tableau of poem or stanza which is then performed as it is read. | Provides concrete focus for understanding and reading. | 'My Parents Kept Me From Children Who Were Rough' by Stephen Spender. |
| Underline favourite/most striking words and phrases/images. | Emphasises response and exercise of choice prior to analysis. | 'Fairground' by Vernon Scannell. |
| Substitute other words (e.g. colours/verbs/adverbs/adjectives/metaphors). | Draws attention to effectiveness of poet's choice of words. | 'Hard Frost' by Andrew Young; 'Wind' by Ted Hughes. |
| Examine first (and subsequent) drafts of poems. | Highlights writing process. | 'Anthem for Doomed Youth' by Wilfred Owen. |
| Compare two poems. | Can highlight contrasting content and features of form. | 'A Negro Woman' by William Carlos Williams; 'The Fat Black Woman Goes Shopping' by Grace Nichols. |
| Compare translations of same poem. | Draws attention to nuances of meaning. | 'First Ice' by Andrei Voznesensky. |
| Create storyboard or cartoon strip representing poem. | Highlights structure and narrative content of poem. | 'Flannan Isle' by Wilfred Wilson Gibson. |
| Focus on fragments which have been selected by the teacher before reading the entire poem. | Encourages active reading; useful 'way in'; may focus on particular aspects, e.g. imagery. | 'Porphyria's Lover' by Robert Browning. |
| Present poem gradually, in small sections (e.g. two lines at a time), in sequence. | Deepens response to poem by slowing down reading. | 'Futility' by Wilfred Owen; 'The Naming of Parts' by Henry Reed. |
| Reconstruct two poems which have been cut up. The titles are given. | Focuses on tone and style. | 'The Next War' by Wilfred Owen; 'Does It Matter?' by Siegfried Sassoon. |
| From extracts of direct speech taken from the poem try to work out the speaker and the context. | Arouses interest; raises questions about context. | 'My Last Duchess' by Robert Browning. |

**FIGURE 10.2**

note the ideas of other groups and add their own. When they have seen the whole poem they receive their first fragment and can now add to it or adapt it. After this introductory activity the entire poem can be subject to other different activities; for example, giving it a title, discussing specific questions. Working with poets' drafts (Dymoke 2003) is an excellent way of drawing pupils' attention to the craft (as opposed to spontaneous expression) element of writing poetry and will help them with their own drafting process.

One of the purposes of these tasks is to encourage pupils to be active in their approach to reading, to engage with the form and content. The *Cambridge Critical Workshop* (Wood and Wood 1995) provides a useful structure for a more formal, systematic approach to texts. Questions could be asked about form (tightly organised, irregular), tone (tender, ironic, harsh), rhythm (steady, irregular), tempo (quick, moderate, slow), diction (formal, colloquial), texture (smooth, coarse), imagery (literal, figurative), impact (dramatic, understated, impersonal).

## Writing poetry

A central challenge in teaching poetry is to maintain a balance so that due attention is given to both the subjectivity of the reader and the objective text. The same tension is present in approaches to writing poetry. In the belief that creativity (interpreted largely as originality) should be respected, pupils were often told to 'write a poem' with little or no further guidance or direction. The implicit romantic view was of poetry as a 'spontaneous overflow of powerful feelings' or that genuine poetry is 'composed in the soul'; the emphasis was primarily on the expression of private emotion. There was correspondingly an insufficient emphasis on the craft of writing, on the drafting process, and on a sheer delight in language. There is some danger that emphasis on form without sufficient motivation and engagement will promote mechanistic writing devoid of any real sense of meaning or purpose; all teachers will be familiar with the contorted meanings which some pupils produce in the pursuit of a rhyme. However, working with particular formal constraints can be very liberating and expressive because the framework is already given. The following list represents some examples of more structured approaches to writing poetry; a more detailed discussion of these and other methods can be found in the further reading section. It goes without saying that teaching poetry writing is about understanding the process and not just about implementing a series of tips. When pupils feel liberated in their writing they can go on to more ambitious work.

### List poems

Composing a poem as a list of single words on each line based on a single topic is an accessible way of getting started. The following simple example of how a list poem might begin is based on the title 'moth'.

Fluttering
Eerie
Flickering
Light

Drunken
Movement

The lack of concern with syntax and word order can be liberating. A second stage could be to work up each word into a line.

## Provide an opening phrase or line

Pupils faced with a blank page often find it difficult to get started. An opening line or phrase may be all that is needed: This is the place where . . . ; I am the man who . . . ; It is always late at night . . . ; At the bottom of the cupboard . . .

## Turning prose into poems

Pupils can begin by creating the line breaks but then can be encouraged to condense meaning and add phrases as with a draft of their own. Here is an example based on a prose passage:

During the blitz, many Londoners slept on platforms of underground stations because they felt safer there away from the bombs. The picture shows people taking refuge in Holborn underground station. During the worst part of the bombing, almost 180,000 people slept in the tube stations each night. The story goes, that the loud snoring in the tunnels sounded like the wind.

'The Blitz'

Underground station.
A sanctuary
From the bombs.
Two thousand refugees
Hoping to return home
Safely
A loud snoring wind
Echoes through the tunnel.

## Found poems

Collected writings in the environment (shops signs, notices, overheard conversations) provide the raw material for crafting a poem.

## Using a poem as a model

Here the form of a poem is used to give pupils a structure and suggestions for content. Adrian Henri's 'Without You' is a popular model. Lines such as 'Without you the *Sunday Times* colour supplement would come out in black and white' and 'Without you the first Martian to land would turn around and go away' can be easily imitated.

The popular poem 'Daily London Recipe' by Steve Turner takes the language and format of a recipe for a cooking dish to represent the city with people packed in buses, left in work for eight hours and then tipped in to terraced houses.

It could be used as a model for a poem called 'Exam Recipe'.

Take a number of empty heads
Then cram with facts
Add some droning and moaning
Then test, test and test again.
Transfer mixture to large open space
And leave for three hours.

## Brainstorming

A simple brainstorm – for example of words to describe feeling 'cold' supplemented by a thesaurus (chilly, freezing, icy, frosty, bitter, wintry, perishing, arctic . . . ) – may form the basis for a poem based on each day of the week getting colder using a different metaphor for each day.

## Kennings

This was an ancient technique used in Old Norse and Old English poetry which described something in an indirect way without using the name, e.g. cat might be a 'toe-nibbler, dark-dreamer, paw-padder, floor-scratcher' (Brownjohn 1994: 81).

## Using a simple structure

Brownjohn (ibid.: 286) asks pupils to write about their memories of childhood, the things left behind as they grow up, 'When I was a child . . . ' and then to look forward to adulthood, 'When I am adult . . . '. The result can then be shaped and structured.

## Sound effects

A poetry writing workshop can be conducted using sound effects. The writing can be built up slowly from first impressions, to the inclusion of similes and metaphors, to specific thoughts which can be later crafted and then spoken over the recording of the sounds.

## Summary

To summarise, a successful practical approach to poetry in the classroom will involve the following:

- creating a rich poetry environment;
- combining reading with writing of poetry;
- reading a wide variety of poems, some of which are chosen for their accessibility;

- retaining flexibility in approaches to reading and studying poetry;

- choosing appropriate methodologies for particular poems and eschewing any advice which is intended to apply to all poems;

- asking pupils to do things with poems instead of asking them questions all the time;

- recognising that many poems need familiarity before they can be properly experienced and analysed;

- recognising that close textual study is more fruitful after pupils have experienced the poem;

- focusing pupils' attention on poetry as genre in comparison with other forms of writing in a spirit of exploration.

The way a poem appears on the page invites us to speculate about meaning, purpose, ambiguities and complexities and makes us think about language itself and respond to it more sensitively.

Poetry is the most 'natural' form of language not just because it has affinities with our experiences as young children but because it provides an insight into its true nature – it is the primary form of language. Common sense can mislead us into thinking that language is a transparent device for conveying meaning in simple ways.

A 'poetic' view of language and meaning needs to inform all English teaching.

## Further reading

Dymoke (2003) *Drafting and Assessing Poetry* addresses a range of issues including poetry writing, drafting strategies, assessing poetry. Pike (2004) *Teaching Secondary English* contains a chapter called 'Popularizing Poetry'. Andrews (1991) *The Problem with Poetry*, Dias and Hayhoe (1988) *Developing Response to Poetry*, Benton *et al.* (1988) *Young Readers Responding to Poems* provide excellent discussions of the teaching of poetry drawing on critical theory. The last publication provides examples of small-scale research projects. Marsh (1988) *Teaching Through Poetry* and Tunnicliffe (1984) *Poetry Experience* are useful books which deal also with the writing of poetry. Buchbinder (1991) *Contemporary Literary Theory and the Reading of Poetry* is stimulating and has helpful sections on further reading. Hayhoe and Parker (1988) *Words Large as Apples* contains useful discussion and practical ideas. Styles and Triggs (1988) *Poetry 0–16* is inspiring and full of valuable information. The HMI publication (DES 1987) *Teaching Poetry in the Secondary School* is still worth reading. For inspiring books on teaching the writing of poetry see Pirrie (1987) *On Common Ground*, and Brownjohn (1994) *To Rhyme or Not to Rhyme*.

## Resources

The following websites provide useful ideas and links: www.poetryclass.net; www.poetryzone.ndirect.co.uk.

Dymoke (2003) *Drafting and Assessing Poetry* contains a useful list of anthologies and websites. Styles and Triggs (1988) *Poetry 0–16* has an excellent guide to those published up to 1988, including poetry from around the world. See in particular *I Like That Stuff* and *You'll Love This Stuff* (ed. Styles), Cambridge University Press, and *Black Poetry* (ed. Nichols), Blackie. *The Poetry Pack* (ed. Bleiman), English and Media Centre, is full of interesting ideas for exploring poems at GCSE and A level. See also *The Poetry Video* from the same source containing over fifty poetry readings and *Studying Poetry*, a secondary course in poetry. *The Poetry File* (Ainsworth *et al.*) from Stanley Thornes contains printed poems as well as activities. See also Owen (2003) *The Poetry of Ted Hughes*. The anthology *Axed between the Ears* has an accompanying resource pack, published by Heinemann. *The Forms of Poetry* (Abbs and Richardson), Cambridge University Press, provides a guide to literary forms of English. *The Cambridge Critical Workshop* and the *Cambridge Poetry Workshop* (Wood and Wood) from the same publishers have useful activities and assignments. *Poetry Workshop* (Benton and Benton 1995), Hodder & Stoughton, has a good collection of poems by theme and author and is useful for wider reading.

## 11

# Media education

*The media network has its idols, but its principal idol is its own style.*

John Berger

## The nature of media education within English

LIKE DRAMA, MEDIA EDUCATION DOES not have an independent identity as a curricular subject within the National Curriculum; both subjects are subsumed under the English Orders. Media education particularly, as a relatively recent phenomenon with its own barely established pedagogy and conventions, could be regarded as under threat in this context. There is in fact a striking parallel between this sense of insecurity and that experienced during the early history of English, less than a century ago, in its relationship with classical studies. Some are relieved that media education appears at all in the National Curriculum, pointing out that in the ideological climate of the 1980s its very existence – like society itself in Mrs Thatcher's famous remark – was called into question. Other commentators show concern over this position; Davies (1996: 59), for example, protests:

> As far as I am concerned, the most extraordinary thing that is currently being said about the latest version of the National Curriculum for English is that it allows far more opportunity for studying the media than had been anticipated and, in this respect, is almost as good as the first version of the National Curriculum for English. Which is fine, except that the first version did not actually do all that much to promote media study and had minimal impact on the practice of English teachers and, if this second version is nearly as good, that means it is nothing like good enough.

Despite Davies's view, the inclusion and promotion of media education in the original National Curriculum for English did achieve significant advances in ensuring at least that all English departments took this area of the subject seriously. It is worth looking back at the Cox (DES 1989) conception of media education, its place in the subsequent official orders, and what commentators made of it. By so doing, we may uncover useful approaches to the rather less detailed – some would say less satisfactory – account in the current orders. Cox was able to make full use of the expertise of the British Film Institute, then as now pioneering the cause of media education, by quoting from its publication (Bazalgette 1989: 96) of primary phase curriculum policy:

> Media education . . . seeks to increase children's critical understanding of the media . . . How they work, how they produce meaning, how they are organised and how audiences make sense of them, are the issues that media education addresses. [It] aims to develop systematically children's critical and creative powers through analysis and production of media artefacts. This also deepens their understanding of the pleasure and enjoyment provided by the media. Media education aims to create more active and critical media users who will demand, and could contribute to, a greater range and diversity of media products.

This provides us still with a series of useful guiding principles at once wide-ranging and encouraging depth of study. In terms of the original National Curriculum, published a year later, the fundamental principles were adapted into three approaches (to be found in probably the most useful section entitled 'Non-Statutory Guidance'):

- Approach 1: Media Languages:
    - How do we make sense of a media text?
    - What conventions are at work in it?
    - How do we categorise it in relation to other texts?

- Approach 2: Representation:
    - Is this text supposed to be like real life?
    - Do you find the characters and setting convincing?
    - What roles are there for different groups (e.g. women) in this story?

- Approach 3: Producers and Audiences:
    - Who produced this text and why?
    - For whom is it made and how will it reach them?
    - What will they think of it?

For many involved in promoting media education at a time when the English curriculum certainly appeared like a battleground, this seemed indeed like 'three steps to heaven'. You may notice the similarity to our recommended approaches to the reading of texts in Chapter 5, and this underlines the fundamental unity of English. As the English Orders came to be modified (many would say eroded) English teachers have been determined to safeguard what is most valuable in media education. As ever, this opportunity was and remains elusive, but none the less real. McGuinn (1995: 157), writing just before the revised English Orders were published, makes an important point:

> English teachers must meet a number of important challenges. The first is to treat the English Order as an enabling rather than a restrictive document. The problem is, these opportunities are largely implicit rather than explicit – a series of hints to 'those in the know' rather than clear guidance for the uncertain.

English teachers need to be enterprising and resourceful here; the guiding principle must be that approaches to texts derived from the mass media should not be qualitatively different from those taken to literature, although of course each text – and, more broadly, each genre – will have its own idiosyncrasies.

The term 'media education' implies breadth of teaching and learning, and must be distinguished from 'media studies', which has come to mean rather more specialised syllabus-based study, usually at GCSE, AS or A level. It is the former that we shall be mainly concerned with here, exploring the possibilities of creative media-based activity as central to the English curriculum. In this context there is a cross-phase element, and a great deal of inspiring media education is taking place at Key Stages 1 and 2 in many primary schools which may be successfully built on in the secondary school. There are also strong cross-curricular possibilities and much pioneering work has already been carried out by expressive arts and humanities departments in this field. So media education, perhaps more than most areas of English, may crop up in a variety of times and places. It should be an important part of both Key Stages 3 and 4 of the National Curriculum, and may have further implications as a media studies examination option at GCSE which is often, but not exclusively, taught by English specialists. The place of media studies as a free-standing subject in the options system varies considerably between the schools which offer it, and it is well worth keeping a watchful eye on how it is positioned in the all-important options columns at the end of Key Stage 3. An alternative approach, adopted successfully by several schools, is to organise the Key Stage 4 English curriculum around the central 'core' of English GCSE itself with 'satellite' options, which may include English literature, media studies and drama, with the teaching groups organised accordingly. There are also some rather more vocationally orientated alternatives developed in some schools under the general title 'Arts and Media Services' and increasingly subsumed into the GNVQ framework; indeed, given the number of vocational opportunities in the media, it is a little surprising that development here has not been more widespread. Whichever system, if any, is used, there are clear implications for the preparation of pupils in broadly-based media education at Key Stage 3 in a way similar to that generally used for, say, English literature.

## Tensions in the teaching of the media

As we have already noted in the context of other aspects of the English curriculum, there may be a tension between immersion in the subject and the keeping of a critical distance. The position for media education may exaggerate this tension, in that, almost by definition, it is the area of the curriculum likely to be most familiar to young people (and, by the same token, least familiar to their teachers). The mass media are frequently focused on the young, and are enjoyed by them without too much concern over keeping a critical distance: indeed it would seem strange if otherwise. Traditionally, this may have led to a view of young people as passive victims of cynical media operators; Buckingham and Sefton-Green (1994) explore this idea:

> The view of young people as 'dupes' of popular media has a long history, and is regularly espoused by critics of all political persuasions. For many on the Right, the media are often seen

as a major cause of moral depravity and violence, while they are routinely condemned by many on the Left for their reinforcement of racism, sexism, consumerism and many other objectionable ideologies. Yet what unites these otherwise very different views is a notion of young people as helpless victims of manipulation, and as extremely vulnerable and impressionable. In this account, the text is seen to be all powerful, while the reader is powerless to step back or resist: 'reading' or making sense of media texts is regarded as an automatic process, in which meanings are simply imprinted on passive minds.

This model of passivity, which arises from a rather patronising, dismissive judgement of the very media probably most enjoyed by pupils, needs to be avoided in teaching. It is important to find a way both of being critical and of finding pleasure in the media artefacts being studied. In studying a film the teacher may wish to pause the tape to analyse camera angles, only to be greeted by calls from the class, who are enjoying the film as a change from the rest of the curriculum, to be allowed to continue watching. This may be a familiar scenario, and it would usually be resolved in the give-and-take spirit of good teaching. For example, a simple warning at the start that the watching of the film will be interrupted may be enough.

A worthwhile way in to media education, and one especially suited to an English teacher's fascination for words themselves, is to pose the question, what do we in fact mean by the word 'media'? It is a short step from there to ponder on the idea of the medium in its other contexts: as in 'the happy medium' or as used in spiritualism, for example. Useful discussion may be stimulated on the nature of a medium as a means of transmitting a message, and with carefully chosen examples (the more immediately topical the better) it should be possible to go from there to an exploration of how the medium affects and is affected by the message, the sender of the message, and of course the receiver. We are here in the realms of semiotics, but such an exploration need not be over complex. We need to establish that the medium is not neutral or transparent and is bound up in an intimate and influential relationship with the three other components and with the overall context and purpose.

In discussing these ideas we are laying the foundations of media appreciation which may be at once enjoyable and analytical; the two need not be mutually exclusive. It may be helpful here to consider Brecht's concept of alienation, used by him in relation to the theatre, but undoubtedly applicable to media education in the liberating combination of full enjoyment of the spectacle with critical appraisal. Brecht himself maintained that 'Alienating an event or character means first of all stripping the event of its self-evident, familiar, obvious quality and creating a sense of astonishment and curiosity about them' (quoted in Brooker 1994: 191).

For Brecht there was a dialectical relationship between theatre and spectator, with meaning arrived at through synthesis. His own term 'Verfremdung' might in this context be better translated as 'de-familiarisation' or 'estrangement', as has been pointed out by Brooker (1994) in his illuminating essay on Brecht's key words, with fewer of the rather negative connotations of the word 'alienation'. Particularly appropriate here is Brecht's insistence that the process of 'Verfremdung' should be thoroughly educational, but also thoroughly engaging, even celebratory, and potentially liberating. In the context of media education this may be an important relationship; a tension between immersion and critical distance may of course remain, but it should be a healthy tension leading to greater understanding and, ultimately, a deeper enjoyment. If we consider other fields of human activity, such as music, sport or motorcycle maintenance, it is surely true that the more we become interested in a particular area, the more we seek to understand its workings – it would be difficult to conceive it otherwise – and the greater the resulting enjoyment. Media education, like other aspects of education, should have greater enjoyment as its end: we are back to Traherne's insistence that we consider always our ultimate ends.

In media education, as with English, there has to be a balance between critical analysis and creative production, with the one constantly influencing the other. Here again, however, the relationship may not be as straightforward or unproblematic as appears at first sight; Medway (1996: 131) highlights this:

> Immediately, we are confronted by a striking asymmetry and an apparently insurmountable constraint . . . the semiotic artefacts produced in the one classroom are not the same sort as are analysed in the other . . . There are good reasons for this of course. It would be impossible for students in schools to produce newspapers, advertisements, TV documentaries, commercials, soaps and the like that are in any way equivalent to those produced by the media industries. It is not simply that professional technology is largely unavailable to schools. A more basic problem is that it is impossible for students to experience the sort of economic and institutional environment that informs mainstream mass media production.

## Media workshop approaches

In effect this means that we cannot hope to educate our pupils in the ways of the media entirely through 'hands on' experiential learning. It is a fairly common experience for pupils – and their teacher – to be seriously disappointed by the fruits of several lessons' labour in, say, making a video or recording a radio phone-in. In an age of accelerating media sophistication, such disappointment is perhaps inevitable, but it should be confronted as an opportunity to examine exactly what is needed for professional production, not only in terms of technological expertise but also the 'economic and institutional environment' Medway refers to above. The workshop production element in media education remains all the more fundamental in this context, and provides an important taster of the methodologies and technologies involved. For both teacher and pupils, there are important class and equipment management issues here, especially when, as is generally the case, there is not enough equipment to go round. Pupils may well at first need to be convinced that the adage 'successful production is nine-tenths planning and preparation, one-tenth execution' is true, but the results of early failures may be helpful here. We learn from our mistakes, not by simply being told. With careful planning and timed allocation of the resources available it is possible to convert the classroom into a successful media workshop, and the necessary trust shown in allowing pupils to use expensive equipment relatively independently may enhance the spirit of collaborative learning. In the end, it is the production side which many pupils remember most fondly in their media education, and its importance should not be underestimated or avoided through fear of failure or resources management difficulties. The potential to bring together the arts-based and critical-appraisal models of the subject English is perhaps greatest through the agency of media education.

Davies (1996: 60) provides a useful statement of intent for media study:

Media study should look at how meanings about the world are:

- made
- sustained
- contested

in all forms of human communication. It should study what those meanings and beliefs are, where they come from, who makes them and why.

This kind of English operates on the principles that:

- the more those forms or media influence us (by determining our thinking and actions) the more we should study them;
- the more we benefit from them (by gaining understanding, and means of expression) the more we should learn how to use them positively;
- it is not the job of media study to teach people what the right meanings are, or what the right pleasures are – its particular task is to teach people to examine how meanings are made.

This appears to be a positive starting point for the structuring of media education throughout the secondary English curriculum, although we would emphasise more strongly the production side of classroom activity, including the celebratory. Apart from anything else, it is the creative aspect of the curriculum which may usefully counter the danger of a too earnest approach to, for example, the manipulative power of advertising. The sheer size and breadth of the mass media in all their complexity mean that we must keep the underlying structure of media education firmly in mind. Consider the variety of genres that constitute the media or, better still, have a class 'brainstorm' ideas. The list is likely to include:

- film adaptations of books, including a fast increasing number of 'classics';
- popular music in an incredible variety of guises;
- TV soaps, sit-coms, mini-sagas, drama series and serials;
- popular magazines, increasingly focused on highly specific readerships;
- TV commercials, including those loosely based on continuing narrative;
- the vast range of radio programmes, both commercial and BBC;
- advertising in magazines, on hoardings and in other contexts;
- the 'popular' (tabloid) and 'serious' (broadsheet) press;
- computer games and CD-ROM software;
- pulp fiction and non-fiction;

- popular films in a range of genres;
- public information and charity campaigns through the media;
- TV documentaries and news programmes;
- pop music videos;
- 'fanzines' from the worlds of football, other sports, and popular music.

In fact the list is endless, with each item on it capable of infinite subdivisions of ever more subtly distinctive genres. Teachers, clearly, face a genuine learning experience here, adding to the excitement of media education; certainly, in my own experience I have been introduced to some fascinating examples of fanzines and styles of music which would have been otherwise entirely unknown to me. So much for the teacher as expert. As for other areas of the English curriculum previously noted, we have to collect our own resources as well as relying on those available to pupils, and there is no shortage of opportunity if we keep our eyes and ears open.

It is sometimes claimed that media education is particularly relevant to boys, especially the practical, productive side with its range of sophisticated electronic equipment. P. Thomas (1997) provocatively sees male fascination for such gadgetry as symptomatic of a particular world view unsuited to the reflective and sensitive writing so often called for in English:

Men like controlling things. They enjoy gizmos like computers and cars and mobile phones because they can operate and control them. Cars are the ultimate in gizmo control, with limitless scope for supplementary gizmodification: turbo, mobile phone, CD HiFi, 4WD and remote control demist on the tinted glass wing mirror. The car, for men, is not simply transport or carriage – it's for driving, a verb which needs no preposition.

Thomas cleverly links this characterisation to styles of narrative writing, but the relevance to media education is clear. There is, of course, a great danger of stereotype reinforcement here if we simply pander to the most overt elements of what is in the end more of a caricature than a characterisation. It is sometimes suggested that boys tend to miss out the reflective stage in learning, preferring to leap straight from the descriptive/informative to the active/speculative. If this is the case, the production of media artefacts is likely to be less than satisfactory, for, as we have already seen, it is the reflective stage – careful planning and preparation – which is all important. Nevertheless, it may well be that pupils – and they are often boys – who are reluctant readers or writers perform creatively with media-based equipment. If a vital part of education is the giving of space, especially to adolescents, then media activities may be particularly valuable.

## Further practical implications

The English curriculum is now so crowded throughout the years of secondary schooling that any opportunity to cover different requirements through one central area of study must be seized gratefully. Such is the breadth of media education that much of it can be inventively combined with other aspects of English: literature, for example, or language study. In the activities which follow, the idea is to give a 'taste' of what is possible rather than to define a rigorous curriculum. The various connections to other areas of English will be self-evident.

In the early years of the secondary curriculum it may be best to start with a reasonably open-ended project based introduction to media education, such as the one outlined in Figure 11.1.

A broadly based scheme of work such as this allows for considerable flexibility, and implies opportunities to assess pupils in all three of the English attainment targets. It also allows for the development of pupils' interests, although the teacher's role will be vital in guiding these into a form of media education through purposeful teaching. At later stages of secondary schooling, similar open-ended investigative and presentational work could be set, considering one aspect of the mass media, on such topics as 'Images of Youth in the Media' or 'The Representation of Women in the Media'. Again, the stimulus and guidance offered by the teacher will be instrumental in ensuring sustained and questioning activity.

A different approach to media education might be to focus on contrasting film versions of literary texts, of which there is certainly no lack. Again, it is clear that a variety of elements of the syllabus may be covered, including, at Key Stage 4, GCSE coursework and preparation for English and English literature examinations. Film adaptations of Shakespeare can be particularly exciting, and expose the plays to a multiplicity of interpretations. From the media education angle, the question to ask is how a particular

---

### YEAR 7 ENGLISH ASSIGNMENT: MEDIA-BASED ENTERTAINMENT

A four week project on any aspect of media-based entertainment you wish to work on, either individually or in pairs. For this purpose, entertainment includes sport through the media, pop music, radio, television, films, computer games, videos, magazines, or another area of interest by negotiation with the teacher.

- You will need to focus on a particular aspect of your chosen subject which interests you, and plan carefully how you intend to develop the project.
- Your project must include some of the following:
   information researched from books, magazines, CD-Roms, TV, etc.;
   survey work and interviews, carefully planned and then taped;
   your own views on the subject;
   a detailed description of how the media present the subject of interest, who the intended audience is, and what the effect is.
- Apart from your written and illustrated project, you will need to give an active presentation on your work to the rest of the class. This should include the following:
   a spoken explanation of what your project involved and what particular areas of interest you covered;
   demonstrations and examples illustrating the subject – e.g. songs and music, taped or live; video clips from films etc.; taped interviews; home-produced video material; posters and other large-scale visual material.

FIGURE 11.1

interpretation is realised on film. Comparison of the two film versions of Golding's novel *Lord of the Flies*, frequently taught, could focus on questions like these:

- What is the significance of the opening sequence in each film?
- What part does the music play in creating atmosphere?
- Does the fact that the original film was made in monochrome and the more recent one in colour have any implications for our understanding?
- One film emphasises the British public school background of the children, the other places them as American Military School pupils: how are these contrasting portrayals made clear in the films?
- What are the major deviations from the plot and characterisation of the original novel? Are these justified?
- What symbolism is apparent in both films (e.g. Jack's survival knife or Simon's 'wand' in the later film)?
- Which film did you enjoy more? Why?
- Would you try to film the novel differently? How?
- How does either film compare with others you may have seen dealing with similar themes, such as youth interaction, violence, survival, or destruction of a social order?

There are plenty of excellent resources available, some of which are listed at the end of this chapter, to help in teaching the media, including the practical and technical aspects. There is not space here to go into detail, and there is in any case no need to replicate what is readily available elsewhere in an attractive, palatable form for both pupils and teacher. The following list of possible approaches to media education, then, is intended as a stimulus for further exploration and development in the context of a resourceful and inventive English department:

- 'storyboarding' different media texts, either as the planning of a video-film or as an end in itself, using one of the templates available in many publications or created using ICT;
- cross-genre adaptations, such as a film version of events normally portrayed in a documentary – the Comic Strip TV film *Strike* is a marvellous example of a tongue-in-cheek Hollywood version of the miners' strike;
- given a list of a day's 'newsworthy' items, creating an evening news broadcast and subsequently comparing it with what real news programmes made of the material;
- a similar exercise using newspapers, focusing on the distinction between tabloids and broadsheets, and then contrasting newspaper and television presentation of 'news';
- detailed step-by-step analysis of still pictures, starting with one small portion and then progressing to the 'whole' picture, asking how the inclusion of more detail alters interpretation and understanding (along the lines of the British Film Institute's Reading Pictures material);

- discursive use of newspaper and documentary presentations of contentious aspects of the world of the mass media, e.g. press intrusion into personal lives; censorship and the relationship between screen and real-life violence; the exploitation of women in tabloid newspapers;

- analysing positive and negative images in TV programmes, as a preliminary to storyboarding and/or shooting a short film focusing on either attractive or unattractive aspects of a school or local area;

- the study of advertising targeted at specific audiences in 'special interest' magazines, and the subsequent creation of a series of ads promoting a product to an unlikely group of consumers;

- role-playing the planning of an evening's TV schedule, given the constraints (such as the nine o'clock watershed and limits on the number of American or Australian imports) with which schedule planners have to work;

- photo-storying (examples of which may be found in many adolescent girls' magazines) an unlikely subject, such as a 'classic' literary text;

- study of the media promotion of a new pop group (the latest boy band should provide plenty of exemplar material), including the all-important 'image' and the perhaps less important 'music', as preparation for an imaginary promotion campaign;

- analysis of the presentational styles of several disc jockeys for different audiences, programmes, types of music and radio stations, and the planning of a short sequence of linked records for a particular programme;

- cross-curricular possibilities, including expressive arts departments' use of the media for presentational purposes, the humanities' concerns for historical, social and moral aspects of the media, and the technical expertise to be found in science and technology subjects;

- cross-phase approaches, especially appropriate to study and production of media artefacts aimed at younger children.

As with all such approaches and activities, the onus is on the English teacher, working collaboratively with colleagues where feasible, to integrate and develop them as part of a cohesive curriculum. In particular, there needs to be a balance between the responsive and the productive within each activity where possible, and certainly over the whole structure of the course.

## Further reading

Buckingham's *Media Education: Literacy, Learning and Contemporary Culture* (2003) is invaluable: comprehensive, helpful and appropriately challenging. *The Media in Britain: Current Debates and Developments* (Stokes and Reading 1999) provides a useful theoretical framework. Potter (1990) *Reading, Learning and Media Education* gives plenty of helpful background information, as does Inglis (1990) *Media Theory: An Introduction*. Goodwyn (1992) *English Teaching and Media Education* and Bazalgette (1991) *Media Education* make explicit links between English and media education. Less concerned with the English connection, Masterman (1992) *Teaching the Media* has become something of a standard text. Clarke (1987) *Teaching Popular Television* is helpful; the more recent study of the same subject, Goodwyn (1997b) *Understanding Television*, concentrates on the needs of the post-16 student. A further publication from the English and Media Centre offers practical guidance for teachers: Buckingham *et al.* (1996) *Making Media: Learning from Media Production*. Andrews's survey of recent research and theoretical developments, 'Viewing Still and Moving Images' (in Andrews 2001) is helpful, as are the chapters 'Media in English' (in Haworth *et al.* 2004) and Hardman's 'What do we mean by Media Education in English' (in Williamson *et al.* 2001). Goodwyn's *English Teaching and the Moving Image* (2003) is practically orientated, with many good teaching ideas. The following books also provide valuable contextual information concerning the teaching of the media, and are well worth exploring: Brereton (2001) *Continuum Guide to Media Education*, Burn and Durran (2007) *Media Literacy in Schools – Practice, Production and Progression*, Hart and Hicks (2002) *Teaching Media in the English Curriculum*, Marshall and Werndly (2002) *The Language of Television*, and Stokes and Reading (1999) *The Media in Britain*.

## Resources

Published material tends to date rather quickly but a great deal is available specifically for classroom use. There are several general introductions aimed more at Key Stage 4: *Media Studies: An Introduction* (Dutton 2000); *Media Choices* (Mills, Mills and Stringer 1991); *Media Studies for GCSE* (Wall and Walker 2002); and *Examining the Media* (Connell, Brigley and Edwards 1996). Other publications focus more directly on specific aspects of media education – the following photocopiable resources are from the English and Media Centre and are all very helpful, with self-explanatory titles: *The Soap Pack: A Study of 'Brookside' from Script to Screen* (with accompanying video, EMC 2005); *Production Practices: Media Simulations* (EMC 1998); *Picture Power* (also available as a CD-ROM, EMC 2006). *Teaching Television: 'The Real World'* (Hart 1988), and *On and Off the Record: The Language of Reporting* (Rumsby), Nelson, are also well worth using when teaching about these areas of the media. For summaries of topical articles from the press – useful as stimuli for discussion about reporting styles and the content itself – Carel Press publish regularly updated Essential *Articles*, while Collins issues articles from *The Times* on the CD-ROM *Changing Times*. Hodder Murray publishes impressive media textbooks for AS/A level use, linked to the OCR specification but relevant beyond this, and Heinemann has interesting books for KS3 and GCSE: *Developing Media Skills* (Barton 2001) for the former, and *GCSE Media Studies* (in two versions, for AQA and WJEC), alongside *MediaStage* – an interactive software application. Nelson-Thornes and Longman have also recently extended their ranges of media textbooks, with some very attractive titles suitable for the 11–18 age range

Apart from book publishers, there are plentiful other sources of media education material. Film Education, for example, is a registered charity devoted to the enhanced public understanding of film and provides excellent resources, mainly free of charge, to anyone on their mailing list; especially valuable are their film guides to popular films as they are released, often coinciding with short programmes to video-tape from television, and sometimes with CD-ROM materials. The British Film Institute (BFI) has a wide range of excellent media materials advertised at www.bfi.org.uk/education. Further resources can be obtained from the two main media-based museums in the UK, The Museum of the Moving Image (MOMI) on the South Bank in London, and The Museum of Film and Photography in Bradford; both make excellent venues to visit with school parties, and have active education departments.

# 12

# ICT

*The status of knowledge is altered as societies enter what
is known as the postindustrial age.*

Jean-Francois Lyotard

## Thinking about ICT

THIS CHAPTER PROVIDES a range of practical examples of the use of ICT to support the
teaching of English, after some discussion of its general impact on the subject and on
education more widely. As with other topics in this book, devoting a separate chapter to
ICT emphasises its importance but runs the risk of implying that it should be treated as
a discrete area rather than integrated into other aspects of English. Presenting the book
as one continuous text that does not follow a simply linear pattern but instead allows
the reader to move from one topic to another as these arise in context could solve this
difficulty. Of course, this is precisely the facility afforded by computer technology with
its system of hyperlinks. Another challenge when writing about ICT is that, even more
than other aspects of English, the subject matter can become out-of-date as technology
develops. The answer would be to have the facility to update and edit text on a regular
basis. Again, this is precisely the facility afforded by web-based publications.

It is worth examining these two examples more closely. The system of links on an
Internet text, which allows the reader to move easily between subjects, is of course
predetermined. They may appear to give a natural, organic flow to a text but they are
all pre-planned according to the author(s) preoccupations and values. They may take
the reader on a predetermined course that is in fact more limiting than the browsing
afforded by a book. The example however does highlight the fact that the relationship
between ICT and English should not be seen in a purely functional way. Computers do
not only provide an easier and quicker way of doing the same things as one would with
a pen but actually may change our conception of the reading and writing process (seeing
these as more dynamic, fluid and collaborative). The second example provides an ideal
of constantly updated publications, but anyone who has spent time on the Internet will
almost certainly have been frustrated by the presence of material which is wildly out

of date. This can become more problematic than the printed word because in the latter case the convention of dating publications is more clearly established. The example is a reminder that ICT is dependent on human agency and its value is largely determined by critical and discriminating use.

An underlying theme of this book has been to promote a balanced approach to what are often seen as competing ideas on the teaching of English, such as explicit and implicit knowledge about language; structure and experience; child- and subject-centred learning. A balanced approach to thinking about ICT means not being too evangelical or uncritical but also not underestimating its impact or value. Technology changes rapidly but so do attitudes. Whereas a few years ago it was not uncommon to find English teachers actively hostile to the use of ICT, this is now rarely the case. To be against ICT is a bit like trying to resist the impact of the wheel or electricity.

One of the important changes that has occurred in recent years has been the renaming of IT (information technology) as ICT (information communications technology). This change situates technological aspects firmly in human contexts and appropriately widens the field to embrace elements such as video and audio recorders. This chapter therefore needs to be read in conjunction with that on media. Another term that has been adopted is 'e-learning', referred to as 'the blending of traditional and ICT-based forms of teaching and learning' (DfES 2003: 2).

The importance of properly integrating ICT with teaching rather than seeing it as a bolt-on extra has always been stressed but only made properly possible in recent years. At one time, use of ICT meant booking the computer room well in advance and making a special visit perhaps to type up work which had already been written in pen. The increasing use of interactive whiteboards, laptops and other technology makes integration a reality.

It is wise to be suspicious of statements about ICT which are too dogmatic and generalised, because the reality is invariably more complex. The use of email may make some users sloppy in their writing habits but it may also motivate pupils to write who have hitherto shown reluctance to do so. The use of grammar- and spell-checkers does not have to induce hysteria about falling standards but may suggest that their sensible use is a fitting subject matter for English teaching. Easy access to a mass of information about authors and texts suggests that active approaches to analytic and critical reading are more rather than less necessary. Early fears that technology would replace face-to-face communication seem unfounded. Computers can have the effect of isolating people socially but also allow instant communication across the world. Use of ICT has the potential to engage and motivate pupils, but it would be unrealistic not to be aware of the dangers that pupils may use it as a substitute for original thinking. It is necessary to guard against plagiarism, but this danger is sometimes overemphasised especially when a teacher has good knowledge of the capabilities of individuals. Many teachers have had the experience of pupils proudly handing in a print-out of pages from the Internet, but this sometimes occurs because of misunderstanding and limited experience of using the technology rather than simple deceit.

Sadly there has been an increasing need for guidance on Internet use which is 'safe and discriminating'. Schools are relatively 'safe areas' for children to use technologies, as they are likely to have filtering and/or monitoring software, and classroom supervision.

Access to the Internet at home, however, may not be mediated by such safety mechanisms. There is no fail-safe technological solution that will protect children from all the risks they may encounter online. Children therefore need to be taught safe and discriminating behaviours that they can adopt whenever they are using the Internet.

Practical advice on teaching Internet safety is available from the Becta website (address is given in the further reading section). With the increasing use of computers in primary schools pupils are likely to have been advised on such matters, but it is wise not to take this for granted. It is always a good idea to consult school policies and specialists within the school about the use of ICT.

Before considering some practical examples of the use of ICT in English lessons, it is worth giving some thought to the wider impact of ICT in education. Rather than indulge in futuristic speculation it is perhaps more helpful to draw attention to growing trends. Technology is having an increasing impact on school administration and lesson planning, from computerised registration and the use of spreadsheets and databases in order to record and track pupil progress to the use of technology to store and present lessons in dynamic and imaginative ways. Departments have found that sharing and, importantly, adapting resources has been greatly facilitated. Technology is increasingly being used to support assessment processes. The increasing use of ICT has the potential to transform the way teaching and learning is organised in schools, with more interaction between teacher and small groups, more use of independent individualised programmes and one-to-one mentoring.

The wide use of technology has brought frequent references to the 'knowledge society'. The mass of information that is available at the touch of a button has implications for the way we think about education and teaching. The ready convergence of text, image and sound in digital technology suggest that it is important to think about truth and knowledge being conveyed by means other than in its traditional formulation in propositional language (with implications here for assessment as well). It is perhaps helpful to distinguish between 'knowledge' and 'information'. The Internet brings unprecedented access to information, but for this to be transformed into knowledge it needs critical selection and understanding. Far from reducing the need for teaching, as was once thought, technology makes it more subtle.

Access to technology also has the positive effect of challenging the authority of traditional texts. The fact that young people are now able to produce their own professional-looking publications incorporating sound and image means that they may be less likely to be seduced by the surface features of text. Contrary to some opinions that technology elevates style over content, the reverse may actually be the case. There was a tendency in the early days of using ICT for elaborate presentation to mask paucity of content, but as the use of ICT becomes more widespread and more transparent, attitudes to presentation are likely to be more balanced, their significance neither over- nor underestimated.

## ICT and English

When thinking about the broad relationship between ICT and English it is useful to distinguish between

- teaching *for* ICT
- teaching *through* ICT, and
- teaching *in* ICT.

These are not absolutely clear-cut categories but tend to overlap. Teaching *for* ICT refers to the teaching of generic skills (keyboard skills, operation of email, sending attachments, etc.). Only a few years ago a teacher might have taken a class to a computer room to work on a project such as the creation of a newspaper front page, only to find much of the lesson taken up with teaching basic skills such as accessing programmes and saving files. This is now less likely to occur as pupils are increasingly acquiring basic computer skills in primary schools and at home. Of course, as with all learning, there will always be variation in prior knowledge in a class but the National Curriculum levels and programmes of study for ICT ensure a greater level of continuity. There may be exceptions when for example a particular facility (e.g. split screen within a word-processing package) needs to be explained, but the English teacher is less likely to be concerned with teaching ICT skills per se.

The term teaching *through* ICT refers to the use of technical aspects of ICT to extend and enhance the pupils' learning in English. In some cases this is a matter of being able to perform tasks (e.g. sequencing a poem or doing a cloze activity) more quickly and efficiently. The use of ICT however makes new activities and approaches to the teaching of English possible. Most of the practical suggestions for using ICT in this chapter will come within this category of 'teaching through'.

Teaching *in* ICT refers to the way in which the implications of using ICT become an object of study in its own right in English. For example the use of emails raises interesting questions about changing conventions of communication and levels of formality/informality. Spell-checkers need to be seen not just as functional devices; their use should be actively discussed. The way in which 'reading' starts to become redefined when conceived in relation to multimedia CD-ROMs and hyperlinked texts can be discussed with pupils. The Internet needs to be understood in more than just technicist terms but needs to be seen in terms of its effect on human relations. Is the use of Internet leading to a more open and democratic society or is the opposite the case with more potential for manipulation? Is the use of the pen likely to disappear? When is the use of a pen preferable if at all? Are there any ethical questions about the use of personalised letters by companies for advertising purposes?

The use of ICT in English needs to be seen in relation to established principles of good practice in the subject. The possibilities of writing for a real audience with a sense of purpose become much wider with the use of email and publishing packages. The potential for integrating speaking and listening, reading and writing can be enhanced by use of interactive multimedia resources. Emphasis on the writing process, which has been an established principle for many years but in practice has been tedious for pupils, is far more natural with ICT. Most importantly ICT, because it can engage pupils to work actively on language both when reading and writing, has the potential to highlight the way in which meaning is constructed in use.

A further revision of the English National Curriculum might well see more emphasis on what has been referred to above as teaching in ICT.

## Using ICT in the English classroom

The following suggestions are given to stimulate further thought and ideas. Some are fairly familiar and well-established techniques. As with all practical ideas and suggestions they need to be used with critical discrimination.

### Reading

- The familiar cloze exercise in which words from a text are deleted so that pupils can fill in the blanks is more flexible using a computer. Drop-down menus can be created to provide pupils with a choice of words. Cloze activity is sometimes overused with low achievers. Why not try it with gifted and talented or post-16 students using for example a Dylan Thomas or Auden poem?

- Many complete texts (Shakespeare plays, novels, narrative poems) can be accessed from the Internet or CD-ROMs. The entire text can be searched (use 'find') for particular words, for example use of 'nature' in *King Lear* (there are 40 references), the use of 'death' in *Macbeth* (there are 20 references). This initial search can lead to a finer categorisation of types of imagery. For this kind of search it is useful to have the play set out on one page as in http://the-tech.mit.edu/Shakespeare/. The search facility can also be used to highlight the way repetition can work in a text.

- The 'find and replace' facility on word-processing programmes can be used to change a novel extract or poem. Appreciation of the subtlety of an author's choice of words is more easily shown rather than explained by having pupils replace words by ones which very clearly do not fit as well. Find and replace can also be used to create new, absurd or startling texts. Using technology can facilitate an appropriately 'playful' approach to text and language. The 'thesaurus' facility can also be useful for working on a text.

- Comparing the same news story published in different newspapers, a long-established activity in English lessons, can be given a fresh impetus by downloading these online. They can be compared on screen using split screen and manipulated by for example swapping headlines to see the (often inappropriate) effect. Simulation of the creation of a newspaper front page is an established activity in many schools and makes the process of editing very real.

- Access to the Internet allows pupils to search for relevant background information related to any text being studied – biographical details, social and historical context, textual notes. If such research activities are set as homework it is often a good idea to give the pupils specific questions so that the research is more purposeful and focused.

- As a way of helping pupils to view information derived from the Internet with caution they can be set the task of finding material related to a particular text which is wrong or misleading. This can be good fun. They may light on discussion groups treating *Macbeth* as a whodunnit or, bizarrely, wondering whether Macbeth and Lady Macbeth were actually really married! Alternatively, pupils can be set the task of finding contradictory interpretations of a text.

- Many directed activities related to texts (DARTS) activities can be employed more easily with computer technology: underline key words; highlight words and phrases in particular colours; annotate texts using 'comments' or 'track changes' facility. These activities can be conducted with the whole class using an interactive whiteboard or set as individual or group tasks.

- The 'table' facility on word-processing packages can be used effectively for tasks which require pupils to categorise different texts. For example, pupils can be given a range of sentences and asked to place these within the most likely 'genre' categories (narrative, instructions, informal letter, etc.).

- Asking pupils to search and select photographs and pictures to accompany a piece of text is a form of comprehension. They are in effect creating a new text based on their understanding of the original.

- Guided reading can be effectively supported by the use of interactive whiteboard because it is easier to manipulate text – breaking it up into sections and highlighting key features.

- Annotating text using the 'comment' or 'footnote' facility on word-processing packages can encourage pupils to make inferences and read between the lines.

## Writing

- As suggested above, a word processor is better used for the drafting process rather than just typing up work already composed in class. Saving different drafts means that pupils can later reflect on the writing process, print out various drafts for display and share thoughts about the composing process with a partner or the whole class. Pupils need to be taught possibilities – from changing individual words to changing the order of whole paragraphs.

- The 'track changes' facility in word-processing packages is also a useful device for allowing pupils to examine the drafting process more closely. A teacher can, using a whiteboard, take the class through the changes that have been made to a particular piece of writing, discussing ways in which the text has been improved (or not). A pupil can do the same with their own work.

- The traditional approach to pupils for whom writing was a chore was to face them with threatening blank sheets of paper lesson after lesson. Alternative ideas can be enhanced by the use of ICT. The use of writing frames is made easier by computer technology as these can be adapted for the individual or class. A teacher can use the computer to create other templates for writing either for use on screen or for printing:

(e.g. postcards, heart shapes, character templates/silhouettes, animal shapes, speech bubbles).

- Another alternative to the 'blank page' syndrome is to present pupils with a text that has already been written for them to work on: continue the writing, create a title, rewrite the middle paragraph. They can be asked to use the 'find' facility to identify all the 'ands' in a piece of poorly written prose and improve it by changing the text.

- Enhanced presentation of work, made possible by word processing and desktop publishing, should not be underestimated both as a source of motivation and as a means of learning about the effects of different methods and styles of presentation: the insertion of paragraph or section headings is a way of thinking about the structure of their writing; newspaper and magazine articles often have a summary in a text box – this is a way of making the task of précis more meaningful; the choice of title formed in a larger, different font is a way of drawing a reader's attention to the central meaning of a text.

- Pupils can use ICT to create a particular text type in a more realistic way. For example, a newspaper article can be presented in columns, with justified text and headlines; an information leaflet can be produced using a template; a compilation CD cover can be created using a 'wizard' in a publishing package.

- The draw facility can be used to create speech bubbles on pictures. This allows pupils to create and superimpose imaginative written text. The same device can be used by teachers to create worksheets to practise the use of speech marks.

- Pupils as well as teachers can access websites such as that provided by the QCA to view samples of pupils' work with grades and comments on ways it could be improved. Pupils can be asked to provide their own comments on a piece first before accessing the commentary.

- In the traditional English classroom, particularly in primary school, the invitation to 'draw a picture' after writing was often seen as just a time-filler or reward for the pupil who had finished quickly. But the task had more educational potential than was often realised; at its most positive it was in effect asking pupils to select key elements in a piece of writing and think about conveying meaning in visual form. Now pupils can choose pictures and photographs electronically to accompany their writing, retaining the creative element and removing the tedium.

- The storage capacity of hard disks and CD-ROMs opens up all sorts of possibilities of archiving and sharing pupils' work.

## Speaking and listening

- ICT provides pupils with an effective support for presentations using PowerPoint and multimedia.

- Digital recording and editing facilities allow the creation of 'vox pop' programmes with pupils speaking directly to camera.

- Video recording of group discussions and playback can also be an effective way of encouraging self-awareness and critical feedback.

- Whereas games based on sport, fighting and racing are likely to produce little more than grunts or exclamations, problem-solving games or simulation in pairs or groups can do much to facilitate talk.

- The phenomenon of chat rooms erodes some of the traditional distinction between speaking and writing. Printing out an extract from Internet conversations can provide a useful focus for examining these differences.

## Poetry

- Presenting a poem to a class line by line using an interactive whiteboard can create interest, encourage prediction, invite questions and draw attention to form.

- Active approaches to text can be applied to poems as well as prose: match rhymes using a colour font or 'highlighting' facility; identify the stress on syllables in the same way. An alternative to cloze activity is to delete whole lines, not just words, and ask pupils to create possibilities.

- Annotating a poem with questions can be a non-threatening way of engaging with the text and can be a precursor to further discussion and research.

- Poetry reading can be enhanced by choosing appropriate music to introduce the reading, using the volume button to fade out the music as the reader begins. Alternatively, leaving the music playing at a very low volume can be very effective.

- Typing up poetry which has been drafted on paper can be a chance to review punctuation, line lengths, spacing, stanza breaks and general presentation (e.g. choice of font).

- An anthology of poetry can be created from websites with accompanying pictures, annotations and introduction.

- Sequencing poems is a well-established poetry-teaching activity (when a poem is broken into stanzas or lines for individuals or groups to assemble). When this task is performed on-screen different versions can be created, stored and compared.

- Found poems (see Chapter 10) can be created more easily on screen because extraneous words can be deleted in an experimental way. A piece of descriptive prose can be distilled into a haiku.

- Split screen is useful for comparing a poet's two drafts of a poem or two versions of a translated poem: 'First Ice' by Andrei Voznesenky is a suitable poem for the latter activity.

- Pupils can create a sequence of images to go with a poem for presentation. These can be found on the Internet or created using a digital still or video camera.

## Drama

- Changing a narrative into a drama script can be tedious on paper if it involves the copying of lengthy extracts. Converting prose to stage directions and dialogue is made much easier by cutting, pasting and reformatting text

- An extract of play text can be annotated by, for example, including the thoughts (subtext) of the speaker.

- The whole business of writing a play, which can become technically awkward with paper and pen, can be facilitated with the use of a word processor.

- Comparing three versions of a single extract from a play can often be more productive than watching just one version all the way through.

- Pupils can prepare an advertising flyer for a play that is being studied using words and images. This is followed by a discussion of the effect of different font sizes and use of quotations.

## Language

- Using the 'find' facility a teacher can replace all the punctuation in a text (full stops, commas, questions marks, exclamations marks) with different symbols. The task for low achievers is to work out which symbol represents which punctuation mark and replace it.

- The grammar facility on word-processing packages can be used on a text and pupils asked to try to guess what the suggestion might be before looking it up. Pupils need to be taught that the spelling and grammar checks can be totally unhelpful if used indiscriminately.

- The 'table' facility in a word-processing package can be used to categorise text, for example identifying parts of speech.

- Pupils can also be asked to change the font in a text so that different parts of speech (nouns, adjectives, verbs, conjunctions) are each in a different colour. They can be provided with a piece of prose and given the job as editor of improving the style, with particular attention to verbs, adjectives or connectives.

- The use of a whiteboard can enhance the teaching of word-level work by allowing a whole class to see how parts of words are combined (e.g. prefixes and suffixes) or how spelling can be helped by breaking words down into constituent parts.

### Further reading

For an interesting collection of chapters see Adams and Brindley (2007) *Teaching Secondary English with ICT*. For background reading on ICT see Abbott (2001) *ICT: Changing Education*; Blake and Standish (2000) *Enquiries at the Interface: Philosophical Problems of Online Education*; Goodwyn (2000) *English in the Digital Age*. Nicholls (1991)

*Learning to Teach* has a general chapter on ICT. Dymoke (2003) *Drafting and Assessing Poetry* has a chapter on poetry and ICT and details of many websites.

## Resources

The British Educational Communications and Technology Agency (Becta) website has extensive information on the use of ICT and links to other websites: www.becta.org.uk. Other sites with useful links: The Standards Site www.standards.dfes.gov.uk; National Teachers' Portal www.teachernet.gov.uk; Teacher Training Resource Bank: http://www.ttrb.ac.uk/.

# 13

# English at Key Stage 4

*Examinations are formidable even to the best prepared, for the
greatest fool may ask more than the wisest man can answer.*

Charles Colton

## The 14–19 context

BEFORE CONSIDERING SOME OF THE ISSUES related to teaching and assessment at Key Stage 4,
it is important to examine briefly the wider curriculum context. This book has followed
the structure indicated by the National Curriculum in that separate chapters have been
devoted to Key Stage 4 and post-16 teaching. It is important however to be aware of the
increasing tendency for policymakers to think in terms of the 14–19 curriculum and that
reform of the examination system at this level is in process.

One of the reasons for thinking more in terms of 14–19 education is that in the
modern world age 16 should no longer be seen as the culmination of formal education or
training for the majority of pupils. The DfES document *14–19: Opportunity and Excellence*
(2002b) built on the proposals outlined in an earlier Green Paper published in 2002. In
this document concern was expressed at the numbers of pupils who drop out of formal
learning aged 16, the percentage of pupils who do not achieve five good GCSEs at school
and the weakness of the vocational routes on offer. These concerns eventually had
implications for policy changes with the introduction of new initiatives and courses.

As part of the 14–19 reform a new diploma qualification has been introduced that
is intended to combine theoretical study with practical experience. It is intended that
diplomas will cover 17 subjects by 2011. All diplomas will require students to achieve
a minimum standard in English, mathematics and ICT, and all will involve some work
experience. This development builds on the increasing flexibility in the curriculum with
wider choice and more school and college partnerships. Central to the success of the
proposed changes to the 14–19 curriculum is a cultural shift so that courses which do not
fall into the traditional academic mould are not undervalued.

In the short term, as a core, compulsory subject, English is not directly affected by the
broad current changes to the 14–19 curriculum (although the English GCSEs are being
revised for 2010 in accordance with changes to the National Curriculum and will embody
functional skills). However, it is important to be aware of indirect consequences and
possibilities. Viewed positively, the vision in these proposals is of young adults motivated

and committed to a form of learning which suits their own aptitudes and strengths, not tied to a traditional classroom setting but taking advantage of flexibility and choice, including individualised programmes, vocational courses and work placements. It is important that developments within English keep pace with these changes by exploiting possibilities for cross-curricular connections, for example relating language activities to real work-based contexts. It is important also that assessment systems support rather than constrain curriculum innovation.

## Examination and coursework assessment

One of the major contentious issues in recent years was the abandonment in the mid-1990s of so-called 100 per cent coursework schemes at GCSE in favour of a system of assessment by combined coursework and external examinations. In the changes for 2010 coursework will be replaced by controlled assessment (see below). The issue of the abandonment of 100 per cent coursework assessment, perhaps more than any other, outraged many teachers of English at the time and it is important for newcomers to the profession to understand why that was the case. The following discussion is not intended to be mere polemic nor is it simply an exercise in nostalgia; understanding the benefits and tensions associated with particular methods of assessment is not only a valuable means of gaining insight into aspects of teaching English but is also a way of ensuring that current systems are used in ways which are most beneficial for pupils. The change which reduced the coursework component of the GCSE (to a maximum 40 per cent in English and 30 per cent in Literature) had political and ideological motivations but the opposition voiced at the time was based rather more on educational grounds; many teachers felt that coursework schemes allowed the development of more meaningful and worthwhile courses than the ones they replaced.

Chapter 8 described the way in which reliability and validity in assessment can tend to pull in opposite directions. At the risk of oversimplification, reliability is the degree to which a system of assessment yields the same results in different contexts whereas validity refers to the degree to which a method of assessment can be described as an appropriate means of testing what it purports to measure; a multiple choice test in English can be said to have high reliability but poor validity; on the surface it seems that external examinations sacrifice a certain degree of validity for a high level of reliability because pupils are being tested on the same content and tasks. However, even the reliability of external examinations is often overstated. It is relatively easy to ensure a fairly high degree of standardisation with regard to setting examinations by ensuring that the content is the same for everyone and that candidates have the same amount of time to answer questions. Those factors however do not ensure reliability because there is no guarantee that pupils' performance on one or two occasions will be representative of their potential achievement. Also, standardising the marking of the papers is extremely challenging.

Unless English is assessed in a very reductive and mechanistic way (by, for example, judging writing only by surface criteria, and comprehension of reading by the degree to which candidates' answers are correct or incorrect), it is very difficult to standardise marking. The advent of GCSE signalled in all subjects a healthy change of emphasis towards rewarding what pupils were able to do rather than uncovering what they could not. The more complex the examination, the more elaborate mark schemes have had to become in order to ensure comparability of response by examiners. The standardisation of external examinations in English is not much easier than standardising the marking of coursework.

If the degree of reliability of external examinations was overestimated, the reliability of coursework schemes was severely underestimated. Few professionals who were not closely involved in the detailed workings of such schemes had a proper understanding of the rigour with which moderation procedures were carried out. Staples (1992: 114) wrote:

> It is only fair to note, though, that many English teachers are passionately committed to 100 per cent coursework, such is their hatred of one-off summative papers coupled with the pride they justifiably feel in the courses they have been able to create under a very open-ended scheme. There must always be severe doubts, however, over a system which allows so little scope for outsiders to assess a pupil's performance, not to mention any positive effects there might be of preparing pupils to think and write under pressure, as they have to do in controlled examinations.

The comment reveals some fairly common misconceptions: teachers generally had more positive educational reasons for favouring coursework schemes than a 'hatred' of other methods of assessment; there was always considerable scope for outsiders to scrutinise pupils' work. Referring to such methods of assessment as 100 per cent coursework schemes, although common, was somewhat misleading because all of them required at least one submission which was written under controlled examination conditions. The new policy on controlled assessment has parallels with the old 'controlled conditions' assessment. The proliferation of information on the Internet makes the problem of plagiarism of more concern than ever before and the concept of controlled assessment to replace course work has arisen largely for that reason. It is therefore being introduced for more negative than positive reasons. However there are more positive implications because controlled assessment has the potential to replicate some of the more positive aspects of course work, with the potential to assess more complex processes. There will be an element of flexibility. In controlled assessment, the levels of control will be designated at three key control points: task setting, task taking and task marking. In addition, the level of control at each of these key control points will fall into one of three categories: limited, medium or high.

The hope is that the movement towards controlled assessment may develop not as a movement away from course work (the way it is currently conceived) but rather away from terminal examinations.

At the time when changes to the examination system to reduce the course work element were being mooted, teachers gave eloquent testimony to the ways in which coursework assessment influenced their classroom practice for the better. G. Harrison (1990: 3) contrasted the way in which the traditional O level examinations meant that English, which had been a 'lively, enjoyable and stimulating subject' in the first 3 years of secondary school, became an exercise in practising repetitive tasks which would gain the necessary grades (writing at speed; practising comprehension papers; completing context questions and essays on set texts which were learned practically by heart). She goes on to describe the varied and dynamic syllabus which the GCSE coursework scheme promoted, requiring

> a climate, a framework . . . within which every pupil has the opportunity to flourish and to excel. The preparation for further study is immeasurably superior as they become self-reliant, independent, forward-looking students, able to organise, revise and view their own work with some objectivity. This is active not passive learning.

Bousted (1992: 20) wrote with equal conviction about the value of GCSE coursework syllabuses, drawing on specific examples of her own work on Howker's *The Nature of the Beast* and Shakespeare's *The Merchant of Venice*. She described in detail the work she undertook with a multi-racial, mixed-sex class relating their own personal experiences to their reading of the play:

> Teachers could now work with pupils to encourage the confident expression of their initial responses to a text; to then examine the text and see what evidence could be gathered from it to support or challenge these initial responses which, in this process, would often become more considered, and complex. Thus, a more detailed and certainly a more diverse response to the text could be stimulated amongst a class of pupils.

Gabrielle Cliff-Hodges (1993: 69) described the very wide range of reading and writing which the scheme promoted and used extracts from pupils' work to demonstrate the quality of their responses. She compared her practices as a teacher with her own memories of reading in secondary school where there was 'no connection between reading for pleasure and reading for school purposes'. There were many similar letters and articles bearing testimony to the benefits teachers derived from coursework schemes, which can be summarised as follows:

- Teachers were released from the pressures of preparing candidates for examinations and all that entailed (mock exams, teaching exam technique, etc.), which placed severe limits on the time which could be devoted to the actual teaching of English.
- By choosing texts and assignments which were suitable for their own particular pupils (taking into account ability, culture, interests, etc.) teachers were able to ensure more valid forms of assessment.
- A higher level of validity was ensured because the method of assessment was able to judge work which had been produced in more meaningful contexts than the artificial writing and response demanded by timed examinations.
- The trial marking and moderation procedures, through which pupils' work and the actual tasks demanded of them were scrutinised and shared, were invaluable sources of professional development for teachers.
- Coursework assessment promoted more individual, personal and authentic responses than the writing which tends to ensure success in examinations.

Such schemes were not without their disadvantages. Sometimes schools set inappropriate assignments which did not give pupils sufficient opportunity to demonstrate achievement, or the range of reading and tasks offered to pupils was narrow and insufficiently challenging. Controlled assessment has the potential to develop as simply a constant series of terminal examinations, which from an educational perspective would be counter-productive, or it has the potential to preserve some of the better practice embodied in coursework assessment.

It is not the intention here, however, to create an unduly pessimistic view of current systems of assessment at Key Stage 4. The challenge for teachers is how to make best use of whatever system is in place (while still exercising the right to lobby for change if that is felt to be an appropriate course of action). Despite the external constraints, it is very evident that syllabuses have been constructed as far as possible in order to preserve best practice in English teaching. It is important therefore for teachers to keep faith in methods which are educationally worthwhile and avoid the narrowing of the curriculum, which in the past all too often accompanied examinations. The use of model answers, endless dictated notes on set texts and excessive concentration on examination practice should not be necessary.

## National requirements and syllabus design

It is not the intention to provide here details of specific syllabuses. The syllabuses are currently under review and in any case different schools opt for different examination boards and the details can easily be accessed from websites (see further reading section below). However, a useful exercise for new teachers who are not familiar with the details of syllabuses at Key Stage 4 is to consider how English might be appropriately examined at GCSE given the constraints which operate. English syllabuses have to meet the requirements of the National Curriculum and must therefore cover speaking and listening, reading and writing; they must include a substantial amount of literature whether or not the candidates are also taking English literature as a separate examination. (The distinction between English and English literature is not therefore the same as the traditional distinction between 'language' and 'literature', as is often assumed.) Syllabuses must also meet the national GCSE criteria, which specifies the relative weighting to be given to the different dimensions.

The syllabuses must be written in accordance with the programmes of study section for Key Stage 4 so need to include, from the 'range and content' element:

### Speaking and listening

- prepared, formal presentations and debates in contexts where the audience and topic are unfamiliar;
- informal and formal group or pair discussions requiring students to take on a range of roles;
- individual and group improvisation and performance.

The range of purposes for speaking and listening should include describing, narrating, explaining, informing, persuading, entertaining, hypothesising, and exploring and expressing ideas, feelings and opinions. The stimulus for speaking and listening activities should include those drawn from work contexts and other real-life uses.

## Reading

The texts chosen should be of high quality, interesting, engaging and challenging. The range of literature studied should include:

- Stories, poetry and drama drawn from different historical times, including contemporary writers.

- Texts that enable pupils to understand the appeal and importance over time of texts from the English literary heritage. This should include works selected from the following pre-twentieth-century writers: Jane Austen, Elizabeth Barrett Browning, William Blake, Charlotte Brontë, Robert Burns, Geoffrey Chaucer, Kate Chopin, John Clare, Samuel Taylor Coleridge, Charles Dickens, Arthur Conan Doyle, George Eliot, Thomas Gray, Thomas Hardy, John Keats, John Masefield, Christina Rossetti, William Shakespeare (sonnets), Mary Shelley, Robert Louis Stevenson, Jonathan Swift, Alfred Lord Tennyson, H. G. Wells, Oscar Wilde, Dorothy Wordsworth and William Wordsworth.

- Texts that enable pupils to appreciate the qualities and distinctiveness of texts from different cultures and traditions.

- At least one play by Shakespeare.

The range of non-fiction and non-literary texts studied should include:

- forms such as journalism, travel writing, essays, reportage, literary non-fiction and multimodal texts including film;
- purposes such as to instruct, inform, explain, describe, analyse, review, discuss and persuade.

## Writing

In their writing pupils should:

- develop ideas, themes, imagery, settings and/or characters when writing to imagine, explore and entertain;
- analyse and evaluate subject matter, supporting views and opinions with evidence;
- present ideas and views logically and persuasively;
- explain or describe information and ideas relevantly and clearly.

The forms for such writing should be drawn from different kinds of stories, poems, play scripts, autobiographies, screenplays, diaries, minutes, accounts, information leaflets, plans, summaries, brochures, advertisements, editorials, articles and letters conveying opinions, campaign literature, polemics, reviews, commentaries, articles, essays and reports.

## Key skills

GCSE specifications in English should provide opportunities for developing and generating evidence for assessing key skills: application of number, communication, information technology, improving own learning and performance, problem solving, working with others.

Other constraints prescribed by the national criteria for GCSE are as follows:

- The weightings for the objectives are: speaking and listening 20 per cent; reading 40 per cent; writing 40 per cent.

- Each scheme of assessment must include a weighting of 60 per cent to examination and 40 per cent to controlled assessment.

- Question papers in English must be targeted at either foundation or higher tier.

This is a formidable list and illustrates the challenge facing examination boards when devising syllabuses to meet all these requirements. If you are not yet familiar with GCSE syllabuses you might like to attempt the following task. Even if you do not succeed in designing a full syllabus (a tall order!), thinking about some of the issues involved will act as a useful 'way in' to critical examination of some of the syllabuses offered by various examination boards and as a way of understanding the decisions which need to be made.

## Task

Using the general criteria and National Curriculum requirements design a syllabus for teaching and assessing English at Key Stage 4. You will need to make decisions such as:

- how many examination papers to have (remember that pupils are under stress from examinations and these need to be kept to a minimum);

- which aspects of the syllabus are best assessed by controlled assessment and which aspects are best assessed by examination (e.g. Shakespeare, poetry, response to non-fiction, speaking and listening);

- related to the above, what forms of writing are best assessed by controlled assessment or examination;

- whether to differentiate for the tiers by outcome, by task or by using different stimulus and reading material;

- how the assessment tasks might be combined to fulfil more than one requirement;

- whether set texts should be prescribed;

- whether some reading material should be pre-released as an anthology.

The syllabus design becomes more complex with the addition of literature as an extra subject. It is possible for some of the coursework element to operate as 'cross over pieces' fulfilling the requirements of both English and English literature. For example, coursework on Shakespeare or prose could fulfil requirements for both.

One of the disadvantages of traditional terminal examinations in English is that writing tends to occur out of context with very little stimulus other than a bald title. One solution which has been used is to link the reading materials in one section of the examination with the writing in another. Thus pupils may be asked to respond to two non-fiction leaflets based on house safety; for example, 'Write down six different things you can do to your house to make it more secure . . . Which of the two leaflets do you think is more likely to get its message across to the reader, and why?' The writing tasks which follow are integrated with the same theme; for example, 'Imagine you are renting a house which you do not feel is very secure from thieves. Write a letter to your landlord explaining in detail what you want him or her to do to make the house more secure. Try to write personally and persuasively.'

The integration of reading and writing in this example is helpful but the tasks are inevitably thin and two-dimensional. Even a theme such as 'security in the home' has more potential interest than the bland and prosaic treatment forced by the examination context: comparison of attitudes to home security over time (interviewing grandparents) and in different cultures; whether it might be in advertisers' interests to promote a certain degree of paranoia about home safety; examining the extended imagery in the police safety leaflet – 'fortress', 'castle', 'defence'; considering the way films exploit feelings of personal vulnerability in the home (*Home Alone, Cape Fear*); whether a leaflet of this kind may be counter-productive, etc. Classroom teaching needs to foster an active, enquiring approach to meaning and language and the strict division between fiction and non-fiction reading fostered by the examination structure is not always helpful. Analysis of texts with all abilities which probes different levels of meaning is likely to be a more helpful preparation for examinations than constant practice of passages in timed contexts.

One of the criticisms of the ways in which traditional examinations assessed reading is that they required either rote learning of set texts or, in the case of language papers, comprehension questions on rather meaningless, decontextualised prose passages. All the current syllabuses inevitably require response to unseen texts of some kind but the use of pre-release material which is studied in advance has been popular

Assessment by examination should not divert teachers from varied, active, exploratory approaches in the classroom. Integrated teaching with an emphasis on meaning, the encouragement of personal response to texts, writing with a sense of audience and purpose and the development of confidence in using language will contribute more to a better performance in examinations than rote learning of prepared answers and practice on decontextualised extracts.

## Preparing for examinations and controlled assessments

Inevitably some practice and specific advice on taking examinations will be necessary but this does not have to dominate the syllabus. General and fairly familiar guidance on sitting examinations will help candidates: read the instructions and questions carefully; leave time to check the paper at the end of the examination; time answers so that all questions are attempted; take heed of the marks which are available for specific questions or sections as these may indicate the relative weighting of time and energy which should be expended on them.

In addition, some specific guidance on approaching the English papers is likely to be helpful: candidates can be helped by examining the structure of the paper in detail so that they know what to expect; they should be prepared for reading stimulus material and advised not to spend too much time on this (some boards specify pre-reading time at the start of the examination); pupils can be advised on making the best use of prompts which give an indication of what should be covered in answers; technical terms can be revised prior to examination (unless these have been acquired in context they will not be understood but some systematic revision prior to an examination is useful); word limits are sometimes set and candidates should be advised not to waste time counting words over and over again – an estimate is all that is necessary. Specific examination practice and advice is necessary but if it dominates an English syllabus unduly it will become counter-productive.

Tasks that are set for assessment purposes have to address the required learning outcomes. Creative responses to literature can stimulate highly innovative work but if not set appropriately may not always allow pupils to show more than an elementary grasp of plot. Diaries or letters in role as a character from a novel sometimes prompt pupils to write little more than summaries. One problem is that it is not always clear to pupils whether they are meant to be demonstrating their own understanding of the text or whether the perceptions should be confined to those of the character through whose eyes events are being perceived. Sometimes assignments are inappropriate to the nature of the text; for example, asking the pupils in role as Piggy to write a letter home misses the point that the absence of contact with adults in Golding's *Lord of the Flies* is an essential ingredient of the novel. The point here is not just that assignments should be set carefully but their purpose, assessment criteria and relationship to objectives should be explained clearly to pupils.

The later years of compulsory secondary schooling do mark a significant period in the development of young people and this chapter needs to consider some of the broader issues which may affect the teaching of English at this level. Some understanding of adolescence will therefore be helpful.

## Teaching young adults

It is important not to make too many over-generalised claims about adolescence. Whereas for some pupils it is marked by emotional upheaval and a crisis of identity, for others it passes relatively smoothly (Head 1997). The attendant physical and emotional development and uncertainty about roles and relationships may cause no more than fluctuations of mood but for some it involves more serious challenges to authority and deviant behaviour. Nevertheless, it is by definition a time of transition and adjustment so that feelings of personal vulnerability, however these are manifested, may be strong.

Because the onset of adolescence varies considerably with individuals, the challenge facing teachers is greater.

Much of the writing on education and adolescence inevitably focuses on more general rather than subject-specific implications. Coleman (1980), for example, in a description of adolescent needs lists the following:

- the importance of a framework of authority in which young people are able to play some part in the decision-making process ('a permissive environment is no more preferable than an authoritarian one');
- the importance of participating as much as possible in the adult world;
- the need to be seen as individuals and not stereotyped;
- the need for help with developing sexuality;
- the importance of involvement in peer group activity.

There are clear implications here for schools: the inclusion of a personal and social education dimension in the curriculum; the value of work experience and extra-curricular activities, which are increasingly being viewed as essential rather than peripheral aspects of school life.

There are also implications for the teaching of English, although these are not clear-cut. Teachers involved in making choices and recommendations for reading for this age group are faced with a paradox which is neatly summed up by Landsberg (1988: 183):

> The urgent message of literature's most thoughtful critics . . . is that the reading of good books can work in a mysterious, compelling way to enlarge the reader's life. Vast numbers of books for beginning and middle readers, both the most praised and the most popular, seem to have exactly that effect. On the other hand a tidal wave of books with an obsessively narrow focus on contemporary teenage preoccupations has inundated the market in the last decade, triumphantly carrying with it the majority of readers in this age group. At precisely the moment when a youngster hesitates on the brink of the larger world, the popular literature for him or her is totally given over to navel gazing and trendy 'problems'.

The challenge of both engaging the immediate interests of pupils and helping them know and come to terms with an external world is particularly pronounced at this stage of development. Although teachers may object in principle to the prescription of texts at Key Stage 4, few are likely to disagree with the inclusion of Shakespeare and other pre-twentieth-century literature as one way of extending the range of reading which pupils encounter. It is important not to restrict pupils' reading to topics which are seen as 'adolescent', thus stereotyping young people and restricting them from full access to the adult world.

Adolescent cognitive development, under the influence of Piaget, is often associated with the onset of more formal thinking, a more advanced tendency to hypothesise and a more pronounced capacity for 'metacognition' or thinking about thinking. There are implications here for the teaching of English. The type of approach recommended in various chapters in this book, which seeks to develop in pupils a conscious knowledge not just of the way language works but of how different genres and texts operate within different conventions, is well-suited to the developmental needs of young people. Pupils of this age will need opportunities not just for reading and analysing texts but for examining these in their broader cultural contexts and comparing a wide range of types of text (cf. Chapters 5 and 10). They are then more likely to become involved in challenging conventional ideas about reading and literature. These are not alternative models to the 'personal growth' pupils are likely to derive from their reading but ways of extending their understanding to reflect their intellectual development.

Adolescence is also a time of increased focus on beliefs and values with a corresponding emotional disengagement from dependence on adults. Personal and expressive writing therefore may be very important at this age. As with reading, there is a paradox in that the need to give expression to deeply personal thoughts may come at a time when pupils feel least able to voice them. Writing in English should never seek to be an overtly therapeutic process nor should pupils be asked directly to share private experiences. This does not mean however that they will not give expression to matters which are deeply personal to them either directly or through metaphor.

This chapter ends with three extracts from written assignments which were submitted to me in my teaching career and which illustrate the role that writing can play in the young person's growth to maturity. The first piece was written by a pupil in a lower set of a Year 10 class in response to an assignment which asked the group to write a diary in role. She chose to write about a suicide:

*Monday 10th July* God I am sick, I've no-one to talk to. No-body understands. Baby John has done nothing but cry all day. I could kill him never mind myself.

*Tuesday 11th July* Mother came for the day, she never shut up going on about Dave telling me I should of never got married baby or no baby, telling me he wasn't capable as a father. No-body cares about me. No-body understands. I've had enough.

*Wednesday 12th July* Sat in by myself all day no-one came, couldn't be bothered with baby John, I bought tablets at the chemist, I never left them they stayed in my hand all day. I haven't eaten for 3 days now.

*Thursday 13th July* I was up early (5.30 a.m.) Baby John was ill not surprising he hasn't hardly had anything to eat. The rain has never stopped the milkman came for his money but I never answered the door. I bought another bottle of tablets today. One bottle doesn't seem enough.

*Friday 14th July* Went out for a walk it was still raining. I passed the river, too many people fishing there, I wasn't out long frightened in case someone saw me. I bought two more bottles of tablets. I should have enough now.

*Saturday 15th July* I stayed in, closed all my curtains and locked all the doors, before I did all this I took the baby next door and asked if they could look after him till tomorrow. I have wrote a letter to him so when he gets older he will be able to read it and maybe understand why I couldn't live any longer.

*Sunday 16th July* Before I die whoever reads this diary please understand why.

*My dear son John,*
*You should now be at an age to understand this letter, I am deeply sorry that I couldn't bring you up,*

*John. I had you at a very young age, in fact I was 15 when I had you, I hope you will grow up to be a fine big lad, someone who knows how to look after thereself not like me I was incapable. John if you go steady with a girl please treat her good and if she was to fall wrong look after her and show that you care for her. Look after yourself John and I hope you have a happy healthy life.*

*Love, Your mam never forgotten and will always be watching over you.*

*P.S. I enclose a photograph of me.*

It appears at first that the pupil used the diary in role to explore situations and feelings which were some considerable distance from her. The piece could be interpreted as an example of a young person using her writing to take a glimpse into an adult world beyond her with its potential difficulties and challenges. The ending borders on the sentimental but the directness and simplicity of the language and the colloquial style give it authenticity. It was in the following year when this girl submitted an autobiography that it became apparent the writing had a more personal relevance: her own mother was only 17 when she was born and had been unable to look after her. The diary can be seen as an attempt to explore the sense of bereavement and loss her own mother may have felt; the photograph may represent her own wish that a similar memento had been left for her. In the light of the information about her own past life, the diary takes on new meaning. Using the protection of role and metaphor as a means of providing objectivity and distance, she has used her writing to help come to terms with her own personal experiences.

The second example was also submitted by a Year 10 pupil in response to an invitation to write about an occasion when someone felt excluded from a group or situation. I had not asked the pupils to draw directly on their own experience; it was up to them whether they chose to do so and whether they would write in the first or third person. One girl decided to write about her parents' divorce which happened when she was 8 years old. The piece is lengthy and written in a very controlled way; there is very little self-pity or heightened emotion and the style is fairly undemonstrative. She writes about her confusion at the time over what divorce meant and the failure of the adults to explain anything:

*When I asked questions about it, or why they were getting divorced I was just told 'You're too young to understand' I think perhaps this hurt me as much as anything else because, true, I did not understand, but I felt I could. I was eight years old.*

She continues to describe the fears she felt about the future and of having to be taken into care. After giving an account of the father's departure she describes a first shopping trip for birthday presents without him. The piece ends with a description of the father's first Sunday visit and an outing to the park where at last he explains the divorce to her:

*I saw he was crying, I had never seen him cry before. We arrived back at the car. We did not speak all the way home. When we arrived he kissed us both, we said goodbye; we got out of the car and he went. That was all I needed. Someone should have explained earlier. Two months was too long to wait. Adults should not presume children are too young to understand. They understand more than you think.*

The writing is very far from being an indulgent piece of self-expression. The pupil uses the task to allow her developing adult self to understand and distance experiences which at the time were bewildering and painful for her.

The same idea of being excluded from and underestimated by the adult world appears in the course of an autobiography written by a Year 11 pupil who had special needs. The pupil concerned was ebullient and witty, very talented at drama but with severe problems throughout his school career with the mechanics of reading and writing. His piece provided a retrospective look at his school career with the benefit of a more sophisticated view:

*School has never been my strong point but it's A thing you have to live with.*

*I first attended an infant school which was all right. All the teachers were a bunch of old bags I hated them. After lunch or break they used to come in the classroom stinking fags or coffee. I think harf the time they were never Interesed in what they were doing. They always picked in me to read out when they knew fine well I couled not read. It was just to mack me look a fool.*

*I can remember one teacher in who every firday aftarnoon she whould show us her skrap book of holydays photographs. she say I'v been hear and I'ev been there as she turned a globe of the worled round. The posh bich had been everywhere. I am shur she would have said I'v been to the moon if she thort we would have believed her.*

*In the third year was good I liked the teacher so I would behive untill one day a sicolligis come to see me and interviewed me made me read ask some silly questions and sent me bake to the classroom. I spent a whole aftrnoon whith her. I did nat know what to think. I was never tould what she whonted.*

*That night I got no sleep by wondring what they were going to do. I was always the thike one in the class. I thort they were going to sened me away.*

*And one day a cared was sent to the house.*

*Saying she was coming to see us. I had a lot of expling to do because I had nere taled my mum or dad. So she came to our house and explaind she wonted to see why I was not progresing at school. This whent on untill the second year of this school.*

In the course of the year the group read Daniel Keyes' *Flowers for Algernon*, a science fiction short story in which the main character undergoes an operation to increase his very limited intelligence. The pupil who wrote the autobiography was very taken with this story and, largely inspired by his enthusiasm and leadership, the group worked on a dramatic representation of it. He played the central character and, as someone who had always been considered 'the thike one in the class', it was both ironic and poignant that his own lively intelligence allowed him to play the part before and after the operation so convincingly. It is not necessary for the teacher to have specific knowledge of how pupils' writing and response to reading at this age may relate to their own personal lives; it is enough to be sensitive to the fact that this may be, and often is, the case.

## Further reading

Although syllabus details become out of date quickly, the insights in publications related to this phase remain valuable. The following books have chapters on English at Key Stage 4: Pike (2004) *Teaching Secondary English*; Protherough and King (1995) *The Challenge of English in the National Curriculum*; Davison and Dowson (1998) *Learning to Teach English in the Secondary School*.

## Resources

The Qualifications and Curriculum Authority website (www.qca.org.uk) provides up to date information on assessment and qualifications. Syllabuses for the three main awarding bodies can be found at their websites: AQA www.aqa.org.uk; EDEXCEL www.edexcel.org.uk; OCR www.ocr.org.uk.

The revised anthology *Klondyke Kate Revisited* contains a range of useful non-fiction extracts. See also *The Beautiful Game*, a non-fiction anthology with language and media units on football. Both are available from The English and Media Centre.

Two NATE publications, *Exploring Pre-Twentieth Century Fiction: A Language Approach* and *The Wider Reading File*, are loose-leaf and photocopiable, focusing on the 14–16 age range. The English and Media Centre also publishes guides on *Gulliver's Travels* (including activities on the film version), *Under Goliath, The Friends*, Janni Howker's novels, *Animal Farm, Of Mice and Men* and others. Further guides on specific texts accompany Hodder English 4. A wide-ranging Key Stage 4 volume *The Language Book* (Shuttleworth and Mayne) and two packs for Key Stage 4 focusing on language and gender under the title *Language Awareness Project, Years 10 and 11* are available from Hodder & Stoughton.

# 14

# Post-16 English

*In seed time learn, in harvest teach, in winter enjoy.*

William Blake, *The Marriage of Heaven and Hell*

## The background

TENSIONS, you will have no doubt noticed, lie at the heart of every facet of the teaching of English; sixth form work is no exception. A and AS Level English teaching – which constitutes most of post-16 English teaching, in schools at least – is often sought after enthusiastically by newcomers to the profession. However, it is also sometimes withheld by heads of department anxious to safeguard academic teaching, though this happens far less now than it used to. In a sense, this state of affairs mirrored the élitist nature of A levels generally, intended as they were for university preparation for the minority. There was no alternative qualification available for the less academic: those disinclined towards academic study were simply disqualified and expected to seek apprenticeships or employment. The move away from this élitist concept is a slow, ongoing process. Curriculum 2000, introduced in response to the recommendations of the Dearing Committee, has done something to broaden the base of the curriculum at this level. The major implications, running alongside other changes, for English at post-16 have been:

- the re-casting of A level into stepped components (AS, usually taken in Year 12, and A2, taken in the following year by those who choose to specialise in English);

- the consequent increase in the number of students taking English in Year 12, at AS, as one of five or more subjects; in many school sixth forms and colleges the majority of Year 12 students take some form of English;

- greater diversity of available courses, including literature, language, and syllabuses combining the two;

- greater emphasis on intertextuality across language and literature courses, partly through the synoptic element in all syllabuses, seeking to evaluate students' knowledge and understanding of the subject as a whole;

- for literature study especially, a stronger sense of the social, cultural and critical context for any given text;

- as for all subjects, more frequent testing of students' progress, at AS and A2 levels and, often, for specific modules; many would say this amounts in effect to over-testing;

- the arrival and promotion of Applied A Level courses in a number of pre-vocational areas, many of which have communications components which may be taught by English specialists.

In many ways, the sixth form seems to provide a most fertile ground for imaginative English teaching, with the possibility of a genuine and voluntary partnership in teaching and learning based on a greater degree of intimacy than is generally possible in earlier years. Greater maturity, smaller group size, a less formal school/college ethos, and significant subject specialism should also combine to create a convivial ambience. Neither is it a matter only of individual learning, for the combination of these factors may lead to resourceful collaboration. It is widespread practice to 'share' responsibility for AS and A level groups, thus making collaboration almost inevitable, even if only at the informal level. The opportunities, of course, extend well beyond the informal, and the best departments plan for a balanced curriculum, in terms of both content and teaching style, and regularly monitor the progress of their students.

The intention in this chapter is to look more closely at the creative possibilities open to English teachers in the teaching of AS and A level courses in English literature and language. There are other qualifications for which English teachers often prepare students, such as Scottish Highers, the expanding but still controversial pre-vocational courses and other A levels such as Communications or Theatre Studies, but lack of space precludes a thorough account. There currently exists also a general state of flux, particularly concerning vocational education, which suggests that any such study be postponed for the time being; in the meantime, many English departments have shown a reluctance to become too heavily involved in, say, the communications 'key skills' of pre-vocational courses. For better or for worse, A levels remain the bread and butter of English teaching in sixth forms and the intention rather is to give a 'flavour' of the potential which undoubtedly exists for creative and effective English teaching at this level.

## The educational context

It may be helpful, however, to look a little more closely at the educational context which has such a profound bearing on sixth form English. One issue impossible to avoid is the vast increase in the number of students in sixth forms, most of whom continue to be attracted – often against careers advice – to A level courses. A glance at some figures illustrates this expansion: in 1939 88 per cent of children left school at 14, and even in 1959 only 10 per cent continued schooling beyond sixteen; the growth of A levels was very much geared to this context, and in many respects the academic basis of the examination-determined curriculum has not been appropriate to the influx of students with quite different needs. At Key Stage 4 the introduction of GCSE has gone some way to bridge the gap between the needs of 'traditionally academic' pupils and those with other aptitudes; but in some respects this has simply pushed the problem up into the post-16 phase. There have been attempts to broaden the base of post-16 education, incorporating both academic and vocational aspects and seeking common ground between the two, but – until now at least – A levels have remained sacrosanct, sometimes (as in the Dearing Report) referred to as the 'gold standard' of the English education system.

The current very public concern for 'lifelong learning' and entitlement to a broadly based education has tended to focus on the post-16 curriculum. Increasingly discussed is the possibility of eroding the significance of GCSEs in favour of a seamless continuity in 14–19+ education, with qualifications at the age of 16 seen as no more than a 'staging post' in the process, possibly reduced to an assessment of 'key skills' in literacy, numeracy and ICT. The development of what amounts to three separate strands in education and training should be seen in this context: the academic strand is still to be based on A levels, with the important development of AS levels giving a degree of breadth; the vocational, previously often termed the pre-vocational, strand is given expression through GNVQs in both schools and colleges; finally, the occupational route, confusingly once known as the vocational, attains accreditation through National Vocational Qualifications (NVQs) largely outside educational establishments. There is supposed parity between these routes, and the rhetoric of politicians emphasises this. Witness, for example, David Blunkett (in a speech reported in the *Times Educational Supplement*, 7 November 1997), 'We need to be imaginative . . . We need to challenge this old world obsession with the professions promoted by people who don't want to get their hands dirty.' In reality, however, parity has proved extremely elusive, and some, such as Tomlinson (1997: 16), doubt the intentions behind the rhetoric:

> A schizophrenic situation has developed whereby politicians repeat mantras of a learning society in which all are educated enough to want lifelong learning, while cementing a system that cuts off large numbers of young people from education at sixteen, and perpetuates the notion that there are separate types of student suitable for separate tracks.

The situation, then, is problematic, and talk of 'tracks' begs the question of how those born on the wrong side of them are to be educated. It is worth bearing in mind these considerations when planning for the teaching of A level groups, as it is likely that their composition will reflect a wide range of interest, commitment and aptitude; some indeed may have been advised to select an alternative 'route' but preferred the traditional security of A levels, perhaps sensing the reality of Tomlinson's words. English is particularly susceptible to these concerns, in that the subject is often taken as a 'safe' second or third option on the basis of enjoyment and a measure of success at GCSE, awareness of the employment market, or even parental insistence on increasing general literacy. These may be sound enough reasons, of course, but not necessarily those of the dedicated, talented student intending to read English at university, who is also likely to be represented in the group and would have been the originally intended client of the A level dominated system. Diversity presents a challenge, and the chance to innovate accordingly to meet the challenge.

The various tensions, contradictions and concerns may be summarised thus:

- the fundamental distinction between education and training as reflected in the three 'routes';
- the wide-ranging needs and aspirations of students;
- the supposed parity between the three 'routes';
- the transition from compulsory to voluntary participation in education;
- the transition from GCSE courses to A and AS levels and the position of GCSE English as preparation for further study;
- the competing claims of different institutions: school-based sixth forms, sixth form colleges, tertiary colleges, FE colleges and others;
- the contradictory claims of specialisation, often vociferously endorsed by students, and curricular breadth, reflected in the introduction of 'key skills';
- the perceptions of the alternatives in post-16 education held by the general public, including parents, prospective employers and higher education;
- methods of assessment – the roles of coursework, modular structures and terminal examinations;
- inter-subject comparisons in terms of possible combinations and perceived difficulty of study.

To these we would add further points relating more immediately to the situation 'on the ground', the day-to-day reality of teaching English at this level:

- implications for selection of students, in that English is often heavily subscribed, and the offering of appropriate guidance and induction;
- pedagogical issues in the teaching of sixth form groups;
- the tension between freedom and restrictions for post-16 students, often particularly keenly felt in school-based sixth forms;
- staffing considerations, including the usual need to work collaboratively;
- students' involvement in their own education and assessment, including such concerns as use of private study time, appraisal, reporting to parents and participatory learning.

## The transition to post-16

Bearing all this in mind may seem rather daunting, but although they are important considerations they should be regarded as secondary to the enthusiasm for the subject with which a teacher of English can inspire sixth form students – often, indeed, the inspiration which has in the first place led teachers to follow that vocation. Given this commitment, much of the rest follows in the collaborative working of a good department; this collaboration should extend to the students themselves, whose involvement may be significant in many of the areas noted above and should serve to alleviate some of the difficulty in keeping all the balls in the air.

It is worth starting this process of participation as early as possible during the course so that it may feed into the teaching and learning from the start, and also establish in the minds of the students the nature of their involvement in their own education. Within the induction period, generally positioned either in the 'fallow' time of June or July previous to the course starting or at the beginning of the new academic year, a survey such as that shown in Figure 14.1 could be used.

---

### SIXTH FORM INDUCTION: QUESTIONNAIRE FOR ENGLISH

Discuss the following questions with a partner. The aim is to encourage you as students and us as teachers to think about the ways in which teaching and learning best take place.
Circle a number 1–5, with 1 denoting 'strongly disagree' and 5 'strongly agree'.

Section 1: Types of learning
(a) I prefer teacher-led lessons to any other                                                    1 2 3 4 5
(b) I like working to given deadlines best                                                       1 2 3 4 5
(c) I like the teacher to give firm discipline, even at sixth form level                         1 2 3 4 5
(d) I work best individually                                                                     1 2 3 4 5
(e) I work best in a small group                                                                 1 2 3 4 5
(f) I thrive on discussion work                                                                  1 2 3 4 5
(g) I like to organise my own notes as against teacher direction                                 1 2 3 4 5

Section 2: Reading
(a) I like to read only for light entertainment                                                  1 2 3 4 5
(b) I like to feel challenged by what I read                                                      1 2 3 4 5
(c) I spend 1=no time, 2=30 mins, 3=1 hour, etc. reading most days                               1 2 3 4 5
(d) I like reading poetry                                                                         1 2 3 4 5
(e) I enjoy shared reading sessions                                                               1 2 3 4 5
(f) I enjoy reading plays as a group                                                             1 2 3 4 5
(g) I enjoy reading Shakespeare                                                                   1 2 3 4 5

Section 3: Writing
(a) I like to draft essays carefully using at least two stages                                   1 2 3 4 5
(b) I enjoy 'creative writing' best                                                              1 2 3 4 5
(c) I feel confident about writing 'literary critical' essays                                    1 2 3 4 5
(d) The more coursework-based writing the better                                                 1 2 3 4 5
(e) I write best under examination conditions                                                    1 2 3 4 5
(f) I write for my own personal enjoyment as well as for my studies                              1 2 3 4 5
(g) I like a lot of choice in the subjects I write about                                         1 2 3 4 5

Section 4: I chose English at A Level because:
(a) I have a great interest in literature, language and ideas                                    1 2 3 4 5
(b) It should lead to good opportunities in employment/HE                                        1 2 3 4 5
(c) It fits in with my other choices of subject                                                  1 2 3 4 5
(d) Current sixth formers enjoy studying it                                                      1 2 3 4 5
(e) It promises to be the easiest subject on offer                                               1 2 3 4 5
(f) The results at A Level are consistently good                                                 1 2 3 4 5
(g) It's easier to get in than for some other subjects                                           1 2 3 4 5

**FIGURE 14.1**

As with all research of this kind, the content and format may be adapted for differing circumstances. The important point is that completion of the survey should lead to further discussion of the issues raised, both with the students themselves and as a focus for pedagogical development among colleagues. It may well be that few clear-cut conclusions are possible, but this in itself may be a powerful argument for diversity of approach. It is also vital, especially in terms of developing credible cooperation, that the discussions are periodically revisited and that they are seen actually to inform teaching and learning. If conducted properly, this sort of approach may be a fundamental part of the course itself rather than yet another burden.

The suggestions and thoughts arrived at will, of course, differ considerably between individuals, groups and institutions – there would be little point in undertaking such an exercise if not. Nevertheless, there are likely to be some key considerations, reinforced by the findings of research (see, for example, that conducted by Morgan at Denbigh School, 1997). My own (unpublished) research in this area, conducted at Thirsk School with both English colleagues and students during 1995–6, corroborated the findings of wider enquiries, and is summarised below:

- Discussion is popularly held to be the most effective teaching method, rather than 'teacher talk'; the related need to listen attentively and encouragingly, and to base discussion on a range of groupings and tasks, is also important.

- 'Active' sessions are much valued as 'ways in' to literature and language: using drama, collage-making, booklets, posters, etc.

- Note-taking is regarded as essential, and the preferred method is to have time immediately after discussions and activities, with just the odd aide-memoire jotted down during the session itself.

- Notes are the students' own responsibility but should be checked periodically by the teacher, perhaps as the focus of a shared activity and an important aid to examination revision.

- The didactic lecture-style lesson has its place in the context of a balanced curriculum; when vital information has been imparted there is a need to revisit and emphasise, especially in lessons immediately subsequent to the lecture.

- There is a generally perceived need for some work to be done on study skills such as summary making, essay writing, methods of reading, research, use of IT, etc., which may or may not be covered generically by particular sixth forms.

- Related to this point is the expressed liking for collaborative essay planning with a sharing of students' – and particularly the teacher's – expertise, followed by detailed and formative marking; many are acutely aware that the eventual grade depends invariably on how well students write.

- Individual tutorials, either informal or linked to some form of assessment, are widely regarded as useful – especially when focused on specific strengths and weaknesses.

- There are some contradictory views on the nature of deadlines for writing, which really have to be worked out in the context of particular sixth form policies.

- Concern for progression from GCSE to AS and A level is widespread, and in some ways justified – we are talking about 'advanced' study, after all – but it may also contribute to the unwarranted and even intimidating 'mystique' of A levels.

- Different teachers have contrasting views on the use of background material and published notes – certainly there is a tension between the need to stimulate a fresh subjective response and the incorporation of recognisably 'literary critical' interpretations and other contextualising information.

Some of these points refer more to literature than to language study, but they have a general validity. English teachers at this level have to be aware that, as McCulloch *et al.* (1993: 25) put it:

> Students can be resistant to the suggestion that they take responsibility for their learning. Feeling more secure with the teacher-as-expert, they are content to take the role of listeners and note-takers. Current pressures on teachers may encourage collusion in this model, but . . . this is ultimately counter-productive . . . until students have expressed their understanding in their own words, neither they nor the teacher can say with any certainty what they have or haven't understood.

In the light of this observation, the suggestion concerning the place of 'lecture' sessions is significant, in that many teachers feel vaguely uncomfortable giving this sort of lesson; we need not do so, as there is a great deal of essential information that can be given in this way and, after all, terminal examinations usually account for 80 per cent of the final grade. However, the rider 'in the context of a balanced curriculum' is vital too, and requires reflective thought and planning. In this, as in so much else, A level teaching is no different from English teaching for previous years: best practice displays a unity of approach across the entire age range and is best characterised by a 'workshop' approach in which all feel able to contribute according to their aptitudes and interests to a full range of activities.

## Implications for English teaching

We need now to examine in rather greater depth what all this might mean in terms of real teaching and learning. We will look at ideas for the teaching of Tennessee Williams's play *A Streetcar Named Desire*, Graham Swift's short story 'Learning to Swim', poetry interpretation for the 'critical appreciation' examination, Brian Friel's play *Translations*, and a range of language activities. This may seem like rather a tall order, given the space available in one chapter, but the hope is that approaches are transferable – not only from text to text but across the age and ability ranges in schools – so that summarised ideas will be sufficient to stimulate imaginative teaching.

We start with *A Streetcar Named Desire*, a play containing a mixture of passion, sex and raw energy, occasionally spilling over into violence. As with the reading of any play, it is effective to conjure an atmosphere of a theatre group working towards a shared understanding essential for some sort of performance. The text then becomes a working script; the preliminary group reading raises questions, displays possibilities of interpretation and enactment, and progresses towards a thorough acquaintance with the play itself. During this reading it may be best to avoid too much detailed note-taking in favour of jotted marginalia (an issue here might be whether the students own their own texts or not). During a second, more detailed reading the group should be discovering what works in terms of the drama, acting sections out and receiving guidance towards the key themes, characterisations, and the twists and turns of the plot: this would be the appropriate time for a more extensive accumulation of notes after each session, with the possibility of additional short-term writing tasks. On completion of this reading, probably taking us up to a half term of study, the group should be ready to adopt a variety of approaches to the whole play. There may be options available at this stage, and the activities are often best summarised on a handout such as that in Figure 14.2.

Various factors will influence the nature of the choices to be made from these approaches. One important consideration is whether understanding of this particular text is assessed by coursework or by terminal examination; if it is the former, the extent of textual knowledge need not be so broad, but the particular assignment chosen for assessment will need to show great depth of insight into the selected aspect of the play.

---

### ACTIVITIES BASED ON *A STREETCAR NAMED DESIRE* (a half term's work)

1. Presentations (working in groups of three) given to the rest of the group on themes within the play, with each using a minimum of six carefully chosen quotations to illustrate the presentation. The themes are:
   - class conflict and the battle between old and new;
   - gender conflict and sexuality;
   - psychological issues and the question of insanity;
   - setting and atmosphere throughout the play.

2. Tableaux: eleven 'frozen moments', each introduced by the appropriate line(s) – one tableau for each scene, enacted to the minutest detail of facial expression. (See Chapter 12)

3. Theatre programme design (working in the groups established for 1.) to include:
   - biographical information;
   - themes of the play (see 1. above);
   - symbolism and staging;
   - design work and illustrations;
   - imaginary cast list and 'pen portraits' of the actors.

4. Hot-seating: a drama activity which involves each character, played in role, facing possibly hostile questioning from everyone else. Preparation in researching the nature of each character should be thorough and imaginative. (See Chapter 12)

5. Whole-group writing and illustration of a 'study guide' booklet for future students of the play, assembling the material and insights gathered from the above activities and using ICT and photocopying facilities for the final publication.

6. Essay titles to be based on the themes outlined in 1. above.

FIGURE 14.2

It is important also, with the arrival of key skills in the A level syllabuses, that students have the opportunity to work on such areas as giving presentations, using ICT and conducting research.

By way of contrast, Graham Swift's short story 'Learning to Swim' is far narrower in scope and would almost certainly be offered as a coursework option unless combined with other material (possibly the additional stories in the Cambridge edition). This edition, as part of the Cambridge Literature series, presents the text with notes and activities along the lines of the five approaches we noted in Chapter 5; this editorial material is particularly valuable in providing ways into the story for sixth formers. In fact, both literature and language students would benefit from close study of the story, the latter in terms of the linguistic conventions used – such as narrative stance and the interior reflections of three separate but linked characters, and as a possible model for students' own creative writing. It is important to emphasise the creative overlap between literature and language, and innovative English departments are developing exciting teaching opportunities in the light of this cross-fertilisation – cemented as it is by syllabus change incorporating the AS structure, key skills, and modular framework possibilities.

To focus again on 'Learning to Swim', additional approaches and activities might include:

- pre-reading activity: plan a short narrative combining these elements:
    - ☐ a dysfunctional mother–father–son family relationship
    - ☐ the family on holiday
    - ☐ the memories of the adults
    - ☐ learning to swim

(The idea here is subsequently to compare students' efforts with Swift's, focusing through discussion and close reading on the similarities and differences);

- stream of consciousness thoughts, ideally expressed in verse, of the characters – particularly appropriate here in that the story centres on three separate interior monologues distanced partly through the third-person narrative stance;

- role-played or written re-creation as 'flashbacks' of the incidents presented through memories – thus bringing in the possibility of cinematic conventions;

- projection of the characters into the future, looking back to the events of the story and presenting these reflections as Alan Bennett-like 'Talking Heads';

- focus on the nature of language acquisition, using the metaphor of learning to swim as described in the story;

- further role-play possibilities such as hot-seating, dream sequences or use of the psychiatrist's chair;

- wider study of other Swift material, particularly novels such as *Waterland* and *Last Orders*.

The 'critical appreciation' section of the literature examination paper, in which candidates respond to poetry or prose under examination conditions without having seen the text beforehand, is now a feature of all literature syllabuses. It attracts controversy: some feel that it genuinely shows what an individual student, unaided, can achieve in understanding and response; others point to the incremental and often collaborative nature of understanding which this paper deliberately precludes, and insist that one slight 'mis-reading', under the pressure of examination conditions, can ruin a student's chances of presenting a coherent response. Whichever view is taken, it is unlikely to be abandoned in the present climate of 'rigour', and English teachers simply have to prepare their students accordingly. It can be done, and adventurously too. The importance of using the entire 2 years of the course in preparation cannot be overemphasised: right from the induction period onwards there should be opportunities for engagement with poetry and prose, building confidence to make coherent, informed and subjective responses. Part of this process of confidence building lies in demystifying literary criticism while providing the appropriate tools and vocabulary to accomplish the task. It is vital to stimulate peer support here, as AS and A level groups are mixed ability in terms of aptitude and confidence: the teacher's selection of working groups and pairs, for example, can be particularly effective. Gradually, using the wealth of excellent resources now available (some of which are discussed in the further reading section), it should be possible for each student to face up to a poem or prose extract alone and unaided – and again there should be plenty of opportunities to practise the skills involved. Perhaps it is not coincidental that this is the very time when many young people take their driving tests, and the combination of nervousness and recklessness may be familiar!

Activities throughout the course, for work on poetry appreciation, may include:

- performance-based interpretations of poems, including mime, music, and role-playing characters;
- 'critics debate' triads, with two students debating opposing interpretations while a third listens carefully, takes notes, and finally reports back with an attempt at consensus;
- playing the poet in role in a hot-seating exercise to face questions, perhaps with a particular teacher-given focus in mind;
- using choral readings with echoes of key words to achieve different effects and understandings, examining through the sound of the verse stylistic features such as rhythm, rhyme and assonance;
- constructing collages, illustrations for different audiences, brainstorm summaries on sugar paper and animated versions to explore interpretations;
- having groups/pairs construct their own questions, both open and closed, to ask each other on the text, subsequently summarised by the teacher;
- selecting quotations to give weight to an interpretation, using them constructively in the context of many of the above activities and others.

Emerging from this thorough preparation must be a creative combination of close reading, fully endorsed by references and quotations, with a freshness of subjective response. The vital principle, kept in sight throughout the range of activities undertaken, is to return always to the text itself – hopefully with new insights and understanding.

Much of the work on the critical appreciation paper outlined above has direct relevance, with adaptation where appropriate, to advanced English language study also, in the sense that it too demands close textual analysis and response. If we look at some of the criteria for achieving an A grade for English Literature (AQA 2002: 52), the position is further clarified:

> Candidates' . . . discussion of texts shows depth, independence and insight in response to the tasks set, and they analyse and evaluate the ways in which form, structure and language shape meanings . . . They are able to make significant and productive comparisons between texts which enhance and extend their readings, and are sensitive to the scope of their own and others' interpretation of texts. Their material is well organised and presented, making effective use of textual evidence in support of arguments. Written expression is fluent, well-structured, accurate and precise, and shows confident grasp of appropriate terminology.

Our central thesis here is that English remains English, with all its exciting possibilities, whether focusing on literature or language – problematic in any case to differentiate (see Introduction). Teachers educated in the literature tradition, who sometimes feel intimidated by the newer language-based syllabuses, need not do so.

A further text for study focusing on both aspects of English is Brian Friel's *Translations*, a play which imaginatively explores the relationship between language and power. The possibilities for inventive teaching and learning here seem endless; a selection might include:

Contextualisation: historical / cultural

- brainstorm ideas on and impressions of Ireland, contrasted with England;
- directed research activities on aspects of Irish culture;
- cross-curricular possibilities – history, geography, RE, languages, music;
- the Irish dramatic tradition – Yeats, Synge, O'Casey, Behan *et al.*;
- investigation of media presentations of Ireland, past and present.

Language and communication

- investigation of the relationship between languages and imperialism;
- language, dialect and cultural / national identity;
- the nature of translation and interpretation – connotations;
- the associations and characteristics of the featured languages (Greek, Latin, Gaelic, English) and, by extension, other languages;
- the significance of naming in a variety of contexts.

Other possibilities

- active exploration through music and oral culture, making use of the plentiful Irish resources available;
- focus on the nature of education and schooling – the relationship between learning, subversion and control;
- exploration of character and stereotype – challenges to stereotypical expectations;
- learning through drama – performance, role-play, tableau, etc.;
- nature of maps and mapping – metaphorical significance and ideas of control;
- writing tasks, both empathetic and textually analytical.

Significant here, on reflection, is just how many of these approaches to this particular text embody ideas central to holistic English teaching in more general terms; this serves to underline the idiosyncratic and wide-ranging nature of the subject.

The blurring of the distinction between English literature and language notwithstanding, we need now to examine some of the specific requirements of the language syllabuses. Off-putting to many teachers more used to literature is the extent and depth of the critical terminology; it is as well to remember here that the syllabuses are in English language, not in linguistics. Certainly we need to use the tools of the trade and to impart their appropriate usage to our students; but the context of their usage is far more important. An analogy may be drawn between linguistic terminology for language courses and literary-critical terminology for those based on literature study: in both cases terms are to be used for the purpose of elucidating textual enquiry and understanding, and examiners are explicitly asked not to credit the occasional candidate's attempt to impress by an extensive, if ultimately pointless, display of their knowledge of such vocabulary. As is the case for literature study, there are some excellent published resources now available, to which can be added teachers' – and students' – own magpie-like accumulation of language materials. There is an additional benefit here of being able to use such resources at all levels of English teaching; indeed as language study comes more to the fore throughout the age range, one of the most effective ways to familiarise oneself with the workings of language and its teaching is to read A level English Language books and then to adapt the approaches and activities for lower-school use. The essential principle, applicable to all English teaching, is that one really understands language only by immersing oneself in it, while at the same time affording a certain critical distance through reflection. In practice this means a close, often analytical, study of language as used, coupled with focused, creative use of language as studied. This parallel approach may be illustrated by some of the activities and teaching ideas below:

- a video or handbook produced by students for a specific audience, e.g. 'A Children's Guide to Grammar', 'An Alien's Guide to Holding a Conversation on Planet Earth';
- role-plays to explore language use in a variety of contexts – the use of jargon at a parents' evening or doctor's surgery, for instance – or to 'test' knowledge of a particular variety of language, such as dialect or creole;

- 'statement games' to spark debate – giving students statements about male or female language use to sort into agree/disagree piles;

- taping of speech in a range of contexts with subsequent detailed transcript analysis and comparison to written English conventions;

- close comparative analysis of contrasting texts, chosen to illustrate language diversity or language change over time;

- study of such features of language as euphemisms, product names, personal names, propaganda, ambiguity and jargon;

- group presentations on researched facets of language, combining if possible the analytical with the active, e.g. a study of the language used for charities' advertising coupled with a simulated (or real?) advertising appeal.

We have examined in this chapter some of the possibilities presented by sixth form English teaching. Perhaps because of the concentrated, intensive nature of the courses on offer in this phase no other area of the English curriculum illustrates so vividly the tension between threats – curricular uncertainty and complex syllabuses among them – and plentiful opportunities. Adoption of an adventurous perspective suggests that opportunities may yet win the day.

## Further reading

Peach and Burton (1995) *English as a Creative Art* may be used with students or to stimulate teaching ideas. Useful too are Brown and Gifford (1989) *Teaching A Level English Literature*, Scott (1989) *Reconstructing A Level English* and a publication from NATE's Post-16 Committee (1990), *A Level English: Pressures for Change*, although recent and continuing changes in the sixth form curriculum have lessened their immediate relevance. Canwell and Ogborn have contributed a useful chapter, 'Balancing the Books: Modes of Assessment in A Level English Literature', in Brindley (1994) *Teaching English*. McCulloch *et al.* (1993) *English 16–19: Entitlement at A Level* helpfully links philosophy to pedagogical practice. For a critical overview of the context of post-16 education in general terms, Tomlinson (1997) *Education 14–19: Critical Perspectives* is both wide-ranging and succinct. Pike's chapter 'Teaching English 16–18: Advanced Level' (in Pike 2004) is helpful, although limited in practical scope to AQA syllabuses.

## Resources

As a contextualising aid to literature study, the well-established *Preface* series (gen. ed. Purkiss), Longman, has a wide range of titles dealing with different authors and periods. Macmillan's *New Casebook* series (gen. eds Peck and Coyle), also long standing, provides more detailed literary critical essays, with account taken of recent critical developments; offshoots of this series are the *Critics Debate* texts (gen. ed. Scott), which are particularly useful for summarising contrasting critical interpretations of key texts. Other literary critical studies suited to A level students' needs include the *Landmarks of World Literature* series (gen. ed. Stern), Cambridge University Press; *Re-reading Literature* titles (gen. ed. Eagleton), which stress recent radical critical positions on well-established books; *Longman Critical Essays* (gen. eds Cookson and Loughrey); and, from NATE, the ever-expanding *Critical Reading at Post 16* series (ed. Dymoke), focusing on practical activities to challenge texts. Three books from the English and Media Centre examine particular areas pertinent to A level literature courses: *Reading Fictions* (eds Mellor, Patterson, ONeill), comprising twelve short stories; *Literary Terms: A Practical Glossary* (Moon); and *Studying Literature: Theory and Practice for Sixth Form Students* (Moon). *Literature, Criticism, and Style* (Croft and Cross), Oxford University Press, is a comprehensive guide to literary criticism and two books from Cambridge University Press concentrate more particularly on preparation of students for the 'unseen' examination paper: *The Cambridge Critical Workshop* (J. and L. Wood) and *Prose and Poetry* (Shiach). *The Faber Book of Parodies* (ed. Brett) and *Imitations of Immortality: A Book of Literary Paro*dies (Parrott) from Viking, are entertaining ways of encouraging stylistic experimentation.

There have been many new texts to aid the teaching of English Language A level. NATE, through Framework Press, publish a practical 'way in' to introduce aspects of language at this level, *English Language A Level: The Starter Pack* (Goddard *et al.*) as well as invaluable guides to specific aspects of language courses: *Researching Language: English Project Work at A Level and Beyond* (Goddard) and *Original Writing: Structured Activities for A Level and Beyond* (Ross). Three books from the Cambridge University Press address further concerns relevant to language students: *The Structure of English: A Handbook for Students* (Newby); *English as a Global Language* (Crystal); and, with accompanying cassette, *Exploring Spoken English* (Carter and McCarthy). There are several fairly comprehensive language study books also available, which make stimulating reading in themselves and may conceivably be used for supported self-study. Five of the best are: *Issues: A Coursebook for A Level English Language* (Turner), Hodder & Stoughton; *Grammar, Structure and Style* (Russell), Oxford University Press; *Meaning in English Language* (Jeffries), Macmillan; *Living Language* (Keith and Shuttleworth), Hodder & Stoughton; *Understanding Language* (Parry and Allen), Cambridge University Press.

Aynsley's *Starters for English Language* (NATE 2004) provides innovative 'ways in' to language teaching. HarperCollins publish an imaginatively wide range of literary and non-fiction texts for post-16 literature use, and Nelson-Thornes have some excellent language-focused texts in their range. Heinemann have published some extremely useful syllabus-orientated texts for AQA A and AS (A and B) specifications in literature, language, and language and literature, alongside Goddard's *Researching Language*. Hodder Murray have also extended their range accordingly: the *Living Literature*, *Living Language*, and *Living Language and Literature* series are all very helpful. Barlow's series with Cambridge University Press, endorsed by but certainly not limited to OCR, *Cambridge Contexts in Literature*, provides very useful practical introductions to context for literature with extracts for illustration.

# Inclusion

*Success encourages them;*
*they can because they think they can.*

Virgil, *Aeneid*

## The concept of 'inclusion'

THERE IS SOMETHING DEEPLY MORAL and humane about the idea of an inclusive school as one which is accepting of all children irrespective of race, class, disability or learning needs. As the National Curriclum guidelines specify, planning for inclusion means thinking about how the curriculum can be designed to match the needs and interests of the full range of learners (http://www.qca.org.uk). These need to be addressed both inside and outside the classroom.

The learners may include:

- children with learning difficulties and disabilities;
- the gifted and talented;
- children who are learning English as an additional language;
- boys and girls, who have different needs;
- children who are in care;
- children with social, emotional and behavioural difficulties.

The Every Child Matters initiative heralded a more integrated approach to the well-being of children and young people. The intention is that every child, whatever their background or their circumstances, will have the support they need to be healthy, stay safe, enjoy and achieve, make a positive contribution and achieve economic well-being. In pursuit of those aims the organisations involved with providing services to children are expected to work more closely together. The QCA website has a section which describes how English is particularly suited to fulfilling these aims, for example identifying the role of literature and reading for pleasure in contributing to mental health and a sense of well-being.

As with other aspects of educational provision, the issue of inclusion is more complex than at first seems. The policy of inclusion is easily distinguished from traditional ideas about segregation, when pupils with particular needs were taught in totally different settings. It also, however, needs to be distinguished from a policy of integration, which was based on the idea that a pupil could be transferred into a mainstream setting when they were thought to be ready. In contrast, a policy of inclusion places the obligation on the school to adapt its practices and environment to be able to accept all pupils. 'It is this default assumption of acceptance which is the defining characteristic of inclusion' (G. Thomas 1997: 103). The move from segregation to integration and then to inclusion has not been uncontested.

Wilson (1999) has pointed out that, although we have the idea that it is wrong if people are excluded from a community, we also need to recognise that a community exists for a particular purpose and has its own aims and values. There may then be a clash between two perspectives: including everybody within a group 'seems inconsistent with fulfilling a particular group's purpose . . . if I am unable to play a musical instrument at all, it seems to make little or no sense to say that I can be included in an orchestra' (ibid.: 110). He suggests that when we see schools as *learning*, not just social communities, some selectivity and exclusion is likely to be necessary. Barrow (2001: 236) makes a similar point when he suggests that a policy of inclusion may 'offend the principles of fairness'. He argues that a policy of inclusion has no 'self-evident moral virtue' and often involves 'a refusal to discriminate on seemingly relevant criteria' (ibid.: 240).

Arguments of this kind are a reminder that we should not be persuaded by generalised rhetoric into ignoring practical difficulties and tensions. For example, some pupils with emotional and behavioural difficulties may not be well served by mainstream provision or there may be a conflict between the needs of an individual pupil and those of the rest of a class. Practical considerations also become very relevant when the provision of specialist services become central to the inclusion of pupils with particular needs. The Special Educational Needs and Disability Act 2001 sought to enable more pupils who have special needs to be included in mainstream schools. It signalled that where parents want a mainstream education for their child everything possible should be done to provide it. It also stated that where parents want a special school place their wishes should be listened to. It recognised that mainstream education will not always be right for every child all of the time but recognised that flexibility should be preserved and that some children might be included successfully at a later stage.

It is important to be aware that the concept of inclusion is used in different ways. Sometimes it refers to the actual physical placing of pupils, but it is also used in a more normative sense to suggest that pupils have been properly received and catered for in the new setting. Thus it is possible for pupils to be included physically in a school but not be included in the richer sense of the term. As Knight (1999: 4) states, 'inclusion in some situations (for example of a student with autism) may be more like exclusion because the student's needs are not being met and appropriate services not provided in the regular classroom'. He goes on to say that the stigmatisation of pupils with labels will not disappear by simply placing students in regular schools.

Just as it is important not to ignore practical issues, it is important not to get so bogged down in arguments about detail that sight is lost of the central aims of a policy of inclusion. If we accept that it would be foolish to adopt a universal policy without looking at individual cases, the ethical dimensions of the concept of inclusion can be more easily identified.

- It is a pro-active concept. It is not just about tolerating difference but about actively seeking to determine and make provision for individual needs.

- It means responding flexibly, adapting the curriculum as necessary and seeking to overcome barriers to learning.

- It means not making premature assumptions about the ability and potential of any pupil.

- It involves recognising the strengths and experiences that people of diverse backgrounds and capabilities bring to a community. This has important practical implications in the classroom. It is not a deficit model but seeks, where possible, to celebrate difference.

- It is about developing a culture of respect and acceptance within an institution. A policy of inclusion has important implications for the attitudes and values of the whole community.

- It means challenging all forms of bullying and harassment.

## Teaching across the ability range

One of the major challenges facing teachers of English is how to make provision for the wide range of abilities and aptitudes likely to be encountered in any one class. The problem is not made easier by the fact that invariably class sizes are too large and classrooms may be under-resourced. It is important to be aware of the degree to which practical constraints of this kind limit what can be achieved. It is all too easy to place the blame for underachievement entirely on pupils' attitudes and motivation or on the teacher's lack of expertise. It is easy, on the other hand, to become defeatist about practical problems and to underestimate the importance of effective teaching, irrespective of the difficulty of the circumstances. As with so many other aspects of teaching English, a balanced perspective is essential.

The concept of 'ability' is not straightforward. Much educational writing has questioned whether it makes any sense to talk about generalised ability or intelligence, suggesting instead that there are different types of intelligence (see, for example, Gardner 1984). Many writers have challenged the idea that ability is something fixed or innate, arguing instead that it can be changed by experience. Such 'nature or nurture' debates, which used to be so much to the fore in educational writing, tend to have less prominence now. For example, many handbooks for trainee teachers are more concerned with the mechanics of coping with pupils of different abilities than with examining the concept of 'ability' itself. One of the reasons for the neglect of much of the research on ability and intelligence is that its practical relevance was not always apparent. No matter what explanations might be offered for different levels of achievement (a form of words which avoids making assumptions about pupils' potential), teachers are still faced with the reality of finding strategies to cope in the classroom.

It is important, however, not to take the term 'ability' too much for granted. The structure and assessment system of the National Curriculum is a reminder that at the very least it is necessary to distinguish between reading, writing, speaking and listening rather than to operate with a global concept of being 'good at English'. Pupils may have an uneven profile across the attainment targets. Within each attainment target it is possible to make finer distinctions, for example between pupils who excel at different types of writing or at different oral activities. It is also important to recognise that performance can vary with context, level of interest and motivation. The following piece was written by a Year 8 pupil who had learning difficulties. The task was to write a story about a 'bank robbery' (the topic was chosen by the pupils themselves) after a brief discussion with the group of four pupils involved:

> *One of our freinds gets some keyes of page of the bank. we can get the money out of the trunk an of our freind can go to get the car ready and one can go in a road work and but some dimate in a box that will explored and the van will stop on a dran then we get the money of the van and someone will shout to the men to come with the car and the we come with the car.*

The second story was written by the same pupil a week later on the same theme but with a different stimulus. This time the pupils participated in a drama (with the teacher in role as bank manager and then undercover policeman) which became the basis for the writing. The version was over four times the length of the first effort and had considerably more coherence and depth. The second story concluded as follows:

> *Then I drove it to the back enterence and there went into the bank and Ian was round the conuter buting the money into the bag, and Nathan was holled a gun at the person at the counter and Malcolm was helping Ian to put the money in the bag and I heard a voice say 'you are surround' give yourself up and but your hand above your hand. and I was still in the car, and I was get counD and he put handcuffs on all of us and we went to jail for 20 years for robing a bank. and Ian got away with it with £100 and he went free for the rest of his life. and before we went into jail I said 'I get you when I get out of jail'.*

Whereas the first piece of writing was barely comprehensible, the second has a clear narrative structure, includes the use of direct speech, and has more human interest, introducing as it does the theme of revenge. The point here is not to claim that the context which gives rise to language use is all that matters – clearly the pupil has considerable limitations with writing, which are still found in the second piece – but the example warns against underestimating the importance of the circumstances which gave rise to the work. The second piece gives more scope for feedback from the teacher and highlights more clearly areas which need to be improved. It is not uncommon for low-achieving pupils to perform at a level which is below their real potential for a variety of reasons: lack of engagement with the task, problems with self-image, peer group pressure or in some cases simply being out of the habit. The examples of pupils' writing at the start of Chapter 8 also indicate the way in which the context affects achievement.

# Differentiation

The concept 'differentiation' is rather more straightforward than 'ability' but there are dangers in its use, which can be illustrated by two examples. The first comes from a primary lesson I observed in which the teacher was so preoccupied with the mechanics and organisation of the process that the worksheets designed for the more able were given to the less able and vice versa. Nobody noticed. The second relates to a student teacher who complained that her course had not addressed differentiation but who revealed on further questioning that a considerable amount of time had been spent on how to cope with different abilities in the classroom. Language can deceive and limit thinking. The use of the label 'differentiation', which has a comforting technical ring to it, can lead to a narrowing of perspective, to an assumption that there is something which should be going on in the classroom which is somehow different from, and extra to, effective teaching. Imagine the dangers of telling a learner driver that there are four ways of achieving safety when driving. The use of the term can also deceive us into expecting simple, mechanical solutions which can be applied irrespective of context. The challenge in the classroom is how to ensure that pupils make proper connections with whatever task or material they encounter; this requires sensitive judgements and attention to how they are responding or are likely to respond to the lesson.

It is common to distinguish between differentiation 'by task' and 'by outcome'. The latter concept is somewhat strange because it yokes together two rather disparate ideas. The term 'differentiation' implies that something needs to be done in order to take account of individual pupil differences, whereas embedded in the term 'outcome' is the idea that no such action needs to be taken because pupils will be able to respond at their own level to whatever task is set. Differentiation by task makes more sense as a concept because it suggests that different pupils will be given different things to do. However, both ideas are in danger of obscuring the fact that the major teaching task may actually lie elsewhere; it may in some cases be more helpful to think about the design of a scheme of work rather than focus exclusively on differentiation in individual lessons. The important question to address is how a teacher's thinking might be influenced by the fact that the class contains pupils with very different levels of achievement.

# Introducing topics for differentiated work

Thinking about how to introduce a new theme, text or aspect of language study is important and has to do with realising that 20 or 30 very different individuals may not necessarily find it easy to focus on the same material at the same time. This idea is not unfamiliar in general accounts of pupil learning and is included in such aphorisms as 'start where the pupils are' or 'relate new knowledge and understanding to what is already familiar', but it is less frequently seen as an important aspect of teaching mixed-ability classes. (The assumption here is that all classes are of mixed ability whether the groups have been set or not.)

Finding an appropriate 'way in' to a theme or literary text which is likely to engage all pupils is helpful for a number of reasons: interest and motivation can to some degree compensate for difficulty of material; having all pupils engaged in a common topic or book (though not necessarily the same tasks) recognises that learning has a social as well as an individual dimension; pupils may be more able to support each other through a shared interest; pupils can be helped to find their own level of work through negotiation within a common framework. Finding a 'way in' is often presented as a mere pedagogical tip but it has a deeper significance related to theories of perception and reading. Phenomenological approaches to reading stress the centrality of consciousness and the convergence of text and reader to create meaning (Iser 1978). The so-called 'objective' world is not perceived transparently but is mediated through consciousness. The teacher's task is in part to mediate whatever text or other content is to be the object of study and to 'frame' the pupils' response. This can be symbolised by the well-known drawing in Figure 15.1. It can be seen as just a set of lines, or the 'reader's' enjoyment can be enhanced by being 'shown' that the drawing contains a picture of both an old and a young woman.

Useful 'ways in' to novels include: asking questions about the illustration on the cover and trying to anticipate what the story will be about; exploring the central theme through drama before starting the reading; examining an extract of dialogue from the novel and trying to guess what is going on; reading other related texts (newspaper article, poem, more accessible short story) on a similar theme. Chapter 7 emphasised the importance of designing schemes of work rather than just viewing them as collections of ideas for lessons. Often your starting point for introducing a theme which is accessible to all abilities can lead to more differentiated work as the topic progresses, as in Figure 15.2.

## Graduated questioning

The same principle of structuring a scheme of work can be reflected in the design of a worksheet or set of questions in which the more accessible tasks come first followed by

**FIGURE 15.1**

| Starting point | Development of theme |
|---|---|
| Discussing what it might it be like to start growing smaller instead of bigger. | Reading extracts from *Gulliver's Travels*; exploring metaphor in expressions like 'feeling small', 'feeling ten feet tall'. |
| Sharing personal dreams and individual's ideas about dreams. | Reading extracts from Orwell's *1984*, Chaucer's *Nun's/Priest's Tale*, *Macbeth*, 'Book of Daniel' in *The Bible*; reading psychological explanations of causes, meaning of dreams. |
| Sharing anecdotes about being wrongly accused. | Creating a 'Rough Justice' television programme; reading extract from *Othello*. |
| Ranking a collection of jokes and cartoons from the newspaper in order from funniest to least funny. | Exploring different types of humour; reading and writing examples of parody and satire. |
| Brainstorming the word 'anger'; sharing anecdotes about being angry; trying to capture anger in an image. | Reading William Blake's 'A Poison Tree'; exploring imagery in *King Lear*, *A Midsummer Night's Dream*, etc. |
| Looking at pictures of people and trying to guess their occupations, characters, personalities from their appearance. | Reading and studying character portraits in Dickens, Conrad, Joyce, Chaucer, etc. and then looking at extracts to confirm or challenge initial impressions. |
| Trying to guess the region from a tape recording of different accents. | Studying the difference between accent and dialect. Comparing different uses of the pronoun in different regions and in the past. |
| Discussing whether it is ever right to tell lies. | Reading Yevtushenko's 'Telling Lies to the Young is Wrong'; studying Miller's *All My Sons*. |
| Improvising a scene in pairs called 'waiting' in which the place and the object of waiting is not made clear. | Starting to read *Waiting for Godot*. |

FIGURE 15.2

those which are more challenging. Traditionally, comprehension exercises distinguished between levels of difficulty in questions: literal (which tested understanding of basic information), inferential (which required pupils to draw conclusions from information presented) and evaluative (which looked for judgement and critical responses). Such hierarchies can be misleading since pupils are often able to express preferences but not necessarily in analytic terms. They often condemned lower-achieving pupils to dealing only with the banal: 'Name the city which John went to when he left home.' The traditional comprehension exercise has largely given way to more active and dynamic approaches to reading texts but the same principle of staging can be employed so that pupils are not alienated by lack of achievement early on. This sometimes has to do with the way tasks are structured rather than necessarily thinking in terms of a hierarchy of skills. Even a traditional set of questions can be graduated in a way which avoids the content being too simplistic: 'Here are three reasons why John left home. Which do you think was the main one?'

## Providing individualised support

Differentiating the amount of support given to individual pupils is an effective response to the challenge of working with a range of abilities in the classroom. As an alternative to the more public distribution of different tasks to different pupils, which is often recommended as the most appropriate method of differentiation, the low achievers can be given more structured support and higher achievers more challenging extension work in the course of the lesson. This can be formalised by using extra worksheets or may simply involve the teacher giving oral instructions and help. For inexperienced teachers it should be part of the planning process to work out in advance what advice can be given to pupils who are finding it difficult to make progress with the task; for example, suggesting the first line of a piece of writing; breaking a task down into clearer stages; providing a model for pupils to imitate. The following example illustrates how the process of supporting and challenging different groups of pupils can be built into the planning.

As an introduction to a unit of work on writing for young children, a Year 9 class has been set a number of questions and tasks. They are given different types of children's story books and asked to consider:

- for which age group each story is suitable;
- which of the stories might be easiest/most difficult for a child who is learning to read;
- what might appeal to children about each of the stories;
- what makes a good story.

The challenge could be extended for some groups by asking them to analyse the language of the stories in more detail; for example, are the sentences simple, complex or compound? Are many subordinate clauses used? What level of difficulty is the vocabulary? Does the writing use standard English? Other pupils could be encouraged to focus more on their own memories of reading, stimulated by the examples provided.

A second stage in the project might be to ask pupils to write two versions of the text of a story to accompany a set of pictures – one version for 6-year-olds who are just beginning to read, the other for 8-year-olds who can read quite fluently. The lower achievers might just be able to write one version without being able to attribute it to a particular reading level; this could be the subject of a later discussion with the teacher or the class. Higher-achieving pupils might be directed to analyse their separate versions of the text, using knowledge acquired in the previous activity.

The next task on the same project might require pupils to prepare an entry for a catalogue of children's books, including details on language, story, pictures, presentation, format, size, print, likely appeal and value for money. Here differentiation might occur through initial choice of text(s).

The final task of writing and illustrating their own stories to be read to pupils in the local primary school could take place in groups so that pupils support each other in the course of the work. A scheme of work which has been introduced and launched successfully will often allow teachers and pupils to find the appropriate level of work for individuals and groups as the project progresses. A project of this kind can be a useful way of focusing specifically on use of language, punctuation, spelling and reading in a context which has a real sense of meaning and purpose.

One of the most controversial questions in the teaching of English has in the past been associated with so-called 'basic skills' and how these should be taught, particularly given that in any one class individual strengths and weaknesses are likely to vary considerably. In the literature on the teaching of English there has been a fair degree of consensus over the years, which can be summarised as follows:

- language does not develop simply by instruction and practice in discrete skills;
- exercises and drills do not give pupils sufficient experience of using language;
- viewing English teaching in terms of skills removes the important dimension of values – should reading be seen simply as decoding or should it include valuing books?;
- there is no guarantee that knowledge acquired separately in routine exercises will transfer to actual uses of language;
- language develops primarily by being used in meaningful contexts.

Advocates of an extreme 'language in use' approach to English made the mistake of assuming that written language was acquired as naturally as the spoken form and as a result they saw little need for specific teaching. By contrast, commentators who clamoured for a 'return to basics' were equally mistaken in that they took a much too simplistic view of how language develops.

The teaching of punctuation and spelling can be enhanced at Key Stage 3 by seeing these not just as 'basic skills' but as part of conscious awareness and knowledge of the conventions of written language; the concept of a 'basic skill' is very reductive, as may be seen in the discussions of punctuation, spelling and reading which follow.

## Teaching punctuation at Key Stage 3

Punctuation should neither be taught as a completely separate aspect of the curriculum nor be so well integrated that it receives no distinct attention. It is desirable to use a variety of methods and strategies which treat punctuation not just as a skill but rather as a convention of the language in its conveyance of meaning. It needs to be related to pupils' developing knowledge about language, including syntax. The following list is a reminder of some of the varied approaches which can be taken.

- Teacher intervention in the writing process: orally or in writing as part of a broad approach to drafting, proof reading, creating successive drafts. This is likely to be the most productive way of targeting individual needs. Different conventions can be used other than simply correcting work, for example underlining mistakes and asking pupils to try to identify what is wrong.

- Examining with pupils 'why punctuation?', for example looking at ambiguities, examining texts without punctuation. Creating ambiguous texts can be a useful way of raising awareness of how punctuation can affect meaning.

- Exploration of punctuation in different texts and contexts (adverts, posters, novels, poems, letters) and focusing on changing conventions. In this way work on punctuation can be integrated into other themes and treated as a topic of interest rather than just a skill. The writing of letters, for example, can be confusing to pupils if they are simply taught one approach instead of being shown different conventions.

- Exploration of texts using both essential punctuation and that which is a matter of style and choice. It will help pupils to become more confident if they know when there is and is not flexibility in use.

- Use of games, for example with younger pupils, creating sentences using sounds for particular punctuation marks.

- Use of exercises as part of a rich and broad approach to language development. Indiscriminate use of exercises can waste the time of those who are already proficient in using punctuation and confuse those pupils who have very little understanding. They are most useful as an occasional method of helping to turn knowledge into regular habit.

- Use of graphics (e.g. cartoons) to reinforce how to punctuate direct speech.

- Use of individual target setting so that pupils can be selective and do not become overwhelmed by what they have to achieve.

- Asking pupils to read work aloud with the appropriate intonation. This helps to give punctuation meaning and purpose rather than appearing as an arbitrary set of rules.

- Exploiting opportunities to explore the way punctuation affects style and tone, e.g. sentence length.

- Individual, group or class instruction. Class instruction is only rarely of use because of the wide variety of competence in using punctuation in any one class. Many experienced teachers will attest to their experience of teaching the apostrophe, only to find more pupils misusing it after the instruction than before!

- Typing out a corrected copy of a pupil's work. It is clearly invaluable for pupils to word process their own work but the impact of receiving a typed, revised version can be effective.

- Individualised sheets with advice and support. These are more likely to be useful with pupils who simply need reminding of certain conventions, rather than those who are very weak.

- Use of available ICT programmes.

## Spelling

Opinions have also been divided in the past on spelling – whether it is 'taught' or 'caught'. As with other aspects of the teaching of English, the reaction against traditional, narrow methods (for example, the rote learning of arbitrary lists) meant that some teachers put too much faith in the hope that merely using language would be enough to ensure that pupils would learn how to spell. Because in the past pupils were inhibited from writing through fear of making mistakes, some teachers reacted against providing any kind of feedback which had negative overtones. Spelling does come very easily to some children but many others (including high achievers in English) need more systematic help. Spelling objectives now constitute a strong strand throughout the English framework of the literacy strategy.

It is important not to be too dogmatic about different methods; some popular assumptions in the past have proved to be unreliable and books on the teaching of spelling sometimes differ in the advice they provide. The idea that all pupils will learn to spell if they read a great deal is simply not borne out by the research, although fluent readers are often good spellers. Learning rules went out of fashion because English spelling was thought to be so arbitrary; it is in fact regular in over 70 per cent of cases and some writers do recommend the learning of spelling rules. Mudd (1994) prefers to call these 'generalisations' because there are always exceptions to be taken into account, but she warns against their unthinking use and application.

As with punctuation, it is helpful to view spelling not just as a separate skill but as a useful convention which is part of a pupil's general proficiency in and knowledge about language.

Spelling can be actively explored in projects which examine:

- the way language (and spelling conventions) have changed over time;
- the way spelling gets 'corrupted' in advertising and popular media;
- the differences between English and American spelling;
- the way in which accent and dialect may affect how individuals spell words;
- the significance of social attitudes to spelling;
- the various attempts which have been made to reform spelling;
- the advantages and limitations of spell checkers.

Rather than condemn individual pupils as 'weak spellers' it helps to diagnose more precisely what kind of errors they are making; whether, for example, the problem relates to a difficulty visualising words or has to do with limited phonic awareness. Such pupils may be helped by a multi-sensory approach involving reading, writing and sounding out the word. A particular pattern of errors may reveal that the pupil can be helped by learning a specific rule. Other common methods of helping with spelling include:

- generating lists from pupils' own writing;
- informal tests of selected words;
- writing words in segments, seeing the patterns within words, e.g. yes/ter/day;
- learning spellings rhythmically;
- using mnemonics;

- using a 'look, cover, write, check' method;
- grouping words;
- concentrating on learning high-frequency words;
- using games to reinforce particular spellings.

## Reading

It is beyond the scope of this chapter to explore in detail the full implications for classroom teachers of the Special Needs Code of Practice, including working with support teachers and writing individual education plans, matters on which guidance is given in the further reading section. In the past it was common to view the teaching of basic reading skills as a job for the primary school or specialist, and thus of little relevance to the classroom English teacher. Clearly poor readers do need specialist help but that does not mean the English teacher should abdicate responsibility. Effective collaboration with support staff (and acting effectively at times as a support teacher) requires some understanding of the kind of specialised help pupils need. Despite the practical difficulties in giving individuals sufficient attention, it is possible to give weak readers some support within the context of the classroom. Knowledge of the issues involved in developing basic reading skills is helpful because the debate replicates some of the other controversies and unhelpful polarities in the teaching of English; beginning reading is not so dissimilar, in terms of key central issues, to the teaching of reading at a more advanced level.

As with other aspects of the teaching of English the question of 'meaning' was (and to some extent still is) at the heart of the debate over reading and relates to many issues explored in other chapters of this book. Reading is essentially an aspect of using language and as such it must be concerned primarily with a quest for meaning. According to advocates of the 'real books' approach, readers need access to material which makes sense and towards which there is some genuine motivation. The role of the adult is to serve as an experienced guide rather than as an instructor in skills. Children must develop reading in much the same way as they learn so much about language before they get to school:

> How do they learn all this? Not by programs or formal instruction. There are no kits of materials and exercises for teaching children how the world uses reading and writing. They learn – usually without anyone being aware that they are learning – by participating in literate activities with people who know how and why to do these things. They join the literacy club. People write with them and read with them – lists, notes, letters, signs, directions, recipes – any of the routine 'literacy events' of daily life in which the child can share.
>
> (Smith 1988: 9)

It can be seen that the 'real books' approach described here fits comfortably with a 'language in use' philosophy and as such it has some of the same limitations. Reading is treated just like speaking, as an ability which is acquired naturally without explicit teaching. The reason this view was held so vehemently by many educationists is that so many of the more formal approaches to the teaching of reading were arid and lacking in attention to meaning. The emphasis was on teaching the mechanics of reading; children were first taught to decipher words or parts of words and then to put these together in order to read. Phonics (an emphasis on sound/symbol correspondence) and 'look and say' approaches (whereby pupils are taught to recognise whole words) are methods which are based on the belief that children need to work upwards from a grounding in basics. It is not dissimilar to the view that children need to be taught the basic mechanics of punctuation and spelling before they can use language in any meaningful way. The result was sometimes that pupils could enunciate words or 'bark at print' (see Chapter 5) without attention to what the words meant. Artificial reading schemes were produced which paid little heed to pupils' interests or to what motivated them.

As with many aspects of teaching English the polar positions on the teaching of reading are not tenable. A narrow emphasis on the skills of reading without attention to purpose and motivation is unlikely to succeed. On the other hand pupils need to be able to recognise letters, letter sounds and combinations of letters and will not necessarily achieve that ability by simply practising reading. The balanced position is usefully summarised by Wray (Wray and Medwell 1994: 59):

1   Reading is an extremely complex process. This means that 'simple' approaches to teaching children to read will probably have little chance of success. The approach of 'put children in a roomful of wonderful books and they will learn to read' is just as simplistic as that of 'teach children to recognise and pronounce letters and they will thereby learn to read' and neither is likely to be successful.

2   Teaching reading needs to build upon what children do well (look for meaning, attend first and foremost to functional aspects of print, learn through stories) before introducing aspects which they find more difficult (apply a range of cues simultaneously, respond to text without relying upon its physical context to give them its meaning).

3   Children need to be taught the technicalities of reading but these must be set into a context of meaning.

Wray goes on to quote Adams (1990: 422), who has summarised a range of research into beginning reading:

In both fluent reading and its acquisition, the reader's knowledge must be aroused interactively and in parallel. Neither understanding nor learning can proceed hierarchically from the bottom up. Phonological awareness, letter recognition facility, familiarity with spelling patterns, spelling–sound relationships and individual words must be developed in concert with real reading and real writing and with deliberate reflection on the forms, functions and meanings of texts.

The teaching of both beginning and advanced reading needs to be based on a view which sees the reader as an active contributor to the meaning of the text. Secondary teachers of English who are confident in handling all types of text in the classroom sometimes claim not to know how to help very weak readers, not realising that many of the same principles apply. The following list provides a reminder of some of the strategies which can be used and considerations to be borne in mind when working with poor readers in the normal classroom:

- use 'ways in' to reading material which may be more helpful than simply presenting a block of challenging text;
- ensure that pupils do not get lost and alienated when reading (a frequent cause of misbehaviour) by checking frequently on understanding;
- remember that asking questions of the whole class which only one or two pupils answer will not provide information on whether all pupils are understanding – try alternative strategies such as pairs work or asking pupils to jot down answers in rough;
- take care to use an appropriately large font size when creating worksheets and do not overcrowd them;
- see pictures and drawings which accompany text not just as decorative but as useful 'cues' to meaning;
- try to create some opportunities for reading with pupils individually – not easy in a crowded classroom;
- try to participate in and support paired or home reading schemes which the school operates so that pupils do not see 'reading' as something completely separate from classroom English;
- take note of mistakes or 'miscues' when pupils read – a guess which bears no relation to the appearance of the word but makes sense may indicate poor phonic awareness; one which takes its cue from the spelling of the word but makes no sense may indicate that the pupil is not reading for meaning;
- motivate reading through interests (including non-fiction).

## Children with disabilities

The Special Needs and Disability Act 2001 introduced new duties and responsibilities which came into effect from September 2002. Schools and local authorities must:

- not treat disabled pupils less favourably, without justification, for a reason which relates to their disability;
- make reasonable steps to ensure that disabled pupils are not placed at a substantial disadvantage compared with other pupils who are not disabled (but there is no duty to remove or alter physical features or provide auxiliary aids or services); and
- also plan strategically for and make progress in improving the physical environment of schools for disabled children, increasing disabled pupils' participation in the curriculum and improving the ways in which written information which is provided to pupils who are not disabled is also provided to disabled pupils.

For the classroom teacher this means planning to ensure that all pupils can participate as fully and effectively as possible. The starting point here is receiving appropriate information about individual pupils and, if necessary, seeking it out; it is not wise to assume that those responsible in the school for passing on details are infallible, and some pro-active questioning may be necessary. Not all pupils with disabilities will have special educational needs. This information should include specific advice on practical strategies which may be needed (e.g. you may need to make yourself clearly visible so that a pupil who is hearing-impaired will be more able to lip read; you may need to use a microphone; a pupil who uses a walking aid may need to leave the classroom just before the end of the lesson). It is important to be aware, for example, that appropriate amounts of time may need to be planned to allow for the completion of tasks. Some pupils may only be able to record work at a very slow pace and may require considerable effort to do so. Others may need to use alternative communication systems to compensate for difficulties in using language to meet the demands for speaking and listening. ICT may be a valuable aid in helping pupils who have difficulty with handwriting. Advance planning and liaison with teaching assistants and other support staff is also an important aspect of ensuring adequate provision.

## Teaching high achievers

Meeting the needs of the 'gifted and talented' is an aspect of inclusion. This means not only employing strategies in the classroom to challenge all pupils but being alert to the identification of pupils with particular strengths in the subject. It might be thought that, by the time pupils reach secondary school, high achievers in the subject will have been identified. However, it is important to be aware that a policy for inclusion includes the identification of those pupils who may be underachieving and who by definition will not have been easy to recognise. Pupils may also excel at one attainment target or one component with an attainment target (e.g. poetry or drama) and their potential therefore may have remained concealed. It is also important to be aware that, as pupils mature, hidden talents may start to emerge.

Making provision for higher-achieving pupils is generally more straightforward than meeting the needs of low achievers because they can be expected to take more responsibility for their own learning and to operate more independently. However, it should not be assumed that they need no extra attention; many of the principles to do with meeting individual needs which are appropriate for teaching low achievers are appropriate for the gifted and talented.

■ As suggested in Chapter 8 on assessment, it was not uncommon years ago for high achievers to go through their school careers receiving little more than bland praise (with low achievers conversely receiving nothing but criticism). Both extremes can be prevented by adopting a policy of always identifying both achievements and limitations. With the very best work this can sometimes feel somewhat artificial and even unjust because searching for something critical to say is not always appropriate. It is often helpful therefore to see formative assessment and feedback more in terms of advice and dialogue rather than pure judgement: 'why not try . . . would this be better if . . . have you ever thought of . . . you might be interested in reading . . .'

- If a Year 7 class is working on structuring a written narrative with an arresting opening and development some of the pupils may in addition be asked to experiment with multiple narration. It is important not to seek salvation purely in extension worksheets, but these can be a useful device if not overused. For example, a scheme of work on Dreams might lead some pupils to reading the sleep-walking scene in *Macbeth* with the task of trying to infer what has happened in the past to make Lady Macbeth disturbed; the theme of 'schools' might lead to reading an extract from Dickens's *Nicholas Nickleby* and continuing the narrative in the same style.

- The importance of teacher/pupil relationships and individual contact should not be underestimated. Making sure that a pupil knows that their strengths have been recognised is an important step in keeping them motivated and engaged. Individual extra reading can be encouraged through informal contact in the classroom. If a particular novel is being studied as a class reader, some pupils can be encouraged to read other works by the same author.

- An ongoing reading log or diary may be a particularly useful way of encouraging pupils to take responsibility for their own learning and may be a way of maintaining a systematic dialogue with individual pupils (rather than leaving this to informal, chance encounters).

- In Chapter 7 on planning it was suggested that a scheme of work may be very tightly structured at the beginning but may become more flexible as it unfolds, particularly if it has been successful and has captured the pupils' imagination. This allows for a greater level of differentiation. For example, a class may be asked to prepare, script and present a television programme related to the particular theme or text that has been studied. The type of programme (straightforward news report, documentary with expert comment, chat show with competing views, reality show) may determine the level of challenge involved in the task.

- It is helpful to be aware of the types of work that challenge higher achievers (although clearly appropriate choices need to be made depending on the individual or class): attention to nuances of meaning and sub-texts when reading; making comparisons with other texts; reading what critics have said about a text; creating written parodies of authors' styles; creating satirical parodies of television programmes in drama; asking their own questions about a text; predicting how a text will develop and justify; rewriting texts in a different style.

- Meeting the needs of pupils has much to do with attitudes, relationships and the culture that is created in the classroom, and is not just about teaching techniques, defined narrowly. It is not overly romantic or far-fetched to recognise that most human beings are capable of brilliance given the right context and motivation.

## English as an additional language

Many children in schools have learned a language other than English as their first language; some may have access to two or three other languages in addition to English. The range of pupils who are learning English as an additional language may be broad. Some may be good orally but have difficulty writing. Others will be fluently bilingual. Pupils will vary in the length of time they have spent in the English education system and whether, for example, they are literate or not in their first language. As with all generic concepts, the group of pupils judged to be 'learning English as an additional language' is quite varied. Additional specialist staff may well be provided but a policy of inclusion means that the classroom teacher has to be aware of individual needs and able to act on them.

- Many of the principles which underpin the teaching of English in general apply equally to the teaching of English as an additional language, particularly the importance of meaningful contexts for language use. Having access to as much of the full curriculum as possible may be a key factor affecting motivation and attitude. Working with support staff becomes all the more important. It goes without saying that a teacher should not make the mistake of judging a pupil's intellectual ability by the stage they have reached in their acquisition of English.

- The classroom should be a welcoming environment where bilingual pupils feel comfortable and able to contribute, their inclusion a source of enrichment rather than a problem. In the same way the school should make parents feel at ease. Respect for the pupils' first language and culture is a prerequisite; the addition of a new pupil to a class is often a good test of its own communal values.

- As always, knowledge of individual pupils is essential. What languages do they speak? What languages do they understand? What levels have they reached? What are their achievements in the different attainment targets of speaking and listening, reading and writing? Are pupils receiving lessons in their home language? How are they progressing in other subjects? Pupils at early stages of learning English need considerable support particularly from specialist, often bilingual, staff.

- It is important to be aware that a pupil's conceptual thinking may be in advance of their ability to speak English, so it is important not to underestimate their potential achievements. On the other hand pupils may have learning difficulties that are not immediately obvious. Close monitoring of how well their understanding of language is progressing is necessary.

- Colloquial English or specialist terms and the language of text books may present a challenge. Some pupils may settle in socially very quickly but may find the more formal requirements of the curriculum more difficult. Other pupils may appear withdrawn because they are shy or nervous.

- Close liaison with other support staff is essential. They are likely to have specialist knowledge and experience that can be shared.

- More advanced learners of English may still need continuing support, particularly as the academic challenges become greater.

- Teacher talk needs to be that bit more carefully planned and structured. Pupils benefit from the oral work and the opportunity to listen to standard English before they are asked to make a response.

- Pupils need to feel comfortable when making oral responses. Rules governing talk in the classroom should be negotiated/established and implemented very firmly so that no teasing or hostility is tolerated in any way.

- Cultural references in texts and dialect forms may present problems to which the teacher needs to be alert.

- Some pupils may need additional support after whole-class teaching sessions, for example, extra help with instructions and tasks.

- The use of visual aids in the classroom can be very helpful. This allows pupils to support their linguistic understanding with contextual clues. This may include technological aids such as PowerPoint and overhead projector, but be aware also of the use of simple objects or pictures to support the exposition.

The same sound principles of assessment should inform assessment of pupils for whom English is an additional language: recognising achievement, drawing on a range of evidence, being aware that achievements may vary across aspects of the subject.

It is important not to view provision for pupils for whom English is an additional language only in technical terms and underestimate the importance and power of what might be termed the human dimension of the classroom. A key factor will be whether the receiving community (school or class) is able to adopt an intercultural attitude which includes being able to see their own culture and practices from a different point of view and not to assume they are the only possible and naturally correct ones (Byram 1997).

## Further reading

The QCA website has produced various documents to support inclusion that are available from the QCA website, www.qca.org.uk. The language policies section of the Council of Europe website provides a range of documents on teaching disadvantaged pupils: www.coe.int/T/DG4/Linguistic/Default_en.asp.

The Teacher Training Agency has produced *Raising the Attainment of Ethnic Minority Pupils*, which provides guidance and resource materials. It is intended for providers of ITT but the information is relevant to all teachers.

For a useful general introduction to special needs which discusses the code of practice, statementing and individual education plans see Chapter 7 of Capel *et al.* (1995) *Learning to Teach in the Secondary School*. Chapter 8 in Harrison (1994) *The Literate Imagination* focuses specifically on special needs in English. The same author has a chapter in Hayhoe and Parker (eds) (1992) on bilingualism. Edwards, Goodwin and Wellings (eds) (1991) *English 7–14: Every Child's Entitlement* is excellent on making English accessible to all pupils and has very helpful further reading and resources sections on multi-cultural literature and linguistic diversity.

# 16 Research and writing

*In order to keep our balance, we need to hold the visible and the invisible together.*

John O'Donohue

## Introduction

SINCE THE MOVE to more school-based teacher training there have been, at national policy level, mixed signals about the role of theory and research in relation to both what becoming a teacher should involve and how the professional role of a teacher should be conceived. The first competence framework for qualified teacher status in 1992 was conceived largely in terms of what teachers should be able to *do*, and was therefore interpreted by many as a denigration both of the significance of theory and research and of the role of higher education in the training of teachers. The move to more school-based schemes seemed to affirm that view. On the other hand, the commitment by the then DfES (now DCSF) to the concept of research-based practice, the support by the Teacher Development Agency for Masters courses in education and, more recently, the introduction of a national Masters in Learning and Teaching, suggests a rather different view.

This ambivalence towards theory and research is perhaps understandable. Academic writing on education can seem remote and irrelevant to the day-to-day practice of teachers. Traditional teacher training courses in the 1960s and 1970s were often thought to be inadequate preparation for the realities of the classroom. They seemed to focus unduly on securing a knowledge base in the various disciplines (psychology, history, sociology of education) without sufficient consideration of the implications for practice. The value of empirical research in education also started to be questioned. There were in the 1990s some notorious expressions of disillusionment with the field. Hargreaves (1996) supported the concept of 'evidence-based practice' but expressed the view that there was little to show for the vast sums of money spent on education research. In 1998 Chris Woodhead, the then head of Ofsted, commissioned a report which questioned the quality of much of the education research that was being produced as being shoddy and inadequate (Tooley 1998). These reports were in turn severely criticised but the questions they raised lingered.

It is understandable that trainee and newly qualified teachers might be more concerned with practical teaching in the classroom than with theory and research, which may seem of little relevance. Behaviour management, planning, assessment and implementation of school policies are key concerns in an early teaching career and making a priority of practical experience over theorising does not seem unreasonable. On a teacher training course the experience of writing assignments that are not purely concerned with practice may feel like jumping through hoops without any real relevance or depth of learning. It may be thought that if theory and research have any useful role at all in education this has more to do with informing national policy, although even in this context the value is not always apparent; research findings rarely seem conclusive and are often contradictory.

These views have to be taken seriously. They raise questions both about the nature of theory and research, its aims and purposes and about what becoming a teacher entails. The purpose of this chapter is to address some of these questions by providing an overview of issues related to the place of research in education and particularly in English teaching. The scope of the chapter is therefore limited. It is intended to be not a comprehensive guide to research methods but rather an introduction to the field and to the vast literature on this subject. It is not a guide to *doing* research but it does offer some practical suggestions on writing critically about research and about one's own practice in a theoretically informed way. Above all it is an attempt to convince the reader of the importance of basing practice on understanding.

## What do we mean by 'research'?

General criticisms of education research are frequently based on a misunderstanding of what it can and cannot achieve. However before addressing that question it is important to consider what is meant by 'research' because the term itself may cause confusion. It will not be enough to resort to simple definitions because these can conceal fundamental differences of opinion that need to be understood. It is more helpful to think about the different ways in which the term 'research' is used.

Some writers assume that 'research' is equivalent to 'empirical research', whereas others use the term 'research' more widely to embrace theoretical enquiry as well. Empirical research is conducted by collecting data of one sort or another by observation, questionnaires, videos, interviews, etc. It may have different sorts of aims, for example to show links between cause and effect (that explicit knowledge of syntax improves writing performance), to provide information about opinion (that English teachers would like to see an end to SATs) or to describe pedagogic practice (what sort of questioning do English teachers use in the classroom?). Whereas empirical research involves going out and looking and listening, theoretical enquiry can be conducted at one's desk or in the library through reading and reflection (philosophy can be viewed as a form of theoretical research). Some writers use the term 'scholarship' to refer to this kind of work and reserve the term 'research' for empirical enquiry alone. However, in the 2001 Research Assessment Exercise, which was conducted to evaluate the quality of research in universities, research was taken to refer to any original investigation undertaken in order to gain knowledge and understanding. This included conceptual enquiry as well as empirical research. In this context the term 'scholarship' was used to refer to such activities as the writing of dictionaries and editions of literary texts.

This seems straightforward enough, so what are the underlying differences of opinion or possible confusions? There is an important principle underlying the inclusive perspective on research. The term 'research' is often used in a normative sense to refer to practice that is thought to be particularly worthwhile. The inclusion of conceptual enquiry or theorising as a legitimate form of research says something important about the way knowledge accumulates. It recognises that there are different and complementary ways of gaining understanding in the world. It forms a counter-point to the view that all that is needed to advance policy and practice in education is empirical enquiry into 'what works'. Education is fundamentally about values and human judgement. Empirical enquiry has an important role to play but it has to be considered in the context of wider theoretical frames of reference. In fact the separation of empirical enquiry and theory is misleading; the best empirical work is informed by theory.

Potential confusion arises, however, when using the wider concept of research because not all forms of writing about education come into the category of research: journalism, polemic, casual speculation or simple accounts of practice do not normally qualify. Instead the term 'research' in an academic context refers to *systematic* and *rigorous* enquiry that advances knowledge by building on what is already known. This applies to both empirical and purely theoretical work. In the context of empirical work technical aspects (such as validity, reliability and probability) become relevant because there is a justified expectation that research should be conducted to acceptable levels of rigour and transparency.

Professional practice, then, may be based on authority ('we do it this way because we have been told to do so'), tradition ('we have always done it this way'), prejudice ('we do it this way because no other way is acceptable') or dogma ('we do it this way because we know we are right'). Research offers a more rational and informed basis from which to operate.

What are the implications of this discussion for newcomers to research? Although research has technical dimensions it should not be seen as something rarefied and remote. Human beings in whatever walk of life are always making judgements and choosing priorities – it makes more sense for those decisions to be informed rather than ill-informed. The inclusion of pure theoretical enquiry as part of what is meant by research strengthens the case for using findings from empirical research within broader frames of reference which include decisions about values and priorities. An example will illustrate this point more clearly.

It might be helpful to know whether it is better to stream pupils or teach them in mixed-ability sets in English. This is a difficult question to address empirically but let us assume for the sake of argument that it is possible to set up an experiment with sufficient controls to demonstrate that one of the two groups performs better in a test at the end of a period of teaching. The experiment appears to demonstrate that one way of grouping pupils is better. What the experiment does not tell us is whether there are social rather than academic advantages of grouping children in a particular way, nor does it tell us about possible long-term negative effects on attitudes to school. It might be possible to set up even more elaborate empirical projects to examine these views but the experimental work on its own does not remove the need for human judgement and interpretation. We also need to be confident that the test used in the project is based on worthwhile outcomes, something that is often ignored in experimental designs. In the original question (is it better to stream pupils or teach them in mixed ability groups?) the word 'better' may conceal all sorts of value judgements that need to be unpacked and made explicit. Empirical research can *inform* practice but on its own it cannot *determine* it.

Sometimes the call for evidence-based practice implies that all that is needed is objective enquiry into 'what works'. The reality is more complex. It was suggested that policy and practice should be based on rational enquiry and decision making, rather than tradition or authority. However, unless teachers have some grasp of research principles they may be vulnerable to a disguised form of authority based on such claims that 'research proves X is the case' or 'research shows that y . . .' The reality is that research rarely *proves* anything so we need to examine how the purpose of research can best be described.

## The purpose of research

Technical issues related to research design and methodology are important because research is not just a matter of 'common sense'. However, it is important not to view research as something totally separate and exclusive from normal practice and to recognise that there is a continuum between the way we normally operate in the world and research activity. This can be illuminated by considering a basic principle of statistics, often viewed as the most forbidding aspect of research. Rowntree (1981: 13) asks us to consider a simple scenario. I tell you that two friends of mine happen to be sitting in the next room. One is 5 feet tall and the other is just under 6 feet tall. What would be your guess as to each one's sex, based on that information alone? It would not be unreasonable to assume that the taller is male. That does not mean you are right but, as Rowntree says, *in the absence of other information*, it is perfectly reasonable to base our inference on what is more probable based on previous experience. Research findings inform our knowledge and understanding in similar ways. He provides another example to introduce the concept of a normal curve of distribution and to show that as human beings we do not need much information to prompt us to make inferences. I am sitting writing in my room when a gnome appears who is 10 centimetres in height. I have never seen a gnome before and I do not know whether I have been visited by a small gnome or a large one. However if the gnome is joined by four friends between 9 and 10 centimetres tall I can start to make a provisional estimate of what the average height of a gnome is. I might still be wrong but I can adjust my judgement as I meet more and more gnomes:

> This idea of generalizing from a sample applies to research in the arts as well as the sciences. For example, one would not need to have read everything by, say, D.H. Lawrence and Joseph Conrad before one could begin generalizing about how they compared and contrasted as novelists.
>
> (Rowntree 1981: 21)

Underlying the decisions here are issues related to sample size and probability (Rowntree's example is an excellent introduction to standard deviation). English teachers are likely to be more at home with words than numbers but the principle of probability that is central to statistics is extremely helpful in understanding general ideas that underpin all research and help us gain insight into the purpose of research. In statistical analysis, because probability is normally expressed in a formula, it can appear that the whole operation is objective and devoid of human judgement. However, what counts as acceptable odds is entirely a matter of convention and context. If someone hands me a gun and says that by shooting at my head I have a six to one chance of being killed or of winning a fortune, that is unlikely to be enough to persuade me to a have a go. On the other hand six to one odds on a horse might seem quite a reasonable bet. The point here is that all research in the context of education (even those that appear highly objective) usually have to be interpreted in relation to a system of values.

As indicated above, not all research is based on showing that one approach works better than another. Some research is based more on systematic description rather than trying to show links between cause and effect. The purpose of education research in whatever form is rarely to 'prove' something once and for all, nor to make claims to certainty, but rather to contribute to a growing body of understanding and knowledge. Researchers do seek truth. This claim is one that many writers would dispute, however, so it therefore needs further discussion.

The view that there is no such thing as truth, or that knowledge is entirely constructed, has gained ground in the last 30 years and is often repeated as a position underlying particular research paradigms. However this kind of relativism arises partly from a confusion of truth with dogma or certainty (Fleming *et al.* 2004). Attempts to find truth do not rule out the possibility of doubt, ambiguity or being mistaken but we need a concept of truth to operate rationally in the world. As an English teacher I need to know whether it is true that covering pupils' work with negative comments is more likely than not to demotivate them. I need to know whether it is true that giving endless decontextualised exercises does little to improve pupils' use of language. For you to be reading this book it is true that someone must have written it. If you find out later that it was written by more than one person or in fact dictated over the telephone, the questioning of the truth hinges on a piece of trivial interpretation of language. If it turns out that the book was knocked up by thousands of monkeys on typewriters it just means the original assertion was wrong. The concept of truth, however, does not disappear. Wittgenstein (1969: 13) argues that the difference between the concept of 'knowing' and the concept of 'being certain' is not of any great importance at all. Eagleton (2003: 103) makes a similar point in relation to the concept of 'absolute truth' which he says adds nothing to the concept of 'truth'.

The purpose of education research therefore is not to arrive at certainty or to prove once and for all that one particular approach is the right way to do things. If that were the case then there would be an argument for individual teachers abandoning any responsibility for reading reports of research and leaving it to policy-makers to determine what is or is not the right approach. The understanding that develops from education research almost always accrues in a more organic than linear fashion. There are occasionally examples of major, large-scale projects that seem to offer a compelling case for changing practice in a particular way but these are rare. Wittgenstein uses the metaphor of negotiating the streets of a city or a labyrinth to represent the development of his thinking. The same issues are repeatedly approached from different directions to provide different insights. The analogy is a much more useful image for the growth of knowledge and understanding through research than a linear proof/counter-proof view. Teachers need to be part of the community of practice that contributes to the understanding of education policy and practice.

## Approaches to research

Many books on research methods make much of the different ideologies, theories of knowledge and ways of perceiving the world that underlie different approaches to research. Quantitative approaches which are based on numerical data are often associated with a 'positivist', scientific, objective view of the world. Qualitative approaches that are based on data that is usually not quantifiable (e.g. recorded talk from interviews) are seen as more subjective because they are more tolerant of different perspectives, ambiguity and interpretation. There is an interesting discussion to be had here (and the further reading section provides examples), but this polarisation of approaches is not always helpful. If we take the view that most research findings are contingent and provisional, this erodes the distinction. Many contemporary approaches to research used mixed methods combining quantitative and qualitative approaches. For example, in research on aspects of English teaching the combination of a closed questionnaire that can provide numbers for analysis will often be combined with in-depth interviews to provide a deeper level of understanding. It is more helpful to talk about fitness for purpose – whether the particular research approach is appropriate for the question which is being addressed. To take a very simple example, if I want to know what GCSE syllabus is most popular in schools in the UK then a simple survey that yields statistics is all that is needed. Whether that project would yield any useful information to inform practice is of course another question.

The purpose of this section of the chapter is to provide some brief comments on the main approaches and concepts that are likely to be met when reading reports of empirical research, particularly related to English teaching. Given that one of the key reasons for including theory and research in initial training courses is to empower teachers and that the exercise of criticality is a key general criterion of work at Masters level, an indication is given of some of the issues and problems that are likely to arise in the context of a particular approach. It should be stressed that the short descriptions which follow inevitably simplify and thereby to some extent distort the topic under discussion. The list also has mixed content of methods, approaches and concepts. The intention is to provide a brief guide that will encourage further reading of particular topics of interest:

■ Experimental research is often thought to be the most 'objective' and 'scientific' approach but it is fraught with difficulties. Its most common form is to take two groups, treat one in a different way and compare the outcomes (e.g. does the use of active drama improve pupils' understanding of a literary text?). Some critical issues to look out for when considering reports of this kind of work are as follows: are measures taken to ensure that the groups are similar enough at the start to warrant the comparison? How can we make sure that any change in performance in the test is owing to the intervention and not the result of a different teacher or natural maturation? How can we be sure that the changes detected are not the result of what happens elsewhere rather than the intervention?

- Action research in education is common because it focuses on the evaluation of a teacher's own practice after the introduction of an innovation of some kind. It is not a method per se but can use all sorts of methods (interviews, observation) as part of the process of enquiry. As an approach it can divide writers. Some see it as not 'proper research'. Others see action research as the most appropriate approach for education based on the view that research should be conducted by insiders in order to improve day-to-day practice and not be something that is imposed by 'experts' from the outside. In judging reports of action research it is important to ensure that any claims recognise the context-specific nature of the work.

- Case study, as with action research, may use different methods. The key is that it tends to focus on one particular case (a school, an English department, an incident) and involves detailed description of the phenomenon being studied. It is largely descriptive in approach and can provide insight into the way an institution or group functions. There are interesting debates about the degree to which generalisation is possible from case studies (see further reading section).

- Questionnaires are particular instruments that may be used on their own or in the context of other broad approaches. Closed questionnaires that, for example, invite responses on a five-point-scale (strongly agree, agree, etc.) can be subject to statistical analysis and may be collated with other variables (e.g. 'are English teachers who were trained in school-based schemes more or less likely to use imaginative methods in the classroom?'). Note here the difficulty with the concept of 'imaginative methods', which illustrates one of the issues with questionnaires: how to ask questions that adequately reflect the construct under investigation. There are other issues to consider. How can we be sure that people who are self-reporting their practice do not self-deceive? Large samples of questionnaires can overcome aberrant responses but the data provided by closed questions can be superficial. When reading reports based on questionnaires be alert to biased questions that invite particular responses and low response rates that may skew the results.

- Interviews provide more in-depth data and thus can be useful for probing a particular topic. They have become universally popular in education research in recent years but they are not without problems. They are often based on the assumption that the interviewer can retrieve information from the respondent that is there waiting to be extracted. But the interview process can itself create the response; the respondent may unwittingly provide what he/she perceives the interviewer to be looking for. It is important to be alert to the degree of transparency that exists when interviews are being reported – there may be unconscious bias in the selection of data. If I interview 12 teachers on their attitude to course work I may report the data in a way that does not do justice to their concerns about plagiarism.

- Coding of qualitative (e.g. interview) data is one approach that is used to minimise the problems of selective reporting. It involves looking for key themes or issues that recur in data and aims to draw these together in a systematic way. Computer software can help in this process but it is not a mechanical activity and needs creativity and intuition in transposing raw data into a conceptual scheme of some kind.

- Observation is a common approach used in education research and can also contribute to action research or case study approaches. For example, if we want to determine whether male English teachers tend to favour male or female pupils in oral lessons the obvious approach is go and look. A systematic approach to the observation (e.g. noting specific instances of questions, affirmations, rebukes, etc.) can serve to eliminate the unwitting bias that might arise in a less structured approach (and can allow several researchers to contribute to the same data set). However, when reading reports based on observation, it is important to keep in mind that behaviour can change when people are being observed, particularly if they are told the focus of the observation.

- Ethical considerations quite rightly place constraints on what researchers can and cannot do. In the case of observation discussed above it might be tempting not to tell the observed what is being examined in order to increase the validity of the findings. However, this would violate a key ethical principle that participants in research should do so only on the basis of voluntary, *informed* consent.

- Narrative and autobiographical enquiry in educational research has gained ground in recent years. As the description implies it focuses on 'stories' as the main source of data and acknowledges a narrative approach to framing and reporting research. To some critics it is anathema to 'scientific' methods because it embraces subjectivity so readily.

## The place of theory

Since the late 1980s curriculum development, which previously took place through experimentation and informal sharing of ideas, has given way to the dissemination of centralised, predetermined structures and schemes. One of the consequences is an over-simplification of educational issues. Wittgenstein's comments about philosophers (quoted in Sluga and Sterns 1996: 6) can be applied to contemporary policy development in education:

> Some philosophers (or whatever you like to call them) suffer from what may be called 'loss of problems'. Then everything seems quite simple to them, no deep problems seem to exist any more, the world becomes broad and flat and loses all depth, and what they write becomes immeasurably shallow and trivial.

This 'loss of problems' in part explains the relative absence of theory in relation to English teaching to which Medway (2002) draws attention when he contrasts the work of writers such as Britton, Dixon and Barnes with the 'limited technicism' of the contemporary scene. It is not that theoretical questions are not being addressed at all (the further reading section contains a sample of titles which do address theory) but for many teachers and writers the implementation of national initiatives has to be the main priority.

The reduced emphasis on theory can also be attributed paradoxically to theorists themselves. One of the central tenets of postmodern thinking is the absence of a unifying 'grand theory' or 'metanarrative'. The tendency towards an exploration of the interplay of ideas rather than the formulation of one unifying, explanatory theory is likely to have had at least an implicit effect on thinking about English. Another reason for the diminution of theory is the demand for the initial preparation and continuing development of teachers to be practical and relevant. Theory, if it has a place at all, has to be seen to underpin practice. This is not an unreasonable demand but the challenge of linking theory with practice in a meaningful, properly integrated way is often underestimated.

It is not enough to assert that the aesthetic dimensions of the subject are important while at the same time recommending that lessons should always begin with three clear objectives written on the board. If concepts such as 'engagement', 'response' and 'art' are to be taken seriously, some of the received wisdom about teaching and planning at least needs to be questioned. Empirical research also needs to take place in the context of strong theoretical and conceptual frameworks. For example, only dialogue and debate will resolve the central question of what the purpose of English ought to be (as opposed to what a group of teachers do or do not think at any particular time). Research based on an observation of 'the methods of effective teachers of literacy' is likely to be circular unless there is some prior agreement on what counts as an 'effective teacher of literacy' or indeed on what counts as 'literacy'. The approach may appear to be objective and scientific but it actually begs some important questions of principle and value. The background to the initial introduction of the National Literacy Strategy has largely been provided in terms of a variety of empirical work drawn from different sources (Beard 2000; Harrison 2002). The research basis has also been contested (Hilton 1998, 2001). A stronger theoretical foundation for the first version of the Strategy would have provided a more solid basis for considered dialogue and exploration of ideas, and might have improved some of its content.

Some of the more recent writing on the teaching of English can be described, at its simplest, as not taking previously accepted concepts such as 'literature', 'reading' and 'writing' for granted. The influence of literary theory on the teaching of English is shown in different approaches to reading; for example, in the way reader-response theories emphasise the importance of the contribution which the reader makes to the meaning of texts. Other aspects of critical theory promote an examination of text and categories of text in a wider cultural context, questioning the exclusive category of 'literature'. In the classroom this might mean exploring different meanings of texts, understanding how readers have to fill gaps in order to read and comparing different texts, such as a novel and a soap opera. These approaches go beyond traditional notions of character and theme when reading literature.

There are a number of reasons then why it is important for teachers to familiarise themselves with research (defined in the broadest sense) and understand the significance of relating theory and practice. If teaching practice is based on simply the mechanical application of particular methods in unthinking ways, teachers will not be in a position to adapt to new contexts or to evaluate new approaches. Understanding the basis for practice is empowering and will make teachers more resistant to the imposition of arbitrary policies and practices based on authority. A greater level of satisfaction is likely to be derived from a profession which has a high level of intellectual challenge and stimulus.

## Writing assignments

There are a number of presentational issues that are important when writing academic assignments, such as use of quotations, observing bibliographic conventions, structuring the work appropriately and paying attention to the assessment criteria. It is likely that most readers will have had plenty of practice in their undergraduate courses on the writing of academic essays. What may be new on an English teacher training course is the emphasis on integrating theory and practice and the use of empirical research as well as pure theory to inform the writing. The ideal masters level assignment will integrate personal reflection, professional practice and critical writing on research literature. Some assignments are designed sufficiently well to ensure that these elements receive their due attention but this is not always the case.

- Avoid lengthy anecdotes based on observation and practice that are not related to the academic literature. This can be tempting because it can be therapeutic to write accounts of difficult classroom encounters.

- It is important, however, to draw on practice – this can often be best achieved by integrating concrete data from school contexts perhaps in an appendix (samples of pupils' work; school policy documents; transcripts of interviews with pupils).

- Try to find a balance between range and depth when drawing on literature. In other words some academic papers may be quoted to support a particular perspective but others need much closer analysis.

- Sometimes it is difficult to know how to exercise criticality when discussing research papers. It is a good idea not to be too intemperate in comments (a common mistake) but instead to probe empirical findings in a critical way.

- Lengthy summaries of the articles should be avoided. Instead highlight the salient points that are relevant to the discussion.

- Avoid being merely descriptive when discussing either research literature or practice.

- Avoid too many quotations from the research literature that are left to speak for themselves.

- Analytic comment helps to demonstrate understanding.

## Further reading

There are a number of books that provide an introduction to research in education and general research issues: Wellington (2000) *Educational Research: Contemporary Issues and Practical Approaches*; Punch (2009) *Introduction to Research Methods in Education*; Walliman (2005) *Your Research Project*; Opie (2004) *Doing Educational Research*; Denscombe (2007) *The Good Research Guide*. Cohen, Manion and Morrison (2006) *Research Methods in Education* is a popular text and is now in its sixth edition.

For a discussion of philosophical issues in research see Pring (2004) *Philosophy of Education Research*. Andrews (2001) *Teaching and Learning English: A Guide to Recent Research and its Applications* provides a guide to research in English teaching.

# Bibliography

Abbott, C. (2001) *ICT: Changing Education*. London: Routledge.

Abbs, P. (1974) *Autobiography in Education*. London: Heinemann.

Abbs, P. (1976) *Root and Blossom: Essays on the Philosophy, Practice and Politics of English Teaching*. London: Heinemann.

Abbs, P. (1982) *English within the Arts*. London: Hodder & Stoughton.

Adams, A. and Brindley, S. (eds) (2007) *Teaching Secondary English with ICT*. Milton Keynes: Open University Press.

Adams, M. (1990) *Beginning to Read*. Cambridge, MA: MIT Press.

Alexander, R. J. (2008) *Towards Dialogic Teaching: Rethinking Classroom Talk*, 4th edition. York: Dialogos. (First edition 2004.)

Allen, N. (2002) 'Too Much, Too Young? An Analysis of the KS3 National Literacy Strategy in Practice', *English in Education* 36 (1), 5–15.

Amis, M. (1991) *Time's Arrow*. London: Jonathan Cape.

Anderson, A., Brown, G., Shillcock, R. and Yule, G. (1984) *Teaching Talk: Strategies for Production and Assessment*. Cambridge: Cambridge University Press.

Andrews, R. (1991) *The Problem with Poetry*. Milton Keynes: Open University Press.

Andrews, R. (2001) *Teaching and Learning English: A Guide to Recent Research and its Applications*. London: Continuum.

AQA (2002) *Syllabus for GCE A/AS English Literature*. Manchester: AQA.

Armstrong, L. and Goddard, A. (1996) *Key Stage 3 Writing; A Language Approach*. London: Heinemann.

Arnold, R. (1991) *Writing Development: Magic in the Brain*. Milton Keynes: Open University Press.

Arts Council (2003) *Drama in Schools*. London: Arts Council.

Auden, W. H. (1963) *The Dyer's Hand and Other Essays*. New York: Random House.

Bain, R., Fitzgerald, B. and Taylor, M. (1992) *Looking into Language: Classroom Approaches to Knowledge about Language*. London: Hodder & Stoughton.

Barnes, D. (1976) *From Communication to Curriculum*. Harmondsworth: Penguin.

Barrow, R. (2001) 'Inclusion v. Fairness', *Journal of Moral Education* 30 (3), 235–42.

Barrs, M. (1990) *Words Not Numbers: Assessment in English*. Sheffield: NATE.

Barton, G. (1992) *English into Practice*. London: Longman.

Barton, G. (2001) *Developing Media Skills*. London: Heinemann.

Bates, R., Goddard, A., Norris, P., Turton, M., Dickenson, S. (1994) *The English Pack: Developing a Whole Department Approach to the National Curriculum*. London: Heinemann.

Baxter, J. (1995) 'General Introduction' in Ibsen, H. *A Doll's House*, ed. by M. Rafferty, Cambridge: Cambridge University Press.

Bazalgette, C. (ed.) (1989) *Primary Media Education: A Curriculum Statement*. London: BFI Education Department.

Bazalgette, C. (1991) *Media Education*. London: Hodder & Stoughton.

Beard, R. (2000) 'Research and the National Literacy Strategy', *Oxford Review of Education* 26 (3), 421–36.

Bearne, E. (ed.) (1999) *Use of Language across the Secondary Curriculum*. London: Routledge.

Beck, J. and Earl, M. (eds) (2000) *Key Issues in Secondary Education*. London: Cassell.

Bennathan, J. (2000) *Developing Drama Skills*. London: Heinemann.

Benton, M. and Benton, P. (1995) *Poetry Workshop*. London: Hodder & Stoughton.

Benton, M., Teasy, J., Bell, R. and Hurst, K. (1988) *Young Readers Responding to Poems.* London: Routledge.

Benton, P. (2000) 'The Conveyor Belt Curriculum? Poetry Teaching in the Secondary School (Part II)', *Oxford Review of Education* 26 (1), 81–93.

Beverton, S. (2003) 'Can You See the Difference? Early Impacts of the Primary NLS in Four Secondary English Departments', *Cambridge Journal of Education* 33 (2), 217–36.

Black, P. (1998) *Testing: Friend or Foe? Theory and Practice of Assessment and Testing*. London: Falmer Press.

Black P. and Wiliam, D. (1998) *Inside the Black Box*, Occasional Paper. London: King's College.

Black, P., Harrison, C., Lee, C., Marshall, B. and Wiliam, D. (2003) *Assessment for Learning: Putting it into Practice*. Maidenhead: Open University Press.

Blake, J. (2006) *The Full English: A Handbook of English Teaching Activities.* London: NATE/ Teachit.

Blake, N. and Standish, P. (eds) (2000) *Enquiries at the Interface: Philosophical Problems of Online Education.* Oxford: Blackwell.

Blake, N., Smeyers, P., Smith, R. and Standish, P. (1998) *Thinking Again: Education after Postmodernism*. London: Bergin & Garvey.

Blake, W. (1995) *Selected Works*, ed. by D. Stevens. Cambridge: Cambridge University Press.

Bleiman, B. (1995) *The Poetry Pack*. London: English and Media Centre.

Blocksidge, M. (ed.) (2000) *Teaching Literature 11–18*. London: Continuum.

Bolton, G. (1992) *New Perspectives on Classroom Drama*. Hemel Hempstead: Simon & Schuster Education.

Boswell, J. (1953) *The Life of Johnson*. Oxford: Oxford University Press.

Bousted, M. (1992) 'Praising what is Lost: The Demise of Coursework in GCSE Literature', *Use of English* 4 (1), 15–24.

Bowie, A. (1990) *Aesthetics and Subjectivity from Kant to Nietzsche*. Manchester: Manchester University Press.

Brereton, P. (2001) *Continuum Guide to Media Education*. London: Continuum.

Brindley, S. (ed.) (1994) *Teaching English*. London: Routledge.

Britton, J. (1972) *Language and Learning*. Harmondsworth: Penguin.

Britton, J. (1994) 'Vygotsky's Contribution to Pedagogical Theory', in Brindley, S. (ed.) *Teaching English*. London: Routledge.

Broadbent, S. (1995) *Key Stage 3 English Units*. London: English and Media Centre.

Broadfoot, P. (1996) *Education, Assessment and Society*. Milton Keynes: Open University Press.

Brooker, P. (1994) 'Key Words in Brecht's Theory and Practice of Theatre', in Thomson, P. and Sacks, G. (eds) *The Cambridge Companion to Brecht*. Cambridge: Cambridge University Press.

Brookes, W. (2002) 'Evidence from Experienced Practitioners', in Goodwyn, A. (ed.) *Improving Literacy at KS2 and KS3*. London: Paul Chapman.

Brown, J. and Gifford, T. (1989) *Teaching A Level English Literature*. London: Routledge.

Brownjohn, S. (1994) *To Rhyme or Not to Rhyme*. London: Hodder & Stoughton.

Buchbinder, D. (1991) *Contemporary Literary Theory and the Reading of Poetry*. Sydney, Australia: Macmillan.

Buckingham, D. (2003) *Media Education: Literacy, Learning and Contemporary Culture*. Cambridge: Polity Press.

Buckingham, D. and Sefton-Green, J. (1994) 'Making Sense of the Media: From Reading to Culture', in Brindley, S. (ed.) *Teaching English*. London: Routledge.

Buckingham, D., Grahame, J. and Sefton-Green, J. (1996) *Making Media: Learning from Media Production*. London: English and Media Centre.

Burn, A. and Durran, J. (2007) *Media Literacy in Schools – Practice, Production and Progression*. London: Paul Chapman.

Burton, M. (ed.) (1989) *Enjoying Texts: Using Literary Theory in the Classroom*. Cheltenham: Stanley Thornes.

Byram, M. (1997) *Teaching and Assessing Intercultural Communicative Competence*. Clevedon: Multilingual Matters.

Byron, K. (1986) *Drama in the English Classroom*. London: Methuen.

Cajkler, W. (1999) 'Misconceptions in the NLS: National Literacy Strategy or No Linguistic Sense?', *Use of English* 50 (3), 214–27.

Cajkler, W. and Hislam, J. (2002) 'The Butler was Dead is Not a Passive Form: How Grammar has been Misconceived in the National Literacy Strategy'. Research reported at British Educational Research Conference in *TES*, 29 September, 31.

Calthrop, K. (1971) *Reading Together: An Investigation into the Use of the Class Reader*. London: Heinemann (for NATE).

Cameron, D. (2007) *The Teacher's Guide to Grammar*. Milton Keynes: Open University Press.

Capel, S., Leask, M. and Turner, T. (1995) *Learning to Teach in the Secondary School*. London: Routledge.

Carlyle, T. (1834) *Sartor Resartus*. London.

Carter, R. (ed.) (1990) *Knowledge about Language and the Curriculum: The LINC Reader*. London: Hodder & Stoughton.

Carter, R. (1995) *Key Words in Language and Literacy*. London: Routledge.

Carter, R. and Nash, W. (1990) *Seeing through Language*. Oxford: Blackwell.

Chambers, A. (1993) *Tell Me: Children, Reading and Talk*. Stroud: Thimble Press.

Clarke, M. (1987) *Teaching Popular Television*. London: Heinemann.

Clarke, S., Dickinson, P. and Westbrook, J. (2004) *The Complete Guide to Becoming an English Teacher*. London: Sage.

Claxton, G. (1984) *Live and Learn*. London: Harper & Row.

Cliff-Hodges, G. (1993) 'Forward-Looking Thoughts: The Study of Literary Texts at GCSE', *Cambridge Journal of Education* 23 (1), 65–76.

Cliff-Hodges, G., Drummond, M. J. and Styles, M. (eds) (2000) *Tales, Tellers and Texts*. London: Cassell.

Cohen, L., Mannion, L., Morrison, K. (2006) *Research Methods in Education*. London: Routledge.

Coleman, J. (1980) *The Nature of Adolescence*. London: Methuen.

Connell, B., Brigley, J., and Edwards, M. (1996) *Examining the Media*. London: Hodder and Stoughton.

Cook, H. C. (1917) *The Play Way*. London: Heinemann.

Cox, B. (1991) *Cox on Cox: An English Curriculum for the 1990s*. London: Hodder & Stoughton.

Cox, B. (1995) *Cox on the Battle for the English Curriculum*. London: Hodder & Stoughton.

Creber, P. (1990) *Thinking through English*. Milton Keynes: Open University Press.

Crystal, D. (1987) *The Cambridge Encyclopedia of English*. Cambridge: Cambridge University Press.

Crystal, D. (1995) *The Cambridge Encyclopedia of the English Language*. Cambridge: Cambridge

University Press.

Crystal, D. (2004) *Making Sense of Grammar*. London: Pearson Longman.

Crystal, D. (2004) *Rediscover Grammar*, 3rd edition. London: Pearson Longman.

Cullingford, C. (1990) *The Nature of Learning*. London: Cassell.

Curtis, D. (1993) *Teaching Secondary English*. Milton Keynes: Open University Press.

Daniels, H. (2001) *Vygotsky and Pedagogy*. London: Routledge.

D'Arcy, P. (2000) *Two Contrasting Paradigms for the Teaching and Assessment of Writing*. Sheffield: NATE.

Davies, C. (1996) *What is English Teaching?* Milton Keynes: Open University Press.

Davison, J. and Dowson, J. (1998) *Learning to Teach English in the Secondary School*. London: Routledge.

Davison, J. and Moss, J. (eds) (2000) *Issues in English Teaching*. London: Routledge.

Dawes, L. (1995) *Writing – The Drafting Process: An Examination of Drafting in Pupils' Writing*. Sheffield: NATE.

Dean, G. (2000) *Teaching Reading in Secondary Schools*. London: David Fulton.

Dean, G. (2003) *Grammar for Improving Writing and Reading in the Secondary School*. London: David Fulton.

Denscombe, M. (2007) *The Good Research Guide*. Milton Keynes: Open University Press.

DES (1975) *A Language for Life* (the Bullock Report). London: HMSO.

DES (1987) *Teaching Poetry in the Secondary School: An HMI View*. London: HMSO.

DES (1988) *Report of the Inquiry into the Teaching of English Language* (the Kingman Report). London: HMSO.

DES (1989) *English for Ages 5–16* (the Cox Report). London: HMSO.

DfEE (1998) *The National Literacy Strategy: Framework for Teaching*. Sudbury: DfEE Publications.

DfEE (2000) *Transforming Key Stage 3: National Pilot*. London: HMSO.

DfEE (2001) *Key Stage 3 National Strategy: Framework for Teaching English: Years 7, 8 and 9*. London: HMSO.

DfEE/QCA (1999) *The National Curriculum for England: English*. London: DfEE/QCA.

DfES (2001) *Inclusive Schooling*. London: DfES Publications.

DfES (2002a) *Transition from Year 6 to Year 7 English*. London: HMSO.

DfES (2002b) *14–19: Opportunity and Excellence*. London: DfES Publications.

DfES (2003a) *Fulfilling the Potential: Transforming Teaching and Learning through ICT in Schools*. London: DfES Publications.

DfES (2003b) *Drama Objectives Bank*. London: DfES Publications.

Dias, P. and Hayhoe, M. (1988) *Developing Response to Poetry*. Milton Keynes: Open University Press.

Donaldson, M. (1978) *Children's Minds*. London: Fontana.

Donne, J. (1950) *Selected Poems*, ed. by J. Hayward. Harmondsworth: Penguin.

Dutton, B. (2000) *Media Studies: An Introduction*. London: Longman.

Dymoke, S. (2001) 'Taking Poetry off its Pedestal: The Place of Poetry Writing in an Asessment-Driven Curriculum', *English in Education* 35 (3), 32–41.

Dymoke, S. (2003) *Drafting and Assessing Poetry*. London: Paul Chapman.

Eagleton, T. (1983) *Literary Theory: An Introduction*. Oxford: Basil Blackwell.

Eagleton, T. (2003) *After Theory*. London: Allen Lane.

Edwards, V., Goodwin, J. and Wellings, A. (1991) *English 7–14: Every Child's Entitlement*. London: David Fulton.

Eliot, T. S. (1954) *Selected Poems*. London: Faber and Faber.

EMC (1998) *Production Practices: Media Simulations*. London: English and Media Centre.

EMC (2005) *The Soap Pack: A Study of Brookside from Script to Screen*. London: English and Media Centre.

EMC (2006) *Picture Power*. London: English and Media Centre.

Entwistle, N. (1987) *Understanding Classroom Learning*. London: Hodder & Stoughton.

Evans, C., Midgely, A., Rigby, P., Warham, L. and Woolnough, P. (2009) *Teaching English*. London: Sage.

Evans, J. (ed.) (2005) *Literacy Moves On*. London: David Fulton.

Evans, P. (2002) *How to Teach Non-fiction Writing*. London: David Fulton.

Finch, H. L. (1995) *Wittgenstein*. Shaftesbury: Element Books.

Fine, A. (1996) Interview given for NAWE: 'Another Little Spanner?', *Writing in Education* (Spring), 6–9.

Flaubert, G. (1956) *Madame Bovary*, trans. and ed. by A. Russell. London: Penguin.

Fleming, M. (1989) 'Drama, Kingman and Cox', *Drama Broadsheet* 6 (1), 2–5.

Fleming, M. (1992) 'Pupils' Perceptions of the Nature of Poetry', *Cambridge Journal of Education* 22 (1), 31–41.

Fleming, M. (1997) *The Art of Drama Teaching*. London: David Fulton.

Fleming, M. (2003) *Starting Drama Teaching*. London: David Fulton. (First edition 1994.)

Fleming, M., Merrell, C. and Tymms, P. (2004) 'The impact of drama on pupils' language, mathematics, and attitude in two primary schools', *Research in Drama Education* 9 (2), 177–97.

Flower, L. (1994) *The Construction of Negotiated Meaning: A Social Cognitive Theory of Writing*. Carbondale, IL: Southern Illinois University Press.

Foggin, J. (1992) *Teaching English in the National Curriculum: Real Writing*. London: Hodder & Stoughton.

Forster, E. M. (1927) *Aspects of the Novel*. London: Edward Arnold.

Fowles, J. (1969) *The French Lieutenant's Woman*. London: Jonathan Cape.

Fox, G. and Merrick, B. (1982) 'Thirty-Six Things to Do with a Poem', in Lee, V. (ed.) *English Literature in Schools*. Milton Keynes: Open University Press.

Friel, B. (1981) *Translations*. London: Faber & Faber.

Fullan, M. and Hargreaves, A. (1992) *What's Worth Fighting for in Your School?* Milton Keynes: Open University Press.

Furlong, T. and Ogborn, J. (1995) *The English Department: Organisation and Management*. London: English and Media Centre.

Gardner, H. (1984) *Frames of Mind*. London: Heinemann. (First published 1983.)

George, N. (1971) 'Creativity in Theory and Practice', *Aspects of Education* 13, 12–19.

Gibbs, C. and Stobart, G. (1990) *Assessment: A Teachers' Guide to the Issues*. London: Hodder & Stougton.

Gibson, R. (1986) *Critical Theory and Education*. London: Hodder & Stoughton.

Gibson, R. (1990) *Secondary School Shakespeare*. Cambridge: Cambridge Institute of Education.

Gipps, C. (1994) *Beyond Testing*. London: Falmer Press.

Goodson, I. (1997) ' "Trendy Theory" and Teacher Professionalism', *Cambridge Journal of Education* 27 (1), 7–21.

Goodson, I. and Medway, P. (1990) *Bringing English to Order*. London: Falmer Press.

Goodwin, P. (2001) *The Articulate Classroom: Talking and Learning in the Primary School*. London: David Fulton.

Goodwin, P. (2004) *Literacy through Creativity*. London: David Fulton.

Goodwyn, A. (1992) *English Teaching and Media Education*. Milton Keynes: Open University Press.

Goodwyn, A. (ed.) (1995) *English and Ability*. London: David Fulton.

Goodwyn, A. (1997a) *Developing English Teachers: The Role of Mentorship in a Reflective Profession*. Milton Keynes: Open University Press.

Goodwyn, A. (ed.) (1997b) *Understanding Television*. London: Routledge.

Goodwyn, A. (ed.) (1998) *Literary and Media Texts in Secondary English: New Approaches*. London: Cassell.

Goodwyn, A. (ed.) (2000) *English in the Digital Age*. London: Cassell.

Goodwyn, A. (ed.) (2002) *Improving Literacy at KS2 and KS3*. London: Paul Chapman.

Goodwyn, A. (2003) *English Teaching and the Moving Image*. London: Routledge.

Goodwyn, A. and Findlay, D. (2002) 'Secondary Schools and the National Literacy Strategy', in Goodwyn, A. (ed.) *Improving Literacy at KS2 and KS3*. London: Paul Chapman.

Grainger, T. (1998) 'Drama and Reading: Illuminating their Interaction', *English in Education* 32 (1), 29–36.

Grainger, T. (ed.) (2004) *The Routledge Falmer Reader in Language and Literacy*. London: Routledge Falmer.

Green, B. (1993) 'Literacy Studies and Curriculum Theorizing; or, The Insistence of the Letter', in Green, B. (ed.) *The Insistence of the Letter: Literacy Studies and Curriculum Theorizing*. London: Falmer Press.

Green, K. and LeBihan, J. (1996) *Critical Theory and Practice: A Coursebook*. London: Routledge.

Griffiths, P. (1987) *Literary Theory and English Teaching*. Milton Keynes: Open University Press.

Hall, N. and Robinson, A. (1996) *Learning about Punctuation*. Clevedon: Multilingual Matters.

Hardman, F., Smith, F. and Wall, K. (2003) 'Interactive Whole Class Teaching in the NLS', *Cambridge Journal of Education* 33 (2), 197–216.

Hardy, T. (1985) *Tess of the D'Urbervilles*, ed. by D. Skilton. London: Penguin.

Hargreaves, D. H. (1996) *Teaching as a Research Based Profession: Possibilities and Prospects*. London: Teacher Training Agency.

Harland, R. (1987) *Superstructuralism*. London: Routledge.

Harrison, B. (1983) *Learning through Writing*. Slough: NFER–Nelson.

Harrison, B. (1994) *The Literate Imagination*. London: David Fulton.

Harrison, C. (2002) *The National Strategy for English at Key Stage 3: Roots and Research*. London: DfES.

Harrison, C. (2004) *Understanding Reading Development*. London: Sage.

Harrison, G. (1990) 'Three Glorious Summers', *TES*, 24 August.

Hart, A. (1988 ) *Teaching Television: The Real World*. Cambridge: Cambridge University Press.

Hart, A. and Hicks, A. (2002) *Teaching Media in the English Classroom*. London: Trentham.

Haworth, A., Turner, C. and Whiteley, M. (2004) *Secondary English and Literacy: A Guide for Teachers*. London: Paul Chapman.

Hayhoe, M. and Parker, S. (1988) *Words Large as Apples: Teaching Poetry 11–18*. Cambridge: Cambridge University Press.

Hayhoe, M. and Parker, S. (eds) (1992) *Reassessing Language and Literature*. Milton Keynes: Open University Press.

Head, J. (1997) *Working with Adolescents: Constructing Identity*. London: Falmer Press.

Heathcote, D. and Bolton, G. (1995) *Drama for Learning*. New Hampshire: Heinemann.

Hertrich, J. (1999) *18 Issues Deriving from HMI's Inspection of the Projects*. Available at: www.literacytrust.org.uk.

Hilton, M (1998) 'Raising Literacy Standards: The True Story', *English in Education* 32 (3), 4–16.

Hilton, M. (2001) 'Writing Process and Progress: Where Do We Go from Here?', *English in Education* 35 (1), 4–11.

Hinton, N. (1976) *Collision Course*. Oxford: Oxford University Press.

HMSO (1921) *The Teaching of English in England* (the Newbolt Report). London: HMSO.

Hoggart, R. (1998) 'Critical Literacy and Creative Reading', in Cox, B. (ed.) *Literacy is not Enough: Essays on the Importance of Reading*. Manchester: Manchester University Press.

Holderness, G. (ed.) (1988) *The Shakespeare Myth*. Manchester: Manchester University Press.

Holderness, G. and Lalljee, B. (1997) *An Introduction to Oracy: Frameworks for Talk*. London: Cassell.

Holmes, E. (1911) *What Is and What Might Be*. London: Constable.

Hornbrook, D. (1988) 'Go Play, Boy, Play: Shakespeare and Educational Drama', in Holderness, G. (ed.) *The Shakespeare Myth*. Manchester: Manchester University Press.

Hornbrook, D. (1989) *Education and Dramatic Art*. London: Blackwell Education.

Hourd, M. (1949) *The Education of the Poetic Spirit*. London: Heinemann.

Howe, A. (1994) 'Perspectives on Oracy', in Brindley, S. (ed.) *Teaching English*. London: Routledge.

Howe, A. (1997) *Making Talk Work*. London: NATE.

Howker, J. (1986) *Badger on the Barge and Other Stories*. London: Lions.

Hoyles, A. and Hoyles, M. (2003) 'Black Performance Poetry', *English in Education* 37 (1), 27–36.

Hoyles, M. (ed.) (1977) *The Politics of Literacy*. London: Writers and Readers Publishing Co-operative.

Hunt, G. (2002) 'Classroom literacy and everyday life', in Goodwyn, A. (ed.) *Improving Literacy at KS2 and KS3*. London: Paul Chapman.

Hunt, P. (1991) *Criticism, Theory and Children's Literature*. Oxford: Blackwell.

Inglis, F. (1990) *Media Theory: An Introduction*. Oxford: Blackwell.

Iser, W. (1978) *The Act of Reading*. London: Routledge.

Jeffcoate, R. (1992) *Starting English Teaching*. London: Routledge.

Johnson, P. (1996) *Words and Images on the Page*. London: David Fulton.

Johnstone, B. (1987) *Assessing English: Helping Students to Reflect on Their Work*. Milton Keynes: Open University Press.

Jones, P. (1988) *Lipservice: The Story of Talk in Schools*. Milton Keynes: Open University Press.

Keats, J. (2002) *Selected Letters*, ed. by R. Gittings. Oxford: Oxford University Press.

Kempe, A. (1990) *The GCSE Drama Coursebook*. Oxford: Basil Blackwell.

Kempe, A. and Ashwell, M. (2000) *Progression in Secondary Drama*. London: Heinemann.

Knight, B. (1999) 'Towards Inclusion of Students with Special Educational Needs in the Regular Classroom', *Support for Learning* 14 (10), 3–7.

Knight, R. (1996) *Valuing English: Reflections on the National Curriculum*. London: David Fulton.

Kress, G. (1995) *Writing the Future: English and the Making of a Culture of Innovation*. Sheffield: NATE.

Kyriacou, C. (1991) *Essential Teaching Skills*. Cheltenham: Stanley Thornes.

Landsberg, M. (1988) *The World of Children's Books*. London: Simon & Schuster.

Lewis, M. and Wray, D. (eds) (2000) *Literacy in the Secondary School*. London: David Fulton.

Lewis, M. M. (1946) 'Spoken English in the School', in De Sola Pinto, V. (ed.) *The Teaching of English in Schools*. London: Macmillan.

Lively, P. (1971) *The Whispering Knights*. London: Heinemann.

Lunzer, E. and Gardner, K. (1984) *Learning from the Written Word*. Edinburgh: Oliver & Boyd.

Lurillard, D. (1993) *Rethinking University Teaching*. London: Routledge.

McCourt, F. (1996) *Angela's Ashes*. London: HarperCollins.

McCulloch, R., Mathieson, M. and Powis, V. (1993) *English 16–19: Entitlement at A Level*. London: David Fulton.

McEwan, I. (1987) *The Child in Time*. London: Jonathan Cape.

McEwan, I. (1989) *A Move Abroad: Or Shall We Die? and The Ploughman's Lunch*. London: Pan Books/Picador.

McGuinn, N. (1995) 'What is Left of Drama and Media', in Protherough, R. and King, P. (eds) *The Challenge of English in the National Curriculum*. London: Routledge.

Macrae, N. (2002) *How to Teach Fiction Writing*. London: David Fulton.

Marsh, G. (1988) *Teaching through Poetry*. London: Hodder & Stoughton.

Marsh, J. and Millard, E. (2000) *Literacy and Popular Culture: Using Children's Culture in the Classroom*. London: Paul Chapman.

Marshall, J. and Werndly, A. (2002) *The Language of Television*. London: Routledge Falmer.

Marshall, R. (2002) 'Revolting Literacy', *English in Education* 36 (2), 1–6.

Marson, P., Brockbank, K., McGuire, B. and Morton, S. (1990) *Drama 14–16*. Cheltenham: Stanley Thornes.

Masterman, L. (1992) *Teaching the Media*. London: Routledge.

Mathieson, M. (1975) *The Preachers of Culture*. London: Allen & Unwin.

Mattenklott, G. (1996) 'Poetry as Play: Rules for the Imagination', in Thompson, L. (ed.) *The Teaching of Poetry*. London: Cassell.

Medway, P. (1996) 'Representation and Making: Student Production in English', *Changing English* 3 (2), 131–46.

Medway, P. (2002) 'Teaching and Learning the English Method', *English & Media Magazine* 47, 4–7.

Meek, M. (1991) *On Being Literate*. London: Bodley Head.

Michael, I. (1992) *The Teaching of English from the Sixteenth Century to 1870*. Cambridge: Cambridge University Press.

Michaels, A. (1997) *Fugitive Pieces*. London: Bloomsbury.

Midgley, M. (1979) *Beast and Man: The Roots of Human Nature*. Brighton: Harvester Press.

Miller, A. (1987) *Timebends*. London: Methuen.

Mills, R., Mills, J. and Stringer, L. (1991) *Media Choices.* Oxford: Oxford University Press.

Mittins, W. (1988) *English: Not the Naming of Parts*. Sheffield: NATE.

Mittins, W. (1990) *Language Awareness for Teachers*. Milton Keynes: Open University Press.

Monaghan, J. E. and Saul, E. W. (1987) 'The Reader, the Scribe, the Thinker: A Critical Look at the History of American Reading and Writing Instruction', in Popkewitz, T. S. (ed.) *The Formation of the School Subjects: The Struggle for Creating an American Institution*. New York: Falmer Press.

Monteith, M. (ed.) (2005) *Teaching Secondary School Literacies with ICT*. Milton Keynes: OUP.

Montgomery, D. (1997) *Spelling*. London: Cassell.

Moon, B. (1996) *A Guide to the National Curriculum*, 3rd edition. Oxford: Oxford University Press.

Morgan, H. (1997) *Motivation of Sixth Form Students*. London: Teacher Training Agency.

Mudd, N. (1994) *Effective Spelling: A Practical Guide for Teachers*. London: Hodder & Stoughton.

Myhill, D. (2001) *Better Writers*. Bury St Edmunds: Courseware Publications.

NATE Post-16 Committee (1990) *A Level English: Pressures for Change*. Sheffield: NATE Publications.

Neelands, J. (1990) *Structuring Drama Work*. Cambridge: Cambridge University Press.

Neelands, J. (1992) *Learning through Imagined Experience*. London: Hodder & Stoughton.

Nicholls, G. (ed.) (1991) *Learning to Teach*. London: Kogan Page.

Norris, C. (1991) *Deconstruction: Theory and Practice*. London: Routledge.

O'Neill, C. (1995) *Drama Worlds*. Portsmouth, NH: Heinemann.

O'Toole, J. (1992) *The Process of Drama (Negotiating Art and Meaning)*. London: Routledge.

Owen, J. (2003) *The Poetry of Ted Hughes*. London: David Fulton.

Peach, L. and Burton, A. (1995) *English as a Creative Art*. London: David Fulton.

Peim, N. (1993) *Critical Theory and the English Teacher*. London: Routledge.

Perera, K. (1987) *Understanding Language*. London: National Association of Advisers in English.

Peters, M. (1985) *Spelling: Caught or Taught?* London: Routledge.

Peters, M. and Marshall, J. (1999) *Wittgenstein: Philosophy, Postmodernism, Pedagogy*. London: Bergin & Garvey.

Pike, M. (2004) *Teaching Secondary English*. London: Paul Chapman Publishing.

Pinker, S. (1994) *The Language Instinct: The New Science of Language and Mind*. London: Penguin.

Pirrie, J. (1987) *On Common Ground*. London: Hodder & Stoughton.

Pollard, A. (2002) *Reflective Teaching*. London: Continuum.

Potter, F. (ed.) (1990) *Reading, Learning and Media Education*. Oxford: Blackwell.

Preen, D. (1999) 'Humpty Dumpty and the Nature of Poetic Understanding', *Use of English* 50 (2), 110–14.

Pring, R. (2004) *Philosophy of Education Research*. London: Continuum.

Protherough, R. and King, P. (eds) (1995) *The Challenge of English in the National Curriculum*. London: Routledge.

Pullman, P. (2002) *Perverse, All Monstrous, All Prodigious Things*. Sheffield: NATE.

Punch, K. (2009) *Introduction to Research Methods in Education*. London: Sage.

QCA (2003) *Information and Communication Technology Teacher's Guide*. London: DfES Publications.

Opie, C. (2004) *Doing Educational Research*. London: Sage.

Quirk, R. and Stein, G. (1990) *English in Use*. Harlow: Longman.

Reid, A. (1985) 'The Aesthetic in the Curriculum', in Ross, M. (ed.) *The Aesthetic in Education*. Oxford: Pergamon.

Reynolds, P. (1991) *Practical Approaches to Teaching Shakespeare*. Oxford: Oxford University Press.

Riding, R. (2002) *School Learning and Cognitive Styles*. London: David Fulton.

Riffaterre, M. (1978) *Semiotics of Poetry*. London: Methuen.

Ross, A. and Hunt, P. (2006) *Language Knowledge for Secondary Teachers*. London: David Fulton.

Ross, M. (ed.) (1985) *The Aesthetic in Education*. Oxford: Pergamon.

Rowntree, D. (1981) *Statistics without Tears*. London: Penguin.

Ruddock, J. (1995) 'Going to the Big School: The Turbulence of Transition', reprinted in Ruddock, J., Chaplain, R. and Wallace, G. (eds) (1999) *School Improvement: What Students Can Tell Us?* London: David Fulton.

Ruddock, J., Chaplain, R. and Wallace, G. (eds) (1999) *School Improvement: What Students Can Tell Us?* London: David Fulton.

Rumsby, R. (1990) *On and Off the Record: The Language of Reporting*. Walton-on-Thames: Nelson.

Sampson, G. (1921) *English for the English*. Cambridge: Cambridge University Press.

Sawyer, W., Watson, K. and Adams, A. (eds) (1989) *English Teaching from A to Z*. Milton Keynes: Open University Press.

Scott, P. (1989) *Reconstructing A Level English*. Milton Keynes: Open University Press.

Sedgwick, F. (2001) *Teaching Literacy*. London: Continuum.

Shayer, D. (1972) *The Teaching of English in Schools 1900–1970*. London: Routledge.

Shelley, M. (1969) *Frankenstein*. Oxford: Oxford University Press

Shelley, M. (1997) *Frankenstein*, ed. by D. Stevens. Cambridge: Cambridge University Press.

Shreeve, A. (ed.) (1997) *IT in English: Resources for Learning*. Coventry and Sheffield: NATE and NCET.

Sluga, H. and Sterns, D. (eds) (1996) *The Cambridge Companion to Wittgenstein*. Cambridge: Cambridge University Press.

Smith, A. E. (1954) *English in the Modern School*. London: Methuen.

Smith, F. (1988) *Joining the Literacy Club*. London: Heinemann.

Sockett, H. (1976) *Designing the Curriculum*. London: Open Books.

Soloman, N. (1990) *Help Your Child to Read*. Cambridge: Cambridge University Press.

Spufford, F. (2002) *The Child that Books Built*. London: Faber.

Staples, A. (1992) *An Approach to English*. London: Cassell.

States, B. (1994) *The Pleasures of the Play*. New York: Cornell University Press.

Stead, C. K. (1964) *The New Poetic: Yeats to Eliot*. London: Hutchinson.

Steiner, G. (1978) *On Difficulty and Other Essays*. Oxford: Oxford University Press.

Stenhouse, L. (1975) *An Introduction to Curriculum Research and Development*. London: Heinemann.

Stevens, D. (1998) 'Finding the Perfect Balance', *English in Education* 32 (1), 38–44.

Stevens, D. and McGuinn, N. (2004) *The Art of Teaching Secondary English*. London: Routledge Falmer.

Stibbs, A. (1991) *Reading Narrative as Literature: Signs of Life*. Milton Keynes: Open University Press.

Stobart, G. and Gibbs, C. (1997) *Assessment: A Teacher's Guide to the Issues*, 3rd edition. London: Hodder & Stoughton.

Stokes, J. and Reading, A. (eds) (1999) *The Media in Britain*. London: Macmillan.

Styles, M. (ed.) (1989) *Collaboration and Writing*. Milton Keynes: Open University Press.

Styles, M. and Triggs, P. (1988) *Poetry 0–16*. London: Books for Keeps.

Styles, M., Bearne, E. and Watson, V. (eds) (1992) *After Alice: Exploring Children's Literature*. London: Cassell.

Styles, M., Bearne, E. and Watson, V. (eds) (1994) *The Prose and the Passion: Children and Their Reading*. London: Cassell.

Styles, M., Bearne, E. and Watson, V. (eds) (1996) *Voices Off*. London: Cassell.

Sweetman, J. (1998) *Curriculum Confidential*. Suffolk: Courseware Publications, updated annually.

Swift, G. (1995) *Learning to Swim*, ed. by R. Hoyes. Cambridge: Cambridge University Press.

Tarleton, R. (1988) *Learning and Talking*. London: Routledge.

Taylor, K. (ed.) (1991) *Drama Strategies*. London: Heinemann.

TDA (2007) *Professional Standards for Qualified Teacher Status*. London: TDA.

Thomas, G. (1997) 'Inclusive Schools for an Inclusive Society', *British Journal of Special Education* 24 (3), 103–7.

Thomas, P. (1997) 'Doom to the Red-eyed Nyungghns from the Planet Glarg: Boys as Writers of Narrative', *English in Education* 31(3), 23–31.

Thompson, L. (ed.) (1996) *The Teaching of Poetry*. London: Cassell.

Tomkinson, W. S. (1921) *The Teaching of English: A New Approach*. Oxford: Oxford University Press.

Tomlinson, S. (ed.) (1997) *Education 14–19: Critical Perspectives*. London: Athlone Press.

Tooley, J. (1998) *Educational Research: A Critique*. London: Office for Standards in Education.

Traherne, T. (1960) *Centuries of Meditations*, ed. by H. M. Margolioth. Oxford: Clarendon Press.

TTA (2000) *Raising the Attainment of Minority Ethnic Pupils*. London: Teacher Training Agency.

TTA (2002) *Professional Standards for Qualified Teacher Status*. London: HMSO.

Tunnicliffe, S. (1984) *Poetry Experience*. London: Methuen.

Tweddle, S., Clarke, S., Scrimshaw, P. and Walton, S. (1997) *English for Tomorrow*. Milton Keynes: Open University Press.

Unsworth, L., Thomas, A., Simpson, A. and Asha, J. (2005) *Children's Literature and Computer-Based Teaching*. Milton Keynes: OUP.

Wall, P. and Walker, P. (2002) *Media Studies for GSCE*. Glasgow: Collins.

Walliman, N. (2005) *Your Research Project*. London: Sage.

Watson, K. (1981) *English Teaching in Perspective*. Epping, Australia: St Clair Press.

Waugh, P. (1992*) Practising Postmodernism, Reading Postmodernism*. London: Edward Arnold.

Way, B. (1967) *Development through Drama*. London: Longman.

Wellington, J. J. (2000) *Educational Research: Contemporary Issues and Practical Approaches*. London: Continuum.

Wilkinson, A., Davies, A. and Berrill, D. (1990) *Spoken English Illuminated*. Milton Keynes: Open University Press.

Wilkinson, E. (1966) 'At First Hand', *Trends in Education* 1 (January), 18–29.

Wilkinson, J. (1995) *Introducing Standard English*. Harmondsworth: Penguin.

Williams, M. (ed) (2002) *Unlocking Writing: A Guide for Teachers*. London: David Fulton.

Williams, T. (1962) *A Streetcar Named Desire* in Browne, E. M. (ed.) *A Streetcar Named Desire and Other Plays*. London: Penguin.

Williamson, J., Fleming, M., Hardman, F. and Stevens, D. (2001) *Meeting the Standards in Secondary English*. London: Routledge Falmer.

Wilson, J. (1999) 'Some Conceptual Difficulties About "Inclusion" ', *Support for Learning* 14 (3), 110–12.

Wittgenstein, L. (1953) *Philosophical Investigations*, trans. by G. E. M. Anscombe. Oxford: Basil Blackwell.

Wittgenstein, L. (1969) *On Certainty*. Oxford: Blackwell.

Wood, G. and Wood, L. (1995) *The Cambridge Critical Workshop*. Cambridge: Cambridge University Press.

Wood, J. (2009) *How Fiction Works*. London: Vintage.

Woods, E. (1995) *Introducing Grammar*. Harmondsworth: Penguin.

Woods, P. (ed.) (1996) *Contemporary Issues in Teaching and Learning*. London: Routledge.

Wray, D. and Medwell, J. (1994) *Teaching Primary English*. London: Routledge.

Yeats, W. (1994) *Selected Poems*. London: Random House.

# Index

# eBooks

eBooks – at www.eBookstore.tandf.co.uk

## A library at your fingertips!

eBooks are electronic versions of printed books. You can store them on your PC/laptop or browse them online.

They have advantages for anyone needing rapid access to a wide variety of published, copyright information.

eBooks can help your research by enabling you to bookmark chapters, annotate text and use instant searches to find specific words or phrases. Several eBook files would fit on even a small laptop or PDA.

**NEW:** Save money by eSubscribing: cheap, online access to any eBook for as long as you need it.

## Annual subscription packages

We now offer special low-cost bulk subscriptions to packages of eBooks in certain subject areas. These are available to libraries or to individuals.

For more information please contact webmaster.ebooks@tandf.co.uk

We're continually developing the eBook concept, so keep up to date by visiting the website.

**www.eBookstore.tandf.co.uk**